BUILDING HEALTHY MINDS

OTHER BOOKS BY STANLEY I. GREENSPAN, M.D.

The Growth of the Mind (with Beryl Lieff Benderly)

The Child with Special Needs (coauthor Serena Wieder, Ph.D.,
with Robin Simon)

*Infancy and Early Childhood: The Practice of Clinical Assessment and
Intervention with Emotional and Developmental Challenges*

Developmentally Based Psychotherapy

The Challenging Child (with Jacqueline Salmon)

Playground Politics (with Jacqueline Salmon)

First Feelings (with Nancy Thorndike Greenspan)

The Essential Partnership (with Nancy Thorndike Greenspan)

The Clinical Interview of the Child (with Nancy Thorndike Greenspan)

The Development of the Ego

Psychopathology and Adaptation in Infancy and Early Childhood

*Intelligence and Adaptation: An Integration of Psychoanalytic and
Piajetian Developmental Psychology*

*A Consideration of Some Learning Variables in the Context of
Psychoanalytic Theory*

The Course of Life—Infancy to Aging, 7 volumes (coeditor)

Infants in Multi-Risk Families (coeditor)

Infancy: Handbook of Child and Adolescent Psychiatry (coeditor)

BUILDING HEALTHY MINDS

The Six Experiences That Create Intelligence and Emotional Growth in Babies and Young Children

STANLEY I. GREENSPAN, M.D.
with Nancy Breslau Lewis

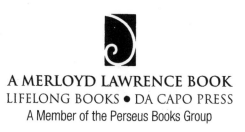

A MERLOYD LAWRENCE BOOK
LIFELONG BOOKS • DA CAPO PRESS
A Member of the Perseus Books Group

Many of the designations used by manufacturers and sellers to distinguish their products are claimed as trademarks. Where those designations appear in this book and Da Capo Press was aware of a trademark claim, the designations have been printed in initial capital letters.

A Catalog Card Number for this book is available from the Library of Congress.

ISBN: 0-7382-0356-4
Copyright © 1999 by Stanley I. Greenspan

Da Capo Press is a member of the Perseus Books Group

Jacket design by Bruce W. Bond
Text design by Jeff Williams
Set in 11-point Minion

First paperback printing, September 2000

Da Capo Press books are available at special discounts for bulk purchases in the U.S. by corporations, institutions, and other organizations. For more information, please contact the Special Markets Department at HarperCollins Publishers, 10 East 53rd Street, New York, NY 10022, or call 1–212–207–7528.

Find us on the World Wide Web at http://www.dacapopress.com

For my brother Kenneth, who taught me about nurturance and caring as we grew up.

CONTENTS

APPRECIATION

I would like to express my appreciation to my wife Nancy, and my colleagues Serena Wieder and the late Reginald Lourie for their collaboration in understanding children and parents; to Sarah Miller and Jan Tunney for supporting the children and families in my practice; and to Merloyd Lawrence for her sensitive and insightful editing and suggestions.

BUILDING HEALTHY MINDS

INTRODUCTION:
WHAT MAKES
THE MIND GROW?

How does your child develop the miraculous abilities to love, think, communicate, and create, as well as to have self-control and feel compassion for others? Many child-development theories focus on only one part of this puzzle, such as a child's genes, cognitive skills, or a new way to set limits. But in fact what gives meaning to all parts of this puzzle and defines your child as a humane and intelligent human being is his continuing relationship with *you*. In the chapters that follow, we will attempt to demonstrate that all the wonderful things you wish for your child do not have to be left to chance, intuition, or genetic endowment. Nor do they require hours of flash cards, educational TV programs, or special computer-based learning exercises. Instead, you'll discover that there are six essential types of experiences that simultaneously promote your child's intelligence and emotional growth. Some of these vital experiences are already likely to be a relaxed and enjoyable part of your daily life together.

High up on many parents' wish lists is the hope that their children will be able learners who can master academic challenges and who are curious about the world. We also want our children to develop a capacity for warmth and intimacy and to enjoy many rich and rewarding relationships. In addition, we want our youngsters to have an awareness of what constitutes appropriate behavior, to have a sense of right and wrong, and to be able to make wise judgments in unfamiliar situations. We certainly want them to feel good about themselves, and to show persistence, flexibility, and creativity. Many parents and educators are searching for ways to "raise the bar," or maximize children's potential, without undermining their emotional vitality and well-being.

We now understand how to interact with children in ways that will foster these admirable goals. We also know how to minimize the odds that they will be side-tracked into negative behavior and feelings. We can help them learn to avoid acting in uncaring, overly aggressive, or impulsive ways, and give them the tools to limit their own behavior. Our children can develop a feeling for subtlety, and learn to perceive the grays in life, rather than becoming all-or-nothing-type thinkers. We can also help them be less prone to weak problem-solving skills, poor judgment, or depression—all of which can lead to risk-taking behavior and trouble with drugs, alcohol, and sex. Instead, they can learn to turn challenges into windows of opportunity that promote intelligence, morality, and emotional health.

The same vital interactions that help build a healthy mind also lead to the actual growth of neuronal connections in the brain. A child's brain grows most rapidly in the first three to four years of life, and will reach two thirds to three fourths of its adult size during this period. Recent research reveals that vital interactions with caregivers literally wire a baby's brain, filling in the broad outlines of his genetic blueprint. For example, your loving smiles, sounds, and tender movements not only teach your baby to look, listen, and love; they also enable connections to form between neurons in the parts of his brain that support intelligence and social skills. Your soothing touch not only fosters your baby's ability to feel close and intimate with you, but also releases growth hormones that enable his body and brain to grow. Pioneering studies by Nobel Prize–winners Torsten Wiesel and David Hubel on critical phases in early brain development suggest that providing your infant with opportunities to look and use his vision during certain early periods is necessary if he is to comprehend his world, and will also reduce the likelihood of his developing visual learning problems.

Not all experiences are equally beneficial in building your child's mind and brain. In one study, for example, it was found that when older children were involved in learning emotionally meaningful tasks, the learning areas of their brains were very active, but when they were given repetitive or boring tasks, or were overloaded with too much information, these same learning centers were not appropriately active. Stressful experience can set up circuits that undermine the growth of a healthy mind and brain.

Since early experience clearly operates as a two-way street, it is vitally important to know what types of experience build the capacities we most desire for our children. Through over 25 years of observations and research, we have identified six types of essential experiences, and we will be exploring them and the developmental achievements they promote in the following chapters.

During the first few months of life, you'll be helping your infant calmly regulate himself while he becomes interested and takes pleasure in the sights, sounds, tastes, and touches you offer him. This ability will help him organize his senses and motor responses and create a deep sense of security.

During his second stage of development, when he is between three and six months of age, your baby will grow in his ability to engage in an intimate, loving relationship with you. He'll experience more and more warmth and pleasure and all the other related feelings that spring out of your engagement together.

By the time he is about nine months old, your toddler will be well into the third developmental stage, and will be exchanging gestures with you in a purposeful way. With your help, he will eventually be able to string together more and more of these emotional expressions, sounds, and actions. Your funny faces and tempting actions, such as covering his favorite rattle with your hand, will inspire him to master the baby version of logic and two-way communication far better than any educational toy or picture book.

By the time he's a year to a year-and-a-half old, your child will be learning to be a complex social problem solver. He will take you by the hand to get you to help him. He's starting to figure out how the world works during this fourth developmental stage, and may even vocalize his own version of words, along with a few real ones, to help you understand his intentions. When he grabs your hand and points to the cupboard to get a toy he wants, he is making his first attempt at social problem solving. As you nod back, he'll motion until you hoist him up in your arms and he's able to nab the toy for himself. Your child will not only be delighted and proud, he'll be on his way to becoming a budding scientist. Your toddler has learned that problems get solved through many interrelated steps, and that the world, including his physical surroundings and his own personality and yours, is made up of patterns. No colorful pop-up toy or computerized light-and-sound gadget can come close to matching the companionable lessons in problem solving that you offer your child as you play and engage in gestural dialogues together.

The fifth core experience that you and your child will share will involve his use of ideas as he explores creativity. This ability will emerge as the two of you become a cat or dog or king or queen in a drama of your child's choosing, rather than from set games or impersonal puzzle pieces.

The sixth stage, or core experience, involves the creation of logical bridges between ideas, or analytical thinking. It emerges from more elaborate pretend play, as well as from debates over bedtime or cookies, and from asking a child about his opinions. Questions such as "Why do you want to go outside?" rather than the rote teaching of letters or numbers will teach your child to connect his ideas and be a logical thinker. In a study carried out in collaboration with Arnold Sameroff of the University of Michigan, we found that children with healthy support and plenty of these kinds of emotional interactions were 20 times more likely than those without them to have normal-to-superior intelligence. We have also found that providing these types of experiences can help children further develop their intelligence and emotional health even when they have significant challenges.

The six essential experiences and the stages of emotional and intellectual growth that stem from them have parallels in the growth of key parts of the brain. We will be discussing these important parallels in the chapters that follow and they are summarized in a chart in Appendix II. Because your child's mastery of these six core experiences is so critically important to his development on so many fronts, we've also devised a Functional Developmental Growth Chart Questionnaire and a Functional Developmental Growth Chart (Appendix I) which you can use to note when he passes each interactive milestone and then compare to a broadly defined expectable rate of progress.

This developmental growth chart is different from developmental charts that simply look at motor, language, or cognitive milestones. Our new chart indicates how well a child puts together and uses all his intellectual and emotional capacities to meet his needs and solve problems. It reveals whether his "team" of mental abilities is working together in an integrated fashion, as well as how the specific contributing components are developing. As you'll see on the growth chart itself and in the accompanying questionnaire, you can chart your child's accomplishments as they emerge and note whether they appear significantly above or below the expectable line. This is a useful tool that can alert you, as well as your child's primary health-care providers and educators, to the developmental areas in which your child is doing well and those where he may need additional support.

In spite of the considerable evidence for the importance of early experience, some argue that later experiences are equally important. However, they are not distinguishing the six early learned essential experiences described above, which help children relate, read social cues, and think (and take years of therapy to even partially learn later on) from attitudes, values, and academic skills which are acquired throughout life. Others argue that genes are relatively more important than experience. Much of the research on identical twins which suggests that behavior is genetically determined, however, is flawed. Because identical twins share similar physical and temperamental characteristics, their caregivers tend to respond to them more similarly than would caregivers of nonidentical twins. Since typical caregivers tend to react similarly to physical and temperamental characteristics, these observations may tend to hold even when identical twins are reared in separate households. Therefore, near-identical interaction patterns, rather than identical genes, may account for the similarities exhibited by these twins. This possibility is usually not taken into consideration in much of the research looking at genetic influences on behavior.

In fact, our clinical work indicates that the more a child's biological endowment presents challenges, the bigger the impact his environment may have on his development. For instance, if a child has low muscle tone and tends to be a little underreactive to sound or touch, he may tend to be more self-absorbed and may have social and intellectual challenges because the sights and sounds and emotional gestures of his caregivers don't easily grab his attention and draw him into interaction. If we woo that child by energetic and lively caregiving into a loving relationship early in life, we can often entice him into robust social interactions and intellectual growth.

Similarly, we find that children's temperamental characteristics are often tied to physical qualities, such as a sensitivity to certain touches or sounds. For example, if a child is unusually sensitive to sound, a cat's meow could reverberate in his ears like a lion's roar. Such a child would understandably appear to be more fearful than another who processed sounds in the usual way. We can, however, gradually expose the hearing-sensitive child to a broad range of sounds while providing him with lots of extra warmth and reassurance. We can also simultaneously encourage him to be assertive, and take an extra step, reach up high for a toy, or playfully wrestle with us instead of passively allowing us to move his limbs as we roughhouse together. If we consistently foster his assertive spirit and provide him with extra security while he slowly masters experiences that frighten him, he can eventually become outgoing and confident and yet retain positive aspects of his sensitivities, such as an enormous capacity for empathy and caring.

We have applied these principles to working with children with severe language, motor, cognitive, and social challenges, including children diagnosed with autistic patterns. We have been impressed with how creating learning interactions based on the way each child's nervous system takes in, organizes, and responds to experience enables even children with significant challenges to progress far more than we ever imagined possible. Many of these youngsters become warm, loving, communicative, and highly intelligent.

Of course, not every pattern can be offset by a certain type of environmental interaction. In our experience, however, we've noted that many of the negative variations we see in children's behavior can be significantly improved and positive variations strengthened by offering a child an appropriate interactive experience that is geared to his unique physical makeup.

This means that even though a child's unique biology (nature) may launch early parent-child interactions in a certain direction, modifying the child's environment by adjusting parenting styles (nurture) can influence the outcomes significantly. After all, a gene can't express itself, or have an influence, without its intimate partner—the environment. In addition, most recent research on how genes work in the body suggests that their expression or influence depends on their interactions with many different environments, including those in the cell, the body, and in the social and physical world; and that these interactions in part determine how we function. Nature and nurture thus appear to interact together seamlessly, in a developmental duet.

One-dimensional, catchy explanations like "It's all in the genes," "The bad seed," "All kids need is more discipline," or "Biology is destiny" may tempt us with their appealing simplicity, but they often lead to poor solutions and worsening challenges when it comes to childrearing. The recent fascination in the media with the notion that peers influence a child's personality more than his parents is another such example of short-sighted thinking. Although peer relationships are important, they build on the early experiences that a child has with his parents. A child learns the basics of how to relate to others and to communicate and think from these early interactions with caregivers. In our practice we've observed that many children who haven't had the benefit of nurturing parental interactions early on have trouble even forming friendships, let alone negotiating the expectable ups and downs of peer relationships.

Recent books that focus on multiple intelligences, or emotional intelligence, or moral development are valuable in illuminating how parents can work with their children's various learning strengths and styles. We are now, however, able to go beyond highlighting different attributes of a child's mind and can help parents to promote healthy intellectual, moral, and social growth actively and in an *integrated* way. By enabling all the members of a child's mental "team" to work together, we can maximize his abilities. We see the effects of unintegrated strengths all the time in the experiences of talented prodigies, who may have phenomenal abilities in chess, piano, or math but reach plateaus or run into difficulties because they are unable to think deeply in other areas or are emotionally immature.

We've also come to understand that most of a child's varying intellectual and social gifts, including his creativity and abstract thinking skills, are not only interrelated, but rest on common building blocks that surprisingly involve emotions. Our own awareness of this was heightened when we studied children with strong self-awareness and reflective thinking skills, and realized that most of them also showed positive self-esteem, demonstrated a capacity for moral judgment, were analytical in their reasoning, and did well in school and with their peers. We sought to understand what helped them become this way, and therefore spoke with them and with other children who had opposite personal characteristics. We learned what we commonly label as intelligence, social skills, and morality was supported by six types of emotional interactions that are negotiated during the early years of life.

For example, when we asked a randomly selected group of eight-year-olds abstract questions, such as what they thought about justice or fairness, their comments were very revealing. Some of the children responded with a rote listing of people who behaved "fairly," such as a particular parent or teacher or television character. However, others gave far more reflective answers, along the lines of "Well, when I hit my brother after he hit me it was unfair for me to be punished, but when I hit him first it was fair for me to get a punishment. If I bump into him by accident, it's not fair to be punished, but if I do it on purpose it is fair."

Not surprisingly, when we looked at the two groups of children more closely, those who gave us the rote list tended to be the ones who were experiencing more problems in their relationships and in their schoolwork. The children who gave us more creative and reflective responses tended to do better in these social and intellectual areas.

We then took a second look at the more reflective responses and discovered that they had two components. This was true whether our test question focused on fairness or any other abstract quality, such as honesty, friendship, or freedom. The first component was that the children's responses always started off with a personal anecdote, an account of *lived emotional experience*. The second component was that the children put these experiences with abstract concepts into some sort of analytic framework and context.

When we later asked this same question of adolescents, they were able to list more categories (five different types of fairness, for example) and supplied an even more worldly-wise analytical framework. But in every instance, and at every age, two components were evident in the more sophisticated replies: lived emotional experiences and a framework, or context. The children who didn't have a lot of lived emotional experiences—due to either nurturing or biological challenges that interfered with interaction, such as difficulties with language, for example—tended to be the ones who responded with concrete lists, rather than anecdotes. Interestingly, we found that the most effective way to teach such children analytic reasoning or thinking was by creating opportunities to have more "lived emotional experiences" and to reason about them. We observed that even children with severe developmental problems, including autistic patterns, could become more creative and reflective when they were exposed to more one-on-one interactions with their caregivers.

It thus became increasingly clear that certain types of emotional experiences seemed to be necessary for generating abstract ideas or thinking.

This startlingly simple concept had been overlooked, because for many hundreds of years it has been a given in Western culture that emotions are separate from intelligence. We have commonly assumed that emotions are experienced as bodily reactions or passions that lead us to do irrational things; and more recently we have also viewed them as the cues that enable us to function socially. Intelligence has been considered to be the vigilant part of our minds that helps us be rational and make sense of the world.

Our new observations suggest that emotional interactions play a far more critical role in intellectual functioning. They can help us go beyond Howard Gardner's important idea of separate, multiple intelligences, or Antonio Damasio's research on the brain which suggests that emotions are important for judgment but somehow separate from academic capacities or overall intelligence. Even Jean Piaget, the pioneering cognitive psychologist, overlooked this vital connection. Piaget observed that when an eight-month-old is accustomed to pulling a string that is attached to a bell and to hearing the bell ring in response, he will eventually stop ringing the bell if it is detached from the string. To Piaget, this sort of behavior revealed that the child is a causal thinker, because he pulls the string only if it leads to his hearing the sound of the ringing bell. Although Piaget's observations were accurate, he did not realize that this was not the child's first opportunity to learn about causality. A baby's first lesson in causality occurs many months earlier, when he pulls on his mother's or father's heartstrings with a smile that brings a responsive smile of delight or some other joyful expression to his parent's face. The child then applies that emotional lesson to the physical world of pulling strings, banging objects, and the like.

At each succeeding stage of development, we have found that emotional interactions like a little baby's smile leading to a hug enable the child to understand how the world works, and eventually to think, solve problems, and master academic challenges. Emotions are actually the internal architects, conductors, or organizers of our minds. They tell us how and what to think, what to say and when to say it, and what to do. We "know" things through our emotional interactions and then apply that knowledge to the cognitive world.

Let's look at some examples of how this works. Consider how a young child first learns how to say "Hi!" as he greets other people. A toddler doesn't memorize lists of appropriate people to say hello to. He merely connects the greeting with a warm, friendly feeling in his gut that leads him to reach out to other people's welcoming faces with a verbalized "Hi!" If he looks at them and has a different emotional feeling inside, one of wariness, he's more likely to turn his head or hide behind your legs.

It is his feeling, or affect, that triggers your child's decision over whether or not to greet a stranger. We encourage this kind of "discrimination," because we don't want our children to say "Hi!" to a menacing stranger in a back alley. We want them to say hello to nice people like Grandma. If your child won't say "Hi" to his grandmother, it's because he's not experiencing a warm feeling inside. If we can teach Grandma how to evoke that warm, fuzzy feeling inside her grandchild, she'll eventually get a friendly "Hi!" back in response. Similarly, if a child learns to greet those people who make him feel warm inside, he will quickly say "Hi!" to a friendly teacher or to a new playmate. He carries his emotions inside him, helping him to generalize from known situations to new ones, as well as to discriminate, or decide when and what to say.

Not only thinking grows out of early emotional interactions; so does a moral sense of right and wrong. The ability to understand another person's feelings and *care* about how he or she feels can only arise out of a series of nurturing interactions that will be described in the chapters that follow. Even something as purely academic and cognitive as math and concepts of quantity is based on early emotional experiences. "A lot" to a three-year-old is more than he wants; "a little" is less than he expects. Later on, numbers can systematize this feel for quantity. Children with math blocks can be helped to become solid students by going back to the early emotional roots of learning about quantity. Similarly, concepts of time and space are learned by the emotional experiences of waiting for Mom, or of looking for her and finding her in another room.

Words also derive their meaning from emotional interactions, as our example of fairness illustrates. A word like "justice" acquires content and meaning with each new emotional experience of fairness and unfairness. Comprehension of a word like "apple" is based on numerous emotional experiences involved in eating one, throwing one, and giving one to your teacher, in addition to its obvious physical characteristics of redness and roundness. Even our use of grammar, which the noted linguist Noam Chomsky and others believe is largely innate and only needs some very general types of social stimulation to get going, is based in part on very specific early emotional interactions. For example, we found that autistic children who did not use proper grammar and repeated only nouns, like "door," "table," or "milk," could learn correct grammatical forms if we helped them first become emotionally engaged and intentional. At the point they learned to experience and express their desire or wish (for example, when they pulled us to a door to open it), they began properly aligning nouns and verbs ("Open the door!").

We found the same patterns evident in children reared in certain Eastern European orphanages or under very deprived family conditions in this country, where there were few opportunities for "intentional" interaction. We also saw that infants growing up under ordinary circumstances required many opportunities to express their desires or wishes in purposeful interactions with their caregivers (such as back-and-forth smiling and pointing) to develop proper grammatical connections between nouns and verbs. This connection between grammar and experience was probably missed in the past because it's easy to take routine emotional interactions for granted unless we also examine more dire situations in which they don't spontaneously occur.

Unfortunately, the compartmentalization of our postindustrial society has tempted many of us into thinking that our minds are similarly compartmentalized. If we want to impart some knowledge, we offer our children facts. If we want to teach loving, we simply say "I love you" or hug. Just as most of us run into a store to purchase a shirt and no longer remember how to grow the flax, pick it, spin it into thread, weave it into linen fabric, and then sew it into a garment, we've forgotten that building a creative, healthy mind in our children isn't a process of one-stop shopping for supercharged "educational" experiences. Just as the linen shirt on your back has its roots in a flax seed planted in the soil, so does your child's personality grow out of the nurturing matrix of your interactions with him.

The more you are able to encourage the integrated growth of your child's mind and brain, the more successful you'll be in laying the groundwork for his becoming an intelligent, logical, socially adept, empathic adult. These important qualities spring out of the fertile soil of your continuing interactions. As you read ahead, you can rest assured that we won't be asking you to complicate your life by piling on more and more outside activities or "cognitive stimulation" exercises into your already busy day. Instead, we hope to inspire you to engage your baby and child, and together create the six experiences that are essential to the growth of a healthy mind.

These core experiences that your child needs to master have their roots in our distant evolutionary past. In comparison to the nonhuman primates and other members of the animal kingdom, human beings enjoy a relatively long period of dependency. For example, we are slower to walk than most of our animal cousins. This long period of dependency provides an opportunity for the brain and mind to grow enormously complex, but this opportunity also brings additional responsibilities. We must appropriately nurture our offspring, with some assistance from other caregivers, for an extended period of time.

We therefore have both a wondrous opportunity and an obligation to enrich the depth and range of our children's thinking and emotions while they depend on us, before they venture out on their own. Our young children require nurturing and interactions with consistent caregivers (as compared to changing ones) for a considerable part of their days and, when needed, nights. We strongly believe that children do best when they can interact with their primary caregivers for at least one half of their waking, nonschool hours. Yet as a society we are failing to address this need.

Why are so many of us moving away from providing these essential nurturing interactions that our children require? Part of the answer may lie in the way our culture views progress. We often focus on the competitive or assertive side of our nature, which has been so important in the mastery of our environment, our economic growth, and for our own survival. However, this single-minded emphasis on one kind of evolutionary fitness has caused us to neglect the softer, nurturing side of our evolutionary inheritance, which actually *creates* the tools that enable us to achieve mastery.

As we increasingly embrace the individualistic, assertive definition of fitness in both our work and family life, we must not lose sight of our children's even more compelling need for intimate, nurturing, interactive experience. Ironically, we can best help our children develop tools for mastery, or a competitive edge, by continually offering them nurturing emotional interactions. These nurturing experiences have helped us create individuals who can build complex, cooperative societies. They will enable those who follow us to develop the tools of reasoning, self-reflection, and cooperation that they will need to master the challenges of the twenty-first century.

If future generations are passive or self-absorbed, or polarized or hostile, or lack the ability to reflect on their lives and experiment confidently with new ideas, we'll have to live in a world where, as Yeats said, "Things fly apart; the center cannot hold." Each time we succeed in raising a child with a healthy mind, we're also contributing to a smoothly functioning, democratic, optimistic, and economically successful society. We increase the odds that the world of the new millennium will be made up of individuals who have empathy and compassion for others, can work in groups, create new breakthroughs, become intellectually robust, and even rear children with healthy minds themselves.

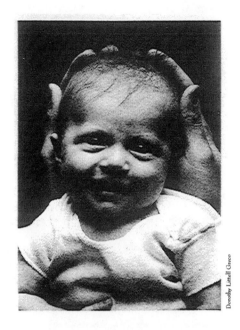

Dorothy Littell Greco

1

STAGE 1:

BECOMING CALM, ATTENTIVE,
AND INTERESTED IN THE WORLD

WHAT THIS STAGE IS ALL ABOUT

When your baby was still safely cocooned in the womb, most of your concerns were probably focused on delivering a healthy newborn. Now that he's lying in your arms, however, a whole new batch of questions has surely arisen. How can you help him develop into a thoughtful, kind child? What's the best way to spark his intellectual curiosity? How will you teach him to be insightful?

At this stage of your baby's development, during these first two to three months, the answer lies in helping him begin to learn to be both calm, regulated, and secure and interested in the world around him. He's already likely to be an adept little learner, taking in all the intriguing sights, sounds, smells, touches, and movements that surround him. Sometimes these sensations will excite him, and you may begin to see his eyes widen in delight, or watch him struggle to turn his head as he attempts to see and hear what's going on. At other times, these sensations may upset or overwhelm him and make him cry. When this happens, your continuing relationship with him and the familiar sight of your face, the comforting sound of your voice, and your gentle touch and movements will provide him with a reassuring sense of security that helps him recover his equilibrium.

During those nine months before he was born, your baby was sheltered in the shadowy, muffled environment of the womb and only gradually became aware of certain sensations. He was comforted by the steady rhythm of his mother's heartbeats, whooshes of arterial blood, and digestive rumblings. A range of sounds and their patterns were registering. While there was not a lot to see in the darkness in which he floated, he could sense when his mother's belly was exposed to very bright light. Tastes were beginning to reach him when the diluted sweet, bitter, or sour flavors from his mother's meals crossed the placenta and seasoned the amniotic fluid that he occasionally swallowed. He likely felt some movement, but was cushioned from all but the roughest bangs and bumps until the final weeks of pregnancy, when his quarters became more cramped and his movements were increasingly restricted.

From the moment he took his first breath, your little voyager has begun to take in and organize a much larger variety of sensations. Let's take a closer look at how he already shows you that he's starting to use all his sensory equipment, pay attention to you, and learn how to be calm and regulated at the same time.

During one of those calm and alert periods between feedings and nap times, take a few minutes to fully enjoy all the wonderful things your one- or two-month-old baby is doing as you play with him. Perhaps you'll find him lying in his crib, looking at some nearby toys with obvious interest. As he looks around the room, gather him up tenderly into your arms and look into his wide-open eyes. You might playfully touch your finger to his nose and say, "Oh, what a wonderful nose my big boy has!" You'll probably notice that his eyes will brighten with interest, and you might continue your game by tilting your head to one side to get closer to his little ear. When you nuzzle his ear and remark, "See how soft my baby's ear is!" he may well turn his head in your direction as if he's trying to capture more of the sound of your voice and the sight of your face.

If you next turn your attention to his other ear, giving it a tiny caress as you say something like "And look what's over here—another delicious ear!" your baby will likely try to turn his head while making a little squeal of delight. When you then hold him at arm's length and look directly into his eyes with a broad smile on your face, watch his lips part as if he's trying to imitate your smile. You'll probably welcome this adorable sight with words like "Oh, look at you, trying so hard to smile right back at Mommy!" Next, you might decide to stick your tongue out, because you read somewhere that infants this age are capable of returning such a gesture in a monkey-see, monkey-do manner. As you say "I bet you can do this, too!" and stick out your tongue once again, your baby will probably move his lips in an anticipatory way, as if he's trying hard to copy you. By his third or fourth attempt, the tip of his tongue will probably peek through his lips, and you'll marvel at his sophisticated social skills.

After the two of you have played for a few minutes, your baby may seem to grow a little weary of all the face-to-face interaction, and become distracted by the whir of a nearby fan or by the glare of an overhead light. You can then offer him some more soothing and rhythmically rock him back and forth in your arms. Or you might alternatively let him relax a few minutes, watching him stretch open his mouth in a tremulous yawn or two. After he rests for a few minutes, he may well glance at you with a gleam in his eye, as if to say, "I'm ready for some more conversation!" Then, you can animate your voice as the two of you get back into a lively interactive rhythm in which he seems to feed off the expressions that cross your face and the sounds that come out of your mouth.

As you're playing with your baby, you'll also notice when he seems to need a longer period of rest. This is likely to occur when he's about ready to go down for a nap or when the two of you have been busy interacting for quite a while and you're both a bit tired. Some babies are particularly soothed when they are rocked at the nice, slow beat of your own resting breathing rate of 12 to 15 breaths per minute. Your baby will usually let you know by his cries or wiggles whether he prefers a slower or faster rhythm. After a while you may feel the baby melt into your arms as his muscles relax, lulled by the steady back-and-forth motion. Eventually, you may become aware that his little feet are pressing into your lap, as if he's indicating that he wants to rock some more. His eyes may seem to sparkle with a renewed look of interest as you continue to rock and talk to him. He may even try to track your eyes as you turn your head from side to side, and you'll know that he's once again ready for some interaction.

Later during that same day, you might take a closer look at all the looks, sounds, touches, and movements your baby shares with you while you do something as simple as changing his diaper. He may energetically kick his feet as you coo to him, and turn his head a little to the left or right to get a better view of your smiling face. You'll probably pick up on a sparkle in his eye that lets you know he's also using his sense of vision, as well as his motor skills, to communicate his delight. As you clean him up he may not like the cool sensation of the wipe-up on his sensitive skin, and may grimace or even cry. In this way he'll show you that he's able to share his unhappy feelings with you, too. In fact, as he cries he may look you straight in the eye, as if to say, "You're supposed to be my friend; what are you doing to me?" After you kiss away his tears, you might flirt with him by smiling and playfully blowing on his belly button until that pleased gleam comes back into his eye. You might even play a little game of "This Little Piggy" and watch him wiggle his body in delight as his toes are tickled. His body language will communicate a clear message of "Do it again, Mommy! Oh, please, do it again!"

Further evidence of your baby's growing ability to take in information through his eyes, ears, nose, skin, and muscles may occur when your spouse joins the two of you. Maybe you'll be standing at the door, noticing that your baby is trying to nestle his head right into the crook of your neck, as if he's helping you to nuzzle him. Your spouse could come up behind you and play a funny-face game with the baby, talking in a silly voice while moving first to the right and then to the left. Your infant would then enjoy the double benefit of interacting at the same time with Mommy and Daddy; enjoying the warm security of one parent's body while playing new visual games with and hearing new sets of sounds from the other parent.

All of this endearing behavior is an indication that your baby is beginning to make use of his ability to see, hear, touch, feel, move, and register emotional reactions as he pays closer attention to the world. When he is calm and regulated, he's especially interested in interacting with you. He shows you that he can focus on your voice, as he turns left and right in search of its source. He may not be able to piece together all of the separate features of your face into a single image, but he can clearly make out the look in your eyes, or the smile on your face, and tries to orient his head to face in your direction. He's even capable of observing a gesture, like sticking out your tongue, and duplicating it. This sort of organized response is no easy achievement; your infant is not only taking in information through his eyes and ears, he's also using his own muscles in an action pattern to imitate your signal. Keep in mind, however, that he can't do other complex imitations yet. Each time your baby's eyes sparkle with a look of pleasure or his mouth quivers or settles into a frown, you're getting a glimpse of his new ability to respond emotionally to the world.

Many babies are blessed with sensory and motor abilities that work in a seemingly effortless way. Other perfectly normal infants have a considerably harder time trying to regulate their senses. Taking in particular sounds and touches, or being exposed to certain lighting conditions, may cause them to become cranky or tearful. Because their senses can so easily become overloaded, they tend be more cautious as they interact with the world, and their parents need to work a little harder to soothe them into a state of focused attention. For instance, a baby with some sensitivity to sound may hear his mother's voice, but be disturbed by its shrill tone. If the baby's mother can deliberately deepen the pitch of her voice and speak in soft, lulling tones, however, it is likely that her child will be able to find comfort in the sound of her voice.

Other babies seem to have difficulties moving their muscles through a sequence of actions. Their parents might mistakenly think that they're a little reserved or distant, since they don't intuitively relax their muscles and mold to the shape of their Mommy's or Daddy's arms when they're picked up for a cuddle. The child who has difficulty sequencing his movements may not be able to turn his head and follow Mommy's facial expressions if she moves quickly, and therefore is less able to communicate his awareness of his mother's presence. While some babies have an easy time figuring out how to suck their thumbs, others keep jabbing their noses or eyes as they try to find their mouths and soothe themselves.

These sorts of expectable variations in the way babies pick up cues from their surroundings and move their muscles mean that there's no one-size-fits-all approach to helping your own child calm down and pay attention to the world. By taking note of your baby's own special biological makeup and interactive style, however, you can deliberately introduce the world to him in a way that maximizes his delight and minimizes his frustrations. Even seemingly fixed biological characteristics, such as a child's tendency to be unusually startled by intense light or high-pitched sounds or by abrupt changes in movement, can be altered by the way in which we behave as caregivers.

We can also enlist the aid of others if our own particular biological makeup doesn't always mesh with our baby's needs. For instance, if you have a high-strung baby and tend yourself to be highly verbal and go through life in a whirlwind of activity, you might turn to your more even-tempered spouse or to a loving grandparent to help you provide your baby with an extra dose of calmness. During later stages of your child's development, when he is a confident, curious preschooler, your dynamic style may be just what he needs. As your baby matures, you'll also be teaching him that he can survive the inevitable bumps and bruises that his unique physical makeup and life's many surprises hand him. With your help, he'll come to experience a full range of sensation and human emotions.

For now, though, the goal is to concentrate on figuring out how to wrap your baby in a basic sense of security while encouraging him to attend to the sights and sounds that surround him. The following pages will provide some pointers on how to settle into this wonderful new relationship with your baby, and how to foster the sort of calm and loving atmosphere that will best promote your child's ability to feel, look, and listen to the world.

WHAT TO LOOK FOR IN THE FIRST FEW MONTHS

It's important to recognize that all young babies vary considerably in how they calm themselves and focus their attention on the world. Some infants will follow the sound of their mothers' voices with their eyes, or even turn their heads, from day one. Others will intently look and listen with excitement at seeing their mothers' faces in the first moments after birth, but may soon retreat into relative self-absorption. Then, over a period of two or three months, these babies may begin gradually to take in and focus on all the wonderful sights and sounds their parents offer them. Both of these very different types of infants demonstrate a healthy, budding interest in the world. The infant who seems to be born with the ability to calmly process sensation doesn't have a significant head start on the baby whose sensory equipment simply needs a period of time and encouragement to get going.

During these first few months, you'll become aware of your infant's own particular style of sharing attention with you. Perhaps he'll get special pleasure out of using his eyes, eagerly looking at your face and other objects. It usually takes a number of weeks, though, before you'll see many outwardly directed looks cross his face. He's just beginning to get used to being out in the world and is still largely preoccupied with his internal, physical sensations, rather than with you. For instance, he experiences his hunger as an uncomfortable, hollow feeling that causes him to tense his muscles and concentrate on what's going on inside of him. As you hold him in your arms just before a feeding, you will probably notice that his muscles feel more taut. Because he experiences fullness as a kind of pleasurable, expansive warmth in his tummy, he's likely to relax his muscles after a feeding and you may even notice a calmer, smoother look on his face.

Within a month or two, however, your baby will probably make you well aware that his hunger is arousing unpleasant, even angry, emotional feelings in him, and not just a muscle-tightening sense of abdominal discomfort. His cries will communicate a real sense of distress. On the other hand, he'll also be letting you know that having a stomach full of milk is a soothing, good feeling. As you nurse him, you'll probably observe that the muscles in his body seem to stiffen with a sense of urgent excitement when he sees an approaching breast or bottle. He'll wriggle around, waving his arms and legs as he attempts to align his mouth and root for the nipple. He may even pull away from the nipple after he nurses and melt your heart with a grin that stretches from ear to ear.

This smile of contentment is a kind of bonus that some parents receive when their baby is as young as one month old, but it more typically appears when babies are between two and four months of age. As you interact with your baby during these months, you'll become aware of other external sensations that he finds pleasurable. You might try exposing him to different levels of light, and see what kind of illumination kindles a spark of interest in his eye or a smile on his face. Try animating your features as you talk to your baby, lifting your eyebrows and dramatically moving your lips. See if he responds to the sight of your lively face with a heightened look of expectancy on his face. Alternatively, try subduing your natural expressiveness and see if your baby seems to prefer it when you move your features more slowly.

Your baby will also be demonstrating his growing ability to stay visually focused for more than just a few seconds. By the time he is three months old or so, he should be able to fix his eyes on yours for 10, 20 or even 30 seconds at a time. He will increasingly focus on your face. There will be a back-and-forth rhythm to your interactions, as the two of you look into each other's eyes, smile or smirk, or burble sounds to each other.

You may notice that your infant will become excited when he hears the sound of your voice, or your spouse's. Most babies tend to develop a preference for their mothers because they seem to prefer the higher-pitched sound of Mommy's voice, and because Mommy is more apt to be holding and feeding them. Your baby's ability to discriminate between different adult voices is an example of the way in which he is becoming a pattern recognizer. This skill becomes well developed during the second year of life, and will be discussed at length in a later chapter.

Some infants, however, are attracted to Daddy's deeper voice, and are more interested in visually tracking his face than Mommy's. Interestingly, when these babies' mothers deliberately lower the pitch of their own voices, the infants seem equally fascinated with their mothers. By adapting your own voice to your baby's particular pitch preference, you can help engage him when he interacts with you.

During these early months you can also pick up on what type of rhythm or cadence most attracts your two- or three-month-old. Some babies have a sophisticated feel for rhythm and can grasp a complex beat like "Bum ba ba bum-bum" after a few repetitions. Their little bodies seem to become more taut, and their eyes may widen in anticipation as they wait to hear the final two beats. Other babies may have a confused, glassy-eyed look on their faces when they are exposed to complex rhythms, but visibly brighten up and respond to simpler rhythmic patterns of two or three beats ("Ba ba . . . ba ba . . . ba ba").

If you can tailor your rhythmic games to your baby's own ability to digest sound patterns, you will gradually see that he will most likely be able to recognize very complex patterns of sound, even if he's only interested in simple patterns right now. As long as you can detect a response, and have a distinct sense that he's able to follow and even anticipate the rhythm of the words or sounds you recite, you'll know that you've hit upon the right combination for now.

You can try interacting with your child's motor system, too, and see what happens when you move his limbs. Does he brighten up and look at you with renewed focus? When you play "This Little Piggy" does he look at his foot or your hand? Does he curl his toes in delight when you manipulate them? Offer him different touches, and see whether he responds to light stroking or firmer belly and back rubs. Notice whether his muscles feel a bit tense and whether his body loosens up as you calm him with rhythmic rocking and soothing vocalizations. On the other hand, if he seems to have a hard time snuggling up into an embrace, try and support his neck and back more firmly and see if that helps him relax into the warmth of your chest or shoulder.

You may notice that certain smells make it harder for your baby to calm down and enter into a state of shared attention with you. If you're wearing a strong perfume or after-shave lotion, does he turn his head away when you approach him? If you suspect that your child may have sensitivities or may be underreactive to various smells, try putting different foods or fragrances near his nose and see if he recoils or frowns with annoyance or fails to show any reaction at all. It's a good idea to check out your baby's olfactory (smelling) responses, since smell and taste are close sensory cousins. Some children with hypersensitivities to smells can't handle food if it is too pungent, while others may need stronger odors and tastes to help them tolerate certain food groups.

As you sharpen your observational skills and pay attention to the times when your baby seems to have more trouble becoming calm and sharing attention with you, you'll begin to assemble a truly revealing developmental profile of your child. You'll start recognizing whether an unpleasant smell, an unexpected hug or cuddle, or a piercing noise overwhelms your child. Don't forget, though, that even a crying, finicky baby is capable of a lot of looking and listening. You may receive some very expressive looks from your three-month-old when he's got a gas bubble in his stomach! If you rub his back while murmuring sympathetically, he may be encouraged to keep using his looking and listening skills even when he's not feeling so good. He may be able to use your soothing sounds and touches to calm himself. Practicing under slightly stressful conditions will make him into a stronger looker and listener later on.

WHY SECURITY AND CALM ATTENTION ARE SO IMPORTANT

Your baby's dawning sense of security and awareness of his environment are crucial for proper brain growth, as these early experiences begin to establish important neuronal connections in the brain. We typically think that learning occurs in school or from reading books to our children, but in fact, the very capacity to learn—to absorb information, discern patterns, and take action in the world—is starting in the first months of life.

Initially, your baby's entire world consists of you and your spouse and any other caregivers who are with him on a daily basis. As he's able to take in the sights, sounds, touches, tastes, and smells that are near at hand and still remain calm, he'll gradually take a more and more active interest in exploring his surroundings. His ability to take in and even see patterns in the sensations and experiences created by his environment will lay the foundation for all of his future learning.

Your baby, like all of us, uses many senses at the same time. He is *simultaneously* looking, listening, moving, and feeling, and sometimes even smelling, tasting, and touching, too. The more your baby is able to make use of information coming from *all* of his senses, the calmer and more regulated he will feel. Paradoxically, when he takes in more information than he can handle, these same senses can be used to calm himself down.

For instance, when your baby looks at your face, he usually sees it as a source of rich, exciting information. If he could use words and think like an older child, he might think to himself as he gazes at your nose, "What's that funny shape in the middle?" He may register your eyes as "those shiny green things looking at me" and your moving lips and voice as the producers of some interesting noise. But if he should become overloaded after too much looking and listening, those same interesting, exciting "green things" can with your help now develop a warm, soothing look to them that will bring him a measure of comfort. The voice that overenergized him can be lowered, and lull him with calming rhythms.

LEARNING TO FEEL SECURE

In this way, your child uses his senses and his motor system to take in sensations from his environment that have the potential both to both intrigue and to soothe him. He is able to take an interest in and become excited by different sensations, yet at the same time he can use sensations in the world to make himself feel calm and regulated. A curious, calm, and regulated baby is by definition a secure baby.

Our adult version of security, while far more complex, still has this dual aspect. We rely on such things as cars that run, bank accounts that are healthy, friendly in-laws, good reports from our doctors, and even political leaders who think as we do to help us feel secure in the world. And if these things that we rely on don't work well, we feel insecure. If our bodies—for example, our memories and stomachs—don't work the way they usually do, we may feel especially insecure.

Your baby is beginning to achieve a sense of security by having control over the seemingly simplest of behaviors: being able to find your face with his beautiful eyes when he hears your voice. But this is no mean feat. He has to first figure out where you are and then activate his muscles and turn his head in your direction.

You can imagine how a baby who has difficulty absorbing the gentle sounds of his mother's lullabies might need an extra dose of rhythmic rocking to bring him back to a state of focused attention when he's upset. Similarly, a baby who is overloaded by various sights might have a tough time recognizing visual patterns and determining whether it is Mommy's or Daddy's face that's hovering over his crib. It's much harder to feel safe and secure in a world in which there are no familiar landmarks. Extra soothing will usually help in such situations.

Offering an overloaded baby simple, soothing sights and sounds may help him recover a sense of regulation. By deliberately putting a peaceful expression on your face and a soothing tone in your voice and facing the baby at a distance that is neither too close nor too far from him, you will likely be able to bring him back to a state of calm interest. As he becomes more aware of his general surroundings, he might eventually notice the shiny necklace around your neck or the colorful hat on your head. However, these sorts of items by themselves aren't compelling enough to sustain his interest and keep him feeling regulated for any extended amount of time. He'll be most fascinated by the richness of his emotional interaction with you.

The importance of this stage is demonstrated not only when babies are able to use their senses to help them regain a sense of security. It is also underscored by those tragic situations in which this early sense of security isn't achievable because there are no consistent, loving caregivers on hand to help babies become interested and engaged in the world around them. Our research with infants whose parents neglect them because of substance abuse or other severe problems points up the critical importance of these early nurturing experiences. We observed that many babies who were very healthy at birth almost immediately began to look at their caregivers, turn to their voices, and even tried to shape their mouths into the beginnings of a smile. However, because their mothers and/or fathers showed little or no interest in helping them focus on their surroundings, within just a few days they lost many of their inborn abilities. The infants became extremely self-absorbed, lost muscle tone, and some even lost their ability to move their heads.

When your own baby is taking in information through his senses, he is also simultaneously experiencing an emotional reaction to those sights, sounds, touches, smells, and tastes that you bring to him. For instance, when your baby hears your voice, he not only begins detecting a vocal pattern that later becomes associated with you and eventually with the word "Mommy" or "Daddy" but that also, in all likelihood, brings him comfort and pleasure.

As we've watched many babies develop over the years, we've come to realize that what have traditionally been described as separate emotional and cognitive (or intellectual) reactions are not so separate after all. In contrast to existing notions, we believe that each time your baby takes in information through his senses, the experience is double-coded as both a physical/cognitive reaction and as an emotional reaction to those sensations. In fact, his emotional reactions may operate like something of a sixth sense, giving each sensory experience texture and meaning.

During this early stage of your baby's development, he will be experiencing basic emotions such as pleasure, comfort, and distress. Over the coming months, you'll see many specific emotions emerging, such as joy, happiness, delight, curiosity, fear, and anger. These emotions will have many subtleties to them, so that eventually you will see your child display an almost infinite range of emotional variations as he attempts to understand his world. Until then, your baby will feel a growing sense of comfort and pleasure in his surroundings, and will gradually come to count on you, his reliable partner, to help him deal with the recurring distress that his hunger and fatigue cause him.

As we mentioned before, your intimate "dialogues" with your child reassure him that his needs can be met and that he can be calmed as well as loved and esteemed. They help him practice using his growing capacities to look, listen, touch, smell, and move, and also promote brain growth that will make him even more capable of retrieving and interpreting the information brought in by his senses. Interestingly, after birth there is a rapid branching of the neuronal connections in your baby's brain as he begins to take in experiences through his senses. The baby's interaction with the world thus promotes the growth of his brain, which in turn enhances his ability to experience and understand his environment. This reciprocal process appears to get more complex as the baby progresses through the early months and years of life, sometimes leading to more brain growth and other times leading to a fine-tuning, or pruning, of the connections and pathways in the brain.

Through the technological magic of brain imaging, we can actually observe how exposure to different sensations affects the connections, or wiring, of the brain. When baby animals are deliberately introduced to more sights, the parts of their cerebral cortexes that are involved in comprehending sight actually develop more neuronal connections. Similarly, if these same animals are immersed in more sounds, those parts of the cortex having to do with coding and understanding sound become more developed.

When you consider that a baby animal living in a forest stands a better chance of reaching physical maturity and reproducing if it is more alert to the sensations that are important in its immediate surroundings, this all makes evolutionary sense. For example, the animal whose brain is richly developed in auditory areas can better discriminate between sounds that mean food and security are near at hand and those that signal danger. As your baby develops a rich network of neuronal connections for sight, sound, taste, smell, and touch, he becomes be better equipped to meet the demands of any environment in which he finds himself. Your tender caresses, empathetic facial expressions, and soothing voice are facilitating the adaptive growth of your child's brain and the eventual blossoming of all of his higher-level learning, social, and thinking skills.

HOW TO HELP YOUR BABY BECOME CALM AND ATTENTIVE

As you and your baby begin to settle into your new relationship, take a close look at how he handles various sensations and controls the muscles in his body. You'll be making use of the information-gathering tools that both of you are born with—the body and its five senses. It's also a good time to make sure his physical environment (such as his crib, toys, mobile, and clothing) is safe and protective. (See Appendix III for some often ignored safety considerations.)

EXPLORING YOUR BABY'S PLEASURE IN DIFFERENT TYPES OF TOUCHES

For the first few weeks of your baby's life, try to concentrate on his needs for comfort in a new environment. You already have much that he needs to ease his transition from the womb into the world—a warm body, loving arms, and a steady heartbeat. As you cradle him in your arms, or nestle him against your chest, recognize that he's feeling the body warmth and heart rhythms that were familiar to him in the womb. Remember, too, that touching and being touched are new sensations for your baby. His skin is exquisitely designed to receive sensation from his surroundings, and you want to make sure that the stroking he receives from you feels good. Most babies enjoy touch that is tender, but firm.

The simple touch of your fingers will not only soothe your baby, it may help him grow! Studies conducted by Duke University researcher Saul Schanberg and his collaborator Tiffany Field appear to indicate that soothing touch releases growth hormones. However, many newborns need to sleep as much as 20 hours a day, so you shouldn't let your loving touches interfere with your baby's need to rest. In later weeks, however, if your child continues to sleep that much you'll want to increase the amount and variety of the touches as well as the sights and sounds you are offering him, to entice him into his wonderful new world. You might consider gently kneading your baby's hands, arms, legs, and feet and see if the baby responds pleasurably to the sensations your hands bring.

It seems that loving touch can also reduce the stress a baby may be experiencing. Megan Gunnar of the University of Minnesota has gauged children's reactions to stress by measuring the levels of a steroid hormone called cortisol in their saliva. By the end of one six-week study in which babies were given twice-weekly massages, cortisol levels markedly decreased. The babies also were less irritable and slept better, too.

Make sure to let your baby's fingers come into contact with different textures—soft and cushiony, smooth, and bumpy—and see if he brightens up. (Ultrasound research has revealed that babies already have had a lot of touch practice from pulling and squeezing their umbilical cords while they are in the womb.) Offer your infant toys that are easy to grasp. By three months, he may be able to reach toward and latch onto a rattle. His fingers will be unclenched and open three quarters of the time he is awake, and you'll want to offer him interesting objects to grasp as he explores the world around him.

HOLDING, HUGGING, ROCKING, AND ROLLING

The way you hold your baby can also have an impact on his sense of security. Some babies curl up like kittens as you hold them against your chest; others flail their limbs or seem stiff-legged and tense when held in that position. Try varying the way you hold your infant to see which position allows him to relax best.

How you move while you hold the baby in your arms also affects his ability to focus calmly. Most babies, during the first weeks of life, are overwhelmed by up-and-down jostling that is too brisk or jerky, and are soothed by rocking and gentle side-to-side movements. Try swaying slowly, taking four to five seconds to move from one side to the other and see if the motion lulls your infant.

As their muscles develop, many infants enjoy rhythmically bouncing in your lap as you hold them. Most also show obvious delight as you hold them up overhead and smile into their eyes. Other babies, however, seem less flexible and their parents have to be a little more inventive in learning which touches and movements best comfort them. Vary the positions you use when you hold your baby and see which ones allow his muscles to relax the most. Does he show any special pleasure when he is moved horizontally or vertically through space?

For most babies, swaddling (gently but firmly bundling the baby's arms and legs in a receiving blanket wrapped around their bodies) is soothing. Other babies enjoy a body massage in which their limbs are gently flexed and extended. Like school-age children who are more attentive in class immediately following recess, these babies seem to need a little sensory and muscular activity to bring them to a state of calm, focused attention.

If your baby seems to be distressed by an embrace that seems quite natural to you, remember that he is not rejecting you. Up until recently, scientists assumed that all human beings experienced sensations in similar ways. We now know that individuals perceive the same stimulus very differently. Your feathery touch could feel tickly and irritating on your newborn's skin, while another baby might take delight in the same caress. Naturally, you may feel a little disappointed that your intuitive approach didn't immediately work, but you can experiment and find a touch that feels right for both you and the baby. It may take a while to hit upon the right balance, and you will no doubt feel frustrated and exhausted from time to time, just as your infant does. Always keep in mind that comforting your baby and slowly introducing him to new sights, sounds, and touches in the first few months of life is an inexact, learn-as-you-go process for everyone involved.

There is one part of an infant's body, though, that almost invariably provides your baby with a sense of comfort and security. Babies take enormous pleasure in using their mouths, and some suck their thumbs even before they are born. The dense nerve endings around the lip area makes moving their mouths and sucking an especially pleasurable activity. You'll soon become aware of your own baby's sucking style. Some infants seem to suck only when hungry or to ease gas pains, while others do it more often. Some suck with vigor as if they're always ravenous; others seem less involved. If your baby doesn't seem to settle himself and relax while sucking, or has difficulty sucking, be sure to mention this to your pediatrician. Occasionally, difficulties in sucking can indicate potential motor challenges that can be helped most effectively when identified early in life.

HELPING YOUR BABY TO LISTEN

As you watch your baby find solace in sucking and calm down as you gently massage him or rhythmically rock while holding him in your arms, you'll probably intuitively murmur to him in low, soothing tones. Your baby's ability to hear and respond to your voice is one of the primary ways in which he learns how to take a deep breath, calm down, and pay attention to you and the world.

Babies react to sounds even while they are still in the womb. During the third trimester, a fetus will actually turn his head in the direction of a noise. At some point during these later months of pregnancy, nearly every mother notices that her baby seems to wake up a little and kick when music is being played nearby. Some studies suggest that talking to your baby before birth, and even singing songs, facilitates later language acquisition. It is unclear, however, whether the baby's reported ease in later comprehending and using words is tied to having heard these muffled sounds while in the uterus. What may be occurring is that parents who talk to their fetus may form an earlier emotional bond that paves the way to more relaxed face-to-face interactions after the baby is born. Continuing observations and research will clarify these issues, but it's important to emphasize that postnatal parent-child dialogues are a foundation for all later intellectual growth—including verbal skills.

At birth, it is apparent that a baby's sense of hearing is better developed than his ability to see, although sight is also developing rapidly. Newborns can already tell what direction a sound comes from, and parents often report that their babies soon try to orient their heads and necks toward their parents' voices. In just a few months, your baby may move his mouth in response to your own cooing and babbling, as if he's trying to imitate the sounds you make. Young infants also seem to enjoy music, just as they did in the womb.

TUNING IN TO YOUR BABY'S PREFERRED WAVELENGTH

We tend to assume that all babies hear the same way, but as with most other things, the way we hear often varies from individual to individual. As you interact playfully with your baby, observe how he reacts to sounds. For the most part, you'll be picking up on styles and preferences. However, if your baby doesn't pay even fleeting attention to ordinary sounds when you play with him, or to loud noises that are near at hand, be sure to consult with your pediatrician to check whether there is a physical problem with hearing.

As your baby develops during the first three months, try to discover the pitches and rhythms he enjoys. Most infants prefer high-pitched, but not screechy, vocalizations, so you can usually entice your infant's attention by using typical baby talk. Experiment with different cadences, and notice whether the baby turns toward you. You might imitate the coos and chirps the baby makes and see if he tries to reply in kind. Be playful, have fun, and take mental notes as you enjoy your baby's interest in you.

Some infants seem to overreact to high-pitched voice patterns and respond far more pleasurably to lower, even guttural, sounds. Occasionally a baby will find the sound of a high-pitched maternal voice so aversive that his body stiffens and he may actually turn away from his mother in a panic. It's as if the sound of her voice grates on him like fingernails on a chalkboard. Such behavior naturally upsets the mother. In response, she may then inadvertently speak even more rapidly and at a higher register because she is nervous.

Parents should realize, however, that a baby who is sensitive to sounds can be just as attentive, loving, and relaxed as any other baby. You might try slowing down your vocalizations and lowering both the intensity and pitch of your voice. As you rock back and forth with your baby held against your chest, quietly intone a few syllables over and over again. Let your baby feel the humming vibrations in your chest while you murmur to him. Your modulated voice, gentle touches and facial expressions, and rocking should all help to soothe your infant. Over time, he may develop interest in the range of pitches, cadences, and volumes that previously overloaded him.

If, on the other hand, your baby seems underreactive to sounds, you'll have to try to be more dramatic as you speak to him. You'll know that he has to be wooed a little if he doesn't wriggle his limbs in excitement or look toward the source of a sound. Be animated, not dignified. Speak as though your every sentence were punctuated by exclamation marks! Vary the pitch and rhythms of the sounds you use, even while you sway with him in your arms or playfully massage him. Greet him with lively facial gestures to cement your connection. Then gradually increase the energy level of your voice.

Why is it so important to help your baby process the sounds he hears? The answer is a simple one: enjoying sounds helps him to relate to you and others, and to learn to communicate and think. Also, your continued willingness to reach out to him and look for ways to entice his sense of hearing will firm up his sense that he is important to you. This is doubly important, since parents whose babies have challenges in the way they hear may understandably feel rejected and discouraged by a situation in which their child seems to avoid their voices, and unconsciously buffer themselves from these feelings by pulling away emotionally.

Your baby doesn't know the meaning of the words he hears right now, but by the time he is 12 to 18 months old he will gradually, and often very visibly, be able to figure out the emotional tone of your words. For instance, when he hears you say in a happy tone, "Oh, look at my big explorer!" as he opens up a box, he will beam with pride and know that you're proud of his behavior. Hearing Mom's or Dad's voice and understanding whether they are approving or disapproving helps toddlers feel connected to their parents from afar, and in that way more free to explore their surroundings and become independent.

Helping Your Infant Enjoy the Visual World

Gradually, over the first few months, babies become better and better at seeing shapes, patterns, and, most importantly, you. After a slow start, when babies tend to be farsighted, their eyesight improves very rapidly. Usually within a few weeks after birth, babies can follow objects moving on horizontal and vertical planes with their eyes. They prefer black and white, hard-edged figures to colored ones. By about two months of age, infants will stop crying when they see their mother, and may smile in response to a smiling human face—and may even respond to a drawing of a face.

Infants seem to find the human face naturally fascinating. Young babies will gaze longer at a picture of a face in which the eyes, nose, and mouth are positioned appropriately than they will at drawings where facial features are placed randomly. By three to four months, your baby's vision is approaching 20/20, and he will try to reach out toward nearby objects. He now has the world in his view and at his fingertips.

Checking out how your infant uses his vision is as easy as sticking out your tongue. Try making a silly face; lift your eyebrows and drop your jaw. See if your baby prefers one expression over another. Vary the visual games you play with your baby. Have him track a bright object as you move it from side to side.

Your baby finds your face more fascinating than any toy. Let him gaze deeply into your eyes as you hold him or nurse him. The sight of your face calms and organizes him, and enables him to absorb and not be overwhelmed by the new sights that greet him every day. However, don't feel as if you must constantly entertain your baby or lock eyes with him. Both of you need brief breaks from each other, so give your baby a variety of things to look at, especially when you're not around. A few simple toys painted in bright, contrasting colors or in bold black-and-white designs will encourage your baby's interest.

Some infants may be hypersensitive to bright or normal light conditions, or become upset by certain facial expressions. If your baby seems tense when his room is flooded with sunlight or when an overhead light shines on his face, try dimming the lighting and see if he appears more calm. Moderate your vivacity if he seems a little overwhelmed by your enthusiastic facial expressions.

If, on the other hand, your baby seems disinterested in watching your face or in tracking moving objects, try to make his environment more visually exciting. Put a bright hat on your head or a red ball in your mouth. Become more visually interesting by shining a light on your face. If your baby seems to relish physical handling, bring your face down close to his as you massage his arms and legs. Over time he will associate the pleasure he takes in that activity with the expressiveness of your face.

As your baby's visual abilities grow during this first year, watch him begin to follow your hands as well as your face, and then look to the floor as you drop his favorite rattle. When he's nearing eight months of age, try hiding something he wants in your hand and see if he will look, react, or even touch your closed fist. In his second year, enjoy treasure-hunt games where the two of you search for hidden toys and navigate through obstacle courses. Before long, during the preschool years you will be building block-towns together and marveling at your junior architect's creativity.

ENCOURAGING MOVEMENT AND MUSCLE CONTROL

In these early months, your baby is slowly beginning to gain some control over his movements. He is far more advanced in what he hears, sees, and feels than in his motor responses to those sounds, sights, and touches. He is clearly adept at crying and sucking, and can certainly influence you and his world with those two behaviors! However, he's only just beginning to learn to cuddle and turn his head and move his arms and legs. Over time, as his muscles develop, he will be turning his head toward your lively or soothing voice, and rhythmically moving his arms as you talk to him. You can help him learn to come to an upright position and to hold his head up by having him recline against your propped-up knees as you hold his hands and gently pull him toward you.

READING YOUR BABY'S CRIES

By the time your infant is two months old, he may stop crying when he hears your footsteps heading his way. If so, he is already learning that his cries bring a quick response from you. As this stage of his development progresses, you will notice a change in the timbre of your baby's cries. His lungs are maturing, the muscles of his lips and mouth are growing, and his tongue will change shape the more he uses his voice. You'll soon be able to pick up differences in the levels of happiness and distress he expresses. Cries of real hunger and pain will have more intensity than the cranky wailing of sleepiness. Most parents also learn to recognize when their infant is in need of immediate comfort or when he just needs to ventilate some frustration.

At the same time, your baby is becoming more sensitive to your reactions to his cries. A soothing, soft tone will comfort him, while an anxious or angry voice will cause him to startle and tense his muscles. (Interestingly, he may not react at all to loud, nonhuman noises like thunderclaps or sirens.)

Always bear in mind that your baby's cries are his only way of letting you know that something is causing him distress, and are not a criticism of the way you take care of him. As you respond to his wailing and his tears, he learns that when he gets unpleasant feelings he can literally call on you to bring him back to a state of calmness. You are gradually becoming your baby's safe harbor from the sensations that overexcite or alarm him. By soothing him and then encouraging him to refocus his attention on the outside human world, you are teaching your infant how to make his inside world feel better, too.

CHECKING OUT YOUR BABY'S ABILITY TO TASTE AND SMELL

Though the closely related senses of taste and smell have historically received less attention than hearing, sight, and touch, they too are developmentally important. The sense of smell develops almost entirely after birth, yet early on most babies tolerate, and some even show a sparkly-eyed pleasure, when exposed to fruity odors like a lemony after-shave lotion.

Babies quickly come to recognize their own mother's scent. By the time an infant is ten days old, he can distinguish the smell of his mother's milk. Once the association is made between the mother's smell and the taste of her milk, the baby has two new added sources of sensory comfort available to him. Generally speaking, though, it is difficult for parents to observe any subtle sensitivities or underreactivity to taste and smell in infants who are less than three months old because usually only milk or formula crosses their lips.

If you are breastfeeding, you may notice how the foods you eat influence the vigor and length of time of your baby's sucking. Babies in all probability have more variations in their capacities to smell and taste than we have yet discovered. Certainly as babies become toddlers and preschoolers, they show strong preferences based on taste and smell, especially in food choices. This will be an important factor to recognize and work with if your baby turns out to be a finicky eater.

RAISING THE BAR

When your three-month-old can remain in a state of calm for minutes at a time and show brief but very real interest in a variety of sensations, you can create interactive opportunities that will promote his ability to focus and attend. Your goal will be *to interact with your baby during at least half of his waking hours.* These interactions won't tire your baby out, particularly if you vary the pace from low-key and soothing to exciting. They will include all those times when you are changing his diapers, feeding him, and playing with him, and even when you are cooking or cleaning in his presence, too.

When you offer your baby various sights and sounds and patterns of touch and movement that intrigue him, this will often lead to at least a split second more of shared looking and shared listening. Perhaps you'll discover that your baby enjoys high-pitched sounds by noticing the look of glee on his face when you warble, "Ooo, ooo, ooo." Try to build on what he enjoys, and offer him a lower-pitched humming sound, "Mmm, mmm, mmm" followed by a deep, full-throated "Boom, boom, boom." You can similarly expand from simple percussive beats such as "Ba dum" to more complex rhythms like "Ba dum dum dah!" Or you might present your baby with a simple facial expression, perhaps quizzically raising your eyebrow, and then adding a wrinkled-up nose and pursed lips to the mix.

The point of all this activity is to help your baby engage his senses, motor skills, and emotions in a single activity. If he is looking, listening, experiencing touch, and moving his muscles in an emotionally relevant way, he will truly be learning. For instance, the next time you rock your baby in your arms, make a point to gently move your head back and forth in rhythm with the beat of the nursery rhyme you're singing. See if his eyes follow yours as your head sways from right to left and back again; notice if his face brightens in pleasure as you stretch out a silly-sounding syllable for emphasis. Try cupping his feet in your hand as you rock, and watch how he reacts when you give them a playful squeeze. This sort of activity gives your baby practice in connecting sights, sounds, touches, and movements in a more organized way, even as he is being drawn into an increasingly special relationship with you.

OVERCOMING CHALLENGES: A BLESSING IN DISGUISE

After noting how your baby typically reacts to a range of sensations, you'll begin to get a feel for his sensory and motor characteristics. You may see certain patterns emerging that seem to point to some difficulties in the way he processes various sights, sounds, touches, tastes, and smells. Perhaps you've noted that he struggles a little to move his limbs fluidly or to hold his head up sturdily.

The exciting news is that you can adjust your behavior as you interact with your child and actually influence the way his nervous system is biologically designed to function. Although you certainly didn't cause any processing and sequencing differences or sensory sensitivities in your

Dos and Don'ts as You Help Your Baby Maintain a Calm Interest in the World

🦶 *Don't* just stimulate your baby with exciting mobiles, rattles, music boxes, and other toys.

🦶 *Don't* leave him to placidly gaze at the world on his own for very long stretches of time.

🦶 *Do* discover how your child's senses work. What sights, sounds, touches, and movements bring him pleasure and delight? Which senses keep him calm and foster his interest and attention? Does he prefer soft or loud sounds? Slow or fast rhythms? Bright lights and complex designs or soft lights and simple patterns? Explore each sense and create experiences tailored to his unique nervous system.

🦶 *Do* help him use his muscles to turn his head, stick out his tongue, cuddle, and gradually move his arms and legs in rhythm with your voice.

baby, your ongoing interactions with him can be an important part of his developing mastery. By becoming more aware of the pros and cons of your own intuitive interactive style, you'll become better able to help your baby overcome challenges to emotional engagement.

Sometimes a family's ability to adapt to a baby's individual needs may be undermined by financial and marital problems, or jealous or needy older children. Your efforts may sometimes be exhausting. But every minute you spend helping your child maintain a sense of calm interest in the world is crucially important, because all of his emerging skills will rest on this ability.

Let's take a look at a few families who grappled with the challenge of helping their babies relax and engage with life. We'll be following these five children as they move through the six developmental stages. You'll notice that some of the parents are already beginning to observe their children's characteristic way of interacting with the world very early on, but aren't always sure about what to do when these patterns present challenges. Before too long, all of the parents will be discovering ways to help their babies master some of these expectable challenges.

BABIES WHO ARE SENSITIVE TO TOUCH AND SOUND

Steve and Ellen were both in their thirties when Ellen gave birth to their third child, Kara. With the confidence born of raising four-year-old Joey and six-year-old Rachel, both Steve and Ellen eagerly looked forward to adding another child to their family. They were realists, though, and expected the first few months to be a little rocky.

Kara was a wiry infant; both Steve and Ellen noticed right away that her body felt less cuddly than Joey's and Rachel's had at the same age. Their older children had both seemed to mold their torsos effortlessly to their parents' chests when they were held upright. Kara, on the other hand, was all knees and elbows, usually flailing her arms and legs when she was picked up and hugged.

When Kara nursed, she seemed ravenous, taking big, shuddering gulps. Ellen was pleased with her success at breastfeeding, but was hoping that the baby would learn to sleep at longer intervals. Kara would fall into a deep sleep as soon as her hunger was satisfied, but would awaken with a start, and start howling when she was placed back in her bassinet. This began to frustrate her parents, who had counted on her down periods to free up some time to focus on their older children.

Steve was less tentative than his wife as he held Kara, and he routinely swaddled her in a receiving blanket after he changed her diaper. Before long, both parents realized that the baby calmed down more readily when Steve handled her, as if she needed the firmer control over her muscles that he provided. Kara also seemed to be quieted by the deep pitch of his voice.

Ellen was unnerved by Steve's relative competency with Kara. With six years of mothering behind her, she was frustrated to think that she was having difficulty parenting her new baby. Although she was a little jealous of Steve's success, Ellen eventually tried copying Steve's firmer touch and also consciously lowered the pitch of her somewhat shrill voice.

Before many weeks had passed, Ellen began to be reassured. Kara was clearly relaxing in response to being swaddled and spoken to in low tones. She still had difficulty sleeping more than a couple of hours at a time, though, and would awake from her short naps with colicky cries. The family's pediatrician said that the baby was probably swallowing air because she nursed so aggressively. Although they still had to contend with their chronic fatigue, Steve and Ellen were relieved to know that nothing was seriously wrong with their baby.

Three months after Kara's birth, both Steve and Ellen knew that although they could help her with her sensitivity to touch and higher-pitched noise, it would be awhile yet before they were successful in calming her down enough to nurse more slowly, and sleep more deeply. They were drained by the unexpected challenges Kara presented, but were cautiously optimistic that they'd get a breather in the next few months. After all, both Joey and Rachel "had really seemed to get their acts together" by the time they were three or four months old. Steve and Ellen felt that they were adapting to Kara's needs and building a foundation for more flexibility.

BABIES WHO ARE UNDERWHELMED BY THE WORLD AROUND THEM

Brian weighed in at nearly nine pounds when he was born. His parents, Stuart and Tammy, were thrilled at his robust size and easy disposition. Everyone who saw Brian remarked on how round he was! Since Stuart and Tammy had listened to their friends' war stories about babies who never seemed to sleep, they felt unusually blessed to have a little boy who slept most of the day away. Tammy was especially grateful for the reprieve, since she had had an emergency cesarian section and was still recovering from the surgery.

Twelve weeks later, Brian's parents felt that they "had this parent thing pretty well nailed down." Not only did their baby routinely sleep a solid eight hours each night, he only rarely had fussy periods. In fact, Brian didn't require too much attention from his parents, and seemed to enjoy his own company. Stuart and Tammy did notice that when they wound up the mobile hanging over Brian's crib, he would remain mesmerized by the whirling animals for long periods of time.

Brian was sweet and soft and a pleasure to show off to relatives and friends. He didn't seem particularly interested in the world outside his crib, though, and seldom craned his neck up above the bumper pads to get a good look. Stuart and Tammy simply assumed that he was a contented little soul whose chubby body made using his muscles more trouble than it was worth. As Stuart put it, "Frankly, we're grateful to have a baby who's so undemanding!" However, after a while, both of Brian's parents began to wonder whether he would ever respond to their adoring gazes with any signs of interest of engagement.

At a time like this, it's very helpful for parents to begin exploring different sounds and sights and intensities of emotion (energetic or soothing, for example) to woo their babies into an interest in the world. In the following chapters we'll see how Tammy and Stuart discovered their own talent at doing this.

BABIES WHO CRAVE STIMULATION

Emma was born with a crop of red curls and a temper to match. Her parents, Mike and Laura, had married late in life and were in their early forties. They were ecstatic when Laura experienced no difficulties in becoming pregnant and carrying the baby to term. However, dealing with their redheaded infant was a lot more than they had bargained for.

Emma came into the world "like a live wire," according to her father. Even as a newborn she seemed to crave sensation. Her arms and legs would wave around whenever she was awake, as if she were eager to get a move on. Emma cried a lot, and her parents sensed their baby's frustration but were at a loss to explain her distress. It was clear, however, that eating wasn't the source of Emma's agitation. She handled her bottle feedings efficiently and only rarely had stomach upsets. Her sleeping patterns seemed normal. By three months, the baby slept in four-hour blocks of time during the night, and Laura and Mike took turns spelling each other with the 4 A.M. feeding.

Why did their baby seem so irritable, then? Mike noticed that Emma did seem to brighten up a little when he played a "bicycle" game with her. As the baby lay on her back, Mike would cup each of her feet in his palms and push them in a peddling motion. He was surprised at the strength of her pushes and made a comment about it to the baby's pediatrician. The doctor told him that some particularly active babies seemed driven to using their extensor muscles, and enjoyed the sensation of pushing.

Now that they knew that a certain type of exercise and body massage brought pleasure to Emma, both Laura and Mike tried to incorporate more of it into the rhythms of their baby's daily life. Diaper changes provided them with frequent opportunities for playful exercising, and Emma showed obvious excitement as she arched her back and extended her legs. She would cry in a fury, though, when the playtime ended. Emma's parents began to wonder whether they were spoiling her, since giving her the exercise she appeared to require only quieted her down for short periods of time. Would their baby ever be able to relax enough to give them the quiet moments of loving feedback that they were yearning for?

As we've discussed, some babies seem to love extra sensations, and parents like Laura and Mike can gradually learn how to proactively supply their baby with opportunities for thoroughly enjoying her senses and emerging motor and social skills. In the coming chapters, we'll see how Laura and Mike continue to discover what techniques work best for Emma.

BABIES WHO TAKE IN SIGHTS, BUT TUNE OUT SOUNDS

Although he was a buttoned-down communications lawyer by profession, Dan was a frustrated rock musician at heart. When his wife Lisa was pregnant with Will, their first baby, Dan would adjust his audio system and flood their apartment with Eddie Van Halen's riffs. He was looking forward to sharing his love of hard-driving music with his son. (Prenatal tests had already revealed the baby's sex.) Dan had immediately mapped out an imaginary future involving lots of father-son bonding, with a focus on Orioles games and trips to the guitar store. Lisa, who had recently taken a leave of absence from her job as a travel agent, was far more concerned about simply surviving the chaotic next few months as she and her baby learned to adjust to and love each other.

When Will was born on December 31, Dan bragged that "he was not only the best-looking kid in the nursery, but the most thoughtful. Now we can claim him as a dependent and save a bundle on last year's taxes!" This baby was an eagerly awaited addition to Dan and Lisa's life, and they were looking forward to their new role as parents.

From the very start, Lisa felt as if Will was using his eyes to try and absorb as much as he could of the world around him. She knew that a newborn's vision was blurry, and that he couldn't possibly comprehend much of anything he was seeing. Still, by the time Will was a little over two months old, Lisa could see that he was unusually attracted to bright colors. He would even try to orient himself toward the light shed by a nearby floor lamp. As the weeks went on, Will grew increasingly caught up in studying her face, which brought her a profound sense of joy. Lisa's own facial expressions grew more animated as she interacted with her baby;

when she'd arch her eyebrows in mock surprise, Will would furrow his brow and try to copy her expression.

Dan was having a tougher time settling into his new role. In fact, he had the distinct impression that he wasn't even a blip on Will's horizon line. Dan would hold Will in his arms and sing a whole medley of Motown love songs, but Will would look right through him. Desperate to get his attention, Dan would try holding him at arm's length, tilting him from side to side as he recited nursery rhymes. Dancing with the baby only seemed to agitate him further.

Dan was getting worried about his ability to connect with his son. "I don't know; it's as if Will only has eyes for Lisa and couldn't care less about me. I really try to give it my best shot when I'm with Will, but he just tunes me out." Lisa was upset, too, since she knew her husband was feeling hurt. Both parents had their fingers crossed that this was just one of those inexplicable, quirky things that babies go through from time to time.

It's important to remember that babies like Will usually aren't personalizing their preferences; it's simply a matter of being attracted to certain types of sounds that bring them more pleasure and comfort. As parents explore different varieties of sounds, they come to realize that they are able to provide their baby with sound patterns that will entice him to enjoy their tones. In the chapters that follow, we will see how Dan and Lisa accomplish this.

BABIES WHO TAKE IN SOUNDS, BUT HAVE A HARD TIME FIGURING OUT SIGHTS

Lynn and Jonathan were scarcely more than newlyweds when they found out they were going to have a baby. Neither had planned on starting their family so quickly, so it took a little while to get used to the idea. Lynn suffered from terrible bouts of morning sickness, and even had to be hospitalized at one point during her pregnancy. It seemed ironic, then, when their baby's birth was unexpectedly easy. After just three hours of labor and a few big pushes, all eight pounds, two ounces of Max made his way into the world.

From the start, he was a big, beautiful, and very noisy baby. Even as the nurses marveled over his black curls and chubby cheeks, they said things like "Just listen to that baby roar!" The crying didn't let up when he got home, either. Lynn and Jonathan were upset by his obvious distress, especially when his hands and knees would tremble as he wailed. When the pediatrician diagnosed a classic case of colic, and advised them to expect weeks more of the same, they were actually relieved to know that they hadn't done anything "wrong" or caused the problem.

Still, the crying made everyone anxious and exhausted. Lynn did notice, however, that Max seemed to be comforted when she hummed into his ear and held him against her chest. His little hands would slowly unclench and his breathing would become more regular as she rocked back and forth, crooning. The two of them would rock together sometimes for a half hour at a time, and the baby would drift back into sleep until gas bubbles triggered off another round of howling tears.

Jonathan didn't seem to have the same magic touch with Max, however. When he attempted to distract his colicky son by waggling his fingers in front of the baby's face, or by having a brightly colored puppet dance just inches from his nose, Max would just screw up his eyes and cry all the louder. Lynn would then rush over and try her own hand at comforting the baby. She was a little hurt, though, when Max would sometimes turn his head away from her hovering face. On one of those occasions when even her crooning voice didn't seem to bring him any solace, Lynn turned on the "white noise" machine that she had bought as a study aid when she was in college. Max's cries abruptly stopped when he heard the sound of waves crashing against a shore and the call of sea birds. His brow was still furrowed in pain, but it was obvious he was listening to these new sounds, and that they were intriguing him.

During these quieter times, Lynn and Jonathan began to realize just how much Max was soothed by certain sounds, and that he would sometimes turn his head to hear where their voices were coming from. He didn't seem to take any comfort in looking at his parents' faces, however, and often gazed at objects rather than at their facial expressions or gestures. In this situation, Max's parents were confronted by two challenges. First, they wanted to help their baby regain calm after he was beset by colic pains, and as you'll see in subsequent chapters, he was able to get past the worst of his discomfort before too long. However, a second related challenge also was becoming clear: Max wasn't beginning to use the sight of his parents' faces either as a way to calm himself or as a source of pleasure.

Sometimes it's helpful to give a baby like Max extra practice in focusing on his parents' faces by offering him a combination of interesting facial expressions and soothing and intriguing rhythms of sounds during those periods of the day when he is both calm and alert. Rather than becoming discouraged when your baby disengages from you with just a brief glance, try to let him to refocus on something and then join in with whatever he's looking at. For instance, if he seems to be looking over your shoulder at a colorful block, you might try putting the block in front of your face and accompanying your action with a combination of rhythmic sounds and animated facial expressions. Simply try to extend your interaction for just a few seconds more.

If your baby doesn't look at or focus on you or any objects, consult with your pediatrician about scheduling a visual examination. Once any physical problems have been ruled out, your baby may still continue to have a difficult time finding pleasure in looking at your face, either because he is over- or undersensitive to sights or because he has difficulty in making sense of what he sees. You might try approaching him slowly with animated facial expressions and sounds, and notice whether he seems better able to focus on you when you're at a particular distance from him. It is helpful to be patient, relaxed, playful, and persistent. Many babies who are slow to develop a comforting sense of pleasure from their parents' faces eventually become enamored at the very sight of Mom or Dad coming into view. A consultation with a developmental specialist can often help if by four to five months of age you are not seeing signs of delight in your baby's eyes.

In the coming chapters, we'll be examining how early parental interactions can foster emotional, social, and intellectual growth for babies like Kara, Brian, Emma, Will, and Max. It's important to remember that *all* infants—those with expectable sensory differences as well as those facing more significant challenges—can be brought into deepening relationships with their parents.

COMMON FAMILY CHALLENGES IN THE FIRST MONTHS

The most important step in helping your baby maintain calm and focused attention is to calm yourself down first. Forget any notions you may have had about perfect babies who come into the world cooing and ready to sleep and eat in nice, tidy intervals. Many new parents have little or no experience with infants and are shaken when the early months of parent-hood force them to abandon their formerly scheduled lives. When your baby's cries awaken you and you're still bone-tired, when no amount of creative burping brings him relief, when your mother-in-law offers unsolicited advice and even your spouse says, "I told you so," try to remember, "This, too, shall pass."

You may be lucky and feel an enormous sense of love for your baby the first time you lay eyes on him. For many parents, though, love and con-nectedness take weeks and even months to build. Love emerges out of the thousands of face-to-face interactions and cuddles that you'll be sharing with your baby. For now, settle for tender regard and protectiveness, and revel in your baby's astonishing newness. Listen to the words of some new parents:

I can't tell you how disappointed I was when the nurse first put the baby in my arms. To tell you the truth, my first thought was that she looked like raw hamburger meat. This was definitely not the Gerber baby I'd been expect-ing! . . . When they brought her back to me once I was up in my room, though, the first thing I did was unwrap her blanket and count her fingers and toes, just like you see in the movies. I remember tracing my finger along her cheeks, real slowly, and stroking the skin behind her earlobes. This in-credible bolt of tenderness went right through me. In all my life I had never, ever, felt anything so soft and new as the feel of her skin. What I felt wasn't really love—I was still so wiped out from fourteen hours of labor that at that point I was more interested in someone loving and babying me. But I know that I felt like this funny-looking little baby was mine, mine, mine.

I'll be honest with you. My wife said she loved the baby the moment they put him on her belly in the delivery room, but it's different for me. I mean, I re-ally enjoy holding him, and I get a kick out of the way he looks when my wife brushes his hair so that it stands straight up on his head and sticks out like a fuzz ball. . . . Sometimes I'm amazed at how natural it seems to have a lit-tle baby in the house these past couple of months, but I can't say I feel love for him, the way I love my wife. Some things really get to me though, like when the baby pokes his head up and it sort of bobbles around, when I come near his crib in the morning.

It was the smell of her skin and her breath that really got to me. Is that weird? My husband says that I'm a Mother Earth type and I guess it's true. All I know is that her newness really sent me over the moon. It sounds ridiculous to fall in love with your baby because her breath is so sweet, or because her skin smells like warm butter, but I did.

Here's the thing. I really do love him now, so I can say this without feeling too guilty. He was the sort of newborn that's every parent's nightmare. I mean, he couldn't sleep. He wouldn't sleep. We'd rock him and walk with him and drive him around in the car, but none of it worked. He had trouble breastfeeding, so we switched him to formula. My wife felt like a failure and I had to deal with her, too. On top of everything, he's supersensitive to noise and the wall of his bedroom is next to the garbage chute just outside our apartment door. Every time someone dumped cans or boxes down the chute he'd go nuts. I mean ballistic, with his face beet-red and his fists all balled up, legs kicking—the works. The good news is this past month the baby has really started to calm down. We get a solid five to six hours sleep each night after his last feeding at midnight, so we both feel more human. Plus, he really seems to know who we are now. When I give him his bottle he sort of arches his neck to get a better look at me and sometimes even stops drinking just to flash me a smile. What can I say? He's got us both wrapped around his little finger.

These parents have learned that sometimes focusing on as few as one or two of your baby's pleasing characteristics can help you build up a tolerance for other disappointing or frustrating behaviors. The tenderness and fun of sharing intimate glances, touches, and even sniffs with your baby can make the sloppiness and stresses of this initial "getting-to-know-you" period seem less overwhelming. You've paid your dues these first few sleep-deprived months, and now your baby's newfound ability to settle himself down and focus will soon be paying off in a big way. He's ready to fall in love.

MAINTAINING CALM, GETTING FOCUSED

Help your baby calm down, look and listen, and begin to move!

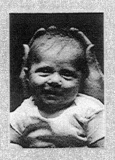

FUN AND GAMES

🎐 The "Look and Listen" Game

Enjoy face-to-face games with your baby in which you smile and talk to him about his beautiful lips, sparkly eyes, and button nose. As you slowly move your animated face to the right or left, try to capture your baby's attention for a few seconds. This game can be played while you hold the baby in your arms, or you can hover near him when he's reclining in an infant seat or lying in your spouse's arms.

🎐 The "Soothe Me" Game

Settle into a comfortable rocking chair and enjoy slow, rhythmic rocking with your baby when he's fussy or tired, or during other times when you simply want to cuddle. As you soothingly touch your baby's arms, legs, tummy, back, feet, and hands and relax into the lulling back-and-forth rocking rhythm, try to gently move his little fingers and toes in a "This Little Piggy" type of game. You can move his arms and legs, and fingers and toes as you change his diaper, too.

2

STAGE 2:
FALLING IN LOVE

WHAT THIS STAGE IS ALL ABOUT

Falling in love with your child is a gradual process that often begins before your baby is born. By the time she is about two to four months old, your baby is poised at the brink of making her own loving feelings more overt. Your first inkling of this may come when you notice that your infant seems more intensely involved with you. There may be special moments when she looks longingly, without blinking, into the very depths of your eyes. Sometimes she may flash you a radiant, loving smile, or coo and grin at you when you pick her up for a cuddle. Or your attention may be caught by the way she brightens to the sound of your voice or wiggles in anticipation when she hears you approach.

These special smiles and looks may bathe you in a flood of tender feelings as you realize that your infant has discovered the joy of loving another human being, namely you, and wants to be a partner in the intimacy. There is now a wonderful shared sense of bliss between the two of you. Your baby is no longer simply a receiver of love; she's an active participant in a loving relationship. The emotional give-and-take between you and your baby can make you both feel unique and valued. You may even be reminded of the wonderful, deep feelings of your courtship days, or if you were fortunate, of your own childhood.

Throughout this stage of development, which loosely spans the period from first smiles to crawling, your baby becomes more and more focused on you and other persons and things outside herself. During the first few months of life she was more easily distracted by the gas bubbles and hunger pangs she experienced inside her own body. After thousands and thousands of interactions with you, however, she has come to link your presence in her life with a whole range of pleasurable sensations. You fill her with milk, give her warm physical contact, and soothe her when she becomes distraught. Now she is ready to respond to your loving overtures with affection of her own.

Your delightful task during these months will be to promote pleasurable feelings between you and your baby. As your child develops more sophisticated ways to communicate her feelings, you can help her receive and send as many loving messages as she can. You can also help her explore other feelings that are starting to pop up as she intimately relates to you. Curiosity, anger, sadness, excitement, and joy will appear more and more frequently to heighten the love you are now experiencing together.

Though the above description captures the pleasures and drama of falling in love for many babies and their caregivers, not all of us discover love in such an idyllic manner. In fact, many infants are still fussy or colicky at this stage and experience only moments of relaxed bliss. Some babies are more laid-back and require lots of wooing. Numerous new moms and dads feel exhausted or worried for lots of valid reasons. We'll be discussing these and other situations later in this chapter.

Remember, there are many ways to fall in love. Sometimes it takes a while for love to blossom; sometimes there are lots of bumps along the way. What's important is that your shared intimacy is gradually growing.

You have plenty of time to cement a loving relationship with your child, as long as you stay emotionally involved.

HOW YOU KNOW YOUR BABY IS FALLING IN LOVE WITH YOU

You'll know that your baby has reached a new rung on the developmental ladder when she resonates with the emotion you express to her with *an emotional reaction of her own.* Her ability to love you and to respond in many different ways to your emotional overtures also reveals just how adept and smart she's becoming. For example, if you greet her with a big, bright smile, she may beam with delight. If you wrinkle your brow, she may look perplexed as though she were imitating your worried facial expression. When you make clucking noises, your baby may struggle to work her mouth into a shape that mimics yours, even though she can't yet duplicate your sounds. You can try to get a duet going between the two of you that consists of shared smiles, frowns, other facial expressions, and rhythmic arm and leg movements.

A second and equally important indication that your baby is emotionally responsive is *the obvious pleasure or joy she takes in your company.* Her loving smile or yelp or gleeful sounds when she first sees you in the morning and the excited squeals or waving arms she produces in response to your voice are all her ways of showing you her loving feelings.

By five months or so, your baby will show you (and other key caregivers) her growing capacity to form a loving relationship by behaving in a variety of ways. Some of these include:

- Responding to your smiles with a big one of her own
- Initiating interactions with loving looks and smiles
- Making sounds and/or moving her mouth, arms, legs, or body in rhythm with you as you move in rhythm with her
- Relaxing or acting comforted when you hold her or rock her
- Cooing when she is held, touched, looked at or spoken to
- Looking at your face with rapt interest
- Anticipating with curiosity and excitement the reappearance of your face or voice
- Looking uneasy or sad when you withdraw in the midst of playing with her

- Becoming angry (with a furrowed brow or piercing cry) when she's frustrated by something you are doing
- Recovering from distress, with your help, within 15 minutes

Your baby may even show very specific preferences, and radiate excitement when *you* amplify her pleasure by:

- Talking and babbling to her, using a variety of high and low pitches and soft to loud tones
- Offering her a range of different facial expressions while talking and babbling
- Touching or massaging her, using gentle touch while telling her what you are doing
- Gently moving her arms and legs while talking to her and looking at her
- Moving her horizontally or vertically, fast and slow, through space while beaming at her with big smiles accompanied by lots of sounds and words

As your baby relates to you and expresses loving feelings, various motor, sensory, language, and cognitive achievements are also often taking place. The milestone of falling in love usually organizes and gives purpose to these skills. For example, when your baby is physically capable of reaching out and grasping something, she will more often attempt to reach for something that she is interested in and takes delight in. There's nothing more interesting in her world than you, and her love for you will continue to spur her on as she learns to reach, grasp, sit, and eventually crawl toward you, the object of her affection.

Similarly, her maturing senses help her recognize you in more and more ways. Over the past few months, your baby has become able to see your entire face clearly, and can recognize you from a distance. Initially she could only perceive your nose, mouth, or eyes as isolated features. By the time she is four months old, she may be able to see the pattern formed by the features on your face and hear more sound patterns, as well. Now, when you greet her with a cheery "Good morning, little Anna Banana!" she may be able to associate this rhythm of sounds with your reentry into her world each day.

In short, your baby's growing use of her muscles and senses, and her ability to respond to patterns of sights and language are all promoted and

A Baby's Developing Skills

MOTOR SKILLS

- Pushing up on extended arms
- Shifting weight on hands and knees
- Readying her body for lifting while being picked up
- Rolling from back to front
- Reaching for a toy
- Sitting with support
- Cooperating in being pulled to a sitting position
- Bringing hands together
- Grasping objects voluntarily

SENSORY SKILLS

- Reacting to a piece of paper placed on her face
- Looking toward a sound
- Tolerating gentle roughhousing

LANGUAGE SKILLS

- Regularly localizing the source of a voice with accuracy
- Vocalizing two different sounds
- Responding to your expressions and sounds with vocalizations

COGNITIVE SKILLS

- Focusing and paying attention for 30 or more seconds
- Looking and scanning for objects and faces
- Smiling at her own face in the mirror
- Looking toward an object that moves out of her visual range
- Looking at her own hand
- Manipulating and playing with toys, such as a rattle or key ring

somewhat organized by her growing involvement with and love for you. In turn, these same abilities help the baby express her love for you, and further cement your intimate relationship. The vital role love plays in this process is made tragically clear when we consider the plight of some Eastern European orphans who were warehoused in institutional settings and deprived of steady one-on-one relationships with loving adults. Although they may have mobiles hanging over their cribs, babies and children in these conditions rarely give them a glance and become increasingly self-absorbed. Over time some of these children lose the ability to move energetically because they have no one to reach out for. Many show severe weaknesses in their cognitive, language, sensory-processing, and fine-motor skills. Some fail to gain weight and some even die. Without the nourishment of love, a whole variety of developmental skills simply will not blossom. That's how important love is.

The chart on the preceding page recaps the various motor, sensory, language, and cognitive achievements that occur during this stage of your baby's emotional development. Remember that as exciting as these new skills are, they are organized and given meaning by your baby's growing ability to relate and give and receive love.

WHY FALLING IN LOVE IS
SO IMPORTANT

Why are we placing so much emphasis on your baby's ability to form a relationship, rather than on her cognitive or motor achievements? Helping her build a sense of love and trust would seem reason enough, but there is another equally compelling fact to consider. Emotional interactions are also the source of her intelligence, morality, and self-esteem. The loving, intimate connection forged between you and your baby sets the stage for your child's higher thinking skills.

Luckily for parents, cognitive skills are best developed through loving, one-on-one interactions with their children, and not in self-conscious "enrichment" programs. Many popular parenting books urge parents to buy flash cards, fancy mobiles, computer software, and educational toys to stimulate their babies' intellectual growth. All of these items, however, pale in importance when compared to your baby's need to be wooed into a loving and playful relationship with you. When your baby flashes you a joyful smile, she's conveying a whole wealth of information about herself to you. As she melts you with her grin, she's not just passively radiating her love for you. She wants to see you so much that she's shifting her body and learning how to use her muscles to better focus on you. She's also turning to the sound of your voice because she is excited by your voice and wants to see where the sound is coming from. Your baby displays her yearning for you in the way she strains to prop herself up on her forearms, or rolls over to get a better look at you, or eventually tries to remain sitting upright without falling. She is driven to practice these new physical milestones because she has taken a passionate interest in you and the world you introduce to her.

Your baby's happy smile of recognition thus reveals the fact that she can understand the rhythm of your words (a cognitive, or intellectual skill), can coordinate her body in her search for you (a motor skill), and can recognize you by sight (a visual-spatial capacity). Her beaming smile lets you know she is doing all these wonderful things. Think of it this way: the most reliable way to tell if the weather is beautiful is to step right outside and take a look. You don't have to monitor the barometric pressure or humidity, or glance at a wind sock, to know that atmospheric conditions must be nearly optimal and contributing to your general sense that the day is bright and balmy. At this stage of her development, your baby's shared joy and interactive smiles are evidence that many of her cognitive, sensory, and motor skills are all working together, under the direction of her loving interest in you and the world you bring to her.

Interestingly, when your baby is between two and four months old there are growing neuronal connections, particularly in the portions of the brain that are involved with emotions and relating, connecting vision with the other senses, emerging motor skills, and making sense of and eventually creating patterns related to looking, listening, moving, smiling, crying, and other expressions of affect. This facilitates the baby's ability to begin to make more sense of what she feels and sees and to gradually construct three-dimensional images. She is then better able to comprehend the emotional, visual, and auditory patterns that make up *you*, the person she loves. As your baby signals her joy and happiness to you, as well as her sorrow and annoyance, important portions of her brain get activated. In fact, her entire preverbal communication system is in part supported by these developing neuronal connections.

Your joyful interactions with your baby may spur brain growth in those areas that involve emotional expression and signaling, which in turn facilitates her ability to fall in love and build an increasingly complex relationship with you. Over time, your loving, nurturing relationship will foster your child's verbal abilities and problem-solving and reasoning skills, and the development of parts of the brain that support language. Here we see evidence of a wonderful sort of reciprocity: aspects of brain growth related to loving, emotional interactions lead to relationships and interactions that in turn promote a flowering of aspects of brain development involving communication, verbal reasoning, and logic skills.

These research findings support the importance of early experience for the growth of the brain and the mind, though we should remember that the specifics differ from individual to individual. Each person's brain may react to and organize these experiences differently. In fact, various portions of our brains can be used to perform the same functions, as we observe when some children grow up with parts of their brain missing and yet learn how to relate, communicate, and think.

The interactions you share with your infant not only foster connections within her growing brain that enable her to express her emotions, but they also offer her a first taste of logic and lay the foundations for future altruism and caring. As your love magnetically pulls her into the world, your baby becomes more excited about the sights, sounds, touches, and tastes that surround her crib. You'll be literally enticing her into an awareness of things outside her own body. Obviously, the more sensations your baby can tune in to, the richer her understanding of the world will be. Because she loves you, she is drawn to those things outside her own body that are a part of you, including the sound of your voice, the look on your face, the smell of your breath and skin, and the tenderness of your touch. As her trust and confidence grows, she can pursue her own budding interests in the world as well.

Similarly, your baby's first lessons in being logical, or understanding that she can make something happen (which will be further developed in the next stage of her development), arise out of the way you interact with her. When you exchange smiles with her, she'll come to realize that by catching your eye and grinning in a certain way, she can count on a return grin. The more involved your baby is with you, the more opportunity she has to learn these first lessons. Her desire to understand things, and to learn to use her wondrous eyes and ears and little hands, comes in part from her relationship to you and her other caregivers. If she could sing now, her theme song would be "Love Makes the World Go Round,"

It may be hard to see how your child's sense of morality, or eventual ability to make good choices and to want to do what's "right" rather than what's "wrong," comes from her love for you. But, as we will later discuss at length, the mutual caring you experience together leads your baby to sense that human relationships can be worthwhile. Briefly put, your baby experiences loving compassion and caring from the gentleness of your touch, the warmth of your smile, and the rhythmic soothing of your rocking. Your caring teaches caring. Because you don't reject her when she's cranky, or pull away when she's distressed, your child learns that physical closeness and love can be found in your arms. Out of such seemingly ordinary experiences as being embraced even when she's angry or sad comes your baby's dawning sense that human beings like herself are worthy of being cared for and loved even when they are cranky. Over time, a deepening regard for other people may take root. As she develops an eventual sense of shared humanity that "they" are like "us" and "we" are like "them," and appropriate reasoning skills, she can begin to care about how "they" actually feel.

The courtship now under way between you and your baby will in many ways contribute to the kind of adult she will grow into. Your patient, involved wooing helps her know the powerful intoxication and comfort of human closeness. By drawing your child into a loving one-on-one relationship with you now, you will be enabling her to eventually extend this sense of shared humanity to other family members, friends, teachers, and mates. Infants who are denied the ability to experience empathy and love with at least one compassionate caretaker may be more likely to grow into self-involved, aggressive children or adults, indifferent to the feelings of others.

Your baby's budding sense of self is forming as well. She now feels part of a relationship and is sensing that the world of emotional relationships and interactions is different from the world of things. Positive self-esteem also blossoms during this stage of development. Your baby learns that you are patient and don't desert her when sleepiness or an upset stomach make her whiny or tearful. When you try to comfort your baby with loving looks and tender touches, she knows—even before she can express the sensation with words—that she is valued and esteemed. She feels a gut-level acceptance of her self, in all its uniqueness, in the relaxed way you hold her close to your heart.

HOW TO WOO YOUR BABY

READING YOUR BABY'S CUES

If you're like many parents, you've been intuitively offering your baby the smiles, nonsense sounds, and funny faces that entice her pleasurable responses. If you're already receiving your baby's smiles in return, just relax and enjoy them. Continue to do whatever brings forth the baby's chortles and grins, and try to woo your baby into more and longer states of pleasure.

Since every baby's response to parental overtures is as individual as her fingerprints, try to notice which type of interaction brings your baby the most pleasure. Does she respond more when your own mood is upbeat and you're talking up a storm? Or does your baby seem happier when you're quieter and use gentle motions? Notice whether she has a happy look in her eye or a lip that quivers with excitement when you pick her up. Does she use her whole body to express her attachment to you, by kicking and waving her arms and legs? Perhaps your baby uses squeals and coos to draw you to her side, or nestles into your arms in a cuddle that brings both of you joy. Try to deliberately use the looks, tones, and gestures that bring your baby the most pleasure.

Wooing your baby is as heady an experience as falling in love with your mate. In some respects, the connection feels even more intimate. There will be many times when you feel intoxicated just by looking at your sleeping baby. Her relaxed fingers and open palms will stun you with their beauty and vulnerability. Her growing emotional responsiveness will continually surprise you during her waking hours. Where did this evidence of a unique personality come from? Suddenly your baby is able to coo with delight or bounce in excitement as you approach her in her crib. Even her ability to use snorting sounds and squeals has a new, playful quality. She has learned how to produce certain noises which are guaranteed to elicit a response from you.

At first you will probably be taking more of the initiative in reaching out to your little partner, though this may soon change. You'll be extending tender kisses, soothing hugs, soft murmurs, and glances that are full of love. In return, you'll become aware of your baby's growing love for you. In the early months her focused attention on your face, shifts in position to get a better glimpse of you, and imitative smiles were the first indications that she had entered into an essential partnership with you.

With your baby's growing ability to interact with the world around her, as well as to calm herself, this partnership blossoms into a full-blown love affair. It's a great time to solidify the love between you and your baby, because she isn't yet focused on crawling or preoccupied with a need to physically explore her environment. By taking advantage of the many opportunities for interaction that occur throughout the day during playtimes, feeding times, and diaper changes, you'll be building up a foundation of love and trust between you and your child.

INTERACTING WITH YOUR BABY ON HER OWN TERMS

Timing is everything. Your baby will establish her own special rhythms as she interacts with you. She may flash you a big smile and wiggle her body in delight for a moment, and then retreat a little. Or she may suck on her fist and stare off into space for a while before turning back to you for 30 seconds' worth of intense involvement. These behaviors will ebb and flow, building to a peak of involvement before dying down.

You'll be following your baby's lead in this courtship dance. As the weeks go by, try to help her stretch out these intimate interactions. Notice what kind of play brings her special joy, and come up with variations that keep her engaged with you. You'll see an eager, expectant expression on her face that wasn't there a month ago. If peekaboo is a hit, try to vary the game by popping up on "*boo!*" in a different spot each time. Your baby relishes both expectation and surprise, so vary the length of time she waits in anticipation of hearing "*boo!*"

Remember not to exhaust your little playmate. Follow her lead when she wants to ease off, but try to help her enjoy ever-lengthening periods of connection with you. Take note of those times when your baby shies away from you. If you are separated from the baby for part of the day, or for an entire day, does she become a little cooler, even aloof? Does she need an hour of your concentrated wooing to be won back, or does she seem bright and responsive with just a few minutes of your undivided attention? Try spending more time together or consciously warming up your interaction if your child seems cool or disinterested in your relationship. Try not to get discouraged if your efforts result in just a few brief moments of warm connection. Each additional second you manage to engage your baby can, with patience, be extended over time into longer, loving interactions.

DISCOVERING WHAT MAKES YOUR BABY HAPPY

Have fun playing with your baby! Make a funny face and watch what she does. See if you can build up a visual game in which you copy your baby's gestures and expressions, and see how she responds

Your baby may be entranced by simple verbal patterns. If you accent a funny sound, or raise the pitch of your voice on a different syllable, she may look surprised and pleased. She can produce her own vocalizations and may offer them up to you as the two of you exchange noises. Although she does not yet have the ability to understand the content of the words you use, your baby is very attuned to the warmth of your tone. Her growing emotional interest in the sounds you make gives you a way to engage her attention.

Continue to explore the pleasures of physical touch. Does your child like you to blow gently on her tummy? Tickle behind her knees? Does she relax when you firmly stroke her arms and legs, or does she seem more lulled by rhythmic rocking? Is the warm water of her bath exciting, or soothing? Your baby may indicate her enjoyment with a wide range of behavior. She may respond with robust smiles—even chuckles—a cooing voice, or synchronous arm and leg movements. Or she may simply study your face with an eager expression. Your baby will enjoy novel (but pleasant) physical sensations, and take comfort in the skin-to-skin contact you give her.

You may notice that your baby stays actively involved with you when you present her with lots of silly faces, but drifts away when you babble nonsense verses. Or perhaps she hangs on every syllable of the lullabies you croon, but seems totally disinterested in mirror games. Follow your instincts and play to your baby's strengths. Forging an emotional link with her through her strongest senses is your first priority. However, be sure to sprinkle these activities with extra practice using the senses that the baby needs a little work in. As long as you keep playtime fun, your baby will actually enjoy exercising her weaker senses.

Just as you are bringing your baby's senses of sight, sound, and touch into the wooing relationship, you can take full advantage of her growing ability to regulate her movements. Your baby can now use her body to arch toward the sound of your voice or to snuggle into the crook of your arm, and can reach out to you with her hands. She may practice these motor skills because getting physically closer to you makes her happy. Similarly, your baby can now hold her head up with confidence while locking eyes with you. Her ability to organize her mouth and facial muscles into a dimpled smile deepens your emotional attachment to each other.

Before you know it, your baby will be ready literally to experience the world from another point of view. At around five months, she will often remain in a sitting position for quite a while if you have supported her with pillows. Because she is now able to sit up, you can play more elaborate interactive games with her. Her love for and interest in you make her want to sit up and explore your face with her fingers, while her strengthening muscles and increased motor skills promote her interest in relating more warmly to you.

Many six-month-olds can roll completely over by themselves and use their hands in a more coordinated way. Babies this age are capable of simple motor planning, like bringing their hands together and grasping a favorite toy or rattle that you hand to them.

By the following month or two, most babies will be able to sit steadily for long periods of time after being helped up into a sitting position. A little later on, they may begin to crawl. Some babies can pull themselves into a standing position by 8 months or so, and early walkers may take a first step by 9 or 10 months. The eager, expectant look on your face as they eventually toddle into your arms encourages them to make more use of their muscles. However, most babies will take their first faltering steps between 12 and 15 months, and some perfectly healthy infants wait until they are a year and a half before they are really off and running.

KEEPING THE INTIMACY GOING

During the first months of life, your baby's attention span could be measured in a few seconds, but it is growing rapidly, along with your relationship. Her newfound ability to "stop, look, and listen" permits her to take note of your smile and the tenderness of your caresses. A growing sense of inner security and trust fuels your baby's capacity to build (and even expect) intimacy, and keeps your favorite interactions going. If you should become distracted while you are interacting with her, you may see the smile fade from her face and her whole body droop in sadness. Try to engage in longer and longer "conversations" and avoid abrupt halts in your playtime together. Don't rush to pick up your phone on the first ring if you are having fun with the baby. Let the answering machine pick up, and give yourself time to gradually taper off the happy dialogue you've got going.

Take advantage of your baby's growing cognitive skills and have fun with peekaboo games. Hide a toy under a cloth and then reveal it to her with a flourish. Play "Here I am" games as you move this way and that, and tempt her to follow you with her eyes and smiles.

ENJOYING ALL YOUR BABY'S FEELINGS

Although it's easy to focus on the explosion of positive feelings—like love and delight—that develop between you and your baby during this stage, it's equally important to help your baby tolerate negative feelings. By four or five months, most babies show anger when they're frustrated. If, for ex-

ample, your little girl is ravenously hungry but in desperate need of a diaper change, she may become infuriated if you attempt to lay her down on
her changing table before giving her a bottle. Her cheeks may start quiv-
ering, and her jaw may tremble with rage. She may start flailing her arms
and legs or howl in protest.

There is clearly a new level of intensity in the distress your baby feels
when she doesn't get her own way, and you need to acknowledge that as you
try to comfort her. Let her know that you understand that she's angry;
soothingly tell her that you know it's "so, so hard to be still when you're
tummy's growling." Your calm tone will let the baby know that you don't
mind her assertiveness. By using the calming techniques discussed at length
in Chapter 1, you'll be helping your baby regain a sense of equilibrium.

By being animated and emotionally responsive, you can woo your baby
not only when she's happy or angry but also when more subtle feelings,
such as disgust, emerge. At around four or five months of age, your baby
may crinkle her nose and shiver when she tastes something that is unpleasant to her. She may be startled at the new sensation, and cry. Although your first reaction may well be to think that she looks so cute that
it's hard not to laugh, try to offer her lots of sympathy. Use your own expressions to let her know that you understand her reaction. After she's
calmed down, you might try to expand her tolerance for the unpleasant
taste by playfully pretending to take a taste yourself. Let her see you raise
your eyebrows and smack your lips in mock delight, and see if she'll try to
copy you. If her aversion to the new taste persists, call it a day for now. The
important message that you'll be giving your baby is that your love and
connection to her aren't threatened by the inevitable bad feelings that she
will experience as she explores the world.

Most babies can be reengaged after experiencing emotional upset or
anger with some loving, soothing overtures from you. Help your baby
learn early on that strong feelings can best be dealt with by engaging, and
not by withdrawing, from people. Even upset, high-strung babies can be
wooed into intimacy.

FOSTERING INTIMACY AS
YOUR CHILD GROWS OLDER

Engagement isn't a one-time accomplishment that your baby achieves
when she's four months old. This skill is going to be further strengthened
as she progresses through the various stages of development discussed in

the following chapters. For instance, when your baby becomes a preschooler, you'll be wooing her as you play pretend games with her. Although she'll be utilizing new developmental skills as she takes on new roles as a wicked witch or a beautiful princess, she'll also be enjoying intimacy at the same time. With your help, she'll calm herself when the fantasy play gets too exciting, and then flash you a smile that reveals how much your intimate relationship means to her.

RAISING THE BAR

As you and your baby spend more and more time in loving interaction, you'll start to notice the particular ways she expresses her love and interest in you. Perhaps your baby prefers to use her visual sense, and keeps her eyes glued to your face as you woo her. Maybe you've noticed that she seems to like bright colors, but doesn't particularly like to look in your eyes. If so, she may enjoy playing a game in which you put a purple spoon in your mouth. It would be surprising if that sight didn't pull her eyes right to your face with an accompanying look of delight.

Does your baby readily turn toward the sound of your voice? Does she respond to a wide range of sounds, from high to low pitches? If she's more attentive to high-pitched noises, see if using a Minnie Mouse voice will entice her. On the other hand, use a lower tone if that seems to bring her more pleasure.

Notice whether your baby uses a variety of motor gestures. Does she reach for your hand with hers? Does she use her head and neck muscles to turn toward you when you speak to her? Try to position yourself so that your baby's physical efforts will result in face-to-face contact with you. Does she readily swivel her head to follow you as you leave the room? Try swooping to the right or left, or bouncing up and down as you exit. She'll enjoy watching you and will orient her body toward you at the same time.

After you start focusing on your baby's own special features, her unique physical profile will become more apparent. You'll be making a mental checklist of which senses she uses most easily and with the greatest flexibility. The key here is to tune in to your baby's individual profile by tailoring your overtures to her strengths.

Use your shared love and your baby's obvious pleasure in using at least some of her senses as the starting point. You can then orchestrate some games that will introduce other senses or movements into your interactions. Help your baby use many of her emerging skills together, just as an orchestra conductor helps weave all the various musical sections into a seamless symphonic sound.

Let's assume that your six-month-old has shown you in many ways that she's soaking up the world through her eyes. They shine with delight each time she catches sight of you. Even the talking heads on the television screen seem to capture her interest. Connecting with her visually is easy, and you've already intuitively come up with many silly-face games that bring you both pleasure.

Next, try to mobilize all of her senses to work together. Remember that our brains can absorb information from many sources at the same time, and your baby can simultaneously look, listen, move, and feel. In fact, *it is the ability to exercise all of these systems at the same time that really strengthens and organizes your child's nervous system.* If you continue to encourage this ability as your baby develops, you will be helping her improve her capacity for intellectual, social, and emotional functioning enormously.

Gradually introduce some interesting sounds into your face-to-face play together. You will then be playing to your baby's visual strengths while giving her extra practice in a sensory area that she uses less. You might make funny noises each time you alter your facial expression, building from a simple rhythm to a more complex one as the game continues. In addition, observe whether varying the range of sounds from soft to loud affects your baby's pleasure. Your baby may only tolerate softer noises, like muffled claps, initially.

Next, woo your baby into continuing this pleasurable interaction by appealing to her delight in movement. As you rhythmically clap and scrunch up your face into silly new expressions, slowly move around your baby in a half circle. Watch her move her legs and arms in an attempt to follow the sights and sounds you're offering her. You're inspiring your child to use her seeing, listening, and motor skills all together in a manner that will stretch her not only physically, but also emotionally and intellectually.

Try to help your baby take even more initiative. As she moves into the second half of the first year, you may notice her wanting to do such things as holding her bottle or a toy more independently. Admire her initiative and build interactions around it, such as commenting on a particular toy she's reaching toward. See if you can be so appealing that she moves in rhythm with you and woos you with funny faces, sounds, and arm and leg movements of her own.

RECOGNIZING MAGIC MOMENTS

Once you are attuned to your baby's natural sleeping/waking schedule during the day, you can recognize the times when she is most available. This may be after her meals, and midway between her naps. These 15-to-20-minute blocks of time, when your baby's most urgent needs have been met, are her "magic moments," when she's willing to see what you and the world have been up to. Seek opportunities to interact actively with your baby; don't let her stare off into space or zone out in her crib for long stretches of time. Look for feedback, whether it's a warm, relaxed set to her face, an exuberant waving of her arms and legs, or a series of hoots and cries.

Now that some of the colicky fussiness of the early months may be behind you, many magic moments can occur throughout the day and evening. Reserve at least a part of the evening for you and your baby. Let it take precedence over doing the dishes and other chores. Loving intimacy will flower as your baby is given time enough to trust the steadiness of your interest in her and your responsiveness to her physical and emotional needs.

If you are relying on out-of-home child care, it's important to recognize that the hours you spend at home before work and before bedtime have to provide your baby with ample opportunities to interact emotionally with you and/or your spouse. There are simply no shortcuts when it comes to cementing a loving relationship with your child. Set your alarm a few minutes earlier in the morning to give yourself more time for a leisurely playtime or bath time with your baby.

When you're back home from work, your baby may be aloof or clingy for a while. Be patient and know that she may need a period of wooing and comforting before she is ready to fully reconnect with you. Keep her near you in a safe place and talk and wave to her as you cook dinner. Keep the television off and make time for lots of cuddly interaction before she goes to bed. Woo her when she's annoyed; woo her when she's happy. Finding the energy for intimate moments with your baby may be a tall order when you're tired and frazzled, but no other single activity is more key to assuring your child's emotional and intellectual growth.

WOOING THROUGH BAD TIMES AS WELL AS GOOD

Your baby's reactions to you may now be growing increasingly rich and detailed. Her smile, in response to yours, may be expressing a deep feeling

Dos and Don'ts for Raising the Bar

~

- *Do* woo your baby.
- *Do* find out what experiences bring pleasure and joy to your infant.
- *Do* gently persist in wooing, even if your baby seems to be content to be on her own. Find those magic moments when she is calm and available.
- *Do* help your baby recover from crying or annoyance with pleasurable intimacy.
- *Don't* ignore your baby when she is alert and awake and ready for play.
- *Don't* try to get your baby to do only certain prescribed behaviors; tune in to her preferences.
- *Don't* take it personally if your baby seems a little aloof or distant. Some babies are more sensitive and require more patient wooing. The rewards are worth it!
- *Don't* blame your baby if she is fussy. Help her become calm.

of warmth and interest. If your baby's responses seem less than joyful, take a look at your family patterns and wooing efforts. You might try becoming either more expressive if she seems detached, or more soothing if your baby pulls away from your overeager expressions or gestures. If you do not feel a deeper connection with your baby, take a look at your family relationships, or whether you're tired or preoccupied when you interact with her. Try to carve out even more time for you (and other family members or caregivers) and your baby to simply relax together and enjoy each other.

By now your baby may be able to maintain a loving exchange for longer periods of time. Just as significantly, your baby may now be able to quickly rejoin your dialogue after an interruption like a sneeze or a slammed door. If it takes your baby a little longer to recover from interruptions and maintain a joyful engagement with you, you can woo her by first using whatever techniques best calm her—a gentle smile, lulling voice, or firm massage. Once she has recovered her equilibrium, see if she tries to copy you or woo you back. With practice, your baby may learn to rejoin loving interactions more readily.

BUILDING YOUR BABY'S SENSE OF SELF

During this second stage of development, your baby's sense of self is increasingly tied to your emotional interactions with her. Thousands and thousands of these interactions help the baby exercise all of her senses and motor skills together while experiencing a growing range of emotions with you. These emotions provide a kind of glue that helps the baby organize all of her various experiences.

Her sense of self is intimately tied to times of shared joy and bliss. Her most intense feelings are reserved for those people who love her. She clearly prefers your sounds, sights, smells, and rhythms to anyone else's. Your compassion for her and her compassion for you will help her learn to feel compassion for others. Your baby is learning that shared feelings of joy, as well as annoyance, are part of a special human relationship that is quite different from the world of inanimate physical objects. Her sense of self is no longer part of all the sensations around her, nor is it yet fully defined. It is emerging out of the shared feelings she experiences while relating to her most intimate caregivers. Your baby's eventual sense of right and wrong is also rooted in this capacity to experience a shared sense of humanity.

Children who are deprived of intimacy and shared bliss with a caregiver over a period of time often do not develop caring and empathic feelings for others. Not surprisingly, infants and children who have been shunted from one foster home to another can become antisocial or withdrawn. Such youngsters are often helped by mentoring programs that foster a warm and trusting connection with one adult.

With all of these implications, it is easy to see why fostering loving, one-on-one interactions is so important. It is crucial to keep this in mind when assessing child-care options. Most day-care centers do not have the kind of infant-to-staff ratio, training support, or salary structure that fosters long-term (over many years) relationships to form between babies and their caregivers. At a later stage of your infant's development, group day-care settings may promote the development of certain motor and cognitive skills, but truly ongoing, intimate emotional interactions, during "magic moments" as well as at other times, may be quite difficult to achieve when a caregiver is responsible for four or more babies. Furthermore, because of low salaries and training support, there may be lot of turnover in the day-care staff. In addition, babies usually change caregivers each year as they move from the infant room to the toddler room. Warmth, affection, and physical care may be present, but babies this age need many moments of loving interaction during the day. They also need relationships that span years, not months. In a busy, understaffed day-care setting, the easygoing, placid baby may be left on her own because caregivers are often diverted by more demanding babies. Well-intentioned staffers may assume that such a "good" baby is receiving more than adequate intimacy at home. Parents locked into hectic schedules may similarly suppose that day-care providers are filling the interactive void.

OVERCOMING CHALLENGES: A BLESSING IN DISGUISE

Some infants have challenges in forging emotional relationships with their parents. You may notice that your baby will be more sensitive to certain sights, sounds, or touches, or look puzzled by some of your facial expressions. She may even subtly pull away from you and appear to keep her distance. She needs to know that she is the center of your universe, even when she appears to shy away from intimacy.

All babies have unique nervous systems, and you can learn how to tailor your parenting skills to mesh with your own baby's individual profile. There's no one-size-fits-all approach to wooing your baby into love. Every baby deserves a custom fit! Your ability and readiness to make adjustments in the way you interact with your baby can help her experience the world more fully, in all its nuanced wonder.

BABIES WITH HIGH OR LOW MUSCLE TONE AND CHALLENGES IN SEQUENCING MOVEMENTS

You may notice that your infant's body feels a little loose, or somewhat tight. It may be that her muscle tone needs to be coaxed into becoming more taut, or more flexible. By focusing on your baby's particular muscular profile, you can learn how to help her gain confidence in her own body and to return your hugs. Her emotional development doesn't have to lag just because her muscles need some practice.

What exactly is muscle tone? It is, literally, the balance between a person's flexor and extensor muscles. The flexors are the muscles that we use to bend our knees and bow from our waists. Flexor muscles pull our necks forward. Extensor muscles help us stand erect and permit us to arch our back and stretch. Every human being has a particular tone to his or her muscles, and as adults we long ago made adjustments in how we move. Some of us will never be able to touch our fingertips to our toes while we bend from the waist. Your baby, however, may become frustrated if holding her head up to look at you requires too much work because her muscle tone is low. You might find yourself becoming impatient and feeling rejected because your baby with low tone doesn't reach out for you like other babies her age.

Sometimes physical milestones like learning to hold her head up, or sitting without falling, may simply take your baby a little longer to accomplish than other babies. Through your loving interactions, she can develop the ability to tolerate the frustration she may encounter when her muscles feel unreliable.

How can you help your baby learn to use and trust her own muscles to get her where she wants to be? First, make an informal survey of how "loose" or "tight" her body feels. Let's assume your baby, although obviously reactive to sights and sounds, seems to have loose muscles when you hold her. She may not move to mold her body to yours. Perhaps you've noticed that her legs seem unusually relaxed as you change her diaper, and she doesn't draw her knees up toward her chest when she cries in anger. It's as if her muscles are a little stretched out. Appreciate that gaining muscle control over her face and smiling may be a far harder task for your baby than it is for you. Know how much harder it may be for her to hold her head up and watch you make silly faces and nonsense sounds. She may take delight in your presence, but find it difficult to respond in kind. She may take a little longer to follow you with her eyes when you move around, even though she may want to look at you right away.

Try supporting your baby's neck as you hold her face-to-face. Use animated, loving expressions as you playfully interact with her. By helping her control her neck you'll be increasing the odds that your baby will take pleasure in the social interaction you're sharing. Be patient and very animated as you give her time to look at you from her left, and then from her right. Give her muscles a gentle workout while engaging her with a soothing song. While supporting her neck and back, let her feet gently push against your lap as you raise her up and lower her down.

What if your baby's body feels tight? An infant with high muscle tone may find it hard work to relax enough to melt into your loving embrace. Help your baby become more flexible by playing gentle bending games as you hold her on your lap. Bring her knees toward her chest as she lies on her back. She may find it difficult to position her head accurately. If your infant seems to overshoot your face as she looks at you, shift your own body to be into a position where you can capture her gaze. The loving connection you will achieve during this period with extra patience and wooing can help your baby be motivated to practice turning, looking, smiling, and making sounds. After all, she is turning to or smiling at you!

Babies with low or high muscle tone may find it hard to sequence actions; that is, to do a few things in a row such as turn and look, or snuggle and hug. Here, too, patience and practice while having fun are the keys to developmental progress. Although it's sometimes hard to watch your baby become frustrated as she tries out a new behavior or skill, let her reach out again and again for the toy just beyond her grasp. Nudge it a little closer only when you sense that she's nearing her limit, and let her savor her achievement. Your baby needs to learn new skills on her own. If she is not progressing with your help and practice, it's best to consult your pediatrician and consider an evaluation with a developmental specialist.

Perhaps your baby's muscle tone seems sturdy enough, but she has exhibited a bit of a sensitivity to certain sights, sounds, or touches. Let's take another look now at Kara, Brian, Emma, Will, and Max, the babies we introduced you to in the previous chapter. Like you, their parents are learning to adjust their wooing styles to better match their babies' unique physical makeup.

BABIES WHO ARE SENSITIVE TO TOUCH AND SOUND

Kara's parents, Ellen and Steve, had made real headway in calming Kara down the past few months. They continued to use firm touch when they handled her, and she relaxed when her parents consciously lowered the pitch of their voices and slowed down their speech. At seven months, Kara remained extremely sensitive to high-pitched sound, and would stiffen and cry when her brother Joey's playmates made screeching noises as they crashed their trucks on make-believe freeways. Kara would greet her brother with excitement and clear affection whenever she saw him, waving her arms and crinkling her face in a big grin. When Joey's excited screeching started, however, she would become anxious and cry brokenheartedly. As much as Steve and Ellen wished Joey would pipe down and moderate his sound effects, they also recognized that he had a right to his fun, too. They were willing to modify their own voices to help Kara with her sensitivity, but they also felt that she had to begin to reach some kind of accommodation with a world that was filled with noisy screams, whistles, and kid brothers.

Sleepiness continued to be a problem for Ellen. Kara was still nursing, and gaining weight, but she continued to be something of a prima donna when it came to eating and sleeping. She would lunge for Ellen's nipple with gusto and nurse so quickly that her mother felt as if her baby were starving. Exhausted, Kara would soon drop into a deep sleep after nursing, but never for more than five hours during the night.

A new battleground emerged when Kara graduated from being bathed in her portable plastic tub. Now that she was able to sit unsupported for long stretches of time, her parents introduced her to the bathtub. To their dismay, she cried hysterically whenever she was fastened into the tub's portable safety seat. Her face would be contorted in rage and her back would arch as her parents attempted to quickly bathe her. Ellen noticed that Kara did, however, keep her eyes glued to her parents' faces even when she was distraught, as if she were saying, "How could you do this to me! Just get me out of here!"

Kara's parents were stumped. It was hard to remove from their minds the old parenting tapes that had served them so well with Joey and Rachel, their six-year-old daughter. Some of Rachel's happiest playtimes had been spent splashing in her bath, and Ellen and Steve couldn't help but feel that none of the old rules held for Kara. They had congratulated themselves on intuitively adjusting their style to mesh with Kara's needs for firm touch and lower-pitched voices and sounds, and had assumed that she would settle into a more scheduled, easier style as she matured. Her sensitivities persisted, though, and even popped up in situations that puzzled them. After all, what could be so alarming about sitting in a bathtub filled with warm water and colorful toys?

Both Steve and Ellen continued to feel unsure about how to help Kara relax and enjoy herself more. They yearned to feel that their love for their baby was reciprocated, and wondered what they had done "wrong." Not only were they frustrated, but they also felt a growing sense of guilt over the amount of time they spent focusing on Kara's sensitivities instead of interacting with their two older children. It was time to seek professional guidance.

After observing Kara as she and her parents interacted during several sessions, a developmental specialist explained that because Kara was so easily distracted by certain pitches of sound and needed firm touch to calm herself, she had a tendency to experience the world in disorganized little pieces. He went on to spell out just how hard it was for Kara to take easy comfort from many of the noises and touches she received.

This new understanding about Kara's feelings led her parents to both be more flexible with her and to reexamine their own ability to tolerate uncomfortable feelings. After a few suggestions from the therapist, Ellen and Steve came up with an alternate bathing routine. While Ellen held Kara's body, she made sure to firmly support her baby's back, almost encircling the infant's body with her arm. Looking right into Kara's eyes, her mother crooned soothing words like "I know you don't want to take a bath right now, my little one, but we'll make you feel so clean and cozy, and soon you'll be in your soft, snuggly bed."

Sometimes, though, Kara would still break into angry howls the moment she was lowered into the water. Steve and Ellen soon figured out a way to help ease Kara's adjustment to the feel of her bath water. First, they moistened a washcloth with warm water and slowly massaged Kara's feet. They gradually dipped one of her feet into the water, then the other. As Kara was smoothly lowered into the tub's anchored baby seat, Ellen continued to soothe her with soft murmurs and gentle hugs.

Because both Ellen and Steve remembered just how focused on their faces Kara could be, even while she was angry, they tried offering her more visual support during her baths. Steve made funny faces and handed Kara a new ring filled with brightly painted plastic keys as soon as she was settled in her tub seat. The key ring was easy to grasp and fun to shake, so Kara found her new toy intriguing.

Bath times soon became less of an ordeal. Kara never loved her bath the way her sister and brother had, but she was able to tolerate it, and even give her parents a smile or two if they enticed her with particularly goofy faces.

Ellen also decided to try to apply some of these soothing and diverting techniques to the way she nursed the baby. She knew that if she could just prolong the time they spent together at each nursing session, Kara might relax enough to slow down and fill her tummy with enough milk to be truly satiated. With a full stomach, there was a good chance that the baby would sleep at longer intervals.

After Kara voraciously gulped her mother's milk for a minute or so, Ellen would gently disengage her nipple from the baby's mouth for a few seconds of face-to-face interaction. Initially Kara was confused by this change in their routine and would desperately root for her mother's nipple. After a while, Ellen could hold Kara's interest for over a minute at a time, offering smiles and coos and even playfully sticking out her tongue. Kara began to return some of these smiles, and stick out her own tongue in response. Then she would remember that she was hungry and return to her mother's breast. Eventually, Ellen was able to extend each nursing interlude to nearly 15 minutes and Kara managed to sleep from midnight to seven each morning. Both Steve and Ellen felt as if they had turned an important corner in learning to relate to their third child.

Babies like Kara, who have sensitivities to sounds and touches, may not warm up to new interactive techniques right away. If your baby has a similar profile, you must keep on empathizing, engaging, and offering patient love even when she doesn't give you an immediate emotional payback. If you're there for your baby through the frustrations of everyday challenges, she'll come to rely on your ability to ease her distress and learn that she can experience a wide range of feelings.

BABIES WHO ARE UNDERWHELMED BY THE WORLD AROUND THEM

Connecting with a quiet, underreactive baby is equally challenging. Brian is a good example of this sort of child. His parents, Stuart and Tammy, felt as if their seven-month-old son was barely interested in them, despite the love and attention they lavished on him. This was especially upsetting to them because they had relished the first four months of Brian's life. Brian was a placid baby who nursed well, and quickly slept through the night. He made very few demands on them. In fact, their friends often told them that Brian was a "perfect" baby.

As Brian approached five months, though, his parents noticed that he seemed content to remain sleepily in his crib, staring at his hands or quietly looking at his mobile. He would sometimes reward his parents with a brief smile, but he never seemed to seek their company. Brian's parents began to lose confidence in their ability to reach their baby and felt guilty because they had equated his passivity with "good" behavior. They also feared that he wasn't developing a "normal" affection for them. Their pediatrician suggested that they consult with a developmental specialist in the area.

It soon became clear that Brian was unusually self-absorbed. The specialist reassured Stuart and Tammy that their little boy was not rejecting them; Brian simply needed a lot of encouragement before he would literally sit up and take notice of the world around him. Brian's parents were urged to ratchet up the energy level of their voices and to offer more physical enticement. They began to realize that Brian was far less sensitive to a variety of stimuli than they had assumed. He wasn't willfully tuning out his parents; he hadn't yet been able to consistently tune in and follow the pitch and rhythm of their voices. It was easier for him to happily respond to his parents' smiles. However, even the mere act of smiling required more than the usual amount of effort, because his muscle tone was low.

To understand the world of a baby who tends to be self-absorbed, imagine that you're swaying on a hammock on your front porch on a sultry summer afternoon. The sun is so strong and the heat and humidity are so high that you feel as if you're functioning at half-speed. The world's a little off-kilter, and it takes too much energy to focus on much of anything. Brian was similarly unresponsive and he was quite content to idly drift, much as you would while swaying on your hammock. No child wants to isolate himself in his own world—it's just easier to withdraw than to strain and have to work hard to pay attention.

Brian's parents gradually learned to more actively woo him into a relationship with themselves and with the world in general. The solution was to offer Brian a whole range of exciting sights, smells, touches, and sounds. Stuart and Tammy would bring out a collection of bells and toy drums and put a bell on top of their heads to draw Brian's attention to both their faces and the new sounds. In this way, Stuart, Tammy, and Brian explored different rhythms of sounds coupled with funny faces. Brian's parents also firmly-but-gently massaged his arms, legs, tummy, and back, and enticed him to reach for his favorite colorful rattle when they held it near their mouths. These activities often brought Brian into greater engagement with his parents.

After a time they learned to be patient, because their baby might need 10 or 15 minutes instead of just a few seconds to respond to the new sensations and movements. Stuart and Tammy also kissed Brian more exuberantly, sang with greater enthusiasm, and danced with him in their arms.

As they transformed themselves into virtual one-man bands to catch their baby's emotional interest, Brian's parents appealed to his visual responsiveness by continuing to give him lots of smiles and making time for many loving face-to-face interactions. Slowly, slowly, progress was made and by the time Brian was a year old and walking, he was a far more responsive child. It required a change of tactics and much energy, but Stuart and Tammy succeeded in waking their baby up to the pleasures of experiencing the human world.

BABIES WHO CRAVE STIMULATION

Unlike Brian, seven-month-old Emma, the redheaded whirlwind, was always trying to move. By the time she was eight months old, she was already crawling and leading her tired parents, Laura and Mike, on a merry chase around their apartment. Both parents regarded her presence in their lives as nothing short of a miracle; neither parent had anticipated that a baby could bring such joy to their middle-aged lives.

However, running after their baby was exhausting. Emma seemed to require nonstop movement once she mastered the mechanics of crawling. Her parents had realized early on that she seemed to need a lot of tactile stimulation and muscle exercise, and had made a point of playfully pushing and pulling her limbs during her first few months of life. Her response was enormously gratifying; she would kick and wave her legs and arms, with her mouth open in an "O" of pure excitement.

Once Emma was up and away on her hands and knees, though, Laura and Mike found it increasingly difficult to deal with their baby's fury at being hemmed in. Emma didn't just cry when she was picked up; she howled. It was hard for Laura and Mike to catch Emma's attention and pull her into another activity once she was set on moving. As much as they were charmed by her obvious zest and energy, they also needed more quiet times with their baby. As Laura wistfully put it, "I had always dreamed about having the baby nestle her head against my neck and pat me on my shoulder. Somehow, that seemed like a perfect picture of love."

Mike and Laura decided to consult with a specialist to get a better understanding of Emma's development. He attempted to describe for them how it must feel to be an active infant like Emma. He explained that although it seems counterintuitive, a baby like Emma may feel compelled to literally throw herself into the world because she is *underreactive* to certain sensations. In other words, Emma craved an inordinate amount of touch and movement precisely because it was difficult for her to process milder sensations. Her muscles were taut and springy, and gross motor activity brought her a lot of pleasure. As much as Emma needed to move and take in the world's sensations, she needed to be drawn into a nurturing, secure relationship with her parents even more.

The specialist's advice to Laura and Mike was simple: Encourage and join in Emma's explorations, not only to create a lot of interaction, but also to help her learn to enjoy slower rhythms of interaction. Joining Emma's active style was the relatively easy part; helping her slow down was often more difficult.

Laura and Mike discovered ways to balance their baby's need to move and their own need to share loving, intimate moments with her. When Emma awoke from her naps, her parents took full advantage of the five minutes it took to change her diaper. They worked at making faces and sounds that would catch Emma's interest, and rewarded her with big smiles when she locked her eyes with theirs.

Then Laura and Mike were off and running, following their baby's lead—even getting down on the floor to give Emma a sense that her kind of fun was their kind of fun, too. The specialist urged them to increase their own energy level, even if just for a short while. The parents gamely cooperated, although Mike remarked, "I'd try anything to make Emma happy, but just remember I'm not a twenty-five-year-old anymore!"

When it was time to shift to another activity, or to run errands, or simply to relax, Laura and Mike began to see Emma's flood of tears as a standard response and not as a rebuke. This helped them to feel more confident about setting the limits that were necessary for their own sanity and also freed up their energy for more creative playtimes with Emma.

BABIES WHO TAKE IN SIGHTS, BUT TUNE OUT SOUNDS

Unlike Emma's parents, who both had been frustrated by their baby's need to literally move away from them, some mothers and fathers find that their infant develops an easy rapport with just one of them. This is obviously a painful situation for the rebuffed parent and can even lead to rifts in a couple's relationship. After nearly eight months of parenting her son, Will, Lisa felt as she and her baby were in sync in every way. She could "read" his facial expressions well and could tell when his interest was about to flag, or if he needed a quick cuddle to comfort him. Will had a way of lunging toward her face with drooly lips as if he wanted to return the kisses she covered him with. His responsive smiles and obvious attachment made her feel blessed.

Lisa was getting worried, however, about Will's relationship with his father, Dan. Dan was the noisier, more sociable half of the couple, and his considerable charm had served him well in his law practice. But his playful singing, dancing, and gentle roughhousing somehow held no pleasure for Will. Dan's feelings were hurt, and he was baffled by Will's apparent indifference. Will so obviously preferred his mother that Lisa sometimes felt guilty. In fact, a new tension had entered the couple's relationship that had Lisa and Dan worried. They decided to get some outside help and take a closer look at the Will, Lisa, and Dan triangular relationship.

As the therapist met with Lisa and Dan and watched them interact with Will, he was initially puzzled by the baby's disinterest in his father. Dan's warm gregariousness was very engaging, in sharp contrast to Lisa's more subdued interactive style. As the therapist carefully observed Will, however, he saw that the baby was having trouble paying attention to the barrage of hearty sounds coming out of his father's mouth. On the other hand, Lisa's quieter, more visual approach seemed to capture Will's interest. The two of them seemed to feed off each other's faces, exchanging warm looks. Clearly, Will's ability to pay attention to visual cues was far stronger than his fleeting attention to complex verbal cues. Because Will had difficulty processing the sounds that he heard, he found it easier to simply tune out.

Dan's rambunctious style of loving and interacting with his son had inadvertently collided with Will's difficulty in paying attention to complex auditory stimulation. The dad who liked to sing all the verses to "I Heard It Through the Grapevine" while noodling on his guitar never dreamed that his own baby needed to listen to smaller sound bites before he could pay attention to the music of the world.

The therapist explained to Dan and Lisa just how hard it apparently was for Will to use his listening to focus and attend. For many people like Dan, auditory attention is quite automatic. Dan derived so much pleasure from his verbal abilities and love of music because the sensations he received through his ears were compelling. But when those sounds are difficult to engage with or comprehend, as they were for his son Will, paying attention becomes an unrewarding, minute-by-minute struggle. It was far easier for Will to simply drift away from the source of those sounds.

The therapist suggested a number of simple changes that Dan could make to coax Will "Back in His Arms Again." First, Dan could gear his interactions to his son's strong visual sense. Playing games with big, shiny balls, using flashlights in the dark, and exhibiting silly faces were a big hit with Will. Next, Dan could simplify the songs and conversations he shared with his seven-and-a-half-month-old. Will wasn't yet ready to respond as pleasurably as other babies his age to complex rhythms and sound. Dan could try to offer simple, singsong phrases instead of stanzas. A "Where's my BIG boy?" repeated three or four times as he picked the baby up, would be far more likely to engage Will's interest than a whole song.

It was equally important to work with Will's motor system, since the very act of listening involves organized, purposeful movement patterns. A baby orients his head and body toward the sounds he hears. If sequencing a series of actions (such as those involved in crawling) is difficult for an infant, it is easy for him to become distracted. Dan increased the amount of time he spent in physical proximity to Will by simply rolling on the floor and lying side by side with Will. He soon found himself crawling on the floor next to Will, practicing moving on all fours. He was delighted to see that his son seemed intrigued by this new state of affairs.

Lisa's already close relationship with Will suggested another way to help him pay more attention to sounds. Babies like Will need extra practice in listening, and Lisa was happy to spend an extra ten minutes each day talking and sometimes singing to him, while using animated facial expressions. Will then felt secure enough to attend to the simple sounds and cadences she offered. Now that Dan as well as Lisa had found a way to playfully engage Will's attention and affection, the jealousy and self-consciousness that had arisen between the two parents (which fortunately they had a chance to explore with each other) started to ebb.

Babies Who Take in Sounds, but Have a Hard Time Figuring Out Sights

By the time Max was six months old, his parents, Lynn and Jonathan, had taken him to two different pediatric ophthalmologists. Both doctors tried to reassure the young couple that their baby's eyesight was perfectly normal, but Max's parents couldn't shake the feeling that something was wrong. Max seldom looked at his parents, and seemed disinterested in most of his toys and the mobile hanging over his crib.

And yet—Max took obvious delight in the world around him. He would smack his lips in happy satisfaction as his mother fed him cereal each morning, and would bounce to the beat of the Barney theme song each time he heard it on the television. Max's black curls framed a pudgy face that begged to be nuzzled and kissed, and Lynn and Jonathan didn't need any prodding in that area. They were totally infatuated with their firstborn, but were increasingly uneasy about his reluctance to meet their gaze.

Although their pediatrician felt that their anxiety was excessive, he referred them to a developmental specialist. After several sessions, in which the therapist observed Max interacting with his parents, the specialist felt that there was a strong possibility that Max might have some difficulty comprehending what he saw. He explained to Lynn and Jonathan that a baby with challenges in making sense of the visual-spatial world may find it easier to focus on simple, nonmoving images. He suggested that they consciously try to slowly bring their faces in from afar and see at what point Max would focus. When Lynn and Jonathan spoke to Max, they refrained from bobbing their heads too much, and their little boy seemed to respond to this. The therapist explained that a baby like Max might be able to look at his parents' faces more easily when they simply smiled at him, rather than smiling and wiggling their hands at him at the same time. He also suggested that they put a brightly colored object on top of their heads as they chatted with Max about the interesting colors. Lynn and Jonathan could then move the object close to Max's eyes, and next place it at varying distances from him. Then they could note whether Max could focus on the object or not.

The goal was to pare down the amount and complexity of sights they offered Max. In addition to avoiding using distracting gestures when they spoke to their baby, Lynn and Jonathan could try to reel him in visually by first engaging his listening. Once he was drawn into intimacy by his pleasure in sound and his love for his parents, Max could probably be cajoled into increasing the use of his sense of sight.

Lynn came up with the idea of humming the Barney song to Max as she held him in her arms. After he relaxed for a while, Lynn decided to try and increase his interest in her face by first shining a flashlight on her eyes, then her nose, and so on. Max's interest was piqued, and Lynn was thrilled to find him studying the novel play of light on her face. She softly continued to sing the Barney song, spotlighting the different features on her face in time with the music. Max's fondness for music, and the comfort he found in his mother's arms, were tools Lynn could take advantage of as she helped him to pleasurably exercise his weaker visual sense.

Jonathan tried using Max's love of puréed bananas as a lure to locking eyes with him. He thought he might hold the dish of bananas up near his own smiling face as he spoon-fed Max. Perhaps Max would start glancing at Jonathan's face and associating it with the source of his pleasure. By using his son's love of food as a magnet to attract Max's attention to his own face, Jonathan was establishing a visual connection with his child. Both Jonathan and Lynn felt encouraged by their newly discovered ability to help Max visually decipher the world.

COMMON FAMILY CHALLENGES TO INTIMACY

Most of us have natural talents as well as challenges, which can influence the way we are interactive. Sometimes a parenting style or unconscious fears can inadvertently interfere with joyfully wooing a baby. A parent may have feelings of inadequacy or too easily feel rejected. Just recognizing and acknowledging such uncomfortable feelings is the critical first step in correcting the problem. Paying attention to what you do to buffer yourself from these feelings is an important second step. You'll then be ready to create new ways of establishing intimacy with your baby that will bring pleasure to you both. Let's examine some of the bumps that may await some parents on the road to establishing true intimacy with their child.

TOLERATING ANGER AND FRUSTRATION

Parents sometimes have to learn how to tolerate new levels of anger and stress in their own lives before they can effectively help their infants tolerate the same feelings. It is helpful to acknowledge to yourself that you may feel angry or frustrated when your attempts to soothe your baby fail. Accept that feeling tired or strained by the pressures of being a new parent is entirely normal and can be overwhelming at times. Try not to blame yourself when you become tired of wooing and want your baby to woo you for a change. Pay attention to your own feelings, and don't be afraid to get the support of other family members. Remember, we are all entitled to feel anything, and remember too that a feeling is very different from an action. In fact, the more we are aware of our feelings, the better we are usually able to regulate our actions.

COMMON PARENTAL FEARS

Some parents delight in the doll-like, miniature proportions of their baby's body. Others are made nervous by their baby's small size and dependency. If you find that you fall into the latter category, it's important to acknowledge this feeling. For instance, you might suddenly become anxious as you gently roughhouse with your baby, and then abruptly put her down for a nap. You may be feeling fearful that your enthusiasm could somehow hurt her. Talking about such feelings with your spouse, best friend, and pediatrician can be very helpful. It can also help to pay attention to the numerous ways your baby shows you how sturdy she is. Notice how firmly she grasps your hands, or how strongly she arches her back or even sits up. Become aware of how assertive she's becoming: howling when she's angry or banging a bottle when she's thirsty. Over time, with supportive discussions and learning about your baby, your fears will usually lessen. If instead they seem to increase, you may wish to discuss getting a referral for additional help with your pediatrician or family physician.

Just as in any other courtship, adults may unconsciously reenact old scripts when they become increasingly intimate with their babies. The blurring of emotional boundaries that occurs when an individual falls in love can initially feel scary to some people, rather than intoxicating. Sometimes mothers or fathers, although they yearn to love their babies, feel fearful or even smothered by the closeness and intimacy of the relationship. They may feel very uncomfortable with the sense of merging that occurs, particularly while they feed or nurse their infants.

Some parents adjust smoothly to their new role during their baby's first few months of life, but become unsure of their sense of self when they start to "fall in love" with their four- or five-month-old infant. In the past, intimate relationships may have led them to lose their sense of who they were, and who their partners were. They may have felt extremely uncomfortable with this sense of fusion, and may have asserted their independence by starting to pull away as soon as their relationships intensified. Such parents might become anxious when their six-month-old affectionately reaches out for them. They might then abruptly move away in response, rationalizing that they are teaching their baby to be strong and independent. If parents can identify their discomfort with closeness and focus instead on their baby's smallness and helplessness, they can often begin to respond and gradually initiate intimacy.

Most of us revisit old fears and hesitations each time we fall in love or grow more intimate with another person in the course of our lives. If you can acknowledge these fears to yourself, however, it is a helpful step that fosters your own and your child's growth. It is both natural and human occasionally to feel anxious, or even fearful, as you find your way into each other's hearts.

FALLING IN LOVE

Woo your baby into pleasure and delight as she looks at you, smells you, listens to your voice, feels your touch, and rhythmically rocks with you.

FUN AND GAMES

🍼 The Smiling Game

Enjoy using words and/or funny faces to entice your baby into breaking into a big smile or producing other pleased facial expressions such as sparkling or widened eyes. You can chatter about the spoon you've stuck in your mouth, or the rattle you've placed on your head, or simply about how "bee-yoo-ti-ful" her hair is!

🍼 The "Dance with Me" Sound and Movement Game

Try to inspire your baby to make sounds and/or move her arms, legs, or torso in rhythm with your voice and head movements. You might say, "Are you going to dance with me, sweetheart? Oh, I bet you can—I know you can!" while looking for a gleam of delight in her eyes.

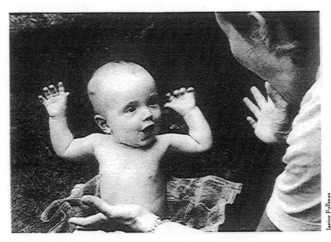

Janice Fullman

3

STAGE 3:

BECOMING A TWO-WAY
COMMUNICATOR

WHAT THIS STAGE IS ALL ABOUT

How does your baby learn to be purposeful and logical? When does he start using his ability to communicate to make things happen? When does he first discover the differences between "me" and "you"? All of these important advances are emerging during this vitally important stage. When your baby is between three and ten months of age, he'll start to show you that he expects more out of your relationship. His ear-to-ear grins are produced not only in response to your wooing, but to entice you, too. They reveal just how much he wants to be in charge and make things hap-

85

pen. Because he trusts and loves you, he looks to you to exchange signals. It's as though love is no longer enough; now he wants a dialogue, too!

Your baby is becoming a two-way communicator. He may already be reaching out to you with his arms and hailing you with a steady stream of babble that's sure to bring you running. Soon he'll propel himself across the floor to be near you, and search your eyes for a response. Long before he is able to talk, you'll be responding to his smiles, frowns, and body movements with gestures of your own. A preverbal but amazingly expressive kind of gestural language will be developing between the two of you.

Most parents still operate under the mistaken assumption that their baby's initial spoken word is the first real sign that language ability is developing. We eagerly record those *da-da*'s, *ma-ma*'s, and *bye-bye*'s in our children's baby books, and worry that there is something very wrong if our baby hasn't produced his first word by the time he is a year old or so. If he is a late talker, we try to reassure ourselves with the thought that even Albert Einstein didn't say much until he was nearly four years old. But we still have an uneasy feeling that our baby may be "slow" or unsociable if he isn't precociously chattering.

We now recognize that all the preverbal gestures your baby uses purposefully, and not only the syllables he lisps, are the real signposts of his growing ability to communicate. The back-and-forth smiles, frowns, giggles and looks of surprise, annoyance, or delight that we sometimes take for granted are the true source of his growing logic, sense of self, and intelligence. All babies, from slow learners to eventual winners of the Nobel Prize, must master the purposeful use of gestures, ideally during this period. If mastery isn't achieved now, it must be reworked at a later stage of the baby's development. In fact, when we see older children in our clinical practice who show various difficulties in using words to communicate, we often observe that aspects of this more basic, gestural ability are missing. We then work with them to use and respond to a wide range of gestural signals, such as hand motions, finger pointing, shoulder shrugging, facial expressions, and vocal tones.

Your baby will be sending you countless gestural, nonverbal messages about his needs and intentions long before he is able to utter his first word. *Your baby's ability to use a rich variety of facial expressions, actions, and sounds in a back-and-forth dialogue with you during these months will enable him to interact with the world in a purposeful and logical way.*

In the coming sections we'll be detailing how to encourage this sort of "can do" spirit in your baby. As you play give-and-take games with him, you'll actually be helping him give purpose and meaning to many other experiences he is having. When your baby reaches for a toy you offer him, he's simultaneously learning to pay attention to the sound of your voice as you encourage him, and to adjust the position of his hand in response to what he sees as you hold the toy up in the air. He's practicing his sounds and motor skills in a purposeful way, even as he's having fun playing a give-and-take game.

When your baby touches your face and puts his fingers in your mouth while you are making mooing or clucking sounds at him, and you playfully lick his fingers, he's not only fine-tuning muscle skills but also realizing that pleasure, delight, and even downright silliness can be part of a back-and-forth communication. He's learning to be a purposeful sender, and not just a receiver, of love. His love for you motivates him to search your face, body, posture, and voice for signs that you're reading him loud and clear.

Your baby's preverbal logic is forming right before your eyes. As his facial expressions elicit a response from you, and as his touches and pats prompt your return hugs, he's beginning to learn that his responses are intentional and lead in turn to other reactions. If he could talk he might say, "If I do this, she'll do that. Hey—I can make things happen! The world can be purposeful and logical." In fact, as you play give-and-take games with your baby, he's also learning that his intentional looking, listening, smelling, and reaching skills can all work together. This ability to bring together, or integrate, all of his behavior will be more fully developed in the next developmental stage, when he is approximately 9 to 18 months old. In the meantime, you'll be surprised at how much his mastery of gestural communication broadens his sense of purpose and supports the beginnings of his logical understanding of the world. Your baby's actions really will speak louder than words.

HOW YOU KNOW YOUR
BABY IS COMMUNICATING

By the time your baby is eight to ten months old or so, it may become more readily apparent that he has been gradually interacting with you in a purposeful way. You'll know he's ready to open up the lines of communication with you, and not merely mirror your behavior, *when he responds to your gestures with gestures of his own.* You'll probably focus on this new ability when your baby reaches out to you to be picked up for the first time. Up to this point, when you've approached his playpen with a hearty "Let's go for a ride in the stroller now!" your baby may have brightened at your approach but may never have indicated that he would be eager to do something or go somewhere with you. Now, he's likely to lift his arms up in anticipation of an adventure when you greet him with "Let's go!" He may not understand your words, but he can read the enthusiastic tone of your voice and your expectant body language. His upraised arms let you know that he wants to join in on the fun.

Along about now, your baby may start responding to your rhythmic words and noises in a back-and-forth way with some sounds of his own, rather than simply joining in with noises when you sing nursery rhymes. Your happy singsong cadence may prompt a playful look to cross your child's face before he starts warbling in response. As part of this dialogue, he may produce a wide variety of different sounds, ranging from Bronx cheers to single syllables formed with consonants and vowels from the front of his mouth (*ba, da, ma*).

Besides vocalizations, you can offer your baby interesting facial expressions. Sucking your cheeks in to make a funny face can elicit either a delighted sparkle in his eye or a look of puzzlement. We've seen that even tiny infants try to mirror their parents' facial expressions, but now they are capable of showing a new sense of purpose when they respond. You'll be able to see a whole range of emotions cross your child's face before he tries to make a funny face back. He may respond to your silly expression by waving his arms and legs in excitement, while his face remains calm. On other occasions he may furrow his brow in rage or fear, or burst into a flood of angry tears. You'll be keeping your eye out for responses of any kind, and shouldn't expect your smile always to elicit a smile, or a wave of your hand to be answered by a movement of his arm.

All your baby's senses and many different actions may come into play during your preverbal conversations together. The very simplest two-way "chat" may involve the sense of touch. When you touch your child, he often touches back. Even very young babies nuzzle their mothers and reposition themselves so they fit right into the curve of their mother's arms. By six months they may fondly pat their parents on the back when they are picked up. Your gentle tickling may cause your baby to arch his back in delight and then glue his eyes to yours while he waves his arms and legs. It's as if he's saying, "More, Mom, more!"

When you playfully lift your baby overhead, or swoop him up in your arms, he may look you square in the eye, wave his arms, and chuckle with delight. You'll probably beam at his shining face and nod your head in shared enjoyment. Guess what? You've just had a real conversation with your child. No words were exchanged, but your actions were met with actions from your baby that let you know that he received your message.

Your baby now knows that his reactions will cause a response from you, and that what he expresses and does can have an impact. He has learned that he can make love happen, and that he is a competent, lovable being. From merely sharing gestures with you a few months ago, he's now determined to convey his intentions to you, and therefore *he initiates interaction with you.* One day, as you lovingly nurse your baby, you'll discover that he will spontaneously reach for your nose and give it a playful pinch. Later on, he'll thrust his hands in the direction of a favorite toy.

These very visible behaviors will be your cue that it's time to energize yourself and look for even more opportunities to exchange gestures with your baby. You will intuitively be accompanying your own gestures with words, of course, but your baby will be making his wishes and feelings known through his body language, actions, facial expressions, and sounds. (See "What to Look For" on the following two pages.)

When infants aren't offered opportunities to participate in these two-way chats, they can become more passive and less organized or emotionally expressive. If you'll just recollect how you feel when you speak in front of a group of people, and how dependent you become on those nodding heads or smiles to keep you going, you'll immediately empathize with your baby's reliance on gestures. It's easy to see how a child whose signals are continually misread can start out life feeling less purposeful or logical. If you attend to a child in a random way, and not in relation to any action or gesture he makes or as part of two-way interaction, he may well start behaving in a manner that Martin Seligman, a psychologist who has explored both optimism and pessimism in people, has termed "learned helplessness."

Your baby thrives on your nods, glances, and vocalizations to let him know that he's been heard. That's why it's so important to enjoy the signals your child sends out to you. His positive messages of a smile or babble or reaching for you are easy to respond to. Negative purposeful actions are harder for most parents to deal with. For example, let's imagine that when you return home from work after being gone all day, your baby seems to turn his back on you and temporarily ignores you. He may be sending you a clear signal that he's miffed. Will you be able to let him know that you understand this message? He may reveal that he's upset in

What to Look For

~

Your baby may open up gestural dialogues with you by initiating such actions as:

- Reaching out to you to be picked up, or hugging you back when you hug him.

- Smiling, vocalizing, putting a finger in your mouth, taking a rattle from his mouth and putting it in your own, or touching or exploring your hair.

- Pushing undesired food off a high-chair tray with an accompanying angry look, screaming when a desired toy isn't fetched quickly enough, or wiggling out of your arms when he has no interest in getting dressed. (His angry face, shouts, and squirming body clearly communicate his sense of protest or anger.)

- Looking for the toy that fell to the ground or (toward the end of this stage) looking in your hand for a hidden, desired rattle.

- Showing caution or fear by turning away, clinging to your leg, or looking scared when a stranger approaches too quickly.

other ways as well, including looking aloof or self-absorbed, or even staring at the wall. He may also exhibit disorganized, random behavior.

Do you take advantage of his apparent disinterest and start cooking dinner or thumbing through your mail? Or do you realize that your baby needs you to sit down on the floor with him, follow his lead, and begin interacting? You might want to entice him into your arms or get a give-and-take funny-face game going, or see whether he will take a spoon from your mouth. Such interactions will let him know that you understand that he's upset and that you're glad to see him.

At this stage of your baby's development there is nothing more important than helping him become a great communicator. Security and love are now elevated into two-way communications, as are new feelings of as-

- Crying more deliberately and calming more deliberately. (Your baby's cries now sound more intentional when he wants to communicate a sense of anger, and more plaintive when he's feeling helpless. He can now usually calm himself down after a few minutes of gestural interaction with you. Offer him gentle sounds, eye contact, and back rubs, not merely to comfort him but also to reestablish a back-and-forth dialogue.)
- Purposely expressing a range of emotions, from joy, anger, and fear to surprise and anticipation.

Your baby may now respond with gestures of his own when you signal him by these kinds of actions:

- Enticing his interest and action with toys or desired food.
- Vocalizing (varying your pitch, volume, cadence, and words).
- Engaging in a wide range of facial expressions.
- Touching (your baby may try to grasp your hand when you tickle him).
- Moving him up and down and sideways through space.

sertiveness and curiosity and a range of new interests. Naturally, the first time your baby creeps, crawls, or utters a first recognizable word may qualify as an exciting Kodak moment. However, these events don't hold a candle to your baby's newfound ability to use gestures to communicate intentionally with you.

Although he wasn't born knowing that he could cause things to happen, when he makes a sound and you make a sound back, he not only begins to know that his sound leads to yours but also learns the difference between your sound and his own. You may be surprised to learn that just a few months ago your infant was unable to distinguish whether a sound he heard came out of his own mouth or another person's. Now he's also becoming aware that the smile his lips produce can cause the smile he sees on your face. As he learns the difference between his smile and yours, your baby is starting to know the difference between what is a part of him, and what is not a part of him. This will eventually help him to separate "me" from "not me," or "you." In a very real sense, your responses to his signals enable him to begin to define a boundary between parts of himself and the rest of the world. That's quite an impressive achievement for such a little guy! It is also the beginning of his later ability to understand the difference between reality and fantasy, or make-believe.

As your baby learns that he can cause your face to become wreathed in smiles or to blanch in fear, he can also apply this lesson of cause and effect to the broader physical world. When he bangs a toy or drops a block, for example, it makes an exciting clap of sound. Similarly, when he knocks food off his high chair tray, it goes *splat* and may even make a colorful mess on the floor. Your baby is connecting the movements of his arm and hand with the sounds and sights that follow. He's learning that he can make all sorts of interesting things happen.

It used to be thought that babies developed the ability to think logically by physically interacting with objects in their environment. In a famous experiment conducted many years ago by Jean Piaget, the founding pioneer of modern cognitive psychology, an infant learned how to pull a string that was attached to a ringing bell. When the bell and string were disconnected, the baby soon stopped pulling the string because it was no longer connected to the sound of the ringing bell. Piaget inferred that the infant's early ability to purposefully manipulate his environment was an indication of the beginning of a preverbal "sensory-motor" capacity to link cause or means (pulling the string) and effect or ends (hearing the ringing bell).

Our observations in recent years, however, suggest that early logic is learned by a very different process. Months before a baby is capable of pulling on a string to ring a bell, or throwing his food from a high chair to create a *splat*, he can elicit a hug, kiss, or smile from you by his smile. Therefore, it's likely that the first lessons in logic, or causality, arise out of the many emotional interactions between parent and child that occur much earlier than his physical interaction with the world. One reason for this is that the child can signal with emotions long before he can move his arms or legs with lots of purposeful control. He then applies those emotional lessons to the physical world. It is fascinating to realize that your child's eventual ability to become an engineer or physicist may stem from his early emotional interactions with you, as well as from his very important explorations of the physical world.

When we talk about the development of logical thinking in an infant, we do not mean to imply that the baby is actually talking to himself with thoughts ("I'm going to smile at Daddy to get him to smile back at me"). That sort of purposeful, interior dialogue doesn't emerge until a child is three or four years old and can think symbolically. Instead, the kind of logical thinking that a baby develops is an appreciation of certain preverbal sequences. Most of our social behavior and daily interactions, ranging from negotiating with peers to circulating at a social gathering, are based on these early learned capacities.

While you and your baby are mastering the basics of back-and-forth communication, some of the physical changes that occur in his body will aid him in learning how to send and interpret these actions or gestures. This growing ability to purposefully communicate will, in turn, strengthen the motor, sensory, language, and cognitive capacities that typically appear during this period. For example, your baby's ability to reach for objects can become part of give-and-take games with you. His ability to creep or crawl can become part of a "come and get me" game you play together. Can you help your baby use these skills interactively? They include:

A Baby's Developing Skills

MOTOR

- Sitting up with good balance
- Holding a toy while sitting
- Reaching up in the air for objects, while sitting
- Shifting from lying on his back to a sitting position
- Going from a sitting to a stomach position
- Creeping or crawling on his stomach or his hands
- Using a thumb and finger to hold a block or toy
- Scooping a Cheerio or small object into his palm
- Playfully banging his hands or toys
- Transferring objects from hand to hand

A Baby's Developing Skills

SENSORY

- Feeling and exploring textures
- Noticing when an object (such as a toy) is put on various parts of his body
- Selective response to some sounds and sights
- Enjoying movement in space

LANGUAGE

- Responding to his name and/or some simple requests (such as being told "No")
- Using sounds to convey intentions or emotions (such as a pleasurable "Mmmm")
- Responding to sounds with different vocalizations or behaviors
- Imitating a few sounds (tongue clicks, or a "raspberry")

COGNITIVE

- Focusing on a toy or person for one or more minutes
- Exploring and examining a new toy
- Making sounds or creating visual sensations with a toy (cause-and-effect playing)
- Discriminating between different people (as indicated by different responses)
- Looking for a toy that has fallen to the floor
- Pulling on a part of an object (such as a piece of cloth) to get the object closer

WHY THIS FIRST TWO-WAY
COMMUNICATION IS SO IMPORTANT

The seeds of many important aspects of your baby's personality, including his social skills, intelligence, and morality, are sown when he learns to use gestures purposefully and becomes a two-way communicator. In addition to enabling him to be purposeful and logical, your responses will let him know that you welcome his assertive attempts to express his needs. You will also be letting him know that his emerging feelings (such as assertiveness and curiosity) can be purposeful and part of a logical dialogue. When your baby reaches up to your hair and twirls it, he's nonverbally expressing his curiosity with a "What is this stuff?" gesture. Try to encourage his inquisitiveness by offering him some gestures in return that indicate "Yes, it's safe to explore the world with me. Go for it!" Catch his eye and smile, then lower your head to make his explorations a little easier. You'll be showing your baby that you respect his curiosity, and that he's been successful in communicating his needs to you.

You build your baby's self-esteem by the exchange of such simple gestures all day long. He's receiving the heartening message that you applaud his efforts to do things, and that his gestures will be understood. By responding to your baby's signals in ways that he can clearly observe and feel, you teach him that he can have a pleasurable impact on the world. This is one way you bequeath the precious gift of optimism to your child.

At the same time, you're arming him with a skill that will help him make intuitive, split-second judgments as he matures. When you foster his ability to read another person's body language and tone, you tap into some of the most primal survival skills human beings possess. When we get an intuitive feeling about a person, it's largely based on the messages his face, posture, and movements convey. His words may be charming or persuasive, but if we sense a tension in his muscles, or see his eyes dart away from ours, we're instantly on guard. We believe in the truth of these physical gestures more than any words.

The social signaling skills that babies learn during this stage of their development are the first steps in a process that can help them become more cooperative and attentive when they reach school age. Children who are adept at sending and receiving gestures find it easier to sense when a classmate's interest is wandering, or when their teachers are losing patience, because they can intuitively read and understand the meaning of hundreds of gestures. A disinterested glance, an exasperated tone of voice, or a shoulder sagging with exhaustion speak volumes to them. They are able to follow rapid changes in vocal tone, figure out patterns, and make quicker judgments about what they see and hear.

Dan Goleman, a psychologist and journalist, recently coined the term "emotional intelligence" to refer to this quality of social adeptness, and his book *Emotional Intelligence* caught the interest of the American public. One way to think about the critical importance of this developmental stage (and the two prior ones as well) is to realize that these early months of a baby's life are when the building blocks of emotional intelligence, as well as traditional cognitive abilities, are first laid down. But contrary to traditional views, we believe that emotional and cognitive abilities are not separate types of intelligence, but are parts of the same pattern of growth. We have found that certain basic experiences simultaneously spur emotional and intellectual capacities.

Some parents tend to place less emphasis on emotional and social skills and focus more on the kind of intellectual training that will lead to A's in science, English, and history. They rationalize that there are trade-offs in life, and that you can drill your child in math concepts and "enrich" him intellectually, or you can concentrate on helping him feel good at the expense of academic success. To them, the choice seems clear: either emotional nurturing or intellectual competence.

Our new way of thinking about how academic strength develops offers parents a third, more reassuring option: The very same things you do with your baby that make him feel secure and loved will also make him intelligent! The funny faces you exchange with each other, and the give-and-take games you now get going, do more than simply build his self-esteem and give him a sense that life is a feast. They also help develop your child's sense that he can make things happen. As he plays with you, he is taking the first steps on the road to being a creative and logical thinker. His early nonverbal play is an important part of his later scientific and analytic ability and also of his social and emotional skills.

Part of the confusion and tendency to separate different types of intelligence comes from thinking about cognitive capacities, such as the ability to memorize new facts, too narrowly. If we focus on the most important cognitive capacities, to create and to reason, we see that it is these capacities that make other skills like learning new facts meaningful and useful. We also see that emotional and cognitive thinking are part of the same process.

Two-way communication also helps your child become empathic and eventually distinguish between right and wrong. As you respond to him, you increase his sense of engagement and security. The nods and glances and exuberant smiles the two of you exchange let your baby know that he is part of a relationship. He begins to learn that his actions and feelings have an impact on you, and starts to value you as a caring person, separate from himself. Your baby tentatively begins to sense that you have feelings, too. This budding awareness of you as a caring person will blossom over time into a sense of caring about you, and through you, others. Out of mutual caring comes a sense of morality. Like emotional and academic intelligence, moral thinking emerges from the fertile ground of wordless communication.

Your baby's mastery of two-way, gestural communication is also associated with branching between neurons in the frontal and prefrontal cortex of his brain. The neurons in that portion of his brain form a rich network that supports his ability to plan or sequence actions, and to express a wider range of emotions, including surprise, pleasure, subtle forms of flirtation, and fear. As your baby purposefully communicates with you using emotionally expressive gestures, the connections between the nerves in his frontal and prefrontal cortex are expanding. This in turn further fosters his ability to interact with you.

Studies of babies' brain-wave patterns at this stage of their development reveal that infants become more selective in their response to certain sounds as they become more purposeful in their actions. For example, they respond more (by turning their heads) to the sounds of the language they hear every day than to the sounds of other languages. It appears that as babies become capable of more purposeful and organized communication with their parents, the neuronal connections in their brains become more fine-tuned, or "pruned," and may in turn facilitate more selective responses to environmental cues.

HOW TO HELP YOUR BABY COMMUNICATE

READING AND RESPONDING TO YOUR BABY'S CUES

How does your baby let you know what he wants? Can you tell when he's mad at you, or when he needs a cuddle? Does he show you that he wants a particular toy, or that he's hungry and thirsty? Every baby has his own gestural style, and some are clearly more theatrical than others. Maybe your baby has already demonstrated what a ham he is by the vividness of his facial expressions. He doesn't merely grin; he beams. When this child is angry, you get all the bells and whistles: wrinkled brow, trembling lip, and tears of rage. There may be a full display of kicking and flailing limbs, accompanied by indignant howls.

Babies who are clear signalers are more likely to get what they want because adults don't have to work at interpreting their gestures. If your infant is able to rely on his muscles he won't hesitate to reach toward you, and you'll know that he wants your company. If his facial muscles are similarly cooperative, he may find it easy to imitate the many expressions he's seen cross your face, and use them as he responds to you. Clear signalers usually have no difficulty expressing their feelings because they can readily use their senses of hearing, vision, touch, and smell to pick up the cues you send to them, and then use their muscles to send a return message. They'll preen in your direction, giving you a flirtatious look to let you know that they're ready, willing and able to interact with you. When a baby is this eager to communicate, it won't take very much practice on your part to learn how to read his squeals of joy, lunges for toys, or looks of disgust when he tastes lima beans for the first time.

Many babies offer less flamboyant cues when they express their feelings or respond to your overtures. If your baby has a more subtle style, you'll have to sharpen your observational powers. When your child wants to be picked up, he may not fix you in his eyes and reach out his arms. Instead, he may use a low-pitched whiny tone, or rattle the sides of his crib. He's using gestures that come easily to him to let you know what he wants, and over time you'll come to recognize his signaling pattern. Don't assume that your baby isn't responding to you or expressing a feeling just because he's not using the body language you had anticipated. Look for behavior that's easy for your baby to do—whether it's smiling, moving his limbs or babbling—and use it as the basis for your dialogue with him.

Some babies are highly intentional, even when they are a little slow in their motor development. You may find that your baby will wiggle and roll across the floor to get to you, even if he can't crawl yet. He'll stare up at you with big, round eyes and you'll realize that he's asking you to pick him just as surely as if he raised his arms and said "Up!"

Other babies are more laid-back and exhibit more subdued responses. They may not answer your enthusiastic vocalizations with sounds of their own, but will smile. The fact that they can use a gesture of any kind to respond to yours is what's key here. Similarly, the particular ways you respond to your baby's gestures are not significant. As long as your child notes that you have received his message—by your head nod, a lilt in your voice, or even a grimace on your face—he will be getting a response, learning to be causal, and feeling secure in his new ability to communicate.

Although it's a good idea to respond to most of your baby's gestures, there's no need to try to reciprocate each and every one of his overtures. He'll be able to figure out the general drift of your responses, and you neither can nor should expect yourself to tune in to all of your baby's behaviors. You won't catch every nuance of his body language and will misunderstand some of his messages. As a result, your child will learn to accept delay and frustration as a part of life. However, only some babies have the fortitude to keep trying to catch your attention by vocalizing louder, clearing their throats, or giving you frustrated looks. You can't count on your baby to be a squeaky wheel when he needs more attention. Be proactive; look for any and all signs, overt and subtle, that your baby is trying to share a feeling or a desire with you.

Finally, parents need to recognize that their responses to their babies' gestural overtures should be not only reciprocal, but also on target. When your baby reaches out his arms to be picked up, the first words out of your mouth shouldn't be "Oh, look, your collar is sticking up!" Your accompanying gesture of smoothing his collar down in no way acknowledges your baby's clear, although nonverbal, desire to be picked up. Always let your baby know that he's been a successful communicator by responding to his gestural overture before you broaden the context of your interaction. Pick him up *before* you straighten his collar. Better still, fight your impulse to spruce him up. It's a losing battle!

FLOOR-TIME FUN WITH YOUR BABY

Your goal during your child's previous stage of development was to establish an easy rapport with him, and to mutually enjoy each other's company. Now you'll be setting your sights on encouraging an ongoing exchange of gestures between yourself and your child. The best way to communicate with your baby and get a fix on his intentions is to get right down on the floor next to him.

Because your baby still has limited mobility at this point, you can capture his attention while you both lie or sit on the floor. Position yourself at least a foot away from his face, so he won't have difficulty focusing on you. Next, you'll be actively helping him open and close what we refer to as "circles of communication." This process involves each of you giving and receiving a signal from the other. A circle of communication is first opened when your baby offers a cue to you.

Let's assume you and your nine-month-old are companionably lying on the floor together, with a bright red ball within easy reach. Watch your baby's eyes light up when he notices the ball and starts to creep toward it. Your child has just sent you a circle-opening gestural cue; the glint in his eye and his wiggling bottom have conveyed his wish to go and explore the ball. Perhaps you'll respond to your baby's signal by moving the ball an inch or two closer to him. As he begins to reach out with his hand, or coos or smiles at the ball, he'll be closing the circle of communication. When he finally gets the ball in his grasp, you'll catch his eye, nod your head, and enthusiastically clap your hands, exclaiming, "What a bouncy ball you've found!" Your nodding head and clapping hands provide your baby with clear gestural proof that you've watched him go after something he desired, and that you celebrate his success in getting what he wanted. The words you say won't have any symbolic meaning for him yet, but he does pick up on the warm tone of your voice. In turn, you baby may grin at you as he takes the ball and brings it up to his mouth, gumming it with gusto. This answering smile reassures you that your child has heard the approval in your voice. Each time he purposefully responds to your gestures he is closing a circle of communication.

These kinds of give-and-take gestural dialogues are big hits with infants of this age. Babies are entranced by games long after most adults' interest has waned. So be prepared to give and take that bright red ball for quite a while! You won't become glassy-eyed with boredom if you focus on the sparkle in your baby's eyes, rather than on the repetitiousness of your actions. While your baby may appear to be mesmerized by repetition, he also enjoys novelty. Try rolling the ball at different angles to the right and left of him, or cover the ball with your own hand from time to time and see if he will look for it. As you make your give-and-take game more fun for yourself, you'll be making it more fun for the baby as well. Encourage your child to show some initiative; wait a while and see if he'll roll the ball off in a new direction. His obvious pleasure in being the boss of your floor-time dramas will bring delight to you both.

Floor-time communication games can take countless forms. If your baby is up on his hands and knees and is already a good crawler, try to get a game of chase going. By the end of this developmental period, your child will probably open a circle of communication with you by crawling away and then coyly looking over his shoulder to see if you're in hot pursuit.

Once you get on all fours and make zooming noises, he'll probably start screeching with delight as he tries to escape. You may even hear him imitating your sounds, as if he's trying to keep your game going a little longer.

There are many traditional action-and-response games like "This Little Piggy" and peekaboo that bring your baby a lot of delight, but offer him fewer opportunities to take the initiative. When you play these games with your baby, try to introduce a little novelty into the action from time to time. Most babies respond with predictable glee to each step of the story of "This Little Piggy." Try facing your baby as you recite the rhyme, so he can see your facial expressions and respond to them as well as to the rhythm of your voice and the tickling sensations of your fingers. As you recite each line, look up at your baby's face and respond to the expressions you'll find there. Your child will be learning that his responses lead you on to the next exciting step of the game. Skip one of his toes as you play, and see if he notices. When he's rewarded by the "Wee, wee, wee, all the way home" extended tickle and hug at the end of the nursery rhyme, occasionally blow on his tummy, too. Keep him guessing about the kind of fun he'll be receiving at the end of your game. Think of how much communicating takes place during just one game of "This Little Piggy"! Not only does your baby open and close numerous circles of communication as he interacts with you, but he is also learning to enjoy the delicious pleasure of anticipation, too.

These interactions are bona fide conversations, based on the give-and-take of gestures. When your baby is about eight months old, he may be able to open four, five, or more circles of communication in a row as he gesturally interacts with you. By about a year and a half, he may easily be nonchalantly opening and closing 20 to 30—or more—circles in a row. The key is to gradually entice him into producing a continuous flow of opening and closing circles. Head nods, smiles, arched eyebrows, and other gestures will punctuate every conversation.

KEEPING THE COMMUNICATION GOING

Practice makes perfect. Now that your baby is starting to use a variety of gestures and vocalizations, you'll be consciously setting up situations in which he can use his new skills to let you know what his wants and feelings are. First, you might look for ways to join him in his interests. As you play floor-time games with your child, allow him to initiate activities as often as he wishes, and then react to his initiative. Your goal will be to get your baby to act, and not to act for your baby, as he explores his world. Sometimes parents get sidetracked into pleasurable activities with their babies that are too one-sided. Small doses of tickling or gentle roughhousing are fun for your child, but they do need to lead to interactions that strengthen his new ability to use a series of gestures to communicate.

For example, try placing a few sheets of wrapping or tissue paper on the floor before you invite your child to have a little floor-time fun. Put him on the floor an arm's reach away from the paper. He will no doubt be attracted by the colorful paper and launch himself toward it. His pointed finger may well lead the way, since his thumb and finger now function like extensions of his mouth, and he uses them to explore everything in his vicinity. In fact, he is growing quite expert in his handling objects, and loves to try to pick up tiny things like Cheerios, bugs, and dust balls.

Once your child successfully nabs the paper, watch his face light up with obvious pleasure or his forehead wrinkle in concentration as he hears a satisfying crunch. Face your baby, letting him see your enthusiastic face as you take the paper from him, and ask, "Can I play the paper game, too?" Try offering the balled up piece of paper back to him, and see what new direction the game takes. You can vary this sort of interaction by placing a ticking watch on the floor near the baby to pique his interest, or mimic the "vroom" of a racing car and see if you can get a chase game going. Once the action is under way, however, resist overcontrolling the drama and make sure to follow your baby's lead.

You'll soon become aware of your child's particular rhythm and style of communicating. Many babies this age intuitively use a lot of gestures in a natural ebb and flow. They point, pose their bodies, use hand and arm movements, and readily mug for you. Others may be more reticent, and may need to be quietly wooed before they're ready to take the plunge and reach out. Respect your baby's unique style, and try to match the rhythm of his vocalizations and the general shape of the postures he assumes.

When your interactive style reflects the tone set by your baby, he'll know that you've picked up on the cues he's sending you. If, for instance, your child becomes agitated and lets loose with a stream of staccato shouts, let him know by the intensity of your own gestures that you've understood his mood. Quicken your head nods and vocalizations to match the rhythm of his gestures. Then try to pull him down to a more relaxed, calmer pace by slowing down the rhythms of your own gestures. If you keep your voice soothing, your baby will eventually regain a sense of calm.

Sometimes your floor-time playmate may back off entirely. Give him some space to recover; gestural conversations can be draining, and 20 minutes of interaction may be more than he can handle. If your baby seems tired, change the rhythm of your interaction. Switch to a more structured game, like "This Little Piggy," or offer him a soothing back rub. You can be interactive yet very comforting as you and your baby pat or rub each other's hands or rhythmically rock in each other's arms. Think of how restorative it is when your spouse and you exchange hugs or massages at the end of a rough day.

Another way to draw your baby back into communicating with you is to keep your nonverbal conversations lively, but not frantic. Provide him with twists and small surprises to keep his interest alive. Use animated facial expressions, throw yourself into the spirit of the chase as you play together, and let yourself be as uninhibited and goofy as you like.

Your baby's attention span is growing at an impressive rate. At eight months he can examine an object for 40 to 60 seconds at a time. Help him to stay focused just a few seconds longer each time you interact by offering him information in a way that he can understand. If your baby's attention seems fleeting, experiment by slowing down, speeding up, or modifying the gestures you're offering him.

To summarize: Follow your baby's lead, respond to his cues in an empathetic and timely way, and try to enliven and extend your gestural conversation. As you build your ability to communicate with your baby, he'll pick up on your love and respect for him by the brightness of your eyes, the eagerness of your head nods, the playfulness of your voice, and the high drama of your body language.

HELPING YOUR BABY USE HIS BODY TO COMMUNICATE

By the time they are eight or nine months old, most infants can sequence at least two movements in pursuit of something they desire. For instance, if your baby sees a teddy bear a few feet away from him, he is now able to crawl or creep toward the bear, and then reach for it. His ability to plan several movements, which we refer to as motor planning or motor sequencing, makes it easier for your baby to communicate his intentions. Imagine the frustration and anger he would feel if he saw the teddy bear and wanted to explore it and satisfy his curiosity, but was still unable to coordinate a sequence of crawling and reaching.

As you observe your baby use his motor skills to get within reach of his heart's desire, try to pay special attention to the way he uses his large muscles; for example, how he crawls, walks, and reaches for things. If he seems awkward or hesitant, it may be that he is simply in need of more practice; but it may also mean that he has real difficulty in planning his actions. Observe him over time and see if he becomes more accomplished, or if he still exhibits challenges. If your baby does have a hard time sequencing two movements, he may also be frustrated in his efforts to communicate his intentions to you. You'll find it hard to decipher whether he's feeling assertive, curious, happy, or angry, because he can't direct his body to signal the messages he wants to tell you.

It's harder to feel a sense of connectedness when your baby offers you confusing signals. One way you can avoid misjudging your baby's intentions is by taking a closer look at his motor abilities. Remember to take note of his particular muscle tone. If your child has taut or stiff muscles, he may not be able to control his gestures and may overshoot the mark when he reaches out. His curiosity can be misunderstood as aggression. Perhaps you've seen him try to put his hand on your lips as you eat something interesting, only to have him bop you on the nose by accident.

Similarly, the intentions of a baby with low muscle tone can be misconstrued by his parents. Let's assume that you take a favorite toy out of your baby's hands and he becomes angry. He may have a burning desire to pinch or poke you in his anger, but because of his floppy muscles he still doesn't have the ability to follow through. (By this stage of his development, your baby is experimenting with other physical expressions of aggression besides crying.) He may attempt to poke at you but wind up toppling over, crying in rage and frustration. If you mistakenly assume that he's crying because he's in pain and give him a hug in sympathy, you'll be misreading his clear intentions. His legitimate feelings of aggressiveness and anger will have been ignored.

Should you have continuing concerns about your child's capacity to control his muscles and sequence his actions, be sure to consult your pediatrician or child development specialist. Since your baby's signaling ability, and thus his skill in communicating, rests on the reliability of his motor system, always look at your baby's muscle tone and sequencing capacity before you leap to any quick assumptions about his mood. After all, if he has difficulty letting you know what he wants, that will certainly influence his mood.

Helping Your Baby Express All His Feelings

Responding appropriately to your baby's happy smile may be effortless on your part. However, he needs to rely on your empathic reading of *all* his emotions, including such negative signals as head banging and pinching. He needs gestural feedback from you about all the many different emotions he's capable of expressing. The more you can read and respond appropriately to your baby's signals of pleasure or protest, the more your baby will appreciate subtle differences in his own and other people's emotions. As you empathize with him, and share his joys and frustrations, he will come to know that he's understood emotionally. He'll be expressing his feelings about needing to be close to you (dependency), and about pleasure, love, curiosity, and also assertiveness and anger. You want him to understand that having all kinds of feelings is okay.

Sometimes your baby may act a little withdrawn, or wary. Don't be offended by his temporary aloofness; let him see through your gestures that you understand him. Maintain a sort of hovering warmth when you're near him, using slow head movements and affirming head nods. Then gradually put a sparkle in your eyes and animate the movements of your mouth to bring the baby back to wanting to interact with you. Mild novelty, even something as simple as changing the pitch of your voice, may engage his interest. Above all, don't assume that his temporary withdrawal means that he is rejecting you. He just needs a pause, and then some help in reestablishing the lines of communication between the two of you. He may first need some rest and comforting before you gradually draw him into interaction.

Let's take a closer look at how your baby expresses other negative feelings, such as anger or resentment. These emotions may first emerge when you take something away from the baby that he enjoys. He is now able to feel a sense of loss and anger when things are removed from his vicinity because he is starting to realize that objects can continue to exist even when they are briefly out of his sight. Just a few months ago, he was unable to comprehend that an absent toy still existed, and you could take one out of his crib and know that he'd never miss it.

By the time he's nine months old or so, it's a different story. Your baby may become agitated if he wants something he doesn't have. Or he may bang another toy against the side of his crib in anger. The way you respond to him at these times will deliver an important message about how you feel about anger and assertiveness in general. Try to bear in mind that more than anything else, your baby needs to know that gestural interaction with you can be maintained even under the pressure of intense and angry feelings. This means that you'll accept your baby's right to bellow or glare, but will offer him warm and soothing gestures in response.

We're not suggesting that you coo to him in syrupy tones; when he's angry your baby would only become more frustrated by such a response to his genuine irritation. Instead, respond to his agitated vocalizations and thrashing arms with gestures that convey to him the depth of your empathy. Temporarily match his excited state with quickened head nods and vocalizations of your own. Tell him in an energized voice, "I know you're so, so mad. I can tell you're really angry at Daddy." Then gradually try to pull him down to a slightly more relaxed level where he can begin to open and close gestural circles of communication with you. Try slowing down the pace of your words: "There, there, little guy. Are you feeling better now? Let's take a d-e-e-e-p breath, okay?" This will help your baby to calm himself while he remains in sync with you.

By accepting your baby's right to feel angry, and by responding to his feelings with gestures of your own and then gesturally slowing him down, you teach your child how to return to back-and-forth communication with you. You've avoided using gestures like angry stares or frowns and stiffening your back, which would only cause your baby to be afraid and to disengage from you. You've also avoided patronizing sweetness, which would further irritate him. Instead, you've helped your child cement his new communication skills by remastering the earlier milestones of calming himself and relying on your love, even when he is furious at you.

Another emotional area that is troublesome for some parents is the nine- or ten-month-old's very obvious enjoyment of his body. He will be busy exploring all his various parts during these months, now that his muscle control permits him to reach out and manipulate his fingers. You may find that your baby likes to suck on his toes or pull at his genitals. This very normal behavior upsets some parents and causes them to respond with anxious gestures or angry tones that confuse their babies.

Remember that children at this age are purposeful pleasure seekers, and so enjoy stimulating themselves. If your baby is spending a disproportionate amount of time doing this, he may be attempting to bring a needed level of excitement to his own body. Since your baby will almost always prefer to interact with you rather than to be alone, try to offer him better alternatives to his solitary explorations. Let your baby play with your hair, give him massages, play "This Little Piggy" with his toes. Point your finger at his nose and mouth and stomach and then yours, naming the various parts of his body while adding little tweaks and tickles to your game to delight him. As you and your child communicate with each other, he will learn that interaction can help him explore the pleasure he feels in his own body. Often babies who are involved with self-stimulation need and enjoy extra rocking, as well as more interaction. Try not to be prudish or overreact to your baby's obvious sensual delight. Help him to find a balance between his solitary pleasuring and your companionable interactions.

LETTING YOUR BABY BE THE BOSS SOMETIMES

Now that your baby can proudly set things in motion by letting you know what he wants, he might become a little bossy. He'll find it hard to submit to your control sometimes, and will become angry. This is not the time to take your baby's anger personally. He's learned how to grab your attention each time he expresses a desire through his gestures, and he simply wants to continue asserting himself.

You can avoid many of the power struggles that typically crop up by letting him take a bit more control of your playtimes. Babies want respect and admiration for their assertiveness, and you can lavish it on them as you follow their lead during floor time. If your child wants to bang his toys, let him think that this is your idea of fun, too. Feign enthusiasm if you have to, but you may be surprised at how much you enjoy letting your baby temporarily take over the reins!

Let's suppose your child bangs his block on the floor, and then on a pot lid—all the while looking up at you, waiting for your reaction. You can catch his eye and say, "What a fun game! Listen to those noisy blocks!" Then, you might try reacting to the different timbre of each noise. Cover your ears when the clatter is jarring, and smile when the sound is pleasing, or rhythmic. Your baby will see by these gestures that his initiatives can provoke different responses.

By letting your baby take control of your floor time together, you acknowledge his preferences and broaden his ability to communicate with you. You also share leadership with him in a way that makes him feel valued and important, and avoid power struggles by letting him be in charge.

COMMUNICATING LIMITS

As long as you encourage your child to take the lead during your floor-time interactions, he will develop a deep-rooted feeling that he can be the master of his little kingdom. You should then feel perfectly free to set limits in other areas of his life. Because he is increasingly focused on the exciting outside world and wants to do so many things, your child can sometimes overstimulate himself. He may become overwrought and disorganized, and will need your help in calming himself down.

You've already taught your baby the meaning of your admiring nods and smiles, and now he needs to learn the meaning of your side-to-side shaking head, and the message carried by the words "No, no!" You can display other gestures that convey disapproval, including a stern look accompanied by a pointing finger or a click of your tongue. The gestures and words you use when your baby needs to be distracted from a dangerous or irritating situation will broaden his gestural vocabulary.

After many repetitions, your baby will get the message when he hears your stern voice or sees your disapproving facial expression. Sometimes you'll simply have to run and scoop the baby up (if he's exploring an electrical outlet or trying to pinch another child), but you should recognize that those sorts of expedient moves are also missed learning opportunities.

More minor disturbances will give you plenty of chances to teach your baby how to respond to your gestures. If your baby keeps touching a dusty radiator and getting his hands dirty in spite of your futile attempts to distract him, firmly turn him around and send him on his way in the opposite direction. Remember to shake your finger while saying "No! Yucky!" in a deep voice as you glue your eyes to his. Furrow your brow so that he doesn't think this is a fun "come and get me" game. Also, be prepared to lighten up the serious quality of your voice if it seems to frighten your baby. Some babies will be responsive to just a slight deepening of your normal voice.

By actively learning how to read and send gestures, your child experiences the clear relationship between cause and effect. He'll eventually change the behavior that you disapprove of because he loves you and has come to rely on your warm and loving tone when you're with him.

Your approving gestures mean more to him than his need to investigate all his surroundings. Still, remember that your baby is only just beginning to comprehend your "No!" gestures. He will more fully understand the meaning of "No!" in the next stage of his emotional development.

Until then, continue to help your baby practice observing and appropriately responding to your approving and disapproving gestures. As he learns more about your gestures, over time he will come to accept that restraining himself can make him feel good, as he associates a feeling of approval with your supportive voice and affirming head nods. These positive feelings will eventually mature into true self-esteem.

NONVERBAL COMMUNICATION AS YOUR CHILD GROWS OLDER

The simple gestures that you now matter-of-factly exchange with your baby are creating messages that he will continue to read in the faces and bodies of every person with whom he comes in contact. These nonverbal cues convey crucial information about others. They will teach your child to trust relaxed, kindly voices and to be wary of furtive looks and nervous, jerky motions. Certain tones of voice and postures will warn him of danger, while vacant facial expressions or fidgety limbs will signal him that he's losing his audience. As he matures, you'll be teaching him how to pay special attention to all the unspoken messages that body language conveys. Even when spoken words acquire symbolic meaning for your child, your floor-time play together will still emphasize gestures, because they deepen—and sometimes deliberately contradict—the meanings of the words you use.

One day in the future you and your three- or four-year-old will no doubt reenact the story of "Little Red Riding Hood" together. Your toddler may take on the role of the wolf, disguised in Grandmother's nightgown. As he responds to your "What big eyes you have, Grandma!" with an "All the better to see you with, my dear," you'll see your child widen his eyes and smack his lips with menace. He'll be gesturally communicating his understanding that although his words may be sweet, there's an evil intent lurking behind those words. He's beginning to understand that his actions and gestures can be at odds with the words he utters, and that the truest communication that goes on between people is that which is revealed by our bodies.

What a powerful lesson he'll be learning! In the years ahead, you'll help him refine this notion, and someday he'll be able to discern the difference between a snake-oil salesman and the real McCoy. Remember that while you're teaching your child these subtle lessons, he'll still need the comfort of the warm look in your eye and the lulling of your rhythmic rocking. Continue to calm him and woo him as your dialogues together grow increasingly more complex and entertaining.

RAISING THE BAR

Even the simplest little games involving two-way communication will provide a baby's nervous system with a great, broad-ranging workout. These games also teach him to coordinate many different actions at the same time. Games like peek-a-boo will develop your child's ability to look at your face, hear your words, and simultaneously move his hands. When your baby reaches for your nose and gives it a squeeze, and you pretend you're a locomotive and go "Choo-choo!", your playful interaction is actually coaching your child to look, listen, and act at the same time. He is powerfully motivated to study your gestures and get the story straight because he loves you and experiences joy each time you play together. Your baby can now do more than one thing at the same time, and his ability to integrate these capacities under the umbrella of being purposeful or intentional is what strengthens his nervous system and mind during this stage of his development.

During this first year of your baby's life, you've become ever more aware of the unique aspects of his nervous system and personality. You've come to appreciate which of his senses he prefers to use, and which senses need strengthening. While emphasizing the cues that are easy for him to follow, be sure to offer support for other ones as well. For instance, if your baby seems particularly responsive to the things he sees, rather than the things he hears, start with visual cues, smiles or frowns, or let him help you flick on a light switch that illuminates a sparkling chandelier.

After the two of you have opened and closed a few circles of communication by emphasizing visual cues, it's time to expand the range of your gestures to include more sounds and movements. Try using sounds to indicate that the light will be going on. You might swing your baby in your arms, or bounce to the cadence of a nursery rhyme. See if he will make sounds or move his hands to get you to turn the light back on. Your baby will get a sense that moving and listening can be part of a visual experience, too. Once you've succeeded in snaring his attention by appealing to his stronger sense, he'll be more likely to stay focused on you while you help him exercise his more challenging ones. Conversely, if your baby needs practice visually, focus more on talking and moving at first, and less on dazzling chandeliers. In general, try to tailor the initial cues you offer your child to his stronger sense, and broaden from there.

As your baby learns to respond to an increasing variety of gestures, he'll be integrating what he sees, hears, and touches with movement. If you notice that he doesn't make full use of all his muscles as he interacts with you, offer him exercises that will help him use more of his muscles. Initiate games in which you playfully pop up from a reclining position when you chant a certain sound, and see if he will copy you in a monkey-see, monkey-do manner. Put a birthday party blow-out toy in your mouth, and have him watch the paper tube uncoil while its whistle sounds. This visually intriguing, noisy toy will prompt him to reach out and grab it! Give your baby plenty of incentives to practice seeing, reaching, and crawling at the same time. Also, if he seems to hesitant to pick up small objects, offer him tiny pieces of finger food, and place them with a flourish on his high-chair tray.

As your baby begins to operate like a wonderful one-man band playing his new "instruments" of sight, sound, touch, and movement all at once, it is his emotions and emotional interests that pull all the music together. So be sure to create many opportunities for your baby to trot out his one-man band with pleasure and intention.

MAGIC MOMENTS

Communication skills can't be learned on the fly. Your baby needs your undivided attention every day, many times a day, so that a shared gestural language can fully unfold. If you are away from your baby many hours each day at work, you must make a special effort to carve out several floor-time periods that are sacrosanct. One mother learned the hard way that her baby's need to communicate with her had to take precedence over everything else.

Most afternoons when this mom came home from her job, she could see that her nine-month-old (who was cared for in the daytime by a neighbor) was annoyed with her. The baby would pull at her legs and whine. He could give her the cold shoulder whenever she leaned down to pick him up. The mom would often give the baby a quick hug and a kiss and then put him down so she could unload the dishwasher and start cooking dinner. With her two older children and husband coming home in less than an hour, time was precious.

After a while, the mother noticed that her little boy didn't act clingy or whine when she came home. In fact, he didn't show much of a reaction to her at all. His disinterest was a red flag that made her worry about him. Realizing that her baby needed a sense that he came first, and wondering whether her bustling around the kitchen felt like a rebuff to him, she began to woo him by getting down on the floor, right at his level, as soon as she brought him home. At first the baby crawled around the floor, playing with pots and pans, ignoring her. Gradually he warmed up and seemed to sense that his mother was back in his world for real. He scooted over to her and tentatively pulled at her hair. In response, his mother pulled him into her lap, gave him a big hug, and said, "I'm so glad to be home with you!" The baby and his mother then spent time playing crawling games and exchanging gestures.

After 20 minutes, both floor-time participants were tuckered out but in sync. When his mom went back to cooking dinner, the baby would occasionally leave his pots and pans to crawl near her and babble. She'd return the compliment, and the baby would go back to his play and then come over again. It became clear to this mother that from now on floor-time communication would have to come first, and everything else could wait for a little while. She realized that a floor-time philosophy could still prevail even as she was getting dinner ready.

Some of these "magic moments" come at inconvenient times, it is true, but others can be scheduled at the end of the day, after the baby is bathed and relaxed. In the evening, try to have quieter floor-time sessions that will wrap your baby in a cocoon of empathy and connectedness. Exchange loving touches and soft vocalizations to ease your sleepy baby into his crib.

The more time you spend in play and direct dialogue with your baby, the more fun as well as interesting it may eventually be for you. You'll become more familiar with and attuned to his individual style of signaling. If some of your baby's gestures remain unclear to you, you may need to see them twenty times or more before you can sort them out and know whether your child is playfully squeezing your nose or trying to pinch you with a vengeance.

MAKING YOUR HOME EXPLORATION-PROOF

If your baby feels free to explore his environment, he will become more adept at showing you what he wants. When you put excessive limits on his experimentation, you will almost certainly run up against his wish to assert himself. You can avoid unnecessary power struggles by making sure that certain areas of your home are safe for him to explore by removing small objects, padding sharp corners, and covering switch plates and removing other electrical hazards.

A baby who has lots of opportunity to poke into things doesn't feel more than momentarily aggrieved when some things are forbidden to him. Nor does he stop loving you when you remove dangerous objects from his grasp and tell him "No!" By providing a safe environment for your child you encourage him to show you, through his gestures and behaviors, how much he enjoys exploring his world.

HELPING A DISTRESSED BABY TO COMMUNICATE

Even after your baby has become distressed and gone into meltdown, you can communicate together. One general rule of thumb is to always gently nudge your baby to use his body or his voice to show you what he wants. For instance, when you hear your eight-month-old howl angrily in his playpen, you'll probably rush to his side to see what the matter is. As soon as you determine that he's in no physical distress, resist the urge to pluck him up into your arms. Sometimes waiting several moments before doing anything, while your face and voice are showing your baby your attentive concern, will spur him into action. Give him a lot of additional vocal support, saying, "Do you want Daddy to pick you up? Do you want me to play with you?" Even though he probably won't understand the words you are using, you're giving him a chance to show you what he wants. In those few seconds that you offer him the solace of your words, he may suddenly reach out his arms in a silent request to be picked up. Let your baby know that you empathize with his feelings, but don't jump the gun and anticipate his needs. Give him a chance to build up his repertoire of gestures.

Babies use their motor systems to discharge their frustrations. They may bang their hands on their high-chair tray, or knock down a toy. At this age, a baby may often gesture using his head and trunk because he has the most control over those parts of his body. Many babies need lots of opportunities for robust physical interaction. Get down on the floor with them and incorporate rhythmic movements into your play. Some babies also need practice using their legs and hands so they don't have to rely on their head and neck muscles so exclusively. Other babies are already adept at using their arms and legs, and will kick or poke at you when they are mad. Still others may stare at you silently, or emit shrill cries, or even bite themselves as they attempt to show you how angry they feel.

By responding to most of your child's signals of anger, even when the cues are subtle or silent, you will gradually pull him back into the pleasure of interacting with another person. Letting your child know that you are registering his intentions and feelings—whether it's simply by nodding your head, or curling your lip, or, when he recovers his usual cheer, flashing him a smile as you throw your arms up in jubilation—is vitally important during these months. When you catch sight of his affirming nod, happy grin, or even a pout on his face, you can rest assured that he has received and processed your preverbal message.

Dos and Don'ts as Your Baby Learns to Communicate

~

- *Do* simultaneously exercise as many of the seeing, smelling, hearing, touching and moving elements of your child's nervous system as you can while the two of you interact.

- *Don't* be a ringmaster and direct the way your play unfolds. Follow your baby's lead and help him use his interests to give direction and organization to his new abilities.

- *Do* play lots of emotionally pleasurable games for longer times. The more interactive playtimes you share, the more fun you'll have.

- *Do* seek out the magic moments.

HOW TWO-WAY COMMUNICATING BUILDS YOUR BABY'S SENSE OF SELF

In the early months of your baby's life, he had no sense of being a separate being. His self was experienced as a kind of heightened alertness to the world inside and around him. Over time, his growing relationship with you led to a more intense engagement with the human world. His sense of self increasingly became tied to and part of your emotional connection and interactions with him. Now, during this period of development when two-way, purposeful communication occurs, a new *willful* self is sprouting. Your child is starting to realize that his behavior can cause you to respond to him and help him get what he wants. His sense of self is both a part of your relationship and at the same time is beginning to be experienced as separate and purposeful.

When your baby feels a need to be picked up, he indicates this by lifting up his arms. He doesn't experience this wish in a verbal form, or with symbols, as an adult would. The baby can't think in terms of "I want to be picked up" because he has no words yet. He does, however, feel a sense of intention, or desire, that gets communicated through his gestures. When you respond to him in an appropriate way, and pick him up, his sense of a "me," a self that can make things happen, is given a boost.

Your *No, no!*'s as well as your *Yes, yes!*'s help your baby organize the experiences he is having. These cues from you provide your child with the feedback he needs to know that his willful acts are having an impact on the world. It's as if he's assembling a mosaic-like picture of himself, formed out of all the many experiences he's having. Each time you respond to his overtures, another little piece of the self-portrait comes into place.

Thus, your child's concept of himself as a separate being emerges out of your reactions to his overtures and gestures. When he shoots you a mischievous grin, and you continually return his grin with an accepting smile, he will develop a very different self-image than if you pay no attention or make a habit of offering him head-shaking frowns.

Always bear in mind that different children respond differently to the same cues. You don't want inadvertently to overwhelm your child with sensations that cause him to become disorganized or shut down. Avoid yelling or abrupt gestures. Keep an eye out for signs that your child is overloaded, including the following:

- A vacant, slack set to his face
- Flailing, disorganized limbs
- Glazed eyes
- Staring at a fixed object

When a baby is traumatized or overloaded, the fear or anxiety he is experiencing disrupts his natural capacity to create patterns. He becomes "unglued" in a real sense, and the budding sense of self that was beginning to integrate all the separate pieces of his personality may be temporarily compromised. While in this state, an infant often needs to be soothed and reengaged, and in this way two-way communication can begin again.

Sometimes, however, your baby needs limits. Feedback and two-way communication need to occur in all areas. Limit-setting reactions to your baby's behaviors, if they are done gently, can actually help him coalesce his sense of self just as much as approving ones. When your child tips over his cup of milk for the third time, it's perfectly appropriate to let him see your exasperated brow. Your baby will come to feel the effects of causing annoyance and his self-definition will include the knowledge that he is sometimes a producer of annoyance. Of course, his sense of himself is best built from predominantly positive pieces of experience. Each time he's seen the delight on your face as he explores the contents of a box, or heard the joy in your voice as you greet his sunshiny face each morning, he's been learning aspects of curiosity, assertiveness, and pleasure. He incorporates these emotions into a growing sense of who and what he is. Emotions, both positive and negative, thus form the glue that binds all the separate pieces of a baby's experience into a cohesive picture.

OVERCOMING CHALLENGES: A BLESSING IN DISGUISE

Now that your baby is able to use gestures to express his intentions, you are getting a clearer picture of his personality. Does he often reach out to be held? If he does, he is showing you how much he desires being close to you. Similarly, his exploration of the toys in his crib or the features on your face indicates that he has a healthy curiosity. Each time your baby points his finger at something he wants to eat or handle, he is confidently showcasing his assertiveness.

If your baby tends to be a little passive or fearful, withdrawn, or distractible, it may also emerge during this period. His new intentionality will give you insight into the way he perceives and reacts to the world. By zeroing in on some of your baby's unique features, you can engage in playful interactions that will give him needed practice in areas in which he may have challenges.

BABIES WHO ARE SENSITIVE TO TOUCH AND SOUND

At ten months, Kara was still adjusting to the rhythms of her energetic and noisy family. Her brother Joey, now five years old, and sister Rachel, age seven, stirred up a lot of excitement as they whirled around the house. They particularly liked to squeal with delight as they "accidentally" bumped into Kara. More often than not, this occurred when Kara and her mother were happily playing give-and-take block games on the floor together. Since Kara was clearly sensitive to rough handling and averse to loud sounds, her mother, Ellen, was fast losing patience with her marauding older kids.

It didn't take too long for Ellen to realize that both Joey and Rachel were becoming a little jealous of their baby sister and resented her new capabilities. Those interactive games that Ellen and Kara were playing might be "baby stuff," as Joey and Rachel put it, but both kids clearly wanted in.

Because of Kara's sensitivities, Ellen and her husband, Steve, emphasized floor-time activities with Kara that involved firm touches and soothing, low-pitched vocalizations, as well as the give-and-take of visual gestures. Kara's parents had willingly adapted their parenting styles over the past few months to accommodate their baby's sensitivities, but floor time was becoming particularly chaotic because of their older children's interference.

It became clear that the best strategy would be to enlist the older children as play partners, and to divert them from their exciting role as spoilsports. One day when Kara was down for her nap, Ellen called Rachel and Joey into the family room and invited them to snuggle with her on the sofa. As the children nestled in her arms, she kissed the top of their heads and announced: "Kids, I need your help. You know how little Kara is, and how I have to help her do so many things. She's not as grown-up as you both are, and I'm getting a little tired of playing with her by myself. Would you come and play with us for a little while when she gets up from her nap? Maybe you could teach her some games that are a lot more fun, like "The Three Bears,' or 'Ring Around a Rosy.' What do you think?"

Not too surprisingly, both kids jumped at the chance to show their baby sister how to play some "real" games. Ellen subtly established some ground rules for their joint games that would minimize the high-pitched sounds and rough touches that the baby found jarring. She told Joey and Rachel that one of them could be a papa bear, and one could be a mama bear, but she reserved the role of baby bear for herself. Ellen knew that she could modify the pitch and shrillness of baby bear's high falsetto voice to a timbre that would be more soothing to Kara's ears. She could also keep on eye on her older children's sneaky elbows and knees and prevent the sudden pushes and knocks that sent Kara into a tailspin.

Ellen's goal was to have her two older children tolerate their younger sibling's presence as a sort of sidekick. While Joey and Rachel became engrossed in their pretend play, Kara enjoyed crawling after them and whooping with delight in response to the bearlike rumbles of her brother and sister. Ellen subtly steered some of the potentially upsetting pretend play drama away from Kara, while encouraging all three children to interact companionably during floor time.

Sensitive babies like Kara can become overwhelmed when unnerving sounds and touches come their way. It's important to help such children regain a sense of control, and to assert themselves, too. Give-and-take games are a good way to strengthen these babies' can-do sense, and give them a feeling of competency. For example, ball games can exercise the baby's ability to read such visual cues as the sight of a big red ball coming her way and the anticipatory expressions on Mommy or Daddy's face. They can also strengthen the baby's ability to coordinate arm and torso muscles to reach for the ball.

Since Kara's visual responsiveness and motor skills were excellent, Steve and Ellen could rely on her interest in following a bright red ball with her eyes and reaching for it. Steve developed a routine that carved out some special time in the day when he could play with Kara and focus on her obvious delight in her new ball. When he first came home from work, Steve would pay special attention to his older children and have floor-time fun with them. He would then wait until Joey and Rachel wandered off and pursued their own interests, before turning to his ten-month-old for some more special interaction.

Steve sat down on the floor facing Kara, holding the red ball in his hands. With a glint in his eye, he raised the ball right up in front of his face and exclaimed, "How about a game of catch, sweetheart?" Kara's arms excitedly fluttered upward, reaching toward the coveted ball, and she babbled right back at her father. With an answering wink and a smile, Steve rolled the ball toward the baby's knees, and she lunged toward it. The action continued back and forth, with both Kara and Steve communicating their love for each other and their interest in the game via a whole repertoire of nods, smiles, gesturing hands, and sounds.

When playing games like the one Steve so enjoyed with Kara, it's a good idea to vary the action. In this instance it involved changing the angle and direction of the rolling ball. Babies like Kara should be encouraged to explore and reach beyond what is comfortable for them, because they need to gain confidence in asserting themselves. Because some sounds and touches are so aversive to them, they can become easily overwhelmed as they explore a noisy and bumpy world, and retreat into passivity. Steve found that when he spurred Kara on by using a deep, but warm and gentle voice, Kara stayed involved in their play. Giving her occasional firm hugs when she captured the ball in her hands also helped her persevere.

Once again, Kara's parents relied on the formula that had served them so well during earlier stages of their baby's life. By first tailoring their approaches to Kara's stronger visual sense and need for firm touches, they were successful in establishing an intimate bond of pleasure between them. Once Kara was calm, and felt secure and loved, she was available for a back-and-forth exchange of gestures. Ellen and Steve could then steer their interactions in a direction that would give Kara a real workout and help her to master such emotions as fearfulness and passivity, where she showed some vulnerabilities.

BABIES WHO ARE UNDERWHELMED BY THE WORLD AROUND THEM

At eight months, little Brian was still what his pediatrician called a "low sender." Sweet and good-natured though he was, Brian didn't spontaneously initiate or send many signals on his own. His warm, but lazy, grin never erupted into hoots or shouts, and he seldom lifted his arms to be picked up when his parents approached his crib.

Stuart and Tammy knew that their baby wasn't coolly rejecting them when he sometimes appeared to drift away into his own world. They long ago realized that they would have to send a whole range of exciting signals in their baby's direction before his antennae could pick up even a few. Their earlier efforts to step up the amount and variety of exciting sights, smells, touches, and sounds they offered him had met with real success. Brian had learned to return their loving smiles, took obvious comfort in being held in their arms, and loved swaying to and fro on his baby swing.

Now it was time to increase their energy level once again and help Brian understand that his behaviors and gestures could cause nice things to happen. Stuart and Tammy decided to watch out for even the tiniest gestures their baby made, and to respond to as many of these behaviors as they could. For instance, each time Brian showed even mild pleasure—by deliciously shivering when he had a lick of ice cream, or happily bouncing when a battery-driven toy monkey banged on a drum—his parents would catch his eye, nod happily, and let him know that they registered his pleasure. By constantly reacting to even the smallest gestures that Brian displayed, Stuart and Tammy were teaching their child that his gestures had an impact on them, and on the world in general.

Brian's parents looked for ways to turn the simple exchange of a gesture or two into real preverbal dialogues. Since Brian only rarely initiated gestures, Stuart looked for ways to playfully intrude into his reveries and rouse him into action. He had observed that when Brian appeared unfocused, he would idly wave his hands in a back-and-forth motion. When Stuart and Tammy checked with their developmental specialist, he told them that because Brian's muscle tone was a little low, his motor planning and control over hand gestures was a little delayed. Stuart used these hand movements as an interactive opening. When he got right down on the floor in front of Brian, he deliberately let his own hand get hit by Brian's flapping wrists. His raised eyebrows and startled "Oh!" caused the baby to focus his eyes and look at their colliding hands. This gentle intrusion interrupted Brian's self-absorption and made him available for the back-and-forth exchange of more gestures.

Stuart next grinned at Brian's dimpled face and poked out his tongue at him. When he saw a brightening glimmer in the baby's eye, Stuart proceeded to wiggle his tongue and make intriguing clicking noises. Brian tried to move his mouth in response to his father's gestures. Stuart next gave him a hug, widened his eyes in feigned anticipation, and exclaimed "How about a game of peekaboo?" With Brian's eyes still trained on his own, Stuart gently took the baby's hands and covered his eyes for a moment. Then, crying, "Peekaboo, I see you!" Stuart whisked both of their hands away from the baby's eyes. With that flourish, Brian tilted his chin up and beamed at his dad. Even a low sender like Brian can be jollied into opening and closing several circles of communication in a row.

Now that both Stuart and Tammy were aware of Brian's low muscle tone, they began to see how it affected his ability to express his intentions. They knew that their baby needed to rely on his motor system as he interacted with the world and communicated with them, yet his relatively loose muscles didn't always permit him to move assertively or point out what he wanted. Stuart's recognition that Brian had good control over the muscles of his tongue and neck led him to choose gestures that would be easy for Brian to mirror or respond to during their floor-time games.

Tammy came up with another strategy that would give Brian practice in acting assertively. She looked for ways to exploit Brian's attachment to Duck, a bright yellow stuffed animal that was a favorite and familiar toy. One day, as she and Brian sat on the floor next to the low shelf where

Duck was stored, Brian's waving arm brushed the toy, and Tammy saw a chance to put her plan into action. With a quick, unobtrusive gesture, Tammy threw Duck about six feet away from where they were sitting. She turned to Brian and clapped her hands, saying, "Oh, look, honey—you made Duck fly! Let's go get him." Encouraging him with a lilt in her voice, Tammy waited to see if Brian would show some initiative and crawl toward the toy. She made herself wait for the baby to make the first move, and got up on her own hands and knees as if she were ready to follow his lead. Sure enough, after 30 seconds or so, Brian set off in Duck's direction.

These are only a few examples of how the back-and-forth of floor-time play can build on a baby's natural interest of the moment and help him to become more assertive. The key is to create opportunities for a continuing flow of such gestures as animated sounds, facial expressions, and movements. As an "underwhelmed" child gains confidence in his ability to *do* things, and comes to know the heady excitement of expressing his desires, it is increasingly easy to sell him on the joys of experiencing and interacting with the world.

BABIES WHO CRAVE SENSATIONS

Emma, now ten months old and as saucy as ever, needed no prodding to let her parents, Laura and Mike, know exactly what was on her mind. In fact, she had already mastered a whole range of defiant gestures, including a pouty lip, and a whining trill. She put them all to frequent use when Laura and Mike tried to hem her in. Emma was still an active explorer, busily investigating lamps and chair legs and even drawers in the apartment where the family lived.

Emma's parents often had to rein in her explorations for the sake of her own safety, and they were baffled by the intensity of her anger. They had learned to tolerate her howls of protest when she was younger, and with a lot of patience had managed to repeatedly reel her back into a warm, loving relationship with them. Now, however, just as her increased mobility made safety a real concern, it was becoming harder to calm her down whenever they were forced to curb her explorations. This, of course, was exhausting her middle-aged parents. Although they took delight in Emma's exuberance, they were losing confidence in their ability to tolerate her misery whenever they were forced to set limits. Each time they confronted Emma with stern faces, shaking fingers, and verbalized "No," she became more and more defiant.

A consultation with their developmental specialist gave them more insight into Emma's negativism. He explained that defiance was a very common development at this stage in high-intensity, purposeful babies like Emma. Since movement felt so good, and exploration satisfied her curiosity, why should Emma stop her activities without protest? The specialist went on to reassure Laura and Mike that their parenting skills had already helped Emma master the first two developmental milestones of regaining calm and giving and receiving love. Her exuberance and assertiveness were proof that she was well on the way to mastering the next developmental milestone of gestural communication.

In fact, Emma's scowls and protests were visible evidence that she was adept at communicating how frustrated she felt. Laura and Mike were still wrestling with a tough issue, though. How could they set limits in a way that wouldn't cause the baby to overload and have tantrums?

Laura and Mike were counseled to try two very different interactive techniques with their baby. The first involved upping the amount of physical comfort and soothing they extended to Emma, especially when she was on the brink of a tantrum. The specialist urged them not to withdraw from their baby, even when she was at her most draining. As Mike and Laura shook their heads "No" and physically steered Emma away from danger, they were to be twice as soothing as usual. Tender hugs, lulling voices, and offers of other physical activity were standard operating procedures to follow when Emma was about to lose control.

When saying "No" to one area of activity, it was important to present the baby with a physical alternative that would bring her equal pleasure, but in a safe setting. After whisking Emma away from such dangers as ledges and ladders, Laura and Mike were told to consider creating even more interesting setups, like crawling into a big tube or into a special playhouse. They could also entice Emma into their outstretched arms and give her an exhilarating airplane ride.

This new approach could be boiled down into four simple steps. First, *interrupt* the dangerous activity. Next, *divert* the baby's attention with an alternate movement that she experiences side by side with you. Then, *reassure* the baby of your loving connection with her by your warm words and soothing embraces. Finally, *free her to explore* in a new direction.

The second interactive technique involved offering an even richer variety of gestures to Emma. Instead of waiting until danger was imminent and resorting to shrill cries of "No, no!", Laura and Mike were asked to come up with a few preliminary, cautionary gestures that would give Emma a little warning that a "No" might soon be on its way. Mike decided to use his hands like a traffic cop. After catching the baby's eye as she headed toward trouble, he tried holding his hand out in front of his face, palm facing out, while shaking his head from right to left and back again. Although Emma often continued right on her merry way, Mike's warning gesture let her anticipate that a firmer limit was about to be set. Because she wasn't caught totally by surprise by the inevitable "No!" that soon followed, Emma eventually seemed to tolerate the notion that her parents had to be the boss sometimes. Since she was encouraged to be physically active even after she was rebuked, her underlying sense of autonomy wasn't threatened. She reluctantly learned that she could be the boss of her own explorations most of the time, just not all of the time.

Because Emma was so physically adept, the specialist proposed that the family play another floor-time game that most babies Emma's age are not yet able to do. The game introduced the concept of modulation, to help babies like Emma who crave sensations learn how to tolerate limits and find life fun when it's conducted at less than full throttle. Simply put, the game involved having Emma's parents get on their hands and knees and literally set the pace of a crawling game. At first, they were to crawl lickety-split with Emma at their heels, and then crawl like a snail for a while before speeding up full steam ahead once again. The idea behind the game was to help Emma learn that activity and movement could be modulated (fast to slow) and therefore controlled.

Another change suggested by the specialist concerned the way Laura and Mike read Emma's gestures. He pointed out that a defiant baby's meltdowns were usually preceded by warning signals that eluded many parents. He asked Laura to keep a sharp eye out whenever she sensed that the baby was slipping out of control.

Laura soon noticed consistent stormy-weather warnings. Sometimes Emma got a devilish set to her face, or a knowing twinkle in her eye, when she started to head in the direction of something that was forbidden. Laura also observed that the baby would sometimes scowl or clench her little fists before the floodgates opened and a storm of tears followed. The specialist pointed out that these were the type of early warning signals that Laura and Mike should be responding to. If they waited until Emma's full fury erupted, it would take far longer to help her regain calm and to prod her back into happily communicating with them once again.

BABIES WHO TAKE IN SIGHTS, BUT TUNE OUT SOUNDS

Over the past few months, Will started to use gestures in many new ways. He would excitedly lift up his arms at the sight of his mother, Lisa, each morning, and would try and clap, palm to palm, when his father Dan danced for him. Dan had long since tried to tone down his noisy, hyped conversational style to better mesh with his baby's need for small sound bites. Because Will had some difficulty paying attention to sounds, particularly complex ones, Dan had conscientiously tried to speak to his son in more subdued and tender tones.

Both Lisa and Dan felt comfortable with Will's developmental progress. He was a placid, happy baby who seemed to respond with unusual joy to bright lights. Since Will's parents were in the process of remodeling their basement into a playroom for the baby, they had recently taken him with them as they shopped in a lighting fixture store. His reaction to the light play of hundreds of lamps and shimmering crystal chandeliers thrilled his parents. The baby grew so excited that he started crowing with delight, bouncing up and down in his father's arms.

From their previous experience, Will's parents were well aware that the best way to help strengthen Will's ability to process sounds was first to appeal to his strong visual capabilities. Once the baby attended to something he saw, it was often possible to extend his interest to other touches and simple sounds. Laura and Dan came up with a way to help their ten-month-old focus on and respond to a string of sounds: They could use their voices as a sort of guidance system.

For instance, when Dan and Will sat on the floor together, exchanging comfortable glances and warm smiles, Dan took a brand new toy from behind his back and held it up high for Will to see. And what a mesmerizing toy it was, for a little boy who loved bright lights and color! Laura had found a miniature fire engine, painted a gleaming cherry red, with a flashing yellow light on its roof. As Dan held the toy in front of him, Will's excitement was obvious. Dan put the toy under his hands, and then used the words, "Here I am," to guide Will toward the toy. At times he would move away from Will, hiding the fire engine behind a chair and out of the baby's direct line of sight. Dan would peek out from behind the chair and make pulsing siren noises to guide Will. By appealing to the baby's ease and pleasure in using his visual sense, Dan was able to interest Will in paying attention to simple, rhythmic sounds because the sounds helped lead the baby toward an object his eyes yearned for.

Desires or feelings guide attention, and so search games like the one described above are wonderful floor-time workouts for babies like Will. Babies with auditory challenges can gain needed practice in digesting sounds, while they have the fun of savoring sights.

BABIES WHO TAKE IN SOUNDS, BUT HAVE A HARD TIME FIGURING OUT SIGHTS

Max, now nine months old, continued to both frustrate and delight his parents, Lynn and Jonathan. He showed a lusty interest in certain sensations; sweet tastes made him smack his lips with gusto, and music—the louder the better—caused him to stop in his tracks and bounce in time. He was starting to pull himself upright, too, by holding on to the sides of tables and chairs. His precocity didn't extend to the way he processed what he saw, however. Max still avoided direct eye contact with his parents, and seemed reluctant, or even aversive, to respond to any of the expressions that flitted across their faces.

Even though Lynn and Jonathan had been reassured months before by the baby's opthalmologist that his vision was normal, it was clear that Max needed some help in comprehending what he saw. Max's parents realized that he had to be gently coaxed into trying to visually attend to the goings-on around him.

Since Max loved all kinds of movement, especially the delicious dizziness of swinging to and fro, Lynn decided to entice him into using his eyes by first offering him a ride in his baby swing. She put the baby in the swing, pushed him while standing in front of him, and grabbed the swing each time it returned to her. Looking her baby right in his eye, she warmly exclaimed, "I see you, Mr. Max!" Once she saw the baby's eyes glance in her direction, she immediately set the swing back in motion. In this way, each time the baby reestablished eye contact with his mother, he got another push.

Swinging was fun for Max, and now locking eyes with Mommy became part of the fun, too. Though he was only nine months old, Max was already learning how to enjoy looking and visual processing.

COMMON FAMILY CHALLENGES TO COMMUNICATION

All of us find it difficult to communicate about certain things. As we teach our babies to communicate with us, it's not surprising that we instinctively try to avoid communicating in areas that make us feel uncomfortable. At this stage it's important to become comfortable with your baby's assertiveness. Let yourself experience some feelings of loss if you love to have your baby in your arms and miss him when he crawls from you to explore a nearby toy.

PARENTAL SOFT SPOTS

If your baby's anger, clinginess, or curiosity make you feel uneasy, you can't ignore these feelings. Trying to do so merely drives them underground, where they tend to fester. The best way to defuse things is to honestly take stock of your own particular parental soft spots. If it's difficult for you to objectively analyze your own behavior (and it is for many of us), take a deep breath and ask your spouse how you behave when someone does the following:

- Rejects or moves away from you
- Is angry or aggressive toward you
- Displays curiosity, including in his own body
- Hovers, and doesn't give you enough breathing room

You may want to try to figure out what it is in your own feelings and background that makes you feel uneasy or nervous in certain situations. Reflecting on your own emotional vulnerabilities helps give you a sense of perspective. Even if you don't change your feelings, you are less apt to take your baby's behavior personally.

Let's take a look at a common parenting soft spot. Some mothers and fathers may be diligent about regularly setting aside time to get down on the floor and play with their babies, but find that their overtures are sometimes rebuffed. This may awaken a pattern of feelings that they have experienced in other areas of their lives. For instance, if you have always been sensitive to being rejected, you may feel particularly vulnerable if your child pulls away briefly. If you can realize that you have a slow-healing soft spot in that emotional area of your life, you may be able to say to yourself, "Oh, there goes my sensitivity to rejection again!" Perhaps you then won't confuse your baby's temporary pulling away with a rejection of your love, and you'll be able to woo your baby back into interaction again.

It's hard not to take such rejection personally, and some parents respond by withdrawing from floor-time play so they can ward off painful feelings of inadequacy. They certainly don't neglect the physical care of their babies, or stop loving them, but they may stop seeking a reciprocal sparkle in their child's eye. It's natural to feel a little angry or disappointed with a baby because you have to work harder than some other parents to get a gestural dialogue going. It's possible to change the situation, however, by refocusing on ways to engage the baby's attention. You can look for even the tiniest of gestural responses by getting right down to the baby's eye level and animating your facial expression. It's best to respond right away if you see any sort of gesture. If the corners of the baby's mouth turn up in a tentative grin, or his little fists wave in the air, mirror his gestures with similar ones of your own. The important thing is to keep engaging, keep working at warming up the interaction, and keep responding gesturally to any cues offered by the baby.

Some parents may withdraw emotionally when their babies behave aggressively. They may also mistake a baby's natural assertiveness for aggression, and inadvertently confuse their child. Suppose your nine-month-old is sitting in your lap, idly exploring your face with his fingers. He may trace the flare of your nostril and then decide to explore the inside of your nose. Suddenly his natural inquisitiveness isn't so cute anymore, and you may flinch and draw back. As long as you quickly recover and reestablish physical closeness with your baby, and let him know by your loving gestures that you aren't put off by his curiosity, your dialogue will continue. You can use a gentle voice to tell him to keep his fingers out of your nose because it can hurt you.

It's important that your baby learn that it's good to explore his environment, and that by doing so he doesn't risk losing his communication link with you. Being a co-explorer can be great fun!

Another pattern many parents fall into arises out of their feeling that they have to determine the direction that every gestural dialogue follows. Such parents are doers, not listeners, and it's hard for them to patiently wait for their babies to initiate gestures. Although some of us may be motivated by love as we try to anticipate all of a baby's needs, we may inadvertently deny our infants needed practice in giving and receiving signals.

Instead of trying to do it all ourselves, our goal should be to challenge our baby into making gestural overtures.

On the other hand, some parenting styles reflect a generally passive approach to life. Some of us may prefer to respond to other people's initiative, rather than challenge them to action. If this is the case in your situation, it's helpful to redouble your efforts to entice your baby into assertive interactions.

BECOMING A COMMUNICATOR

Take note of the things your baby is naturally interested in (your funny nose, or the rattle you've placed in your mouth, for example) and then challenge him to express himself with feelings and actions in a purposeful way. In this way you will help him become a two-way communicator!

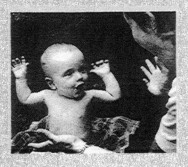

FUN AND GAMES

🍄 The Funny Sound, Face, and Feeling Game

Notice the sounds and facial expressions your baby naturally uses when he's expressing joy, annoyance, surprise, or any other feeling, and mirror these sounds and facial expressions back to him in a playful way. See if you can get a back-and-forth going.

🍄 The Circle of Communication Game

Try to see how many back-and-forths you can get going each time your baby touches a shiny red ball or pats your nose and you make a funny squeal or squawk in response. Or see how many times he will try to open your hand when you've hidden an intriguing object inside. Each time your baby follows his interests and takes your bait, he is closing a circle of communication.

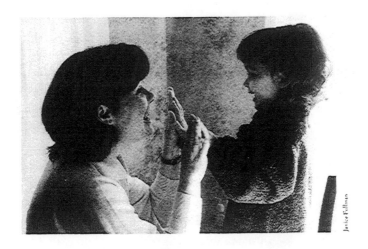

4

STAGE 4:

SOLVING PROBLEMS AND
FORMING A SENSE OF SELF

WHAT THIS STAGE IS ALL ABOUT

Probably more happens during the first half of your baby's second year of life than at any other time, yet typically it is the most overlooked period of her development. Many parents eagerly greet their baby's first kisses and hugs and later on celebrate their toddler's lisping phrases and sentences, yet inadvertently miss a less flamboyant, but equally impressive, developmental achievement that's underway.

Your two-way communicator, who by this time may already enjoy playing peekaboo and funny-face games, is now starting to figure out how to solve problems. She's learning, for example, how to scrunch her face into a silly expression to get your attention when she's in the mood for some fun. She knows how to turn in your direction while motioning toward the refrigerator, urging you to fetch some juice. She may utter a string of pleading sounds that summon you to the playroom, and point toward a toy that's too high up on the shelf for her to reach by herself.

Your child is becoming a problem solver in many areas of her life. She now has ways to get what she wants (a bottle of juice or hard-to-reach toys), to figure out how the physical world works (and pinpoint where Mommy is when she's in an adjacent room, or where a toy is when it's hidden under the rug), and to have fun, too. She is starting to demonstrate an original sense of humor! As the two of you exchange silly hats and put them on each other's heads, she may suddenly pluck one off your head and put it on her foot. Although she's never seen you do this before, your little girl may chuckle with delight because she's come up with a new angle on where to wear her hat. Your child is becoming aware that all of her different needs, interests, original behaviors, and the various parts of her body are merging into an integrated "me," or whole person. A true sense of self is starting to form.

In this chapter, we'll be discussing how your budding problem solver is mastering all kinds of emotional and intellectual lessons during this stage of her development. You may not have focused on these other emerging abilities because during her first year of life you've probably been preoccupied with your baby's happiness, as you should be. You surely were captivated by her ability to share hugs, kisses, and funny faces with you. When she eventually utters a few words, it is such a thrilling achievement that it is easy to overlook the fact that your baby is already communicating in complex ways and figuring out how things fit together in terms of patterns. She is mastering a type of preverbal communication and learning that will provide an essential foundation for her words, thoughts, intelligence, and social skills.

Because so many positive things—ranging from scientific problem solving to developing a more cohesive sense of self—normally unfold during these months, their *failure* to emerge is the first detectable sign of many types of problems. Through our research and clinical observations of many toddlers' behaviors during this stage, we're now able to identify children with severe language problems, learning disabilities, and autistic-type symptoms long before we could expect them to try to use spoken words with any fluency. For instance, we have found that an 18-month-old toddler's inability to take engage in complex problem solving—say, to take someone by the hand and walk him or her to the refrigerator in search of a favorite food or to the toy chest to hunt for a favorite play-thing—can be a warning signal. Thankfully, though, most toddlers exhibit a wealth of problem-solving behaviors. Their drive to explore the world keeps them on the go all day.

Most parents share their baby's intense excitement as she achieves the physical milestone of walking, usually sometime between 9 and 18 months. In fact, few sights are more endearing than watching a toddler take her bowlegged first few steps! However, in our excitement over the child's new ability to walk, we sometimes disregard an equally impressive developmental achievement that's also afoot. Our toddlers can walk *meaningfully* toward and away from things, and can take objects with them, too. Even before learning how to walk, your baby is busy figuring out how to get something she wants, or how to maneuver herself so she can see something interesting.

An ability to solve problems rests on the even more basic skill of seeing and deciphering patterns. It is the ability to understand patterns that lets a toddler know that if she takes two steps here and two steps there she'll be able to reach her favorite toy. She becomes a successful navigator not only because her muscles are coordinated, but also because her growing brain now enables her to understand patterns. Toddlers learn to recognize how one room leads to another, and where you are in relation to them. They can meaningfully explore the world long before they are able to express their wishes and thoughts in words.

Because your toddler is becoming a pattern recognizer, she is learning more about how the physical world works, too. For instance, if she presses a series of two or three buttons that make a toy pop up, or turns a knob one or two extra times to make the volume of a music box increase, she is becoming familiar with some of the infinite number of complicated patterns that exist in physical space. She can understand, for example, how to get to an object that seems out of reach by pulling a chair over and climbing up. She is developing a sense of how close or far things are from her, and thus getting a feel for distance. In fact, you may notice that your child may be quick to get an object that's only one or two steps away, but pout and expect you to be the "gofer" if the object is clear across the room.

Your toddler's growing appreciation for physical space also helps her in her emotional relationship with you. At 12 months of age, your child not only wants to see where you are, she wants to smell you and touch you, too. She needs to physically cling to you in order to feel a sense of close-ness. However, by the time she's 18 months old, your loving looks can make her feel as secure as if she were sitting in your lap. She feels this way because she can figure out the pattern of your smiling glances and feel approved of, even from afar. Her own periodic glances back in your direction and attention to the sound of your voice further help her to feel warm and supported. Although she may not comprehend the exact meaning of your words, she is able to decode the upbeat, admiring pattern of the sounds you utter. "What an a-*maaaa*-zing block tower you've built!" will reassure her that your engagement with her is holding steady from across the room.

Your toddler is obviously not yet able to count the actual number of steps that lie between the two of you, but she has an intuitive sense that you could be at her side in a jiffy. She develops a kind of road map in her mind of where she is in relation to you. Even when she looks away from you for a while, or gets distracted by something else in the room, she knows where you are in space and gets a great deal of reassurance from that knowledge.

In this way, an 18-month-old can have her cake and eat it too. She can experience the excitement of relative independence as she wanders away from you, all the while being soothed by the balm of your loving facial expressions and the supportive tone of your voice. The apparent tension between a toddler's wish to explore (and thus become somewhat independent) and her equal need for the comforts of dependency is something that puzzled many child observers for years. Margaret Mahler, one of the early and most important pioneers in observing infants and toddlers and attempting to figure out what was going on inside their minds, thought that a toddler's need to do such things as move away from her parent's side to explore was at odds with her equally compelling need to hold on to Mommy or Daddy.

Our own research has led us to a very different insight into what has been thought to be one of life's major dilemmas: the conflict between security and dependence, and exploration and independence. The toddler's awareness of patterns, and her ability to see and hear her involved, loving parents across space, supplies her with a portable emotional security blanket that permits her to confidently explore the outer world. She is able to remain wrapped up in the warmth of a parent's love, even from afar. The child's growing ability to create complex patterns therefore provides a solution to this dilemma. Of course, her caregivers need to be engaged and involved in these emotional signals across space to enable this process to occur in an optimal way.

Later on, the child's ability to create inner ideas or images will allow her to carry an image or idea of Mom or Dad inside her head, even when they are out of sight. This makes her emotional security blanket even more portable. As she continues to mature in the years ahead, that inner sense of warmth and security will expand into the kind of feeling that adults experience when they are separated from a loved one. For example, when your spouse is away on a business trip, you may be able to kindle the warmth of your shared relationship in your heart. Even though he or she may be three thousand miles away and you may have to wait until nightfall to hear the sound of his or her voice over the phone, you are able to rely on inner feelings and images that emotionally link the two of you.

Toddlers with visual, hearing, or listening difficulties obviously have extra challenges when it comes to creating their own long-distance security blankets. Like all children this age, they must develop a sustaining, portable sense of security before they can confidently explore their world. Since they may have one less sensory channel to confidently and fully rely on, their task is more difficult, but often very achievable nonetheless.

For instance, a baby who can't hear would have a stronger need to remain in visual contact with her parents as she begins to roam. Mom and Dad could make a concerted effort to make their friendly waves or approving smiles especially vivid to their toddler, even at a distance. They could even make a point of coming over to her from time to time and offering a quick hug or peck on the cheek to reassure their toddler that her explorations won't isolate her from them. A baby who can't see would benefit from hearing lots of encouraging words and vocalizations, as well as touches and smells. In fact, we often recommend interesting games that enable babies who can't see to locate people and objects by touch and sounds, as well as smells. In that way, they can create a sensory road map of their home even though they can't see. The important sense of space and spatial relationships that we all need to feel secure and to navigate can be formed from many of our senses, and not just our vision.

Now let's take a closer look at the remarkable feats of problem solving that may be shown by your child. For instance, when she spies a favorite toy up high on a shelf she may enlist your aid in getting her "lovey" by exchanging a whole range of gestures with you that logically follow each other. Perhaps she'll scoot over to the toy shelves, stop, and look over her shoulder at you. You could give her a nod and a wink and say, "I bet I know what you want!" Watch her spin around, pointing her chubby finger up at the top shelf, grunting with excitement. If you say, "That's it, right?" she'll probably catch your drift and stretch out both her arms toward the stuffed animal she yearns for. You'll reward her efforts by putting the toy in her arms, and will no doubt receive a big smile in return.

Dialogues such as this reveal just how skilled your little girl may be becoming at communicating her intentions to you and solving problems. These skills had their roots in the simple back-and-forth exchanges that she shared with you just a few short months ago. Back then, your baby sensed that her smile could cause you to break out in a smile, too. Her sweet coos elicited loving murmurs from you in return. She slowly became aware that you and she were separate beings, and that her behavior could influence yours.

Now, however, your toddler is more aware of bigger patterns—not just spatial patterns, but also patterns of cause and effect and expectable sequences. She can envision not just a single kiss, or smile, or murmur, but a whole sequence of back-and-forth hugs, kisses, embraces, and eager expressions which may equal the pattern "warm and cuddly Mommy" in her mind. These abilities to recognize and create patterns and use them to problem-solve enable her to become more fully aware of the power of her smiles. She knows that smiling at you, and smiling at your spouse, and smiling at her grandma, and smiling at the grocery store clerk all produce smiles in return.

Because she can recognize patterns, your little girl comes to know you as "Mommy who mostly smiles at me except when I run away from her" and "Daddy who likes to cuddle with me and tickle me with his scratchy whiskers except when he yells at Mommy." Your child is starting to connect her desires and wishes to strategies involving the use of her muscles and gestures ("If I look in Mommy's direction, point and grunt, and let her see I need her help, maybe she can help me reach my lovey"). She can string together a chain of separate acts as she communicates with you, in an attempt to get what she wants. This ability to sequence many actions into a pattern (also called *motor planning*) is helping her feel increasingly assertive. She's busy figuring out patterns of behavior that lead to getting the toys she wants, eating the foods she craves, or receiving the hugs and kisses from you that make her feel secure and loved. She no longer has to rely on your educated guesses about her wishes; she can now enlist your aid to reach her goals.

In a miraculously brief period of time, your child has gone from being a baby just learning the meaning of a smile to devising 10-, 20-, and 30-step "action plans" that enlist your help in getting what she wants. Her ability to use a whole range of nonverbal gestures—crawling or walking, pointing, grabbing, vocalizing, and climbing—has become so polished that she's able to string them together in truly effective ways.

When her throat feels dry and she wants some juice to drink, for example, your little girl can now lead you, step by step, toward the refrigerator instead of woefully crying or tugging on your sleeve in an aimless way. As she bangs on the door with her hand, and you open it in response, she may squeal with excitement while pointing to a juicebox. All these linked actions are driven by your child's strong desires, cooperative muscles, and ability to organize her behavior.

As your toddler communicates with you in these increasingly complex (though still nonverbal) ways, she's starting to know what emotional or social patterns to expect from you. For example, she's beginning to notice which of her actions win hugs and kisses from you, and which ones are met by your angry voice or sagging shoulders. When your or your spouse comes home from work with a playful look in your eye and a lilt in your voice, your daughter recognizes that she's seen this happy sequence of behaviors before and can anticipate some fun. She may mischievously lug your briefcase down the hall, giggling to herself because she knows an exciting game of catch-me-if-you-can will follow. On the other hand, if your mouth is usually set in a grim line when you come in the door, and you collapse on the sofa with a groan of exhaustion, your daughter will instead come to recognize a different pattern of behavior that may lead her to shy away from you.

All of these new emotional and social expectations lead to the dawning of a new sense of self. The "I'm a good sender of hugs and kisses" and the "I'm great at getting Daddy to smile" and the "I'm a clinger-to-Mommy when Daddy gets mad and his voice is scary" pieces of her budding self are all coalescing into a sense of "me." She is forming a clearer definition of self based on how you react to her overtures. Later on in this chapter we'll be exploring just how your child comes to realize that all the separate pieces of herself—the angry me, the hugging me, the loving me, and the whiny me—are part of one person.

Your child is also developing a sense of what to expect from others. If Mommy and Daddy are basically warm and loving, a toddler begins to count on other people being emotionally receptive and available, too. If, on the other hand, a child's parents are usually distracted or aloof, she may come to feel that other people are similarly uninterested in her, or she may develop a countertendency, such as clinging, to make sure that others remain close to her. At this age, a child isn't yet able to think "Oh, I wish Daddy (or Mommy) were more available," or feel as if she's emotionally shortchanged. It is simply a commonplace fact to her that Daddy (or Mommy) will meet her needs only some of the time. This becomes part of the way she sees the world. Many fundamental adult character traits arise out of the expectations—or lack of them—that toddlers develop during this period.

Meanwhile, you're now getting a clearer fix on your toddler's special style. Is she typically a daredevil, or does she struggle to be independent? Does she cling to you, finding a sense of comfort and security only while in your arms? Is she showing a pattern of assertiveness, or a quiet sort of gentleness? Does she have a short fuse and ignite into anger and protest easily? Is she a born flirt, or a wisenheimer?

All of life's basic emotional themes—dependency, assertiveness, negotiating closeness, anger, curiosity, the need to explore, pleasure, dealing with limit setting and frustration—are emerging now. One of your key tasks during the coming months will be actively to assist your toddler in putting together increasingly complex chains of interaction that help her explore not only her physical surroundings but also her innermost feelings. In fact, during these months you'll be functioning somewhat like a teacher of elaborate charades, but the rules of this game allow for the use of vocalizations and words as well. With your help, your child will learn to use a whole range of gestures and words in a logically consistent way to communicate her feelings, wishes, and needs. She may pick up information from your visual gestures, from the pattern and tone of your voice, and from many other features of your communication. Her own behavior will communicate whole messages rather than simple commands or requests, as they did when she was seven months old. Instead of merely raising her arms to convey the idea that she wants to go out, your 17-month-old may well march to the closet door, turn the doorknob, yank the stroller out, look in your direction, and vocalize. As you read and respond to the sounds she utters and to her body English, you will be helping her use her muscles and senses to convey complicated ideas.

In just a few short months from now, your little girl will expand her use of spoken words, relying on phrases and sentences as a kind of shorthand when she wants to express her desires. She will be able to do this because she has already had the experience of successfully communicating her needs and wishes to you. By the time she is about two years old, she will know that when she says, "Love you," the words sum up all the flirtatious behavior and feelings she's shared with you, including hugs, kisses, winsome looks, and fond pats. Your toddler will eventually understand what an abstract term like "love" means because she has experienced not just words, but a whole pattern of behavior that is a part of love. She has come to recognize that other actions mean "love," too, like when you help her recover from frustration, or remain by her side even when she's angry. Your child knows all about anger, warmth, affection, frustration, curiosity, and assertiveness because you've been interacting with her around these feelings. Thus, a concept is first understood through *doing,* and then the words become a label for what is already known. Your toddler knows what love *feels* like at the level of her skin and muscles, in the very core of her body.

WHAT TO LOOK FOR AT THIS STAGE

As we've indicated, over a period of 6 to 8 months or so, your toddler's behaviors are becoming increasingly complex. A 16-month-old, for example, may start up a dialogue by first looking at you and then reaching her arm out toward the toy shelf (opening a circle of communication). You might cock your head to one side, point to a cow puppet on the shelf, and ask, "This one?" Your baby will likely respond, and thereby close the circle of communication she opened, by nodding her head or reaching with both hands for the puppet. She may explore the cow puppet further and chew on the velvety fabric, rub the black and white cowhide design, or try and wedge her fingers inside the puppet. Perhaps you'll offer to help her put the puppet over her hand, or pick up a nearby sheep puppet. The two of you might playfully exchange animal sounds, with your "baa"'s and her "moo"'s eventually dissolving into giggles and a shared tickle or two. After a while she may reach for another puppet, bounce up and down, and make whimpering sounds. You might try imitating her behavior, rocking and whimpering in rhythm with her own vocalizations. She may in turn copy the tone of your voice, or the way you sway to and fro. If your stamina is holding up, you might start crawling on all fours to see if your play partner and her puppet follow suit.

By this point you have exchanged dozens of gestures with your toddler. She has gone from opening and closing just a few circles of communication to perhaps 30 in one sequence, and that's a reassuring sign that she's moving ahead just as she should during this stage of her development. These long sequences of back-and-forth gesturing reflect your toddler's growing ability to organize her own behavior into patterns and to recognize another person's patterns, too.

When a child doesn't seem to be engaging in more and more complicated gestural interactions as the toddler months progress, it can be an indication that a fuller evaluation is needed. Communication or motor problems, or social or emotional challenges can at times interfere with learning how to use gestures to solve problems. Check with your pediatrician if you don't notice a significant lengthening and broadening of your gestural interactions with your child by the time she is about 18 months old.

As your toddler interacts with you in increasingly complex ways, she may energetically use a wide variety of gestures, including the following:

- Interactive social games involving humor and cooperation, as well as defiance
- Back-and-forth vocalizations, and even words, by the end of this developmental stage
- Back-and-forth emotional exchanges that include animated facial expressions
- Back-and-forth touches
- Interactive movements in space (rough-and-tumble play)
- Interactive motor patterns (give-and-take, chase, search, climbing, and imitative games)
- Communication across space (also referred to as *distal communication*) which grows out of early proximal communication using touch, holding, and the like.

By the end of this stage, most babies can remain in voice or visual contact with their caregivers for brief periods of time, even though they aren't in physical proximity. For instance, a 16-month-old may happily bang on pots and pans in the kitchen and vocalize to her mother, who is working nearby in the family room. As the mother chatters in reply, the baby responds by vocalizing and playing, without immediately needing to come over and see or touch her mother. She is able to close the circle of communication she has opened from afar. This ability to remain in touch long-distance, or in distal communication, is one of the hallmarks of most toddlers' behavior by the time they are 18 months old.

IMITATIVE PLAY

As your toddler becomes adept at imitating your behaviors, she is show-ing you that she can make a connection between things that she hears and sees you do and things that she does. She is now able to take in complex patterns of behavior, copy them, and organize her responses. You may find yourself chuckling as you see her pick up her play telephone and angrily slam the receiver down in a perfect duplication of your own actions the night before, when the third phone solicitor interrupted your dinner. Im-itation is a great help for a child learning new social patterns, motor ac-tivities, and sounds, and eventually will be of great help in learning words. You can encourage imitation in many different ways. For example, when your child approaches a door and starts banging on it as if to say, "Open up!" you might try turning the doorknob and seeing if the child will at-tempt to copy your gesture and actually turn the knob herself. If your child is physically unable to turn the doorknob, you could make a twist-ing motion with your hand while standing away from the door, to convey the meaning of "Open!" Once she succeeds in copying your gesture, you could then see if both of you could open the door together as you say, "Let's open the door, okay?" In this way, imitation can be part of routine, purposeful, complex communications between the two of you. If you also play copycat games together in which your toddler touches her nose when you touch your own, or reaches for the sky when you do, she'll have fun and get pleasure out of behaving just like Mommy or Daddy.

Dancing or jumping with your child can also have a lot of meaning. If you turn on the radio and jump and dance, your toddler may be joyfully absorbed in the fun of acting just like you. To be like Mommy and Daddy (touching noses, reaching for the sky, and dancing to the pulsing sounds of the radio), and to experience great pleasure while doing so, is as im-portant as being able to execute more formal copycat behaviors.

Sometimes, though, it's hard to get imitation started with children who have trouble organizing their motor responses. They may see that your wrists swivel, or your arms reach for the sky, but they can't quite copy the motions. You can certainly empathize with their difficulty when you re-member how long it first took you to copy a golf swing, adjust your tennis serve, or do the macarena! For some people, seeing a complex gesture just once is all it takes for them to successfully copy it. Others need the gesture broken down into ten smaller steps, and even then copying it is difficult.

Similarly, some toddlers will readily repeat sounds, while others have a harder time of it. Because it's easy to avoid doing something that's difficult and then give up, such children may move away from you or ignore you as you try to teach them more complex behavior. The best way to get them excited about practicing complex motor patterns of any kind is to start with patterns that they can already do.

Let's say that your child is a good runner. Try to have your first copycat games involve a lot of running back and forth. If she wants to go to the door, suggest that you run there together. If you've noticed that your child likes to raise her arms above her head and make high-pitched sounds at the same time, make this your first imitative game. As we said before, always build on your child's strengths. Take the actions that she already spontaneously performs and bring them under her purposeful control by making them part of an exciting imitation game.

Imitative behavior is extremely important during this period of your toddler's development because imitation allows a child to take shortcuts as she masters complex patterns of behavior. She can learn a lot of things very quickly by simply copying whole patterns, rather than having to learn how to do many small steps in sequence. Usually this ability increases in the second year of life, and reaches a crescendo between 14 and 18 months.

How Imitative Behavior Conveys Emotions

Before too long, your toddler may put on your favorite straw hat, grab your purse, and toddle around the house with a big grin on her face, clearly waiting for your delighted laugh. She has recognized a grown-up pattern of behavior and reproduced it, confident that she will reap a sense of pleasure from your admiring face. This is how your child begins to explore emotional themes of her own choosing. Now she doesn't always have to passively wait for you to dole out happy feelings; she can organize her actions in a way that's likely to prompt a satisfying response from you.

When she feels a need for closeness, for example, she will approach you with her arms outstretched, seeking a hug, or stroke your hair the way she has seen your spouse caress it. When you hug her back, and feel her back muscles relax into the curve of your embrace, a circle of communication in which your child successfully requested and received some loving has been closed.

Similarly, you may observe your child handling anger and distress in patterns of behavior that seem embarrassingly familiar. She may very well bellow at you, try to slam a door, and scoot away in a perfect imitation of your behavior toward your spouse five minutes before. Although initially she may just be copying some of your emotional behavior in a monkey-see, monkey-do manner, soon she will start initiating some of these patterns when she has to let off steam. The important thing to note is that your toddler can now use these learned patterns of behavior to express *all* her feelings. As you help her string together these new behavioral patterns, she will increasingly create her own twists. She may be able to experience and organize interactions around the following kinds of emotions:

Pleasure and Excitement.   When you and your toddler play together with a new toy, or share a joke as she gets dressed up in your hat and shoes, she will use her ability to link gestures to bring herself pleasure. She'll try to catch your eye to share in her delight, and your response will probably lead to further exchanges.

Assertiveness.   When you and your baby companionably explore the house, she experiences a can-do feeling of growing independence. Initially the two of you may do your investigating side by side, but by the time she is about 18 months old, your child will be able to explore more independently. She probably knows the layout of the familiar regions of your house by heart now. She may go into a far corner of a room to push the buttons on the VCR the way you do, while periodically vocalizing or looking over her shoulder in your direction.

Another way in which you'll see evidence of your child's new ability to imitate and recreate "action plans" is her fascination with blocks and large puzzle pieces. She is driven to explore how things relate to each other, or fit together. Just as she now may able to coordinate her large muscles and navigate across all the rooms in the house and still find her way back to you, she is also gaining control over her fine muscles, and can use her fingers to manipulate blocks and create patterns she has perceived. For example, after watching you do it, your baby will probably try and place two, three, or even more blocks in a tower. She is gradually learning how to sequence her behaviors, and learning that one block rests on another.

At 14 months your toddler might pick up a triangle block and try to fit it into all the various holes of her shape-sorter box until one works. Amazingly, your child is already showing evidence of scientific thinking! She is a pattern recognizer who keeps looking for the solution to a problem (which hole will accommodate the triangular block). She may also demonstrate her prowess at using both large and small muscles in a coordinated effort to swipe a tempting gingerbread man off a platter that's placed on a kitchen counter. Your little cookie monster may plan a concerted assault that includes dragging a chair over to the cabinet, pulling herself up on the counter, reaching toward the plate, and nabbing the treat. She has just given you another clear sign that she's becoming a master problem solver.

Closeness.   Your toddler enjoys affection and will offer you wet, drooly kisses and hugs when she feels a need to be close. She will become progressively more coy and charming as she learns to incorporate flirtatious patterns of behavior she has gleaned from watching you into her own repertoire. Through imitation, she'll develop a whole range of facial gestures—from widening her eyes with excitement to teasing glances—that will wrap you around her little finger.

Anger.   Initially your toddler will simply wave her arms in agitation, frown, or bark angrily back at you when she's feeling angry. Soon, she'll use more organized sequences or imitate a pattern to deal with distress by pounding her hands on the floor and yelling after you've just yelled at her. By the end of this stage of her development, she may be able to organize her angry feelings in numerous ways. She may deliberately bite or pinch, throw toys, fling herself on the ground, cry hysterically, or even give you the cold shoulder. She may combine a variety of imitative and novel behavior—frowning, growling, pinching, and running away—in an escalating display of rage. You'll have a real prima donna on your hands!

A WIDE RANGE OF NEW CAPACITIES

Another way in which your child now shows you that she's able to organize her behavior is the delightful sense of originality she unexpectedly displays. As her growing gestural vocabulary offers her more complex ways of expressing herself, she can show you that she's a creative thinker who doesn't have to do things precisely the way she's seen you do them. Suddenly you may become aware that she's got her own view of things. You may be lying in the floor next to your little playmate, building a block tower, when she takes a square block and tries to balance it on your head, laughing. She knows that blocks aren't really hats, and has come up with a joke she wants to share with you. As you giggle in response, and put a block "hat" on her head, the two of you are beginning to play your first game of "let's pretend" together.

Your toddler is showing you that she not only has a creative sense of humor, but that she's beginning to understand that objects have functions. A block is a hard shape we use to build towers; a hat is a floppy piece of fabric that sits on your head. It's fun for a toddler to willfully mix up the proper functions of objects. Not only does your child's playful joke let you know that she can put an original spin on things, it also reveals that she is developing a functional understanding of an object's use. She will eventually apply this understanding to more and more aspects of her world, and will become more of a logical, scientific thinker.

This originality is another sign of your toddler's distinct personality. She is using her new ability to put together whole patterns of behavior to express her emotions, likes, and dislikes, and you'll find her to be quite a character. She is starting to realize that she can be both angry and happy or bold and clinging and still remain the object of your affection. As she comes to experience a whole range of emotions, the constancy of your soothing love will help firm up her budding sense of self.

While you and your toddler are engaged in all these complex gestural games and interactions, her body, senses, and language and cognitive capacities are growing in ways that are astonishing. Organizing behavior and emotions into complex patterns is no easy task, though, and your toddler's ability to negotiate this stage is determined to some extent by her muscles' willingness to get her where she wants to go and her senses' clear reading of cues from her environment. The following charts are guides to a few special abilities that are well known and relate to the main goal of this stage, complex problem-solving interaction. All children develop at varying rates and in the great majority of cases this unevenness is perfectly normal, so bear in mind that these charts are approximate. Even more importantly, don't forget that during this stage of her development, your child's most fundamental achievement is her ability to exchange complex, preverbal problem-solving messages with you. Her communication skills are the real key to unlocking her future emotional and cognitive growth.

Capacities Present from 9–18 Months of Age

MOTOR PATTERNS

AT 9–10 MONTHS

- Walking on own or by holding onto furniture
- Squatting while playing
- Throwing a ball in a forward direction
- Feeding self finger foods
- Stacking two cube-shaped blocks
- Organizing one-step motor-planning sequence, such as pushing, catching, or throwing a ball

BY 18 MONTHS

- Planning motor patterns involving two or more steps, like throwing a ball up in the air and trying to catch it
- Trying to imitate scribbling, or scribbling on her own
- Holding crayon or pencil adaptively (gripping it in a way that makes scribbling possible)
- Putting items in a cup, or toys in a box
- Building a tower with two or three blocks
- Putting pegs in a pegboard, or a round block in a shape-sorter box's round hole
- Removing socks

SENSORY PATTERNS

AT 9–10 MONTHS

- Exploring different foods; tolerating different textures with hands and mouth
- Climbing and exploring off the floor, on couches or table tops

- Showing no particular sensitivity to bright lights
- Showing no particular sensitivity to loud noises, such as vacuum cleaners

BY 18 MONTHS

- Enjoying or tolerating various types of touch, such as cuddling, roughhousing, different types of clothing material, tooth and hair brushing
- Tolerating loud sounds
- Tolerating bright lights
- Tolerating and finding comfort in moving through space

LANGUAGE PATTERNS

AT 9–10 MONTHS

- Understanding simple words like "shoe" or "kiss"
- Using sounds or a few words for specific objects
- Jabbering

BY 18 MONTHS

- Comprehending some simple questions, carrying out simple directions ("Roll the ball here.")
- Imitating simple words
- Using words to make needs known ("Up!"; "Kiss!")

COGNITIVE PATTERNS

BY 9–10 MONTHS

- Focusing and paying attention while playing with you or alone for five or more minutes
- Copying simple gestures like "bye-bye" hand wave and "no-no" head shake
- Finding a toy under a caregiver's hand
- Trying to imitate fine motor tasks like a scribble
- Exploring how toys work and figuring out simple relationships (pulling a string to make a sound)
- Using a variety of sounds interactively

By 18 MONTHS

- Using objects functionally while playing with you (combing hair with a toy comb, vocalizing while holding a toy telephone)
- Searching for a desired toy or hidden object in more than one place
- Playing with you or alone, in a focused manner, for 15 or more minutes
- Imitating behaviors just seen, or seen a few minutes earlier
- Recognizing familiar faces in family pictures
- Using a stick or other tool to capture another object
- Using long sound sequences and some words purposefully in interaction with you

THE CRITICAL IMPORTANCE OF THIS STAGE

Your toddler's new ability to solve problems and understand patterns enables her to make huge leaps in learning to cope with a whole range of emotions, in thinking scientifically, in beginning to understand the difference between right and wrong, and (as we'll discuss in a later section of this chapter) in sensing that she has a self. Let's look at each of these areas in a little more detail.

Coping with Emotions.   The elaborate back-and-forths you exchange with your toddler all day long will teach her that reaching out for another human being with gestures, postures, and vocalizations will get her what she wants and bring her pleasure. Each time she enlists your aid in opening up a box where she knows a favorite toy is stashed, or she repeatedly looks to you for feedback as the two of you fit puzzle pieces together, you are helping her understand that it frequently takes many steps to solve a problem. She's also becoming aware that moving from impulse to satisfaction is often dependent on cooperating with another person.

What an important skill this is for learning to cope with emotions! The child whose parent comes running with a handful of cookies at the first sign of a tantrum never gets a chance to learn the valuable lesson that she has to take many steps and organize her actions to achieve a goal. If, instead, the parent promotes a back-and-forth exchange of looks, sounds, and movements that encourages the child to act purposefully, the child learns that assertive step-by-step behavior can pay off. She will gain experience in being sociable as she engages in preverbal and emerging verbal dialogues with you, and feel confident and proud that she can remain in control and still get what she wants. Her self-esteem is thus given an immeasurable boost each time you take her by the hand, look her in the eye, and say, "Show me what you want."

As a child becomes more and more aware that her own sequenced actions will usually get her what she wants, the more she will come to see the world as a reliable, logical place. She will be attracted to the world, and curious about figuring out her place in it, because of the pleasure and satisfaction your negotiations have given her.

Thinking Scientifically.   Now's the time to focus on the *process* of communicating with your child, and to forget about the specific content of your play. Interactions around food, flowers, sunbeams, toy cars, and spider webs are all of equal import. Be as goofy as you like! You'll know by the growing number of spontaneous looks, frowns, grimaces, giggles, or dance steps you exchange with your child that all her systems are working and that she's learning about the world. The idea is to foster lively back-and-forths between the two of you and to resist the temptation to slip into a show-and-tell mode. Your toddler may very well tune you out if you show her a flower and attempt to label its parts for her.

Instead, offer her a flower and see what she makes of it. If she curiously sniffs it, you might animatedly ask if you could smell it, too. When you do, you might try closing your eyes and looking as if you're whiffing ambrosia. See if she wants to explore another part of the flower. If she plucks off a petal, maybe she'll let you pull off another one. You might comment on the petal's silky softness, or say, "Whee! Look at the petal fly away in the wind!" You'll be a sort of admiring colleague while your child acts as lead scientist during your mutual exploration of the garden.

The choice of objects you use as you and your child interact is incidental; the *play* really is the thing. As you play together, your child's actions should spark a logical reaction from you, but this reaction doesn't have to make scientific sense. When your 16-month-old pushes her toy train along the floor and then kisses the scratch mark she sees on the caboose in an attempt to "make it all better," resist the urge to explain that a toy's "boo-boo"'s don't hurt as hers do. She is learning scientific thinking by seeing patterns, and the pattern she is exploring is how a kiss can make something better. Your toddler is a budding medical investigator! At this point in her life it isn't important to know that plastic trains are inanimate objects. If you engage her sense of fun and adventure while you play, the

facts will take care of themselves later on because she is building the logical patterns that will enable her to figure out and, more importantly, know
how to think with them.

This is an approach to playing that is difficult for some parents. What
most of us don't realize is that there's more educational value in a spontaneous and fun game with our toddlers than in any well-intentioned lecture we may deliver, or computer game we may buy. You needn't worry
that your child will miss out if she isn't immediately acquainted with dry
facts about the way the world works. On the contrary: Because she is now
a pattern perceiver, she understands that objects have intended purposes,
and that hairbrushes go on the top of her head and toothbrushes go inside her mouth. It is her ability to detect patterns and trends that organizes her understanding of the world.

As you nudge your interactions with your child in the direction of emotional problem solving, you will be helping her to think both logically and
abstractly. Such seemingly ordinary accomplishments as your toddler's
ability to find her way back to you as you signal her with silly sounds to
return to your side in the kitchen, or her willingness to moo like a cow and
then chirp like a bird with you because she now comprehends that sharing sounds with you is fun for both of you, are the linchpins of her growing intellect. Because she can now understand and even initiate long
interactive patterns with you, your toddler is becoming a scientific
thinker.

Developing a Sense of Right and Wrong.   During this period of their development, our toddlers have the ability to perceive patterns in parental
behavior that communicate messages about values. Moral concepts about
caring and compassion are conveyed each time you show your child how
to gently pat a kitten, or how to go easy when she rocks her dolly in a toy
cradle. When our gestures show a child how to handle vulnerable things
like pets, toys, and other babies, we are showing a respect for other creatures in the environment.

Children learn how to behave in a caring, moral way not only when you
respond to them, but when they respond to you in the course of the long interactions you now share. When you gesture to your child that she's being
too noisy—whether it's by a downward motion of your hand, by covering
your ears, or murmuring "Hush" with your forefinger placed against your
lips—she will most likely respond with a gesture of her own. Perhaps she'll
quiet down while putting her own finger on her lip, but rev up the noise

level before too long. When you respond with another "Shh!" she'll probably lower her voice once again, because she's starting to take your feelings into account. She's had lots of practice reading and responding to your gestures and feelings during your lengthy dialogues together. Your toddler has a new appreciation that her noise can make you unhappy or uncomfortable.

If your child becomes angry and looks as if she's about to pinch you, you might be likely to frown and wag your finger, saying "No! No!" By gesturing and then urging her to use sounds or actions to show you what she wants, she will learn to avoid taking out her frustration and anger on you. Once she's able to inhibit the pinch, she can be cajoled into pointing to the cupboard when she's hungry or pulling you to the door when she wants to go out. Even though she still may be angry with you, she is also taking your feelings into account because she is responding to your "No! No!" gesture. Through these lengthy interactions, your toddler is learning not only how to regulate her own behavior, but how to do so in accordance with the needs of others. This willingness to change her own behavior is a further indication of your child's growing moral sense.

Sometimes at around 18 months or so, children show signs of what at first glance appears to be altruistic behavior. If a playmate or brother or sister gets hurt and cries, you may see a toddler go over and nicely pat the arm or the top of the head of the wounded child. Most often toddlers are simply copying behavior they have seen others model, but such actions also reveal an intent to do something helpful. Although the child may not understand the full meaning of her gesture now, true empathy will appear later.

When your child behaves aggressively, you have an opportunity to let her know that while her anger may be justified, harmful behavior won't be tolerated. She'll pick up on your attitude toward aggressive behavior long before she learns her first angry word. For instance, a toddler at 17 months may become dismayed if you refuse to remove a food she doesn't like from her high-chair tray. She won't fall for your feigned gusto over the peas or spinach she doesn't like. She may raise her voice and glare at you, and then deliberately tip her dish over. Some children may wait until they have your full attention before sweeping everything off the high-chair tray with naughty pride.

The way you respond to such behavior will send signals to your child about how you and your family view anger and aggression, good and bad feelings, right and wrong. If you habitually overreact and see your child's assertiveness as somehow threatening your own sense of control, and show by your enraged tones, furrowed brow, and tensed shoulders that her aggressive feelings are forbidden, your toddler may link anger and assertiveness to being "bad." She may become overly cautious or rebellious.

As difficult as it may be at times, you can help your child distinguish between acceptable angry feelings and harmful behavior by paying attention to the tone of your voice and your own actions. A firm "No, no!" when she throws her food, coupled with helping her learn to either shake her head "No" or to verbalize the word, may be what's needed. Hitting or biting someone requires immediate restraint. Speak in a serious tone of voice with animated gestures, and show her how to use her own gestures to express anger without hitting or biting. While you are interacting with your child and using gestures to communicate limits, she may also need a brief time away from the toy, activity, or peer that has perhaps overly excited her. The key is to set gentle-but-firm limits while offering her lots of communication at her level, and soothing, too.

The gestures and behaviors we choose to emphasize with our toddlers often convey cultural values. Your child responds to your preferences, which are often a reflection of the culture in which you were raised. The value of gentleness, for example, may be a key concern in one family, and get scant attention in another. One child may be steered toward active, physically robust behavior that is viewed as "good," while another toddler may be taught that being gentle is "good." The very different gestures they both exchange with their family members are beginning to form the basis of their sense of what is right and wrong.

While babies this age are learning to figure out complex patterns involving a full range of emotions as well as those involving time and space, neuronal connections in their brains are continuing to form, just as they did during previous developmental stages, in areas relating to emotional cueing and spatial relations (often in the right side of the brain). For example, finding Mom in another room involves both figuring out space (where Mom is) and connecting that information with the emotional desire to be close to her. Knowing that Mom will give her a hug soon (after she gets off the phone) involves a similar pattern of dealing with emotions and a sense of time.

Developing a Sense of Self.   As your baby increasingly begins to use sounds and words meaningfully, to problem-solve, and to sequence her ideas and actions, more and more neuronal connections are forming in the parts of her brain that deal with language, verbal symbols, and understanding patterns. This brain growth is supported as your baby interacts in more complex ways and as she becomes better able to imitate simple sounds and words. Not only do structures of her brain often facilitate the acquisition of language and the ability to sequence and plan ideas and actions, but they also appear to grow as a result of her increasingly complex interactions with her caregivers and others. Clearly, interaction with the environment and the growth of the brain reinforce each other.

HELPING YOUR CHILD BECOME A PROBLEM SOLVER

ADMIRE AND INTERACT!

The most important thing you can do to encourage your toddler's ability to organize her behavior, communicate her emerging ideas and feelings, and problem-solve is to admire and interact with her. At this stage, your child needs to feel the warmth of your high regard. If she builds a block tower and proudly turns to you, the approving gleam in your eye will encourage her to continue. If, however, you're preoccupied and keep your nose buried in the newspaper, missing all of her glances in your direction, you will inadvertently cut off the exchange. If you tend to be overly fastidious and bossy, your disapproving head shakes and angry exclamations each time your child wants to flex her muscles and climb on the sofa cause her to shy away from feeling assertive and interacting with you. On the other hand, if you join in excitedly with your child as she explores the backyard, she will get a clear sense that you applaud her adventurousness.

One way you can show your child that you love being with her is to act silly. As we mentioned earlier, your toddler may start exhibiting more of a sense of fun during these months. She may use all sorts of babbling not only because she is mimicking the sounds and rhythms of adult speech, but because she is amused by the nonsensical sound patterns that come out of her mouth. By exchanging barks, whinnies, and meows with you, your toddler will feel as if she's the funniest thing ever. She'll continue to seek you out, and try to cobble more and more silly vocalizations together. Even when she's a little cranky or disorganized, your use of funny voices or a little humorous horseplay may rein her back into communicating with you.

If your 18-month-old seems to be repetitive rather than creative and opens and shuts a door again and again, you might try using the following technique that one parent came up with. Get yourself "stuck" behind the door! Act as if you're apologetic to the door, begging "his" pardon for bumping into "him" in a cartoonish voice. Your child may be amused by this by-product of her behavior, and it's a practical way to draw her back into more creative dialogues and a sense that pleasure and silliness are part of human interactions, too.

LET YOUR CHILD BE THE BOSS

As you playfully encourage your child to take center stage, you'll be following a key principle of floor-time interaction: *Let your child be the boss of your play.* Why is it so important for her to call the shots? We promote this rule during floor-time play because we want to take advantage of the child's natural interests. By building on your toddler's interests, pleasures, and delight in certain postures or movements, you help her become assertive and guide her behavior (and, later on, her thoughts) with her own desires or emotions. Connecting wishes and emotions to behavior and thoughts is a key to creative and logical thinking.

For example, suppose your little girl is lying on her tummy, holding her stuffed kitty-cat in front of her face, and making meowing sounds. You could lie down on your stomach, too, so that you're both literally operating on the same level and your child won't feel intimidated by your size. Since she's showing a comfort and pleasure in using her voice to produce the meowing sounds, you might try to keep a playful exchange of meows going. Or catch her eye, and extend your hand to pat the kitty-cat's head. See if she imitates your gesture, pats your head instead, or gets up on all fours in search of the kitty-cat's mommy. Just follow your little girl's lead and help her take her play in new directions.

When you build on your child's interests, you help her feel purposeful. She'll swell with pride because she leads the way and holds sway over you. In so many activities during the day, you necessarily must have the last word, and your child senses her relative lack of power. After all, you are the final authority in matters of bedtime, meals, naps, and schedules. On many levels your control gives your child a sense of security and comfort, yet she also has the very human need to get her own way from time to time. By ceding floor-time control to her, you are helping your toddler exercise behavior that expresses her intentions in an appropriate manner. Because she is doing what she wants to do, her practice will be unforced.

Another fringe benefit of building on your child's natural interests during an exchange of gestures is that you won't have to rely on new toys or gimmicky ideas to enliven your playtimes together. You would soon run out of tricks and would be exhausted and bored if you felt you had to entertain your child all the time. There will be occasions, however, when you'll have to gently intrude yourself into the interaction sequence. If your toddler starts to tune out, or shows a reluctance to initiate any circles of communication, be observant and you will probably be able to detect where her interest has wandered. You can then open up an exchange of gestures around whatever it is that is absorbing her attention.

When your little girl seems to lose interest in crawling like a kitty-cat with you by her side and seems disinclined to play, you can give her a minute or two to rest and regroup. Be patient, and then see what will capture her interest next. Even idle times, such as when she lies on her back and stares at a shadow on the ceiling, or gazes out a window at brightly colored leaves, can provide you with a clue about where your next interaction is headed. Her relaxed behaviors could lead to a lot of energized pointing about the shapes you both detect on the ceiling, or to taking a companionable nature walk outside.

There's often some hint in your child's behavior—a look in a certain direction, for example—that you may not usually associate with play. If she stops playing with a toy while the two of you are outside and picks up a woodchip or two that she finds at her feet, you might refocus your interaction with her around the woodchips. If her attention continues to flag, you might try to inject some novelty into your play by building a block tower made of woodchips. If she truly seems tuckered out and wants to rest for a while, invite her to lie down with you on a lounge chair. Let her hear your voice as you talk about how nice it is to rest together, or simply nestle in each other's arms for a while. The goal is to present your toddler with options and to then follow whatever action—or inaction—plan she chooses. Each time you're successful in extending the chain of back-and-forth's you exchange with your toddler, you're helping her to link up her actions in an increasingly purposeful way. She comes to realize that it's satisfying to take the next step, or fill in the next piece of the puzzle.

HELPING YOUR TODDLER
EXPRESS ALL HER EMOTIONS

Can your child organize her play around a full range of emotional themes? How does she let you know that she wants to be picked up and hugged? How does she indicate that she's feeling feisty or curious? Does she avoid aggressive play, or is she single-mindedly focused on that theme? As you and your toddler interact, try to help her express not only her feelings of happiness, closeness, empathy, and curiosity but also her anger, assertiveness, and sadness as well. If you help her experience *all* her emotions as she naturally feels them and while she's in a safe and secure relationship with you, they won't overwhelm or inhibit her when she's out in the wide world.

Many parents are happy when their children show their love or affection with hugs, or "make nice" by patting Daddy's and Mommy's hands, but are less pleased when their child bangs two dolls or toy trucks together. It's important to keep in mind, however, that all of your child's different feelings have a role to play in healthy toddler development. When she brings these feelings into her interactions with you, she is actually learning how to regulate them. Angry feelings, for example, are no longer just a part of a temper tantrum display. Now they become integrated into your child's play. Eventually, she'll be able to label angry feelings and use emotionally laden words in pretend play or in conversation, and won't have to resort to acting them out impulsively.

One way to help a toddler learn to be patient and to tolerate frustration is to not give in to her demands right away. Delaying will prompt her to exchange more gestures with you about her feelings. Try not to stir up a full-blown tantrum, though. Gradually stretch out your "conversation," and later on when your child learns the magic word "wait," she will already know about patience and how it feels to anticipate getting her needs or desires met, and she will know that she can manage it.

If you notice that your child seems stuck on aggressive themes in her play, you can help her thicken the plot. Imagine that she has been very busy crashing toy cars for the past 15 minutes and even seems to be huffing with excitement as her cars bump into yours. You're feeling good about the length of your play together; there have been lots of interesting sound effects exchanged, and you've even gotten up on all fours pretending to be one of the cars yourself. You're glad she's showing spunky enthusiasm. Still, you recognize that enlarging the context of your play might encourage your child to stitch a more interesting emotional pattern into her interaction with you.

You could expand the scope of your play together by having cars chase each other or by having one of the car wheels "accidentally" fall off. You could then exchange a look of concern with your child and suggest that she help you stick the wheel back on. You might try demonstrating how to fix the wheel, and give her a little assistance as she copies your gestures. Although you have remained focused on your child's interest in crashing cars, you have helped her solve a problem and widened the scope of her play. Her understanding of how things work in her world has also been broadened. From now on, in her mind toy cars won't simply be synonymous with a "vroom" of excitement, or the aggressive thrill of crashing them together. By "fixing" the wheel with you, your child has literally achieved a hands-on knowledge that steps can be taken to find solutions for problems, and that excited feeling states can be calmed.

Some children show a very different tendency when anger and aggression crop up during playtimes. If your child runs away from conflict and wants to kiss and make up too soon, you can guess that her anger may feel too scary for her to tolerate. Help her to stay a minute or two longer with her angry feelings and express what she really wants with her gestures. Because she feels safe and secure in your presence, she will start to learn that just as love and security are part of life, so are anger and conflict.

The same principle holds true for sad feelings. When your toddler conveys her sadness through mournful looks or tears, take the time to empathize with her sadness, just as you did with her anger. Sit quietly with her if she's looking blue because her pink bunny has lost its ear in the washing machine. Let your child see that you're sad, too. Don't rush to wipe away her tears or cheer her up. Take some time to soothe her. You might try gently rubbing her back and murmuring comforting words like "Oh, I feel so bad, too." She may not understand the words you use, but she'll surely pick up on the supportive rhythms of your voice. After a while, you can problem-solve with her and go together to get your sewing kit and make the bunny all better. It's important to let your child know that all of us experience sad feelings from time to time and that she will also.

Helping a child express feelings of closeness, happiness, and pleasure is a distinct delight for most parents. The cozy relaxed interludes when you lie near each other and exchange lazy smiles, or gentle pats and rubs, or silly sounds, are some of life's sweetest moments. Quiet times when the two of you sit together and look at a picture book also warm your child's heart and let her know she is loved.

Something as simple as walking hand in hand together in the park can expose your child to a whole range of feelings. The warmth and security offered by your hand emboldens her to stretch the explorative side of her nature. She may toddle away from you in hot pursuit of a squirrel, or bend down to examine a shiny rock. As she squeals with enthusiasm and looks to you seeking some sign that you approve of her assertiveness, let her know that you're excited, too. You might trot after her when she runs, or hold your hand out and ask to see her pretty rock. In general, try to recapture the joy of spontaneity that you, too, experienced as a child. The more you're able to let your hair down, the more fun the two of you will have.

You can also support your toddler's budding assertiveness by making a fuss over her gestures as the two of you walk along together. You might try to stage a simple sort of hide-and-seek game, and have your arm or leg stick out from behind a tree trunk so she can gleefully find you.

Even pleasant walks may have their share of frustration and anger. One day a quick glance at your watch may remind you that your older child is due home any moment and that it's time to head back. Your little explorer will probably be upset about stopping, however, since she's used to calling the shots during your playtimes together. Her howls of dismay or insistent tugs will let you know that it's time to implement a few limit-setting strategies.

LIMIT SETTING WITH A TODDLER

By the time she is a year and a half old, your baby's need to explore the world and have her own way will run smack into your need to control some of her ramblings. Any self-respecting toddler will be outraged at your attempts to take away the crystal vase she has so patiently climbed up on the cabinet to reach. Sometimes, however, her provocative behavior reflects her intuitive understanding that she needs your feedback to rein herself in. In fact, while she's heading toward the object that she's been repeatedly warned away from, she may be shaking her head and mumbling "No, no!" to herself. Because she isn't capable yet of internalizing the thought "Maybe I shouldn't go get the no-no thing," she thinks out loud to you. Since she isn't heeding her own advice, she'll be needing some help. You might consider acting like a friendly corner policeman, saying, "Stop!" with your palm extended straight out in front of your face. Hopefully, she'll respond to your gestures and you won't have to scoop her up and park her on your hip, out of harm's way.

Without such limits, your child's life would be pretty scary at times. Her anger could overwhelm her, her acting out and explorations could endanger her, and no place would feel truly safe and secure. That's why part of loving a child means providing her with calm, consistent discipline and limits. The "calm" part of the prescription is pretty hard to maintain when your child is in the middle of a temper tantrum or is biting her older brother. However, calmness should certainly remain a goal when limit setting is in order.

Setting limits helps a child organize her behavior and feel in control. Just as you set up baby gates to keep your toddler from tumbling down the stairs, so must you provide her with behavioral "fences" that will guide her toward safe ways to express her feelings and explore her environment. Teaching a toddler about these borders is not the same as punishing her. In fact, once those limits are firmly planted in her mind she'll feel more free to explore the big, wide world.

How do you convey the concept of "No" or "Not now" to a year-old baby? You must speak the gestural language that you both share. She needs to see the seriousness on your face and the forcefulness of your pointing finger, and hear the gravity in your voice as you say "No!" By the time she's over a year and a half old, your child will usually respond to gestural limits, because she is starting to understand how the world works. It may be harder for you to distract her from pursuing forbidden activities now, though, because her sense of determination is more organized and purposeful. It will take more work on your part to deflect her from pulling on the lamp cord she's so enamored with. If you've already tried your corner-cop hand gestures, and trotted out your firmest voice, and she's still ignoring you, you may have to pick her up and take her to the other side of the room. Then, you can try offering the same warning hand motions and speak to her in the same deep voice, and see if you can get her to acknowledge your gestures with one of her own.

Sometimes it will be hard to engage your child's attention long enough to have her hear the seriousness of your tone or see it written on your face. She will learn to respect your vocal overtures if they are persistent, clear, and serious, and if there is enough love and security at the heart of your relationship. When you do recapture her attention, your serious looks and tone will have more meaning and impact on her than they did just a few months ago. Now she is able to associate these gestures with a whole pattern in your behavior that indicates you are in a serious, rather than a playful, mood.

When your toddler disintegrates into a wailing, negative display of flailing fists, recognize that she's probably suffering from her loss of control even more than you may be. She needs your help in regaining her equilibrium more than ever. The best way to do that is to get down on her level and sit eye-to-eye with her. Let her feel that although you're the boss you understand her dismay. You can radiate heat, and not the usual warmth she's used to basking in, without seriously hurting her feelings. Try to avoid behaving coldly or putting an emotional distance between the two of you. Your child will almost certainly continue to voice opposition for a while, which is expectable and normal.

When your toddler is raging, it may be useful to think of yourself as an authority figure along the lines of a Smokey the Bear. You're big and powerful, but not menacing. Your voice is measured and low, not shrill. You convey a sense of gentle firmness, and let your child see that you must reluctantly, but definitely, steer her toward self-control. If she tries to hit and bite you, you need to position yourself in front of her, and raise your voice slightly while intoning "No hitting." Use a stronger voice if she continues to pummel you, and set the muscles in your face more firmly.

It's very important to raise the volume of your voice in stages, starting at a 1 or 2 on a scale of 10. You may have to work up to an 8 before you're done, but slowly going up a scale in emphasis gives your child a chance to perceive the growing seriousness of your voice. It also allows her to show you that she is able to respond to a tone that is gentler than a drill sergeant's. If you use a constant sort of monotone when you speak to your toddler, or fail to intensify your facial expressions or body postures, you won't be taking full advantage of the expressive communication you've so painstakingly established with her.

For example, if your child is on the verge of sticking her wet finger in an electrical outlet, your voice should sound very different than when she is playfully about to take an extra bite out of your cookie. It's important to let her experience these differences in the seriousness of your limit setting, because she's learning about the world and needs to distinguish between true dangers and mild restrictions.

Another reason to offer feedback to your child as you start reestablishing limits is that your own pointing finger or grimace may help warn her that you're ready to blow your top before you actually have to impose a sanction. Similarly, if you pay attention to your child's body language you may see anticipatory signs that she's about to get into trouble. Her devilish expression will give you time to issue a warning before she actually misbehaves. This sort of gestural posturing is highly developed in the animal kingdom. Two stags may bellow and prominently display their antlers in a menacing way, seeing which one will back down so they can avoid a fight. Gestural communication appears to play a similar role in the safe handling of interpersonal conflicts in human beings.

Sometimes you can help your child recover from distress by reinvolving her in a complex negotiation for something she wants. For instance, if she has fallen apart when you've come inside because she wants to go back out and have more fun, you can calm her down by helping her to show you what she wants to do. After speaking to her in a soothing voice and empathizing with her frustration, you can observe whether she's pointing toward the window, or trying to say "Out" or "Go, go." She might run back to the door and knock on it, or try determinedly to turn the doorknob. If, on the other hand, you sense that she's at a loss when it comes to showing you that she wants to go out again, you might try taking her by the hand and leading her to the backdoor. Give the door a push, and invite her to do the same. You will thus be showing her how to make her desires more concrete.

Giving her another five minutes of outdoor fun will let her know that you empathize with her desires and are willing to respond to her gestural conversations with you, but not to her tantrums. She'll come to understand that communicating gets her more results than aimless, disorganized fretting. Sometimes you won't have the time to be flexible and give your child the extra five minutes of play she wants, because real-life concerns will get in the way. An older child might be anxiously waiting for you to pick him up after soccer practice, or a pot may be about to boil over on the stove. These are times when you'll have to set limits that are firm. Still, if you keep your "No"'s persistently soothing and gentle in tone, your toddler will be less apt to react to your limit setting with fury. And even if she does, she is likely to recover more rapidly.

Look for opportunities to reconcile. Seize any gestural openings your child lets slip—they can be as simple as noting that her arm is inadvertently resting on your shoulder as she hysterically sobs—and consider that an invitation to reengage slowly. Avoid relying on time-outs each time your child exhibits too much anger or frustration. When you are forced to implement them, try to keep your toddler in the same room with you. Traditional time-outs typically separate the child from the source of her anger and banish her to another room. Your child could sense that displaying her anger leads to abandonment rather than the possibility of returning to happiness. The alternate kind of time-out that we've found to be more effective involves having your child stop her desired activity and sit still with you nearby, so she can still see and hear you. This is an opportunity for you to "lecture" her a little, using disapproving facial expressions and a determined, heavy voice. Your words may escape her but she'll pick up on the seriousness of your vocal tone. Although you've interrupted her inappropriate behavior, your child still remains in a serious dialogue with you. Because the ongoing relationship between the two of you isn't threatened, your child comes to realize that she doesn't have to be afraid of the fact that a disagreement has occurred.

You won't spoil your child and worsen her angry, demanding behavior by letting her know that you understand the strength of her feelings. You can't spoil her by offering her the comfort of your arms once she gets past the worst of her emotional storms. Being in the room with your child as you experience a time-out together generally will not be rewarding her misbehavior with your attention. This is because you have interrupted her desired activity. If you interact with her throughout the day so that she has the luxury of taking your attention for granted, she won't so crave your attention that any attention, even nonplayful serious gestural conversations, will be rewarding. She will feel the limit of missing out on the game or activity she likes.

It is very important to note that when a child feels rewarded by any type of attention, even stern lecturing, it suggests that you may not have provided enough floor time or nurturance in her life. The goal is for a child to be able to take loving, playful attention, the "chicken soup" of life, as a given. When a child can do this, she feels an inner sense of being filled up, of warm security. She not only will be able to be more selective in the type of attention she wants from you, but may also be able to be more selective with peers and other relationships as she grows.

In general, we tend to spoil our children by not setting limits. Underneath many a spoiled child is an unhappy toddler who feels the need to push and push because no one is giving her the limits she craves. Keep in mind that when tantrums do erupt, the rule of thumb is to work up from the bottom of the developmental ladder. That means that your first priority is always to soothe your child and help her reorganize her upset feelings. Then, you'll concentrate on reengaging her with genuine warmth before exchanging gestures and communicating with her. Later on, when your child is talking, you'll add words to your gestural exchanges. In short, you'll be renegotiating all the previous stages that your toddler has already mastered as you help her regain equilibrium.

Many parents receive confusing advice from professionals about the need to be consistent in setting limits. Letting a child get another five minutes of outdoor play when she's managed to communicate that desire would be viewed by some as either "caving in" or permitting the toddler to manipulate the parent. Remember, however, that the most successful corporate executives, lawyers, and politicians are clever negotiators. They solve knotty problems by coming at them from different angles. You don't want to squelch resourceful initiative at such an early age. Instead, try to convey the message that there are different kinds of limits; some are negotiable and others are not. Eventually your child will learn to respond to the subtle emotional cues that you're sending. The heavier tone in your voice or the stern expression on your face will tell her that she'll simply have to go along with your agenda. Or your bemused smile may encourage her to wheedle you a little while longer. Your flexibility will encourage your child to be a flexible person, too.

As you find yourself increasing limit setting during this period of intense exploration, you should keep a very important principle uppermost in your mind. *Always increase the amount of floor time you spend with your child in direct proportion to any increase in the limit setting you impose.* If you deliberately up the amount of time you make yourself intimately available to your child, she will be better equipped to set up internal limits for herself over time. Even more importantly, she won't bristle as much against the boundaries you impose on her freedom because she doesn't experience a net loss in terms of your warmth and availability. As much as she will sometimes enjoy being defiant, she will usually want to please you even more.

SOCIAL INTERACTION WITH PEERS

If given the opportunity to play with peers during this stage of their development, toddlers can use their ability to open and shut many circles of communication to go beyond simply sitting near another child or engaging in parallel play. We have observed toddlers use the skills from each of the stages they have mastered, including the present problem-solving stage, to interact with peers. They will look, listen, and touch (sometimes assertively) and gradually form a relationship by experiencing pleasurable, and not-so-pleasurable, gestures. They may even send each other angry glances or resort to outright pushing if another peer grabs for a treasured toy.

Their gestures may include looks and touching out of curiosity and affection, or even a pat as well. Once toddlers are about a year and a half old and are familiar with each other, we begin to see them laughing together over silly things like funny noises. Social problem solving among peers can get underway at this time, although it occurs less frequently and with greater difficulty than it does with an adult caregiver.

FOSTERING COMPLEX COMMUNICATION AS YOUR CHILD MOVES INTO NEW STAGES

After your toddler passes through the four developmental stages we have described so far—mastering the ability to calm herself, engage you, exchange simple gestures, and exchange complex gestures—she'll continue to refine these abilities even as she develops more sophisticated ones. In our adult lives, we never stop using the early capacities we acquired as infants and toddlers; we further develop them and add other, later strengths to the mix. Thus, as adults we may be strong gestural communicators just like our toddlers. In fact, we trust that communication system more than the spoken words we also use, because our gestures are learned earlier, and are used for basic emotional problem solving. For example, if you should find yourself in a dark alley with a suspicious-looking stranger coming at you, you would probably react to the menacing expression on his face rather than trust his seemingly innocent request to know what time it is. Similarly, if someone at a party tells you how well you look but you've already registered a fleeting look of dismay on his face, you won't be convinced by his polite remark.

All through our lives, we use this early learned gestural system to convey our emotional intentions. We can read these same gestures in other people, and size up whether someone is happy, sad or angry; nice or mean; or approving or disapproving of us. Adults at social gatherings trade thousands of subtle gestural cues. We may tell an off-color joke to one person, assume a formal and respectful tone to another, and laugh heartily with a third, all on the basis of those individuals' special body postures, facial expressions, and tones of voice. These gestures convey reams of information that we use as we interact.

All the basic emotional themes of life are read and expressed through such complex nonverbal communications. That's why it's so important to be an animated gestural communicator, in addition to sharing long verbal dialogues, as your child progresses through later developmental stages. She will need these skills when she's out playing on the playground with her peers in just a few years. So much rapid-fire gestural communication goes on between children in that setting! When a child turns away slightly from another child, sending a clear message of "Don't bug me!" the second child will usually know right away that she had better go look for someone else to play with. If the child doesn't register the cue and continues to hang around, however, she may be teased and made a scapegoat because she doesn't know when to back off.

Throughout our lives we rely on this nonverbal communication system to convey basic information about whether the world is safe or not, and whether or not we're accepted or rejected by others. We also use the gestural system to constantly give new meaning to our symbolic world, or refine shades of meaning in our words. In our therapeutic practice, we've come to use the acronym WAA–meaning "words, action (gestures), and affect (feelings)"—as a quick way to refer to the process by which gestures and emotions nuance the meaning of spoken words. We urge parents to link their child's spoken words and their own with gestures and emotions that make the child's comprehension richer.

As your child gets older, you'll want to continue to base your conversations on actions she performs. For instance, when the two of you are involved in pretend play, you could steer your dollies' conversation toward commenting on why the dolls suddenly got so sleepy, or why they decided to change their clothes. You can talk about the actions of the drama you and your child engage in, rather than just talking for the sake of talking. WAA conversations snare the child's attention because her feelings, her muscles, and her words combine to give her a more nuanced comprehension of the words she hears.

Mastering complex gestural communication not only paves the way toward developing ideas through pretend play but also facilitates the move toward spoken language. Each time your child opens and closes 30 to 40 gestural circles of communication in a row, she is expressing a wish or a desire that could be summed up in a spoken word or two. In fact, you can think of words as a sort of shorthand for elaborate gestural communications. When your little girl locks onto your eyes, takes you by the hand, yanks you toward the sideboard, and jumps up and down, pointing to an apple, her actions are a choreographed charade indicating "Get apple!"

If you accompany your own responsive postures, facial expressions, and motions with words, your child will gradually understand what your words mean without the clarifying gestures. When she is finally able to use words and commands you to fetch her what she wants by crying out "Want apple!" the words she uses are summary terms for all of the little behaviors that involve getting an apple.

Over time, the word "apple" becomes much more than a word that is tied to the action of fetching a piece of fruit. The child uttering "apple" also knows that she may prefer shiny red apples to yellow ones and also likes rolling them like a ball sometimes. She can now associate other qualities with an apple: apples have different tastes, come in different colors, and are fun to play with.

Throughout every stage of life, a person's verbal, symbolic world will acquire new meaning and value as long as the rich gestural and emotional aspects of communication aren't neglected. In our current understanding of how language develops in children, it has been recognized that children advance from gesturing and performing actions that convey their intentions to using words in a two-step process. First, words are used to summarize an action pattern ("[Get] apple!"); later, the same words develop symbolic meaning in their own right, which may be entirely separate from any action plan. To a three-year-old, an "apple" may be experienced as a sweet or sour taste or smell, or as a round plaything. A four-year-old's emotional experience of "apple" probably has expanded far beyond a round object that tastes good; apples may well be things that you throw at your brother when you're angry, or they may even be a yucky home for worms. To an adult nurseryman, "apple" may come to represent a money-making crop, and to a theologian, "apple" may evoke an image of the Garden of Eden.

Linguists and developmental psychologists have long been aware of this progression toward greater levels of symbolization as children acquire speech. What hasn't been understood until now, however, is exactly *how* young children acquire that high level of symbolization. In our research we have found that *the continuing process of adding new meanings to words is accomplished through emotional experience.* Each new emotional experience with a word or concept enhances its meaning. It is through simultaneous words, action, and affect, or WAA, that we continually refine and expand the meaning of our language.

Adults who have not engaged in adequate gestural communication as toddlers frequently have trouble with certain abstract concepts. Many adults in therapy have a difficult time identifying some of their intentions and emotions. Sometimes therapists make the mistake of trying to help them label their feelings ("Were you happy?"; "Are you feeling sad?"; etc.), working under the assumption that patients can recognize and understand their own actions and feelings. As therapists try to help their patients understand the relationship between the past and the present and achieve "insight," they may inadvertently overestimate their patients' ability to experience a wide range of feelings. The therapist may assume that the patient has already mastered the WAA (words, action, affect) process discussed above.

What we've discovered is that if our patients' words aren't connected with feelings, and with the memories of actual interactive emotional experiences, the abstract words ("happy"; "sad") that we so glibly use in therapy can have no deep meaning. During the course of therapy we discover that some patients have more interactive experience with certain emotions than with others. They may recall many warm exchanges with their parents when they were young, but remember very few discussions around aggression and assertiveness. Their families may have thought that such feelings were dangerous or frightening, and avoided expressing them with their children and with each other.

These former toddlers have grown into adulthood without developing much of a gestural repertoire or comfort level in displaying these avoided, or "constricted," feelings. During therapeutic sessions we may note that whenever such a patient tries to talk about angry or assertive feelings, there is no real feeling tone or expressive body language associated with those sets of feelings. In *Developmentally Based Psychotherapy*, a book about how our new insights into human development can improve the psychotherapeutic process, we discuss strategies to deal with these challenges.

The give-and-take of gestures is not mere child's play. Without a firm underpinning of complex gestures, a person's command of words and ease with emotions remains limited. Many adults do not find it easy to use words to express such abstractions as anger, loneliness, aggressiveness, or passivity. As we rework the early stages of emotional development in therapy with these adults, and as we foster the exchange of gestures with them, we also help them to experience emotions more fully and richly.

Back-and-forth gesturing with emotional signals is a deeply felt experience. It enables a child to first experience complex feelings (through interactions with others) and then describe them to herself and others as ideas. Without experiencing feelings through interaction, it is not possible to fully use ideas to know feelings. By promoting gestural dialogues ranging over many types of feelings during these months of toddlerhood, you will be supporting your child's eventual understanding of abstract concepts.

RAISING THE BAR

How Complex Gestural Dialogues Strengthen Your Toddler's Nervous System

Now that your child uses telling gestures and evocative vocalizations, and can deliberately position herself in space, she is becoming more adept at translating her wishes into action plans. As she uses her senses of touch, sight, and sound to communicate with you, and relies on your feedback and her own muscles to help her reach her heart's desire, she'll be inadvertently supporting brain growth and complexity at the same time.

As the two of you engage in gestural dialogues, you will be promoting this process and helping your child to integrate her emotional-social, sensory-motor, sequencing, spatial, auditory, vocal, and cognitive capacities. It's the *process* of interaction that's important. Your carefree and even silly negotiations with your child teach her how to recognize patterns and solve problems far more effectively than trying to teach her set pieces of behavior. Besides, playing together and problem-solving is a lot more fun than solemnly trying to impart information. As we mentioned earlier, you'll teach your child how to think by playing with her, not by offering her perceptual drills or flash cards. Playing is where the action is during the toddler years. There will be plenty of time in the future to focus on the acquisition of concrete facts; interestingly, facts that are learned as part of problem-solving interactions are usually better understood and retained than those learned by rote.

Another way you can help your child strengthen all the parts of her nervous system is to elaborate each of your interactions and games. When your child lets you know that she's ready for some fun, join right in by following up on whatever sense or physical activity she appears to be favoring. Nothing is quite as motivating to her as her own desires, so follow her visual, auditory, or postural lead during your playtimes together. Copycat games will usually delight her. If your child enjoys raising her arms, for example, try copying her behavior. You could then let your arms relax and rest on your belly, and see if your toddler tries to follow suit. Later on, she may be ready for a more complex gesture, and try to copy you as you touch your nose and ears. By starting with a behavior that comes easy for her, like raising both hands in the air, your toddler is able to feel the pleasure and excitement of being a copycat before being faced with the challenge of having to move her muscles in more complex ways.

If your child likes the sound of her own voice and delights in mimicking animal roars and barks, first see if you can get a dialogue going that's based on these sounds. As she leads you in a game of back-and-forth animal noises, slowly introduce some visual, tactile, and motor activities into your play together. You might try to have a variety of textured play materials—such as Play-Doh, or nappy fabrics, or even a sandbox—near at hand as you play your noisy animal game. Perhaps the barking dogs or mooing cows in your drama could scamper up a sandhill, or wrap themselves in a soft piece of velvet. This is one way to involve your child's sense of touch in your gestural interaction. Maybe you both could also get on all fours and mimic animal-like postures. The important thing is to gently steer your child into using as many of her senses and motor skills as possible as you are interacting and problem-solving, keeping in mind that she always gets first dibs at directing most of your floor-time fun.

Now is the time to ask yourself, What are the most complicated social, emotional, and language-related behaviors your child demonstrates? If she is still playing simple peekaboo games at 18 months, it's time to inject a little more social and emotional complexity into your games together. Try to expand peekaboo, a simple visual game, into a more complex visual interaction by using some props. Hide the toy she has been holding under a small rug and challenge her to look for the toy. You can help your child find the toy by throwing your voice and having the toy chirp, "I'm here, I'm here . . . Come and find me!" By appealing to your child's visual interest first, and then adding some sounds that spur her to sequence her movements in a way that brings her closer to the toy, you are helping her to integrate her senses and to plan actions.

Similarly, if your toddler takes special delight in demonstrating her new walking and running skills, gradually make your chase games more and more elaborate. If you notice that your child coyly nabs your purse and makes a quick getaway to another room, join in the chase. Whoop and holler as you follow in hot pursuit, and see if your child will spice up her game with some yelps of her own. Disappear suddenly behind the sofa and let her find you. As you help your toddler incorporate more of her senses and muscles in games and dialogues that are becoming increasingly complex, she will be getting ready to climb up the next rung of the developmental ladder.

LENGTHENING YOUR INTERACTIONS

Your toddler's ability to participate in lengthier gestural conversations with you rests on her general state of alertness. Her attention span doesn't expand magically, though; it increases in small steps as you add circles of communication, one at a time, to each game or negotiation. When your cues help your child to open and close more circles or communication, she gains practice in being more attentive, since a child who is purposeful is by definition paying attention. If you stay a bit ahead of your child—for example, hiding in a slightly more concealed spot each time you play hide-and-seek—you can gently guide her toward more complicated patterns of interaction. As the two of you stretch out the time you spend interacting, she'll get more chances to practice all her new problem-solving skills.

One way to spin out your play together is to offer many choices to your child. If the two of you go on a treasure hunt in search of an interesting toy, make a point to search a number of rooms together, or consider a number of different toys before selecting one. You might rummage around your toddler's toy chest, turning to her with a puzzled look on your face as you hold up each toy for examination. Questions like "How about the jack-in-the-box?" or "Do you want to play with Barney today?" will spur your child to make a selection. She may continue to forcefully shake her head "No," or say the word aloud, or even tentatively pick up each toy before casting it aside. If you explore the kitchen together to look for some interesting containers to play with in the bathtub, present your child with some clear choices. Saying "Do you want the cup or the pot?" and "Would you like to play with the square box or the round bowl?" as you show her a variety of containers will effectively lengthen your dialogues. The key is to help your toddler gain a sense of purpose and control over her activities while she gets more practice in sending and receiving gestural messages.

Another surefire way to gently extend your play and enrich your gestural dialogues is to stall or get confused, like the TV detective Columbo. It may sound somewhat mean to deliberately frustrate a toddler, but each time we pretend that we can't quite understand her intentions, or encourage her to ask us for something one more time, we build her ability to communicate intentionally. She will be challenged to demonstrate her intentions in different ways. If you remain animated and supportive and let your child know that you are trying hard to understand her, you won't push her so hard that she disengages. If, from time to time, your child doesn't handle your playful negotiations well, back off, offer her a hug, and give her what she wants. You can try again another day.

There are numerous ways to act confused with your toddler. When she makes noise about wanting to go outside, and expectantly takes you to the door, don't open the door immediately. Put a quizzical expression on your face, shrug your shoulders in feigned puzzlement, and ask your toddler, "What do you want to do?" When she pushes against the door and says "Ow! Ow!" (her approximation of "Out!"), and tugs at your sweater, nod your head and announce "Oh, I understand you now! You want to go out of the kitchen to your room, right?" If she violently shakes her head from side to side and pulls you to the back door again, reward her with your wide-eyed, sudden smile of comprehension—"Of course, you want to go to the backyard!" The roadblocks you set up between your child and her goals shouldn't be insurmountable. They should challenge her to practice expressing her desires.

You can also introduce negotiations into many of your interactions. If your 16-month-old toddler squats down in front of her blocks and looks up at you, ask her, "Are you sure you want to play with your blocks now? [Pointing toward a toy train that's sitting on a shelf.] How about making the train go 'choo-choo'?" When she bangs her blocks together insistently and ignores your alternate plan, catch her eye and ask, "How about rolling the big blue ball together?" If you go and fetch the ball and she becomes huffy and pulls you down to the floor where her blocks are strewn, capitulate graciously with "I can tell that you really want to play with the blocks today. That will be fun!" You've succeeded in extending your gestural dialogue and given your little girl's communication skills a boost at the same time.

If it's time for a horsey ride, pretend that the horsey forgot where the barn is. Have your child point and show you the way. If you know your child loves to be jostled on your back as the horsey "gallops," pretend that the horsey's a little tired and see if your buckaroo will kick her heels or otherwise urge you to move faster. When it's time to open the refrigerator and search for the applesauce you promised your toddler, pretend to be confused and search through the wrong shelves for a while. Have your child's pointing finger, adamant vocalizations, or tugs on your sleeve call your attention to the spot where the applesauce is "hiding."

In short, when the mood is right you can sometimes be playfully ob-structive and gently nudge your toddler in the direction of more complex gesturing. If she repeatedly turns away from you as she pushes her toy cars across the rug, hop up and place yourself in the path of the cars. If she's really angry at you and lies face-down on the rug to avoid giving you the pleasure of eye contact, you can pretend that you are a soft and fuzzy blanket that is covering her up. Position your body over hers and tell her that she looks a little cold. Ask whether snuggling under a pretend blanket would feel good. Even if she pushes you away, you've managed to eke out a more direct expression of her feelings from her, and given her an opportunity to make herself clear.

BROADENING YOUR TODDLER'S EMOTIONAL RANGE

Another way to promote your child's ability to use her nonverbal communication skills is to give her practice in expressing a full range of emotions. Ask yourself whether she is happy and enthusiastic. Can she also be angry, recover, get angry again, and finally seek closeness with you during the same play session? Can she be exploratory and assertive and soon after seek warmth and intimacy with you?

Every individual has a desire and need to express aggression sometimes, so help your child find acceptable ways to do this. Suppose you find the front section of the morning newspaper strewn all over the living-room floor, ripped up into strips. You suddenly realize that you had lost your temper about 20 minutes earlier, and had yelled at your child when she accidentally broke a mug. Not surprisingly, your little girl feels angry and misunderstood, and has taken it out on the morning paper. How do you then let her know that what she did was wrong but that feeling angry was a legitimate response to your inappropriate yelling?

First, take a deep breath and get down on her level, face-to-face. As you reengage, let her know that you understand her anger, even if you don't agree with how she expressed it. Show her the shredded paper with a head nod that indicates that you know she was the culprit. you might say, "Are you angry at Mommy?" She may not understand your words but she will probably catch your drift. Then show her with a wagging finger or other gesture that ripping paper is a no-no. If your child is already verbal, help her use the words "I'm mad." Be sure to be soothing and calm. By helping your child reengage with you and your soothing, you aren't stifling her need to sometimes show you a flash of anger. Once you've calmed her, it's a good idea to entice her to help you pick up some of the pieces of newspaper that are strewn all over the floor. Making a game of the cleanup should help resolve any lingering feelings of tension and provide her with a sense of responsibility for ripping up the newspaper.

Although it certainly takes a little time and more than a little patience, interactions like the one above are tremendously helpful in building your toddler's sense that negative feelings aren't shameful or paralyzing. As you prepare yourself to tolerate a wide range of feelings—bad as well as good—when you interact with your child, you are promoting her ability eventually to integrate her angry and happy feelings.

Your willingness to draw her back into physical closeness with you also builds her capacity for intimacy. She senses that her angry feelings, and even her occasional angry behavior, can't be so terrible if Mommy and Daddy still find her embraceable. By confronting angry feelings with your child, and encouraging her to express those feelings in more productive ways, you help her to link negative or uncomfortable feelings with solutions that require assertive, but not destructive, behavior. She is given permission to find alternate ways to express her negative feelings. This is one of the most powerful coping tools you can give your child.

MAGIC MOMENTS

Look for special times during your busy day to connect with your child. Once you've got a dialogue cooking, try to stay focused. If your attention flags or you become distracted by nagging thoughts about the file you left at the office or the groceries you need to buy for dinner, you're likely to miss opportunities to parlay your child's gestural openings into longer and more complex interactions. If you find yourself becoming bored, try some role reversal to liven up your playtimes together. If you're in the midst of helping your toddler build her thirtieth block tower this week, announce that today you feel like a baby and don't remember how to play blocks. Lie on the floor, gurgle convincingly, and watch a look of delight cross your toddler's face. Let her "parent" you for a while and show you how to play with blocks. Both of you will enjoy the change of pace!

Another way to create special, golden moments between you and your toddler is to encourage her to communicate with you from across the room or from upstairs. These kinds of dialogues permit her to feel safe even when she is physically away from you, and encourage the assertive, exploratory side of her nature. A child who is able to communicate across space when separated from the object of her love seems to be wrapped in a flexible emotional security blanket. Exchanging sounds and glances across the room grow to be almost as satisfying to her as sitting in your lap, touching you, or sniffing your familiar scent. With practice, the two of you will sustain a deeply satisfying connection. Your child now uses her listening, looking, and ability to make sounds to feel both independent and secure at the same time. She can have her cake and eat it, too!

THE EMERGING SELF

Your little girl has become an amazing "doer" during this stage of her development. She's not yet experiencing her intentions in thoughts or words, but when she experiences sensations that could be translated as "My tummy is rumbling and I'm hungry!" those feelings trigger a desire to take action. She may do such things as run to the kitchen, or go to you and tug on your sleeve and whine. She may be experiencing different emotions at the same time, feeling both hungry and annoyed. As she connects these feelings with a particular action pattern, she will go on to engage you in a complex series of interactions to get what she wants.

Your child will also experience a feeling of satisfaction when you empathically respond to her signals. The concerned look on your face and such words as "Oh, come show me what you want" will help reduce her anxiety. Once she obtains her cup of milk from you, you can give her the additional satisfaction of holding her on your lap as she drinks it. Your little toddler is now capable of experiencing a variety of feelings, including needs, wishes, and expectations and is also learning how to satisfy these yearnings. A need or wish leads to an expectation, then to satisfaction, and then finally to further expectations that needs will continue to be met in the future. When your child wants to be hugged by Daddy, she'll count on receiving that hug. When she's hungry, she will assume that Mommy will help her find some food.

In all these gestural exchanges, you can see evidence of your toddler's emerging sense of self. Remember, our sense of who we are is based on our inner wishes, desires, or intentions. We experience these as a variety of textured inner feelings that we eventually identify as "me." As a problem-solving toddler, a child is no longer just separate pieces of purposeful behavior, or even the sum of her separate actions. She's starting to weave together these pieces of experience into larger patterns of "me" and "you." The child now has a me which knows that if she's hungry, she can get some milk. When she wants to be hugged, she can go find you. During

Dos and Don'ts As You Raise the Bar

- *Do* engage in long chains of interaction around all your toddler's interests.

- *Do* make a point of exploring a range of feelings: pleasure, excitement, curiosity, closeness, anger, defiance, and limit setting.

- *Do* challenge your toddler to experience different feelings in the same play session so she can make various feelings a part of who she is.

- *Do* let your toddler know what you expect in terms of behavior, much as a corner policeman directs traffic. Use expressive facial expressions, body postures, and vocal tones.

- *Do* challenge your child to solve more and more complex problems, like finding you in a hide-and-seek game.

- *Do* challenge your toddler to show you with her gestures what she wants.

- *Don't* label your child as bad or good.

- *Don't* focus only on playing with blocks, puzzles, or cause-and-effect toys.

- *Don't* become preoccupied with teaching your toddler about discipline and controlling her behavior.

these months, Mommy and Daddy gradually come to be seen as people who not only supply milk or hugs, but who also warn "No! No!" and set limits on her behavior each time she's about to put herself in danger. As your child participates in many different types of emotionally meaningful action patterns with you, she is developing a far more complicated picture of who and what she is and who and what you are.

Back when your child was 8 months old, she certainly experienced sensations and desires (wanting to be fed when she was hungry, for example), but she didn't yet have the ability to integrate these pieces of experience into a pattern. Even at 12 months, she still experienced her emotions in a fragmented way. Her angry self and her contented self weren't two parts of the same whole. To a large extent, those aspects of her personality had not yet come together and therefore were split off from each other. When you got her angry, she may have seen you as an irritant; when you cuddled, she knew you as a source of love and comfort. What she did not yet fully realize was that you and she were the same persons in both situations.

As your toddler becomes adept at organizing and sequencing her feelings and behaviors in a purposeful way, she can merge isolated fragments of emotion, intention, and motivation into a more unified sense of a whole personality. By a year and a half, she has experienced numerous occasions with you in which she became angry, impatient, and finally happy again all in the same episode, and she is also beginning to figure out patterns. Both these developments help her form a fuller, less piecemeal sense of who she and you are. Now, when she enlists your help in finding a cup of milk, she comes to realize that both her anger in feeling hungry and her eventual happiness when she succeeds in getting her tummy filled are parts of herself.

By the time she is around 18 months old, your child realizes that the angry "me" and the loving "me" are both the same person. She has a dawning awareness that the people she trusts can also make her angry. If all goes well, her sense of caring for herself and others will permeate her sense of self and will modulate her rage even when she's frustrated and enormously angry.

This emerging sense of self, made up of a variety of intentions and feelings, is what philosophers and theologians work to define in discussions of will, free choice, and related topics. It is also a key difference between computers and human beings. A computer has no wishes, intentions, or feelings, and therefore no sense of self. Although its electronic circuitry can solve some problems infinitely faster than our brains' neuronal connections, a computer doesn't have the intentions or emotions to tell it what problems to solve. We must program it with our wishes.

In forming a sense of self, your toddler now senses that she is the sum of all her various pieces of behavior and not merely a collection of isolated responses. She is coming to have certain consistent expectations about the core emotional themes of life. If a new person should enter the room showing a facial expression that looks menacing or scary, your child will feel a sense of danger. If another person in the same room is smiling and has a reassuring look about him, she'll probably feel safe and secure in his presence. Your toddler will feel a sense of acceptance and approval if you nod approvingly at her. Every time you shake your head "No, no!" or wear a frown on your face, she'll feel a keen sense of disapproval.

Your child is starting to recognize all the gestural behaviors that signal approval or disapproval, safety or danger, acceptance or rejection, and humiliation or respect because she has become a pattern recognizer. Her own expectations of how other people will react to her contribute to her sense of herself. If every time she attempts to do something new she is embarrassed or teased, she comes to expect that life will be humiliating. Similarly, if every time she is needy or sad she is ignored by her caregivers, she will come to expect that abandonment is her due.

These emotional expectations, which we all struggle with as adults, gradually become part of our sense of self. It is remarkable that this process is well under way when we are less than two years old. Of course, it continues to evolve during the course of our lives. When we see an adult in therapy who is depressed because he fears that if he makes his needs known, his children or spouse will leave him, we suspect that this pattern of expecting abandonment may have been set up long ago, when he was just a toddler. During these critical months of early toddlerhood, children piece together a notion of themselves as being fundamentally lovable or deserving of rejection, safe or endangered, respected or humiliated.

These expectations are the beginning of character formation. Your child isn't thinking this through verbally, but is experiencing these expectations *emotionally*. Even as adults, words only secondarily label what we're already feeling at a visceral level. For example, when we go into a new social situation we may enter feeling excited and confident, or we may be trembling with nervousness, expecting to be humiliated. These underlying expectations about ourselves are forming before we can use words with any fluency and are well along when we are between the ages of 18 and 24 months.

As part of this integrating of patterns, your child is starting to understand that each set of feelings can also be part of a complex pattern. A number of separate experiences are all part of pleasure. Pleasure is no longer experienced as fragmented warm and fuzzy sensations, but as a series of connected interactions that may include going for a walk with you, playing with the dog, or eating a cookie. Your child has an intuitive sense that certain experiences are pleasurable because they are close cousins, emotionally speaking. They have a similar feel to them. Stretching her legs, romping with a friendly dog, splashing in the bathtub, and tasting a

delicious cookie all create a sense of physical excitement and bodily pleasure. Your toddler also experiences you as a source of pleasure in her life.
All the formerly separate pleasures involved in babbling with you, playing
pat-a-cake, and giving and receiving your hugs and kisses are now experienced as part of being with a whole, separate, usually pleasurable person.

Experiences of control and assertion are also linked. Each time your
child manages to pry open a toy chest or boldly shove aside her plate of
food, or succeeds in getting you to push her on the swing for another few
minutes, she experiences a powerful sense of control. When she becomes
furious as she vainly tries to retrieve a favorite toy from her little sister, or
screams in rage when she is deposited back in her crib, her lack of control
links both frustrating situations.

Your child is now forming categories of emotional experience on an intuitive level long before words become a dominant force in her life. As discussed earlier, when these categories of experience are linked with
expectations ("My assertiveness will be met with rejection"; "My needi-
ness will be met with humiliation"; etc.), character is formed. It's important to realize, though, that even the most negative feelings *can* change,
and that the experiences of an 18- month-old don't fix character for life.
Let's hypothesize that during your own toddler years your mother was
physically ill and overwhelmed, or was going through a nasty divorce and
consequently was very distracted. By the time you were three years old,
however, let's assume that she was feeling better and more optimistic and
nurturing when she was with you. Over time, you could very likely be persuaded that the world was a warm, loving, nourishing place rather than
rejecting and humiliating. Your personality can thus change as circumstances alter your experience, just as it does through therapy or when a
new relationship enters your life. Character is always in the process of
forming, but generally, the older you get, the longer it takes to change.

Not only do people develop characters that are optimistic or depressed,
but they can also be trusting or suspicious. Why are some individuals
more suspicious than others? Simply put, you, too, might become very
vigilant and expect trouble all the time if you felt that there were unpleasant surprises lurking around every corner and that life was an unpre-
dictable ordeal.

Luckily, most toddlers are given a fairly sturdy foundation that enables
them to tolerate a range of emotions and experiences. Suppose a child
sometimes has to face sadness and disappointment because she can't have
a certain toy when she wants it. That feeling is soothed and nurtured by

Mommy's empathizing with the child's sadness, and so the feeling ceases to be so overwhelming. As Mommy sympathetically says, "I know you feel bad, sweetheart, but it's your brother's turn to play now. Soon it will be your turn again," she may be rubbing her child's back in a comforting rhythm. Before long it's the child's turn to once again play with the favorite toy, and she can usually cast aside her sadness and experience joy and pleasure.

During another playtime, the child may race a playmate to grab a special toy. Daddy might even foster a sense of competition with encouraging words and animated gestures: "Oh boy, let's see who gets to the toy first!" Both children may initially feel a sense of excitement as they set out on the race, but the slower child inevitably feels disappointed and sad. The sadness can be soothed away by Daddy's hugs and assurance that the child may win the next race. On still another day, the child may feel frustrated because there's no more juice left in the house and she's told that she'll have to wait until Mommy goes to the store to buy some. When Mommy's tone is soothing, and her facial expressions are empathic, the child's frustration usually becomes tolerable.

If a child is soothed by a beloved adult when she feels troubled by sad, angry, and frustrating feelings, the commonality of experiencing upsetting feelings and knowing that the adult can soothe away some of the anxiety associated with those feelings helps the child accept all these separate feelings as part of who she is as a person. She comes to realize that she can be happy, or angry, or sad, or competitive. The comforting, reliable presence of adults and the ability to experience these different feelings within the same relationship becomes a sort of glue that connects all of the child's separate emotions into a more unified sense of self.

Children like the one described above get a lot of experience in putting together the different pieces of the self, so their sense of who they are embraces a fuller range of the human drama. Sadness, pleasure, excitement, aggression, competition, warmth, love, and pleasure all become blended into their personalities in unique proportions. Picture your child's new sense of self as an orchestra in which all the various emotions play their melodies and hopefully harmonize with each other. When one section of the orchestra (rage, for example) threatens to overwhelm the other sections, a child's loving parents—like the conductor—can help keep the emotions regulated. When an emotion becomes too extreme it's hard to integrate it into an organized sense of self, much as a noisy percussion section can drown out the balance of a symphony. Over time the child will take the "conductor" role for himself. It will become a part of his personality that helps keep all the sections in relative balance.

The fact that a child can feel angry, loving, frustrated, excited, and needy with the same person (Mommy or Daddy), and that this person doesn't withdraw or lose control in an angry tantrum, can't help but make the child realize that all these different feelings exist within the same secure relationship. Therefore, these feelings can all be a part of the same "me" that is involved in this emotionally rich relationship. Her "me" embodies many feelings in a unified and complete way because you, her main caregivers, experience these feelings with her and remain a soothing, balancing presence in her life. The commonality of experience with the same caregivers and the soothing quality of that relationship (which makes deeply felt emotions tolerable) are thus enormously important. They help the child develop a sense of self that is both secure and complicated and full of many diverse feelings.

None of us possess selves that are perfectly balanced, nor should we, since none of us enjoyed the humanly impossible situation of having parents who were 100 percent soothing at all times. We struggle as adults, since some feelings are more comfortably a part of us than others. Some of us have difficulty with feelings of aggression, others battle sadness.

Our parents and our own emotional variations create important differences and textures among us that contribute to our uniqueness and creativity. It is only when those textures and differences become so extreme, or are absent because they were not incorporated into our relationships, that the range, flexibility, and harmony of our personalities become significantly limited.

As we are able to foster (in a modulated manner) a fuller range of emotions in our children as toddlers, they tend to have a firmer, more cohesive sense of self as they mature. Individuals who don't tend to integrate the different pieces of their selves may be more vulnerable, especially under stress, because they don't fully sense that their different feelings, such as love and anger and sadness, are all part of the same pattern. For instance, if a child at an older age feels sad because Mom and Dad have gone away for a week's vacation, or because another child at school has been mean, the sadness may feel overwhelming if it is not connected to expectations of being loved or an inner sense of security. There's no sense that "I'm sad today, but I'll feel better tomorrow when Mom and Dad come back home, or when Johnny will be nice to me on the playground."

Mental health, or a healthy sense of self, occurs in part when a child can integrate the different emotional themes of life (love, competition, assertiveness, anger, warmth, sadness) into a cohesive pattern of whom she is as a person. Up until this point, when you've asked yourself whether your toddler is developing a healthy sense of self, you've considered whether she is showing mastery of the earlier developmental stages. How focused and attentive is she? How engaged, warm, and loving is she? How well does she communicate her intentions? How complex are her communications? Now, however, we have something that is much closer to our adult definition of mental health. Is your child beginning to weave the major emotional themes of life in an organized and modulated way into her character?

In all the later years of your child's life, she'll need to deal with competition, sadness, and anger, as well as joyfulness. As these feelings are incorporated into her sense of self, she'll be growing toward a healthy, integrated personality. Even as she experiences one of these feelings, she is aware of the existence of the others. However, if she experiences the feelings in isolation, when she's angry she could be more likely to hurt someone because she wouldn't be aware that the person is also the person she loves. Similarly, when she is sad she might think that the feeling will go on forever, because there would be no sense of a "me" that remembers the experience of pleasure. As an adult, she would thus be more likely to be impulsive or depressed. In the extreme, some adults at times feel so fragmented that they don't know who they are.

We can speculate whether what has been described as multiple personalities may represent a lack of integration of the different emotional themes that constitute a sense of "me." In such individuals, for a variety of reasons, it is as if each emotional theme in their personalities functions as a separate person. Individuals who are very polarized, all-or-nothing thinkers may also share an inability to pull together the complexities of life into one pattern.

Another insight into what's happening during this developmental stage comes from our work with young children who are later diagnosed with autistic spectrum disorders. Many of these children have grave problems in forming a complex sense of self. At the time of their diagnoses at ages three or four, we found that the vast majority of children with autistic patterns—even those who had some use of words and could count—did not fully master the fourth stage of emotional development. Many of their parents reported that their children did not exhibit complex social problem-solving behaviors when they were approximately 12 to 14 months old. Even toddlers who could speak a few words when they were a year old often continued to participate in only the simplest of interactions with their parents.

We have hypothesized that there may be a biological problem that occurs during the all-important second year of life that interferes with the ability of children with autistic spectrum disorders to connect their intentions, desires, and emotions to planning actions and, later on, to using symbols (words). In a sense, a desire or intent tells the part of the mind that plans actions what to do. Without this vital connection, it is not possible to carry out complex problem-solving behaviors and form a complex sense of self.

A child with an autistic spectrum disorder may well engage in repetitive, self-stimulating behaviors for long periods of time. She might spin around in a circle when she wants some juice, or ceaselessly open and close a door when she actually wants to go outside. She is unable to connect her intent to an action pattern. As we work with children with these challenges, employing a comprehensive team approach to therapy (See *The Child with Special Needs* [Addison-Wesley, 1998] for a detailed description of our program), one of our early goals is to help them learn to connect their affect, or emotions, to behavior, and to give the behavior purpose. So, for example, when a child aimlessly wanders around a room, we may follow her lead and try to entice her to dance with us. If she continues to ignore us and drifts around the room, winding up in a corner, we may playfully cordon off the corner with our outstretched arms. As the child pushes against our arms, we are helping her connect her wish to move around with an intention to escape the gentle trap of our arms.

Our aim is to help the child get her heretofore isolated islands of aimless behavior organized into a sense of purpose by a heightened state of emotion or motivation. We do this by following the child's lead and working with her pleasure as we help her solve a problem that we've set up for her. We've had far more success in engaging children with these challenges when we work with them in this way than by using approaches that emphasize more rote learning exercises. More than anything else, children with autistic spectrum disorders need to develop a sense that they have a "me" that is operating on the world with intent and purpose. As we observe children who remain locked in disorganized patterns of behavior and who lack the ability to connect their feelings, wishes, and desires to either behavior or thoughts, we see how very important the fourth stage of development is.

OVERCOMING CHALLENGES:
A BLESSING IN DISGUISE

You've gotten to know your baby for over a year now, and all of her special characteristics are becoming familiar to you. The way she puffs up her cheeks and tries to sniff when she sees a pretty flower, or her look of glee when she pulls the wrapping paper off a new stuffed toy, or even the way she stops in her tracks with a fierce look of concentration as she moves her bowels are all behaviors that are uniquely her own. Other babies may be cute, but few have the sweetness or the flair for the dramatic that your own child exhibits.

Because you've been attuned to the messages she's been sending out to you, you have a sense of any difficulties your child may have in problem solving, in expressing her feelings, or in communicating in complex ways. She'll be needing you to come up with some creative ways to help her overcome some of these challenges.

BABIES WHO ARE SENSITIVE TO TOUCH AND SOUND

Kara was now a year and a half old, and was giving her older siblings Joey and Rachel a run for their money as they played chase games. She seemed "toughened up, less fragile" in her father Steve's eyes, and liked roughhousing with her brother and sister. However, her mother Ellen noticed that Kara still seemed extremely particular when it came to getting dressed. She fussily pulled certain shirts up out of the waistband of her pants, or yanked her cotton socks off in a fury. Since Kara had always seemed to relax and respond to firm touches rather than mild pats or idle handling, Ellen had consciously tried to streamline her motions each time she dressed and undressed her toddler. Still, Kara couldn't seem to stand the feel of certain textures or pressures on her skin. "Loose" socks and scratchy fabrics clearly upset her.

Things reached a boiling point one day when Ellen took her toddler into a shoe store. The salesman, a patient and long-suffering type who was used to squirming youngsters and occasional tears, removed her socks and gave her a playful tickle on the soles of her feet. Kara's initial curiosity and cooperativeness immediately vanished, and she started to wail. The salesman's attempts to distract her only revved up the 18-month-old even more, and she soon dissolved into a full-blown tantrum, kicking her heels and rolling around on the carpeted floor.

Ellen was of course embarrassed by Kara's overreaction, but after raising three kids she wasn't totally thrown by the unexpected. She mentioned the episode to Kara's developmental specialist during their next appointment. He reminded her that while toddlers commonly throw tantrums, this particular storm could have been avoided with a little planning. He urged Ellen to consider just how aversive light, tickling touches felt to her child. Why, Kara even disliked the feel of her loose cotton socks! The specialist suggested that making small changes, like substituting elasticized socks that felt clingy, might be comforting to Kara.

The specialist pointed out that during the next trip to the shoe store they should obviously avoid well-meaning personnel with tickling fingers. Simply warning the salesperson that Kara was sensitive to touch or asking him to tie the laces of the new shoes in a firm, no-nonsense manner would go a long way toward minimizing the toddler's anxiety.

During the consultation with the specialist, Steve mentioned that he was puzzled about his little girl's ability to withstand Joey and Rachel's "playful" pushes and tugs, since she was still so sensitive to lighter touches. The specialist explained that Kara felt safe enough to act aggressively with play partners like her father and siblings, and that she actually enjoyed flexing her muscles when she felt excited and feisty. In fact, these kinds of games involving a lot of gross motor activity help children "defuse" and feel less overloaded by life's routine stresses. In the presence of strangers like the shoe salesman, however, children like Kara may feel anxious and overexcited by unfamiliar, fluttering touches. Their senses become overloaded and they instinctively try either to control or to avoid these situations. An absorbing tantrum, with all its tension-reducing kicking and screaming, becomes a way for the child to temporarily reduce stressful feelings.

When tantrums occur, it's important to empathize with your child and to let her know that you understand that "sometimes it's hard to put shoes on your feet because they make your feet feel tickly." Your compassion will reassure her that even though some everyday things are hard for her to handle, people aren't deliberately trying to bother her. She doesn't have to shut things out and collapse in a heap to feel more comfortable. Mommy's and Daddy's calming interventions can help, too.

The specialist next turned to Steve and asked him to think more about those floor-time chases that Kara seemed to enjoy so much. He asked

Kara's dad if there were any times when she seemed to dissolve into tantrums in the midst of their fun. After thinking awhile, Steve realized that Kara did become disorganized—batting her arms around and sobbing—during those chases in which Joey or Rachel's screams sounded especially shrill or frenzied. The specialist pointed out that just as Kara's sensitivity to certain touches needed special attention from her parents, so did her aversion to loud and high-pitched noises.

Steve and Ellen were counseled to offer Kara more empathy and supply more structure when she was exposed to unpleasant sounds and touches. The next time her brother's screeches disturbed Kara and sent her into a tailspin, Steve and Ellen were to offer her firm, vocal solace, saying something along the lines of "I know you're mad at Joey for roaring at you with his scary voice, but he wasn't trying to make you mad." Kara might not yet understand all her parents' words, but she could hear the empathy and resolve in their voices, and could read sympathetic understanding in the set of their faces and in their nurturing postures. The touches and noises that were more difficult for Kara to handle could eventually be introduced into the flow of their playtimes together, but only after she first had fun using the senses and movements that brought her easy pleasure.

Floor time offered many good opportunities to explore ways to play raucously, but Kara's confidence had to be re-won first. Joey and Rachel were once again enlisted as play partners. Steve and Ellen explained to the older children that their baby sister needed a little help before she was comfortable playing grown-up, noisy games. Since Kara's parents knew that Kara was adept at visual games, they suggested that the three children play games emphasizing soft sounds and use lots of sign language and body postures. They even proposed that the two older children teach Kara mimed gestures along with the words that were hard for her to say. How about bobbing their heads with two fingers pointing up to indicate "bunny"? Or rubbing their tummies to indicate "full" or "delicious"? Maybe pursing their lips into little guppylike "O"'s to mean "fish"?

Family chase games could now emphasize increased visual signaling, which they knew would delight Kara. Furthermore, the new and playful sign language that developed intrigued the older kids and also gave Kara another way to express herself. Mommy or Daddy could announce that they were the zoo keepers who heard that there was a big escape from the zoo. Turning to each child in turn, they asked, "Are you the monkey who climbed out of your cage?" "Are you the zebra who jumped over the fence?" "You must be the fish that swam away down the river!" After receiving wide-eyed nods, sly looks, and eager grins in response, the chase was on. A complex game of hide and seek involving lots of posturing, soft sounds and words, sign language, and fewer shrieks and hoots made the floor-time activity fun for everyone, including Kara.

Eventually Steve and Ellen would add a new angle to the game. Once the animals were recaptured and it was "night time at the zoo," quiet animal voices were heard from every cage. The smallest hoots and tiniest chirps were encouraged from all the sleepy animals, and Kara was gradually re-exposed to softer versions of the noises that used to overwhelm her. Over time, and with many floor-time interactions, the noise level of all the creatures could gradually be stepped up.

In this way, Kara came to recognize that a call to play the "zoo game" meant that she was in store for a lot of fun as she interacted with her parents and siblings. In the context of playing with her family, she felt increasingly comfortable hearing and even producing some of the loud noises that had earlier dismayed her. She was also participating in these elaborate interactions for periods that lasted well over 20 minutes. Kara was now starting to become a major player in the family's dramas.

Babies Who Are Underwhelmed by the World Around Them

At 15 months, little Brian was just starting to tentatively explore his surroundings by cruising along the sides of tables and couches. He wasn't quite ready to let go and walk on his own. His parents, Stuart and Tammy, were by now very aware of Brian's low muscle tone, and knew that he would probably take a little longer than many babies to get up on his feet with confidence.

In so many other ways, however, Brian was quietly communicating that he found the world to be an interesting place. He was excited by his visits to the playground, where he loved to slither down the baby slide and be pushed on the swings. When he wasn't faced with having to coordinate his own awkward muscles, moving through space obviously delighted him. It was as if he were more than happy to love the world, as long as the process did not involve physical exertion on his part. Brian was also capable of entertaining himself for long stretches at a time by gingerly pushing cars and trucks along the floor. He enjoyed fingering toys when they were placed near him, but wouldn't stretch his torso or actively search for them when they were out of sight.

Brian was able to broadcast his feelings and desires to his parents when he didn't have to rely on his large muscles to do so. When he saw Duck, his beloved and well-chewed favorite toy, Brian would excitedly babble, "Duh, duh!" and extend his arms toward the stuffed animal. His relatively good control over his tongue muscles permitted him to communicate his intentions by using many sounds and a few spoken words. Although Brian found it hard to sequence his motions and scramble toward the toy, the twinkle in his eyes and his expectant posture let his parents know how eager he was to play.

Tammy and Stuart knew that they had to look beyond surface appearances when it came to recognizing signs that Brian was using complex gestures with them. Because their son's muscles were less coordinated than those of many other toddlers his age, it would have been easy to fall into the trap of assuming that he wasn't interested in communicating with them. After all, since he didn't wave back immediately in response to their waves, or toddle over to them as soon as they entered a room, why should they assume that he was even recognizing their welcoming signals?

Over the past year, Tammy and Stuart had come to recognize that while Brian used fewer of his voluntary muscles as he interacted with them, he was very capable of exhibiting eyes that glistened with delight and displaying blushes that crept across his cheeks when he was excited. He used different sounds, word approximations, and a few words to show he could open and close circles of communication and problem-solve. He thus expressed many of his feelings even when his arm and leg muscles were uncooperative.

Brian's muscle tone problems naturally frustrated him, because he couldn't adroitly place his limbs where he wanted them. Because he needed extra practice in planning his actions, Stuart and Tammy had conscientiously tried to give him ample floor-time opportunities to stretch his muscles. For instance, Stuart would approach Brian on his knees, so the two of them would appear to be the same height, and would see whether his son would initiate a chase game. Since Brian needed to balance himself by holding on to furniture, Stuart followed his lead and did the same. As Brian giggled each time his father (now hobbling after him on his knees) started to gain on him, Stuart caught his eye and dramatically rolled out "I'm getting closer, closer, closer!" As Brian toddled away, sometimes Stuart would do an end run around his son and let himself get caught, throwing his hands up in surrender. When Brian plopped down on his bottom to "hide," so did his daddy. These exchanges made Brian feel like an equal partner in fun with his father, and gave him much needed practice in sequencing his movements, too. As he basked in the glow of his father's admiration, Brian's self-esteem was also given a boost.

Stuart and Tammy learned not to jump in and direct too much of the floor-time action they enjoyed with Brian. Toddlers with low muscle tone find it harder to make things happen and to assert their will. When their parents rush to bring a toy closer or try to anticipate their child's every need, the toddler loses a valuable chance to assert himself and express a desire or feeling. A low-tone baby may be just as angry as one who has no motor issues, but he may not be able to let his parents know in a timely way that he's mad. Some youngsters may bang their heels against the floor or squeeze their dolls in a fury, but a child like Brian may not be able immediately to summon the energy to coordinate his muscles. He may even come to feel that it's not worth the effort to respond at all.

Stuart and Tammy continually went out of their way to let Brian know that all his hard gestural work would be satisfied by a meaningful response from them. They knew that they would sometimes have to wait extra long for Brian to express himself because it might take him 20 to 30 seconds to show a reaction of anger or joy, while most other babies his age seemed to react in just a few seconds. Brian's parents made themselves wait for a response, and came to understand that an angry flash from his eyes meant that he was as angry as any tantrum thrower. They could then let him know that they "understood how mad he was feeling." Their acknowledgment of his angry feelings let him know that they were reading him loud and clear.

Stuart and Tammy also became patient cheerleaders, rooting for Brian as he tentatively reached for a particular toy. They offered to help him by supporting his back as he stretched toward the toy shelf. They also rearranged certain areas of their home so Brian could follow through more easily on his intentions. For instance, toys were put on low shelves and doors were left a little ajar so he could push them open without having to turn knobs. Stuart and Tammy also bought a number of low, cushioned stools and placed them in various rooms. Brian could then use them to pull himself up to get the things he wanted.

Tammy also tried to help Brian follow simple directions by breaking them up into manageable pieces. For instance, she quickly learned that Brian seemed at sea when she announced that it was time to "pick up all the toys and put them away." Although her 15-month-old might be able to understand the plan of action she was suggesting, he wasn't yet able to sequence his behaviors in response. Brian needed to have even routine tasks broken into separate, simple gestural interchanges that would not only grab his attention but would also permit him to perform a series of linked tasks successfully. Brian then wouldn't be overwhelmed by a task that was initially too big for him to handle.

First, Tammy had to capture his attention by offering him some compelling sights and sounds. "Hey Bri," Tammy sang out in the ringing tones of a circus barker, "it's cuh-leeen-up time!" With an enthusiastic clap of her hands, she announced, "Bring that slippery slinky to Mommy." The slinky toy was lying on the floor within easy reach of Brian's hand, and Tammy knew that he could retrieve it without moving. When Brian grabbed the toy, Tammy brought over a plastic milk crate and set it down about six feet away from Brian—easy cruising distance, if he aligned himself with the sofa. Brian smiled, waited a little while, and then shuffled toward his mother and the milk crate. When he finally reached Tammy, she rewarded him with another clap of her hands, exclaiming, "What a good cleanup helper you are, Brian! Can you put the slinky in the crate?" When Brian nodded "yes," he stretched his hand toward the empty crate and dropped the slinky inside. Tammy looked at him with proud eyes, gave him a hug, and announced, "Let's go find Duck and put him in the crate, too."

Tammy summoned all her patience and provided Brian with enthusiastic support for the retrieval of each toy. By resisting the impulse to rush her little boy, she gave him a chance to master dozens and dozens of sequenced behavioral steps. Before long, he'd be able to understand that "cleaning up" isn't an overwhelmingly complex interaction; it's a doable sequence of concrete behaviors that his muscles can competently perform. Brian's motor-planning issues didn't prevent him from learning how to string together separate behaviors into a coordinated pattern. He, too, was starting to become a problem solver.

BABIES WHO CRAVE SENSATIONS

At 16 months, Emma was exploring the world at full tilt. Slides enticed her to go down headfirst, bookshelves doubled as climbing walls, and china figurines made her fingers itch. Emma's parents, Laura and Mike, were well aware that she sought out physical activity involving a lot of touch, sound, and movements, and her energy level left them gasping.

Over the past few months, Laura and Mike had been surprisingly successful at setting limits when Emma's explorations threatened to get her in hot water. They offered lots of soothing support even when they had to say no to various dangerous activities. Emma's mom and dad deliberately increased the amount of energetic floor time they shared with their child each time they were forced to corral her explorations. They were following the floor-time golden rule: *Whenever you increase expectations or limits on your child, also increase floor time.* Laura and Mike were at last starting to feel as if they were getting a handle on their toddler's high-energy style of interaction.

Recently, however, a new level of defiance had cropped up in Emma's behavior. If a toy frustrated her, she simply flung it away in a fury or pushed her mother or father if they were near at hand. It was as if Emma were thrilled to be able to use her motor system to immediately get rid of any irritants in her life, and had no interest in engaging her parents in a protracted two-way gestural discussion about the problem.

Laura, in particular, was worried that Emma was becoming too aggressive. She sought input from the developmental specialist the family consulted from time to time. After observing Emma's enormous zest and purposeful behaviors for an hour or so, he was able to allay some of Laura's fears. Many of the actions that Laura had assumed were "aggressive" were actually just by-products of her toddler's energetic search for physical sensation. Emma craved input from her surroundings and simply hurled herself at the world. She needed action and movement because it was so difficult for her to perceive more subtle sensations. In her rush to feel, touch, see, and hear, she was literally insensitive to things that stood in her way. If Daddy's leg blocked the way to the backdoor, it received a kick. If Mommy's hair inadvertently covered up a page that Emma wanted to see, Mommy's hair got pulled.

The "aggressive" behavior Laura and Mike observed was actually Emma's search for more sensory input from the world around her. Her parents had to help Emma pick up more cues from her environment that would help her modulate her behavior. The specialist suggested ways they could expand the floor-time crawling and running games that they had been playing during the past few months with their toddler. For instance, they could introduce a story line into their play about a galloping horsey who occasionally got tired, and liked to walk slowly or at medium speed, or who became thirsty, or lost. Emma's parents could thus provide her with the exhilarating fun of running pell-mell, and then offer her the quieter pleasures of slowing down, sipping from a "trough," or bedding down in a stable.

As long as Emma directed most of the drama, she wouldn't balk when Laura and Mike helped her slow down. Now, modulating her activity—fast-slow-fast—could be an integral part of her games. This sort of play generally worked better outside or in a large, uncluttered room. Giving a high-tone toddler like Emma more physical space to play in would provide her with extra leeway as she playfully switched from high to low gear and back again. She'd be less likely to collide with a lamp or another person's nose, and her parents wouldn't have to keep issuing "Be careful!" warnings. Emma was learning to control her activities and behavior while having fun and getting lots of sensory and emotional satisfaction.

Laura and Mike gradually came to appreciate that their little redhead wasn't willfully behaving in an aggressive way, and continued to offer her a great deal of affection. This was critically important, since parents in their situation can sometimes withdraw from engaging their rambunctious toddlers just at a time when their children need loving and limit-setting interactions more than ever. When parents self-protectively distance themselves, toddlers feel increasingly insecure and go on to behave even more provocatively to win back their parents' attention. Overly punitive parental responses can also lead to more problems.

Children who become defiant soon learn to use negative behavior to recapture the heightened sensations that they yearn for in experiences with their parents. They cover their sad, empty feelings with an "I don't need anyone" sense of bravado. Caring parents like Mike and Laura need to reassure their toddlers that even outright defiance and a rough-and-tumble attitude can't undermine a mom and dad's love. Such toddlers need to be reassured that their parents enjoy their companionship. Keeping that in mind, Mike and Laura resolved to expand their playtime with Emma to at least a half an hour at a stretch, and to offer her even more enthusiasm and involvement as they played together.

TODDLERS WHO TAKE IN SIGHTS, BUT TUNE OUT SOUNDS

Will was really coming into his own now. His parents, Lisa and Dan, recognized that their 18-month-old soaked up the visual world like a sponge. His early fascination with bright lights had evolved into a love of manipulating colorful blocks and puzzle pieces.

In some respects, Dan had changed as much as his son during the past six months. A self-admittedly "hard-driving," garrulous man, Dan had made a determined effort to avoid overwhelming his sound-sensitive little boy. Instead of bursting into noisy songs when he came home from work each night, Dan tried to first engage Will's visual interest. Rather than entering the room with a booming "Now where's my rootin'-tootin' little cowboy, my buckaroo Will?" Dan now quietly joined his son (who was often busy playing with blocks and puzzles) on the floor. Dan would turn to Will with a big, welcoming smile on his face, arms outstretched, and his son would crawl right into a big bear hug.

As the two of them sat side by side, a joint construction project got under way. Dan and Lisa had learned to be playfully obstructive when it came to interacting with Will at this stage of his development. That translated into lots of feigned puzzlement whenever Dan turned to Will to see what block they should next select. Dan's raised eyebrows, furrowed brow, and shoulder shrugs would force Will to make a decision and reach for a block of his own choosing. The more back-and-forth's that Dan could drum up, the more practice Will would receive in clarifying his intentions. After Will made his selection, Dan would nod his head in admiration and announce "Good!" and then repeat, very slowly, "That's a pretty color, Will."

Dan was very aware that many sounds uttered in rapid-fire succession confused and sometimes upset his son. As he exchanged dozens of gestures while building the block tower with Will, he was careful first to offer quiet, visual expressions of warmth coupled with slow, rhythmic sequences of sounds. Then, as they played together his simple words of encouragement, offered at an even pace and accompanied by physical affection, also became more and more a part of their dialogue. By taking advantage of Will's visual interest and good eye-hand coordination, Dan found that he and Will could happily "play blocks" together for up to 20 minutes at a time. This gave Will a great mental workout even as he and his dad had fun together. Will's eyes sought out the prettiest colors and most interesting shapes, his hands reached out and his fingers caressed the wooden texture of the blocks, his ears picked up his Dad's vocal cadences, including praise, and his new control over his leg muscles permitted him to scramble up on his knees and place a steeple on their tower. Will's obvious ability to recognize and create block patterns wowed his dad and convinced him that there was a budding architect in the family.

Lisa had always had an easier time relating to Will's quieter interactive style, since she, too, was somewhat reserved. Ever since Will's first birthday, however, when he triumphantly took his first unassisted steps, Lisa had noticed that he seemed a little clingy. The family's pediatrician reassured Lisa that Will's retreat back into her arms, even as he set out to explore the rooms of their house, was typical behavior for a baby his age. He explained that a toddler's increased independence alternately delights and frightens him. As the child investigates his surroundings and begins to figure out how his world is organized, he suddenly becomes aware of his "aloneness" in an unfamiliar place.

Since Will had a harder time than many other toddlers in comfortably holding sounds in his mind, he tended to tune out noises and rely on his visual sense to feel emotionally secure and connected to his parents. When his explorations took him out of their sight, he'd panic and come rushing back to bury his head in their laps. He felt adrift unless he checked back every few minutes for reassuring physical contact. Children with auditory processing challenges like Will's need to be offered rich visual gestures at the same time that their parents send them long-distance verbal cues to help them feel safe and secure. By simply smiling and waving at Will from afar, Lisa could visually communicate her approval of his explorations. If she muddied her supportive gesture with too many words ("Hey, Will— Mommy sees you searching for your blanket and is so proud of you!"), her toddler might tune out the noise, overlook the cheerful wave, and come running back to her instead.

At this point in his development, Will was unable to sequence a whole barrage of sounds while simultaneously watching his mother's gestures. He couldn't tell whether she approved or disapproved of his behavior. However, if Lisa used simple word sequences ("I see you" or "You got the ball") and and kept her visual gestures compelling, Will could eventually learn to figure out her messages and feel relatively secure without anchoring himself to his mother's side.

TODDLERS WHO TAKE IN SOUNDS, BUT HAVE A HARD TIME FIGURING OUT SIGHTS

Like Will, 17-month-old Max was showing new signs of clinginess that had his parents concerned. Lynn and Jonathan noticed that Max often reacted like a stranger in a strange land when he toddled into Lynn's upstairs office or Jonathan's workroom. He would cry out in dismay, as if he were truly lost. Even though his cries seemed a little melodramatic, Max's parents could hear a real sense of panic in his voice. They rushed to comfort him, yet wished there were a way to give themselves a little more breathing room.

A consultation with a developmental specialist shed some light on why Max was finding it difficult to separate physically from his parents. The specialist explained that because Max had difficulty processing certain sights, he never developed a full internal map of his surroundings. If he wandered off his usual paths around the house, he literally didn't know how to toddle back to the kitchen to find his mom. His resulting whining or crying wasn't the attempt of a spoiled, clingy child to have his parents come fetch him; Max truly didn't understand how to find his way back to where he started.

What do you do when a toddler's internal map of the space he needs to negotiate is so blurry? The specialist suggested that Lynn and Jonathan take Max on extra tours of their house, deliberately offering lively auditory and tactile (touch) cues as they pointed out visual landmarks in each room. For instance, when Lynn walked with Max to her upstairs office, she made a point of enticing him to put his hand on the computer monitor on the desk. She knew he could feel the vibration of the machine and would be happy to imitate the whirring sound it made. "Look, Max—see Mommy's noisy computer sitting on her desk? Let's pretend we're computers and make sounds like this one." Together they rumbled and hummed, and then Lynn pointed to the computer and said, "Let's find the way back to the kitchen together."

Each day Lynn and Jonathan staged their floor-time activities in a different room in the house, pinning their games to sounds and touches as well as sights that were unique to each room. The *glug* of the aquarium's motor in the living room, the buzz of the ventilation fan in the bathroom, and the bumpy feel of the contoured carpet in the den all became incorporated into Max's internal map of his home. During their interactions, his parents' animated voices first caught his attention, and then they drew his focus to other sources of information. Next, they used simple visual gestures—lively facial expressions and eloquent pointing fingers—to call his attention to certain landmarks in each room. They helped Max focus on the shiny blue recycling box in the workroom, and the yellow comforter on the guest-room bed. In this way, Max slowly began to build up his spatial understanding of his environment. To help him use his emerging abilities, Max's parents began playing treasure hunt and hide-and-seek games. For example, in one game a toy would be hidden in an easy-to-find spot, and Max would be helped with a picture clue. Over time, more difficult hiding places would be used.

Lynn and Jonathan also wanted to help Max develop a sense of security when he was out of easy earshot of their voices. Like Will's parents, Max's mom and dad needed to encourage their son's inquisitiveness, yet at the same time quell his anxiety as he moved away from them. After a floor-time session in one of the rooms of their home, Lynn and Jonathan gradually introduced him to a new game, which he enjoyed. In this game they would slowly move away to another room, out of easy earshot of their child, and start a "Find me" game. By occasionally calling out firm and comforting words of encouragement in Max's direction, his parents could entice him to follow his new, and somewhat tentative, internal road map of the house. He would eventually be able to find his way back to them because he could use his eyes as well as his ears and sense of touch to recognize familiar routes. Lynn and Jonathan's willingness to stage interactions that playfully challenged Max to use his visual sense went a long way toward helping him recognize some of the visual and spatial patterns that operated in his world.

FAMILY CHALLENGES

A SENSE OF LOSS

Many parents are caught unprepared for the sharp sense of loss they feel at this stage of their child's development. Your toddler's new ability to get up and go has loosened your physical control over her life. Suddenly the cozy balance of power that's existed between the two of you has shifted. Her growing independence and problem-solving skills may make you feel less needed, or even rejected. Some parents may exaggerate imaginary dangers lurking around every corner to justify whisking their child up into their arms once again. It's sometimes very difficult to strike a balance between your child's need to explore and your need to quell your own apprehension.

You can make a point of establishing perimeters within which your toddler can roam relatively freely. If you've done a good job baby-proofing an area of your house, and are attentive, you should be comfortable encouraging your child to explore. You'll lessen the number of times you have to thwart her assertive behavior, and she won't feel micromanaged. When you do have to step in and set limits, your child may very well get angry at you. Don't take her dismay to heart or be indignant. She's entitled to feel disgruntled.

A TAG-TEAM APPROACH TO LIMIT SETTING

If you find that you continually hesitate to implement limit setting in certain emotional areas because you don't want to antagonize your baby, you may very well be replaying old tapes from your childhood. Perhaps you remember clinging to your own mother at bedtime when you were very young, and find it very difficult to calmly take your leave of your own child each night. Try to avoid overidentifying with your toddler. If you continue to feel anxious in the face of her clinginess, let your spouse be the main limit setter in this nighttime drama.

Sometimes, however, a toddler's nightly clinginess can reveal that she isn't receiving enough interaction or nurturing from one or both of her parents. She is in effect signaling you that she needs more hands-on love, admiration, and floor-time activities during the day. Don't confuse her growing physical independence from you with emotional distancing. You're needed more than ever. If you pour your energy into connecting with your child during the day, she may be more willing to part with you at night.

In general, parents find a tag-team approach useful when it comes to enforcing rules because each of us has certain vulnerabilities that can distort the way we set limits with our children. Becoming aware of your own soft spots doesn't guarantee that you won't overreact or avoid certain interactions with your child, so call upon your spouse to be strong in areas where you are weak. For example, once you become aware of your own need to control events, you won't be surprised to find that your toddler's free-wheeling drive to explore unnerves you. Rather than inappropriately shaking your head "no" every time your child asserts herself, let your spouse supervise her on the play equipment at the park.

Your limit setting should be based on your toddler's needs, and not your own. Sometimes our immersion in our babies' lives, and our overwhelming love for them, unintentionally blurs the boundaries between their emotional requirements and our own. If we're reluctant to engage our children in certain emotional areas, we run the risk of making certain feelings taboo. So call upon your spouse, or another loving adult, to help you out in those dialogues and limit-setting situations that make you feel uncomfortable. The important thing is not to inhibit dialogue with your child in any area.

PARENTAL INHIBITIONS AND SEXUALITY

Because your child's behavior and play patterns are becoming more complex during this stage, there are more opportunities for you to misinterpret and distort her intentions. For instance, it's very normal for children of this age to show an interest in how their bodies, and yours, work. Just as they are trying to puzzle out how to open and shut drawers, stack blocks, and turn on the faucet to brush their teeth, 18-month-olds want to explore their own plumbing. When toddlers discover the ins and outs of their own genitals, parents often feel embarrassed or unsettled, and may either deliberately ignore their child's behavior or overreact and exaggerate the intensity of the child's curiosity.

Some parents inadvertently overstimulate their young children, for example, by indirectly rubbing against their toddler's genitals during horseplay or simply revving up too much. If your roughhousing gets too chaotic, reduce the excitement level. Be close and offer soothing rhythmic rocking. You want to make sure that your child feels calm and regulated, rather than overexcited. If she seems preoccupied with stimulating herself, try to offer interesting alternate activities that enable her to enjoy rhythmic movement and exploration. Remember that interest in her body and in moving around is natural, just like all her other discoveries during this stage of her development.

LEARNING HOW TO SOLVE PROBLEMS

Challenge your toddler to interact with you to solve problems—not only those that she wants to figure out on her own, but also those that you present to her. Exchange many gestures as the two of you problem-solve, including sounds or words and actions such as pulling each other in various directions.

Fun and Games

🍎 The Working-Together Game

Note your toddler's natural interest in various toys, such as dolls, stuffed animals, trucks, balls, etc., and create a problem involving a favorite toy that she needs your help to solve. For example, you might have a favorite teddy bear "run away" and "climb" to a high shelf. Your child will have to raise her arms to reach, and gesture for you to pick her up to extend her reach, and you will gladly comply. Such a simple game will involve opening and closing many circles of communication while solving a problem at the same time.

🍎 Copycat Game

Copy your toddler's sounds and gestures, and see if you can entice her to mirror all of your funny faces, sounds, movements and dance steps. Eventually, add words to the game and then use the words in a purposeful manner to help her meet a need, for example, by saying "Juice" or "Open!"

5

STAGE 5:

DISCOVERING A

WORLD OF IDEAS

WHAT THIS STAGE IS ALL ABOUT

By the time your toddler is 24 to 30 months old, he will be displaying a new ability that is nothing short of miraculous. He will be capable of creating richly detailed, multisensory pictures, which we commonly refer to as symbols, or ideas. No longer will he be forced to act on his environment to get his needs met; now your toddler can form a mental image of his wants and desires, and label it with specific spoken words. Instead of plucking your sleeve, dragging you over to the cupboard, pointing to a bag of cookies, and jumping up and down in anticipation, he'll shortly be able to look you in the eye and demand, "Cookie now!"

Your toddler will gradually be moving away from relying on the complex behavioral interactions that he mastered just a few months ago, and will instead be using verbal shortcuts to get his needs met. He has learned to associate a specific collection of sounds, "Coo-kie," with a mental picture that captures the inviting look, sweet taste, chewy texture, and satisfying smell of a particularly yummy foodstuff known as a cookie. Now he can connect the physical sensation of his hunger pangs with a desire to quell that yearning, aching feeling. He can tap in to happy memories of his previous encounters with cookies and act to recapture those experiences by turning to you and uttering a word or two.

Your toddler's transition toward a "life of the mind," and not just a "life of action," is an exhilarating but exhausting development for both you and him. As he makes enormous strides in understanding the world around him, he'll also be frightened from time to time by the barrage of ideas that assault his brain. His imagination will be working overtime, and he may suddenly seem more dependent or clingy, or be beset by nightmares. He'll rely on your soothing embraces more than ever to calm himself as he slowly learns which of his ideas are real and which ones are make-believe.

He'll be busy churning out ideas each time the two of you sit side by side and play "Let's pretend" games together. You'll watch with delight as he tenderly puts his teddy bear to bed inside an empty shoe box, and recognize that your child is starting to grasp that one thing can stand for, or symbolize, another. Because he can picture what a bed looks and feels like in his mind, he is able to pretend that a hollow, rectangular box is a ready symbol for a bed. When you comment that his teddy bear "is sleeping in his bed," he will eventually comprehend that the word "sleeping" stands for the bear's activity in the bed. As soon as he can articulate the sounds, your toddler will himself use the word/symbol "sleeping" to describe an elaborate pattern of behaviors that he has observed.

All of your child's idea-laden play, and his use of words-as-symbols, permit him mentally to manipulate the objects and feelings that surround him. Now he can call out, "Thirsty!" in the middle of the night when he wants a sip of water, without having to cry or stumble to your bed. He can expend less energy to get what he wants than he would have just a few short months ago.

Another way your toddler will show you that he takes pleasure in using ideas is his increased skill at organizing blocks and other objects into meaningful patterns. He'll move way beyond stacking three or four blocks on top of each other and is likely to improvise towers and corrals that become creative settings for the imaginary dramas he creates. In the coming months you may see him building block castles that are toppled by pretend giants or pushing a racing car along a "road" made of rectangular blocks placed end to end. His block play will follow a story line that emerges out of his own fertile imagination.

Your toddler will share his ideas with you in still another way that is more subtle than verbal demands, pretend play, or building designs in space. During countless interactions with you, he has developed a sense that the two of you are collaborators in the world of emotions. Hopefully, you've encouraged him to talk about his feelings and to feel comfortable displaying all of his emotions and intentions during your playtimes together.

For instance, with your input he'll come to recognize that the flip-flops he feels in his tummy are signs that he's a little scared, or that when he's really angry he starts to shake his fists or flail his arms. In this way, you help your toddler to read his own emotional mood and eventually to label the physical feelings and behaviors that are associated with joy, curiosity, sadness, anger, and humiliation. Because he feels safe and secure as he interacts with you concerning desires and frustrations, he becomes better able to tolerate a wide range of feelings. He can pause and acknowledge to himself that he's feeling mad, hungry, or scared, without immediately feeling compelled to act. He may become increasingly able to withstand the urge to hit, bite, or scream because he can derive an alternate kind of satisfaction by using words or pretend play—symbols. He'll come to know that communicating both his good and bad feelings with you is inherently pleasurable. These "reflective pauses" are another sign that he can play out behavior in his mind, or symbolize it, before he feels impelled to carry it out. He's motivated to do this because it keeps him involved in a warm, close relationship with you.

Your toddler may be intoxicated with his ability to share ideas with you. When his forehead furrows as he silently pits good-guy and bad-guy action figures against each other, or he turns to you with an impassioned plea "Go, Daddy!" it is clear that your child has actually been thinking, and contemplating a future course of action.

The transition from operating in a strictly here-and-now, behavioral manner to using ideas and images doesn't happen overnight. It's a gradual process, beginning as early as 16 months in some babies and continuing up to the third year of life. As your child's nervous system matures, he is forming more and more neuronal connections in his brain. He's quickly able to process the mental images that flit across his radar screen, and actually picture his feelings. His repertoire of symbols—arising out of pretend play, block building, conversations, and shared moments of reflection with you—multiplies rapidly.

These mental images form in part in a free-floating manner, like unconnected balloons. Your child experiences them as isolated ideas or feelings, or sensory snapshots of various objects. He stores a vast amount of information; an apple is processed as a round something that is shiny, red, and has a crunchy, sweet taste. As these images are forming, however, very gradually meaning and connections are also occurring. When he is as young as a year and a half, he understands that objects and people have functions. He knows this because he has been involved in countless interactions with you that involve manipulating things in his environment. He realizes that combs are designed to pull through his hair because Mommy has shown him how; telephone receivers are supposed to be picked up when he wants to "talk" to Grandpa; Mommy is there to cuddle and feed him; and Daddy makes bath time and wrestling on the living-room rug exciting times of the day.

Over time, your child's mental pictures of you will expand. He is able to form more vivid, nuanced pictures of you in his mind because he can also recall the proud look or twinkling of your eyes when you praise him, or the scowl that darkens your face or the squeak that enters your voice when you're angry. He is becoming aware of the emotions that accompany or precede your behavior. The multisensory images he has of you, and Grandpa, and a juicy apple become compelling and meaningful to him because they gradually connect with an emotion or intent. The word "apple" comes to have meaning because it is tied to his pleasure in eating one, or to the mischievous delight he experienced in grabbing one out of a bin in the grocery store. These sorts of feelings give meaning to the otherwise neutral new words and mental pictures that his brain is fast accumulating.

Similarly, your toddler's early mental images of you will be based on the intentions and actions you share together—rocking him in your arms, feeding him dinner, and smiling in his eyes as you change his diaper. Later on, he will come to associate the delicious feelings that your rocking, feeding, and smiling arouse in him with the mental pictures he has of you.

Thus, a new sense of comfort and pleasure enters into your toddler's partnership with you. The ability to share meanings, understand another person's feelings, and communicate his own feelings can be exquisitely pleasurable. By simply seeing your face or hearing your name, or eventually just conjuring up a mental picture of your voice, smell, behavior, and appearance, your toddler can tap in to those nurturing feelings. Such pleasures motivate him to keep reaching out to you with words and through symbolic play. In fact, the satisfaction of communicating with someone he loves and being understood (just as you enjoy talking to a best friend) is in part what motivates a child to use a symbol rather than a behavior aimed at direct gratification. Now he can utter, "Want juice" instead of simply grabbing a juicebox.

HOW TO RECOGNIZE ALL YOUR TODDLER'S BUDDING IDEAS

So many ideas are popping into your little boy's head right now! Your delightful task during this stage of his development will be to focus on the expressive behavior and verbal hints that reveal his new ideas. You'll be surprised at how much symbolic information he's able to share with you.

IDEAS IN PRETEND PLAY

Often your child's ideas and emotions are readily apparent. One mother came to enjoy her two-and-a-half-year-old son's fascination with zooming racing cars and desire to win every race. As they sat together playing racing cars, she was able to empathize with her son's feeling and acknowledged it by exclaiming, "Wow! Look how fast your racer is going! It's way ahead of my slow-poke car!" This simple observation let him know that it was okay to elaborate on his heightened interest and express his emotions when he played with Mommy. As a side benefit to his creative play, the child felt less compelled to engage Mommy or his baby sister in a concrete power struggle to prop up his fledgling sense of being powerful and independent.

Your child's imaginative play often focuses on the domestic activities he sees going on around him during the day. His make-believe first develops through simple imitation. He may tuck a doll into bed, stir an empty pot with a wooden spoon, or drag a stick when he's outside and pretend to rake leaves. These behaviors are far more than simply adorable imitations of the tasks he sees you perform, however. His play incorporates things he sees you do and say in a creative way. He will use dolls and stuffed animals and imitative behavior to reenact activities he's observed, but he will put his own emotional spin on it.

When your 20-month-old takes one doll and pretends to hug another with it, you'll know that he has formed an idea of warmth and affection by the way you've lovingly interacted with him, and has applied it to his dolls. When your child pretends to be Mommy or Daddy as he plays with his dolls or action figures, he can explore a wide range of themes and emotions, but at the same time feel comforted by the familiarity of the domestic scenarios he follows. Over time, he'll transfer the emotional lessons he practices as he plays make-believe to real-world situations.

Your toddler's play will often express several different ideas, which may not seem related to each other when viewed through the eyes of an adult. For instance, he may whirl around the room with his arms akimbo, and cry, "Plane, plane!" as he pretends to be coming in for a landing. In the blink of an eye he may announce that the plane is eating a peanut butter and jelly sandwich. To a 30-month-old, there's an internal logic in linking the pleasure of movement with the pleasure of eating. If two very different thoughts, events, or objects happen to be located near each other in physical space, or occur close to each other in time, or seem to have a similar emotional buzz, your toddler may creatively string the two ideas together.

All sorts of ideas get expressed through pretend play. When your toddler huffs and puffs and pretends to blow your house down, he's exercising the assertive side of his nature. When he roars and stomps across the backyard as you flee from him in mock terror, he's feeling as powerful as a mighty Tyrannosaurus rex. You might even observe your child using a cold, deep voice as one of his stuffed animals chastises another, saying, "Never, never do this!" and feel mortified. His play might reveal that he's already grappling with the concept of shame. On the other hand, the loving hugs and kisses exchanged between two of his dolls may reflect his experience of your tenderness and nurturance. His staging of teddy bear "weddings" may give you another glimpse at how important loving feelings are to him.

Each time the two of you explore dark closets and pretend that you're pirates in search of buried treasure, your toddler is using his imagination to indulge his curiosity about things and places beyond those he can see and touch. He is now able to construct a mental picture of a make-believe or hidden object and can feel a genuine thrill of discovery when the two of you pretend that a dusty umbrella stand is really a treasure chest. When you both get down on all fours and gallop away from an imaginary circus ring, your little boy may be experiencing a giddy sense of pleasure.

Sometime soon your child's two favorite Beanie Babies may start bopping each other on the head like Punch and Judy. Or one of the toys may act bossy and bellow at the other. Such pretend play gives your toddler a wonderful opportunity to let off steam and express all the very human and very angry impulses that he feels from time to time.

You'll no doubt see your toddler stage make-believe dramas with you that focus on scary feelings, too. The Power Ranger in your little boy's hand may suddenly whimper and hide under a soft, purple Barney toy when a nearby door noisily slams shut. A doll may comfort another doll that has had a scary dream. Big bears may come and sit on dollhouses. Such frightening images almost always surface in play and should be not merely expected, but welcomed. Pretend play thus gives your toddler a chance to elaborate ideas, become creative, link feelings and ideas, and at times even work through some emotions.

LIMIT SETTING IN PRETEND PLAY

One reason your child may not get overwhelmed by the angry, scary or humiliating feelings he acts out during his make-believe playtimes with you is that he knows that you will help him apply the brakes if the going gets too rough. You'll even notice that he will sometimes introduce limit-setting themes into your floor-time dramas. Bad guys will be sent to jail and stuffed animals will be given time-outs in the corner when they are naughty. This sort of fantasy play shows you that your toddler is identifying with the limits you routinely place on him, and takes comfort in knowing that you won't let him get so angry or distressed or frightened that he could hurt himself or other people. When you see this kind of limit-setting behavior being explored in your toddler's pretend play, it's a sure sign that he's beginning to have some confidence in his ability to control—with your help—his own angers, fears, and anxieties.

BUILDING WITH IDEAS

Not only is pretend play one of the chief ways your toddler gains practice in exercising emotional ideas, but it's also a workshop for understanding how the world works. Your child's increasing dexterity in handling both large and small items and in organizing them into complex patterns is evidence that his spatial reasoning is being honed during these months.

Each time your child transforms a few wooden blocks into a fantasy fort which shields the prince from a wicked witch, he is showboating his new ability to manipulate ideas. He displays a similar delight in lugging cushions and pillows from the sofa to the floor as the two of you build an imaginary fort or treehouse to hide away in. Your toddler uses the physical spaces he creates, both large and small, to experiment with a widening range of feelings and ideas that he discovers as his world grows increasingly complex. In the coming years this symbolic design skill will also help him understand how his body operates in space and will support his grasp of basic math concepts.

HE'S A DREAMER, TOO

As we mentioned earlier, the fact that your toddler may be awakening at night because he is disturbed by his dreams is another indicator of his growing ability to think symbolically. His scary dreams suggest that his brain is experimenting with frightful ideas and wishes as he sleeps. His new preoccupation with pretend play and symbols of all kinds may overwhelm his ability to keep himself calm and regulated.

Bad dreams plague most toddlers from time to time, and you'll be called on to sympathize with your child's fears. He'll need your calm voice and loving embraces to convince him that the robbers, ghosts, and monsters that seem so vividly real to him are only make-believe. He'll rely on your soothing presence and words to let him know that you will protect him and make everything okay.

STORYTELLING

Your toddler's use of spoken language will provide you with the most obvious example of his growing comfort with symbolic expression. He'll continue to use complex gestures to get what he wants or to convey his feelings, but he will also use words as shorthand labels. Some toddlers go through a stage in which they are nonstop chatterboxes, delighting in their ability to produce sounds of all kinds, sometimes quite purposefully and other times not. They may babble streams of nonsense, partly for the sheer joy of doing it, but also in a spirit of pure silliness. You may hear them talk to themselves in their cribs long after the lights are out. Don't be surprised if you overhear snippets of conversations from earlier in the day; your little boy can remember things that happened a few hours before and now can verbalize some of these thoughts. Simple phrases like "Awgone!" (all gone), "Goodboy," "Bye-bye doggie," and "Pick it up" may be sprinkled through his monologues.

Once your toddler begins copying your words in an imitative way, he starts to use them intentionally to get what he wants when he wants it. His "Out, now!" is a foolproof way to at least snag your attention and perhaps to send you scurrying toward the door. Initially your conversations may be largely one-sided, as he may not always answer when you talk to him. With your active prompting, however, and your willingness to continue to open and close new circles of communication with him, the two of you will soon engage in bona fide verbal conversations.

STEPPING FORWARD AND BACK

While noting all the signs of your toddler's new use of ideas—from his enthusiasm for spoken language, castle construction, and fantasy play to his nighttime fears when scary dreams interrupt his sleep—you may also become aware that he's regressing a little in other developmental areas. All his new accomplishments in the symbolic arena may be somewhat overwhelming. He may temporarily feel shakier about being separated from you, or may even fall back into a pattern of temper tantrums.

Remember that your toddler's insecurity about all the exciting new changes in the way he interacts with you is to be expected. Instead, look for some of the following capacities as you watch his development unfold. The key is to observe a trend indicating progress, rather than to be concerned about what he isn't doing at 24 or 30 months.

Use of Ideas in Pretend Play. At 24 months, can your child collaborate with you to construct a simple pretend-play pattern of at least one idea? (One doll hugs another, or feeds the second doll a bottle.) By 30 months, does his symbolic communication (words, pictures, pretend play, motor patterns) contain two or more ideas? (Trucks crash and then they dump rocks; dolls hug and then have a tea party.) The ideas need not be related or logically connected to one another. By 30 months, does your toddler also use symbolic communication to convey two or more ideas in terms of complex intentions, wishes, or feelings?("Daddy play with car"; "No sleep—play!")

Use of Symbols.   With your help, can your 24-month-old toddler use words or other symbolic means (such as selecting or drawing a series of pictures, creating a sequence of motor gestures, or sharing the content of some of his dreams) to communicate a basic need, wish, intention, or feeling ("Want that"; "Me toy"; "Hungry"; "Mad"; "I scared")? By 30 months, can your toddler express a number of ideas that go beyond basic needs and deal with the more complex emotional themes of closeness, dependency, separation, exploration, assertiveness, anger, self-pride and showing off?

Themes of Pretend Play.   Do the ideas and emotions expressed by words or in pretend play cover many themes of life, such as the following:

Closeness or dependency. At 24 months the toddler's dolls feed each other and the child says, "Want Mommy"; at 30 months the child's dolls say, "Hug me" to one another and the child says, "Give you kiss" to Mom.

Pleasure and fun. At 24 months the toddler makes funny faces like the clown he sees on TV and laughs; at 30 months he makes up his own funny words and laughs.

Assertiveness and exploration. The 24-month-old toddler pushes his toy cars, looks at a real car in wonderment and asks "Car?" At 30 months he pretends to be an airplane and zooms around the room.

Cautious or fearful behavior. At 24 months, the toddler says, "Scared!"; at 30 months the toddler stages a pretend drama in which his action figure or baby doll is scared of a loud noise.

Anger. At 24 months the child's dolls hit or fight one another, and the child might say, "Me mad." By 30 months toy soldiers shoot pretend guns at one another.

Limit setting. The 24-month-old toddler says, "No hitting!" to himself; at 30 months the child's dolls may even behave "nicely" at a tea party.

Recovering from distress. The 24-month-old toddler uses pretend play or words to recover from and deal with tantrums or distress; he also uses words and sounds to argue with his caregivers. The 30-month-old child uses pretend play to recover and deal with distress; he may make-believe that he is eating a cookie that he could not cajole from you in reality.

Use of Body in Communication.   Over time, does your toddler demonstrate more complex use of his muscles to communicate symbolically with you? Is there lots of hugging or roughhousing displayed when he pretends to be Daddy during a pretend drama? At 24 months does he show you what to do during make-believe games? By 30 months is he participating in simple spatial and motor games with rules (like taking turns throwing a ball)? At 24 months is he making exaggerated angry faces during pretend play? Does he further refine his acting ability by 30 months?

If your child is moving toward more complex and elaborate use of ideas, he is probably well on his way to mastering this developmental level. Later on in this stage, he'll rely on additional toys and your continued input to play out your joint dramas involving various emotional themes for longer periods of time. Eventually, the dramas he weaves together with your help will become less repetitive. One sequence of activities and words will smoothly lead to another. By then, your toddler will be showing you that he's clearly a master of symbolic expression! He'll also be demonstrating new motor and cognitive skills that will keep you running for your video camera.

During the next year and a half or so, your child will be working through—and hopefully mastering—these related skills, which support his capacity to use ideas and master spoken language and pretend play. The following list outlines some of them in a very approximate way. Remember, the goal with specific motor, language, and cognitive skills is to bring them into your child's new, larger capacity for using creative ideas to convey his intentions. Toddlers do not develop these skills in a predictably lock-step manner, according to fixed guidelines. Simply keep an eye out for signs of your child's forward momentum (see the box on the following pages).

WHY SYMBOLIC EXPRESSION IS SO IMPORTANT

The transition to pretend play and spoken language is one of the most important developmental leaps your child will make. As he loosens his reliance on the concrete world and begins to imagine objects and behaviors in his mind, he can for the first time actually replay experiences for himself that have occurred in the past or in another setting. He is able to stretch his thinking skills by mentally creating new ideas that are made up of bits of behavior or feelings he has experienced before. These multisen-

Capacities Present at
24 and 30 Months of Age

MOTOR

- 24 months: Catches a large ball from a few feet away using arms and hands; jumps with both feet off the ground, balances momentarily on one foot; walks up stairs placing one foot after the other on each step; can run; can stack more than four blocks; can both scribble and make a single stroke with a crayon or pencil.

- 30 months: Throws ball; can walk on tiptoes; stands on one foot; walks up and down stairs; can turn a knob, remove a cap, fold paper, make a tower of more than eight blocks, draw a line with crayon or pencil.

SENSORY

- 24 months and 30 months: Enjoys or tolerates various types of touch, including cuddles, roughhousing, and different

sory images can be held in his mind's eye for increasingly long periods of time, and he can call upon these images to help him make sense of the world. By age two, your toddler's memory is reliable enough so that he's able to deliver simple messages.

Your 28-month-old can thus easily imagine that the unfamiliar sight of billowing curtains in his bedroom are the same ghosts he saw in a spooky cartoon the day before. His mind has perceived a visual relationship between two separate images that seems logical to him. As he matures, he will refine his concept of how things are categorized in the real world. In types of clothing; brushes teeth or hair; is comfortable with loud sounds, bright lights, and movements in space.

LANGUAGE

- 24 months: Understands simple questions ("Is Mommy home?"); uses simple two-word sentences ("More milk!"; "Go bye-bye"); begins to use some pronouns.

- 30 months: Understands sentences with two or more ideas ("You can have a cookie when we get home"); understands directions with two or more ideas and organizes sentences with two or more ideas ("Want apple and banana"); refers to self using personal pronoun.

COGNITIVE

- 24 months: Can attend or focus for more than 30 minutes; can do pretend play alone; can search for favorite toy where it was the day before; can do simple shape puzzles of two or three shapes and can line up objects in a design (make a train of blocks); can point to parts of a doll's body, name some objects in a picture, put round and square blocks in correct place on peg board.

- 30 months: Can make a train of blocks after seeing one in a picture; can name objects in a picture and point to some pictures from a verbal description; can repeat two or more numbers.

the meantime, try to savor his new way of thinking, and recognize that it is a first cousin to the creative fires that fuel the imaginations of poets, writers, and philosophers.

Your child can also substitute symbols for real objects as he plays. One day you may catch him miming Mom's actions as she cooks at her stove. He'll busily stir his paintbrush in a plastic bucket, as if he were a master chef himself. His ability to use substitutes, or symbols, and feel a satisfaction in doing so, is a clear sign that your toddler is becoming an abstract thinker.

With his new ability to manipulate a world of symbols, your toddler has reached a much higher level of communication and awareness. Not only can he think about his behavior; now he is starting to be able to talk about it, too. You help this process along by gently entangling him in longer interactions with you. Instead of rushing to respond to his impatient bangs on the door or bellows for juice, try to maintain a "What's the big hurry?" quizzical expression on your face. Your looks and words can snare his attention, and encourage him to pause a moment before responding to his physical urge to act. He may even take a few seconds to consider a response, and hopefully you'll applaud his attempts to express himself.

The pleasure you both derive from such exchanges will motivate your toddler to communicate more. After all, any activity that is pleasurable tends to reproduce itself. He enjoys these exchanges of symbolic words, images, and behavior, and has a new sense of himself as a great pretender and a creative wordsmith. He's not simply a doer anymore, and is beginning to view you as something more than a loving responder to his needs and wishes. More and more, the two of you will be pleasurably relating through ideas—a real meeting of the minds. Your child will be showing a new social interest in you. He'll be starting to view you, and by extension other people, as an essential part of the fun he finds in pretend play and spoken conversation.

Your toddler also begins to see the world in a new way as he figures out how different images relate to one another and decides what he wants the world to be like. His ability to create his own images and through them to express his own unique thoughts and interests now increases. For example, you may think you know who your toddler's favorite playmate is, and turn to your child with a big smile on your face as you announce, "Danny's coming over." He may surprise you, however, and reveal that he's developed a special fondness for another child in his play group when he replies, "No! Want Jenny!" Now he is able to use his ability to create an image of Jenny in his mind to tell you exactly what he is thinking, even when it contradicts what you're thinking.

In addition, this use of images arms your toddler with the ability to label his emotions rather than being forced to act them out. The more verbal encouragement and pretend play you offer him, the more practice he will receive in picturing his feelings, and elevating them to the world of ideas and reason.

Without this ability to step back and reflect on his ideas and feelings, and eventually to articulate them, your toddler would experience them only as a tightness in his belly, twitching fingers, a trembling in his arms, or as a host of other physical sensations. He might be at the mercy of these wordless sensations and may feel compelled to use his muscles to reduce the uncomfortable tension building up inside him. Like pugnacious barroom brawlers who throw their punches first and ask questions later, such toddlers may become locked into aggressive, physical behavior patterns. Alternatively, they may become passive or inhibited.

Fostering symbolic expression in your child is thus a critically important tool in teaching him to understand the world and to experience and understand and communicate all the emotions that are a part of him. As he hears and uses more words and ideas to express his feelings during this stage of his development, neuronal connections in the parts of the brain dealing with verbal language (often the left side) are becoming more dense. As your child grows older, this specialization may facilitate his ability to sequence language in precise grammatical configurations. A growing density of neurons in the parts of his brain used for visualizing images is also occurring now. This richer neuronal network may support his ability to visualize images in his mind, which may in turn enhance his growing capacity to use his imagination and engage in pretend play, as well as to begin to more fully understand spatial relations.

It is interesting that posterior portions of both the right and left sides of your toddler's brain also show activity during this stage, as he acquires the use of nouns, verbs, and adjectives. Perhaps the part of his brain dealing with emotional meanings is now working together with the parts that deal with grammar and sequencing of words so that his ideas are given meaning by his emotional experience of the world. Nouns, verbs, and adjectives do require lots of understanding and meaning, while grammar may follow more concrete rules. Thus, different parts of his brain may be growing and becoming more specialized and related to each other as language and meanings are blossoming together.

HELPING YOUR TODDLER USE IDEAS AND SYMBOLS

As you watch your toddler's imagination bloom before your very eyes, it's important to remember the power of your own influence. You can help him embrace the whimsical, creative side of his nature and introduce him to language that will help him express all his ideas and fulfill his desires. You'll do this by offering your child countless opportunities to translate his intentions into ideas, or images. These images don't always have to be verbalized; sign language, pictures, or complex gestures may serve just as well.

A child can express his feelings and ideas without uttering a single recognizable word. Visually oriented toddlers with good control of the muscles in their hands can express their feelings using paper and crayons. A three-year-old might reveal his wish to pinch his baby sister through a series of scribbled drawings.

The Importance of Words

Even as you offer your toddler nonverbal ways to express his feelings, it's important for you to use words as the two of you play. By connecting words with his actions and their underlying affects, or emotions, you will help him move into using speech. (Remember the importance of WAA—words, action, affect—which we discussed in the previous chapter.) Words and symbols are learned most quickly if you connect them to your child's gestures, motivations, and strong feelings. Always try to relate the gestural and the symbolic, at least in the early stages of a child's speech development.

For instance, if your little boy is enamored with racing cars, you can zoom your car near his, and excitedly call out the word "Fast!" while you do it. Then your car can creep by his at a snail's pace, while you murmur "Slooow." If you vary your car's speed while using appropriate words to label the action, your toddler may soon take part in the fast-slow-fast game with his own car. Before too long he'll comprehend that your words label the actions that he's able to see and duplicate, and he'll probably lay claim to these new words and use them himself.

New words are quickly picked up in the context of an absorbing activity. If your little boy proudly shows you his mound of jelly beans, devilishly but gently take one and say "Mine!" (Once is cute, twice is teasing and no fair!) See whether he retorts, "Mine!" When your puppy licks your toddler's sticky cheeks and his face lights up with delight, he may learn the words "Doggie licks!" If, as you sternly take a needle from your child's hand, you shake your head and say, "Sharp! Danger!" you'll be increasing the odds that these words will also stick.

You may notice that your child seems eager to use words, but has a little difficulty in getting his tongue in the right position, or in making certain sounds. You might even recognize your own speech patterns in the rhythm of his babble, although individual words may cause him trouble. Enthusiastically encourage these fledgling attempts to use words, and don't be critical of his pronunciation. Just keep him talking and sometimes play copycat games with different sounds, beginning with easy ones that he can do.

Parents quite naturally verbalize the ideas they see in a child's play. For instance, when you see your toddler rummaging through the toy chest in search of a favorite red block to cap off his tower, and hear him muttering "Reh, reh," you might observe, "Oh, are you looking for the red block to put on top?" Your comments give him extra practice in making himself understandable as he tries to respond to you. On other occasions your words may prod your child to articulate a need or voice an opinion. If you announce, "It's time to close down the toy factory. The master toy maker is going to sleep!" your toddler will probably be inspired to say "No, get up!"

Don't forget that children's musculature matures at different rates, and your toddler may just take a little longer than some to organize his mouth and tongue into the shape of the words he knows he wants to use. Other children may be eager to use their new words but take a little longer to comprehend the sounds their parents utter. You can try slowing down the pace of your words, or simplifying your verbal instructions. Be sure to keep up an expressive intonation and speaking rhythm. Utterances in a monotone are harder for your child to understand. The important thing is to make sure that your toddler eventually responds gesturally or verbally to your gestures and words. Every response he gives you means that he is taking in your words or gestures and getting practice in opening and closing circles of communication.

LET'S PRETEND!

Some of the most wonderful times you'll share with your toddler will unfold when you shed your dignity and play with the abandon of a two-year-old. As we saw earlier, playing make-believe games helps your child express many of his ideas while you both simultaneously have lots of silly fun or stage high dramas together. If your child is slow to embrace pretend play, you can inject an element of make-believe into his favorite activities. When the two of you have a tickling match, pretend that your fingers are tickle bugs who are creeping up and down his arms and tummy. When your toddler hugs his teddy bear, grab another stuffed animal and have your toy talk to the bear. When your child climbs up a slide, tell him he's a brave mountain climber, and maybe even yodel. As with all floor-time activities, however, be sure to follow your child's lead and let his interests provide the setting for your little dramas. Don't hesitate to enliven the plot with twists and turns, but let your child develop the story line as much as possible.

Let's suppose that you're working in the kitchen one day, and your budding Ringo Starr is busy banging on an upended bowl with his spoon. After five minutes of this racket you've nearly lost your patience, so that even your two-year-old's winsome smile isn't enough to divert you. Instead of losing it, why not join him? Walk away from your dinner preparations or your laptop for a few minutes, sit down beside your child, and make a little music! Announce with a flourish that you "want to be a member of the band, too." Gather together a collection of boxes, lids, and wooden spoons and introduce your toddler to some new instruments. See if he'll grab a few out of your hands. You could then leap to your feet and march to the rhythm he pounds out. He'll probably want to join the parade, too. By making yourself a key player in a drama that you've spun out of your toddler's concrete banging behavior, you've managed to introduce an element of symbolic fantasy into his play.

When you get down on the floor to become part of your child's pretend play, you can also assume a voice or persona of a character in the drama. This poetic license lets you introduce a conflict or challenge into your pretend play, because your character can have a will of its own.

For instance, one day you and your toddler may be playing a pretend game in which all the action figures in Aladdin's cave seem to be falling off the edge of a cliff. You're becoming a little bored, and want to liven things up. The next time your toddler pushes one of your figures to the brink of the cliff, you might stage a rebellion. Have your figure rise up in protest and cry, "You can't push me—I'm strong!" This challenge to your child's authority will spur him on to take a new step or assert his characters in a different way. Don't be concerned that your contrariness seems negative, or too provocative. By thickening the plot of the pretend drama the two of you have cooked up, you'll broaden your child's verbal and gestural vocabulary. As he gathers together his own response to your words and actions, he'll be picturing in his own mind what he wants to do or say. This is one step on the way to his becoming ever more comfortable with abstract thinking.

One other word about boredom. Don't be hard on yourself if you find that you're bored from time to time. It may mean it's time to introduce some novelty into your make-believe sessions. Your goofy variations will usually keep your spontaneity alive and your boredom at bay.

Sometimes your toddler's play won't simply be repetitive; he may actually seem lethargic. Once you've reassured yourself that he's not ill, you can channel his behavior into make-believe. For instance, if your two-and-a-half-year-old seems a little withdrawn and crawls into a heap of pillows on the floor, you can try turning the lights out, tiptoeing close to him, and announcing in a stage whisper, "Shhhh! It's nighttime and everyone in this room is going to get very sleepy!" You might pick up a collection of his favorite stuffed animals and cover them with a blanket near your little boy. You could then have the animals whisper in various voices, and "talk" directly to your child. Eventually his curiosity about the stuffed animals' intriguing conversation about a sorcerer may overcome his lethargy. As his patience with opening and closing verbal communications grows, even when he is tired or stressed, so may his ability to negotiate the world of ideas.

If your toddler has little interest in fantasy but seems fascinated by tools, try to entice him into using emotional ideas by becoming his play partner. For instance, if your 30-month-old loves his carpenter set and spends a lot of time hammering on his peg board, you could slip a duck puppet over your hand and have the duck admire your toddler's handiwork with words like "Oh my, what a good pounder you are!" You could then have the duck pick up another hammer and bang on a nearby xylophone, saying "Loud, loud!" Your child will be no doubt be intrigued by the duck and the noise he's making, and may be flattered by the duck's appreciation for his pounding skills. He may well imitate the puppet's actions and bang on the xylophone, too. Before you know it, a dialogue may develop between your child and the puppet, or he may try and put the puppet over his own hand and use it to pretend, too. By appealing to your toddler's understanding of how things work and his pleasure in using his muscles, you will have helped nudge him into areas of make-believe where he is reluctant to go on his own.

BROADENING THE RANGE OF PRETEND GAMES

During the toddler years, conversations and make-believe play help your child become comfortable expressing a whole gamut of ideas, themes, and human emotions: love, pleasure, dependency, aggression, competition, envy, hate, anger, and curiosity. Most of us have no trouble exploring make-believe themes of love, caring, and pleasure with our children; we think of ourselves as modeling good and moral behavior when we do.

However, your child has an equally compelling need to experience certain themes that may be mildly frightening to him, such as aggression, dependency, fear, and anger. These very same negative emotions frequently pose problems for adults who join their toddlers in pretend play. Many of us were brought up by our parents to believe that angry or aggressive thoughts were "bad" and that to express a bad feeling or emotion was tantamount to doing something bad. Therefore, many of us face a big psychological barrier when it comes to giving *ourselves* permission to explore and encourage negative emotions with our toddlers.

Why do we have to play along when creepy witches and monsters enter the drama? Why should we persevere with a sad story line that our toddlers introduce? We must explore these feelings with our youngsters because they are part and parcel of every human being's emotional life. As long as we don't dwell on the negative, or focus on our child's worst fears in a provocative way, we can counterbalance his emotional exposure by also emphasizing the symbolic expression of love, closeness, assertiveness, and curiosity. Our goal is to help him elevate *all* his feelings to the world of ideas and to encourage him to bring all these different feelings into pretend play. Once a child learns how to picture and verbalize his feelings, he has the opportunity to reason and make intelligent choices without being forced into concrete, reactive behaviors.

Let's take a look at how sad, dependent feelings might typically emerge during make-believe play sessions. Your little boy might have two action figures in hand, and you might overhear him have one figure say to the other, "Bye-bye. Gone now." He might then immediately switch the action and have some hitting break out among another group of figures. You know that he's been a little droopy since his dad went out of town three days ago, and you sense that your toddler is feeling a sense of abandonment and sorrow when he permits himself to think about his father. It's clear that even when your child isn't consciously thinking or talking about his absent parent, his father is very much present in his little boy's emotional life.

It isn't so surprising, then, that your child wants to avoid directly feeling the sadness that leaches into his pretend play. If he is to learn to express and tolerate these feelings, it will not help to interrupt the imaginative tone of his play by suddenly speculating out loud, "Oh, sweetheart, do you miss Daddy so much?" Instead, stay within the story line the two of you have woven together, and perhaps have one of your action figures wonder whether one of the other action figures will be coming home soon from California. If your child still seems reluctant to play out themes involving missing, one of the figures could idly wonder, "I wonder what that [action figure] is doing now?" You could even set up different houses in different parts of your playroom, and travel by pretend bus from one location to another. Does your little guy want to make a pretend trip to California, or bypass California and visit Grandma in Hawaii? Feelings need not be talked about directly, as long as the drama involves leaving home, trips, and travel.

These make-believe conversations create a here-and-now opportunity for your child to picture his feelings that are connected with his father's travels. Sometime later during the day you might directly talk about Daddy and when he's coming home. By then your toddler will have had a little practice symbolizing and understanding some feelings.

How Limit Setting Helps Your Toddler Express Ideas

Throughout the third year of life, your toddler will insist on what he wants when he wants it, and often at the most inopportune moments, too! He'll probably be showing you a new streak of stubbornness and staging full-blown temper tantrums that may initially shock you with their intensity. Your little boy is feeling his oats now, and exploring new feelings of assertiveness and independence that both exhilarate and exhaust him. Bedtimes may become a struggle, and he may suddenly show a new pickiness about clothing and food that will test your patience.

Even though your two-year-old wants to be the boss all of the time, he has a continuing need for your nurturing support and calm limit setting. As he uses words to explore his feelings, or symbolically acts them out in pretend play, he sometimes gets very rattled and scared. If there are no checks on his angry or aggressive feelings, and you neglect to step in and calm him down, your toddler can become overwhelmed. He may very well precipitate a power struggle with you because he needs to be calmed.

When children are upset at the limits we set, it's important to remember that *crying and unhappiness are not punishable offenses.* We do, of course, want our toddlers to learn how to express sad or unhappy feelings with words or gestures, but we also need to first assist them in regaining a sense of emotional balance.

How do you set limits on your two-year-old's outbursts, yet still encourage him to express a whole range of feelings as he plays and interacts with other people? First, try to show your child that you empathize with his feeling, whatever it may be. Even a simple comment like "Mad, huh?" lets your toddler know that you are aware of his emotions. It also helps him label his distraught feelings, which he may experience in the form of clenched muscles or a churning feeling in his stomach. A calming tone coupled with firm but soothing touches (if he will let you) can help quell some of the turmoil your child is physically experiencing. All of the lulling techniques you've been using to soothe your child since his birth, such as rhythmic rocking or a firm back rub, may help do the trick.

Once you've offered these, and used your most nurturing but firm Smokey the Bear voice to tell him that you can see how upset/angry/sad he is, try to help him to interact in some way. See what he is interested in. You might get your toddler involved in an activity that involves moving his legs, or reaching or stretching his body and arms, to activate some of his large muscles and release the tension that's built up inside his little body.

For instance, if he's infuriated because you've taken his sister's prized hula hoop away from him, and you've already offered him the standard soothing, stroking, and solace, you might scramble to your feet and see if you can distract him by starting a different activity that involves movement. Why not pretend to be part of a human merry-go-round?

Sometimes you'll have to walk a fine line between dealing with your tantrumming toddler's extra need for comfort and security and helping him to learn to cope with frustration and anger. Just remember that he'll be a lot more receptive to your comments about his behavior, and more likely to step back and observe himself, once he's calm enough to get a little distance on the situation. There will be many times, of course, when his behavior is too dangerous or too inappropriate for you to tolerate, and you'll have to act first and explain later.

As long as you've given him daily nurturing interaction during floortime play and conversations, he won't be humiliated by your need to set limits on his behavior when he is really out of control. If during these playtimes you've consciously given your child permission to be your boss and to feel free to express all of his angry, frustrated, and sad emotions as well as his happy and assertive ones, you should feel comfortable setting effective limits when he is overly demanding. He's actually counting on your help to get him back in gear when he's unable to discipline himself.

It will be easier to help your toddler internalize limits if you're able to tolerate more verbal fireworks yourself. Even when you feel strongly about setting certain limits, and know that you'll be sticking to your guns, try not to discourage your child from voicing his opinions. Let him know that you empathize with his feelings, and don't let his angry verbalizations intimidate you. His "doodoo head" name-calling and "I hate you"'s are proof positive that he's now able to use ideas and words, and not simply resort to pinching fingers. So try to be open and listen, even if you ultimately remain firm in your resolve.

Between the ages of two and three your child will come to understand the concept of consequences. Let him know what the consequences of bad behavior are, and remind him again when limit setting is about to be implemented. Sometimes punishments can be avoided altogether by your use of anticipatory comments such as "In two minutes it's time to put your toys away!" Your words can introduce the inevitable, and take some of the sting out of it. If meltdown occurs in spite of your firm, anticipatory words, it's time to set limits. Withholding a favorite toy for a morning, foregoing a trip to the park, or turning off a favorite video will convey limit-setting consequences. If you resort to time-outs, let your child stay in the same room with you so he'll clearly understand that his intense emotions aren't scary enough to cause him to be banished.

Limit setting can help with the goal of encouraging your toddler to use words and symbols to express his feelings rather than acting them out in a physical way. By combining pretend play and one-on-one interactions with necessary limit setting, you'll be letting your toddler know that you truly want to know what he's thinking about, that you enjoy his company, and that you have no interest in permanently clipping his wings. You'll minimize power struggles with him, because he'll know that the two of you take delight in each other's company. Since he knows that he can always rely on you to help him regain his self-control, your toddler will feel free to act spontaneously with you. His imagination will soar.

FOSTERING SYMBOLIC EXPRESSION AS YOUR CHILD GROWS UP

The lessons mastered by your child during this developmental stage will be refined again and again in the coming years. His new ability to form and to hold mental images in his mind will help him understand where things are in relationship to each other in physical space. This will stand him in good stead when he plays in the block corner at nursery school and later on when he's passing the soccer ball to another midfielder. Later still, his ability to calculate RBIs and ERAs will be supported by his skill at mentally storing and manipulating numbers in his head.

His pleasure in symbolic expression will deepen with the years. When he's three years old and begins to move from parallel play to cooperative play with two or three other toddlers, the themes he spins out will have their roots in the imitative and pretend-play sessions the two of you have shared. His skill at staging make-believe games will expand, and before too long he'll discover that other children can act as supporting players in his dramas. He can try on different roles for size as he interacts with his play-group buddies. As they play house he can pretend to be Mommy or Daddy for a while, or be a big bad wolf coming to blow the place down! Your child's delight in dramatic expression will continue to grow as he matures, although he may wind up preferring to applaud from the sidelines rather than be in the spotlight himself.

Your toddler's ease in using words to express himself will grow in amazing ways in the years ahead. You'll probably first introduce him to the catchy rhythms of nursery rhymes, and the colorful images evoked by those simple words will no doubt stay etched in his memory for the rest of his life. Later on, your toddler will recognize some of his own yearnings and fears in the fairy tales you read together.

Clearly, then, your role in fostering your child's comfort with symbolic expression is highly significant and continues far beyond the toddler years. Sadly, many of the adults we see in our therapeutic practice seem to be unable to carry within themselves a soothing, nurturing image that gives them a sense of security. Others are locked into rigid patterns of behavior because they have difficulty using words to label and understand their feelings. They feel compelled to act out aggressively because they literally cannot think about their emotions. The more practice your toddler receives now in separating his thoughts from his actions, the more nuanced and flexible his thinking will be as an adult.

DEVELOPING A SYMBOLIC SENSE OF SELF

Now that your two- or three-year old can create ideas on his own, he's at the threshold of a new level of awareness and consciousness. Because he can hold multisensory images in his mind, his sense of who and what he is, is becoming more complex. He has a new awareness of himself as a talker, shmoozer, play actor, and dream spinner who can exchange ideas with other people through words or pretend play. To a large extent, your toddler is now freed from the tyranny of the here and now. Words enable him to muse about facts, feelings, and fantasies. He can manipulate the pictures in his mind and share a few ideas with you without having to lift a finger. His delight in expressing his opinions and coming up with new plot angles as you play together lets you know that he enjoys this new part of his personality.

Some of the images in your toddler's mind are based on real-world events. When he reaches the top of the hill before you do, and you breathlessly call out to him, "You must have flown up there, Superman!" you'll probably see a wide grin on his face. His view of himself as a fleet, assertive fellow will be supported by his recollection of the speed and power he saw Superman display during a television show. At other times, however, your toddler may use his ability to daydream and form mental pictures to prop up a strong image of himself when he's in fact feeling especially weak or vulnerable. Your three-year-old may boldly nod his head and claim, "Not 'fraid!" when you know he's terrified of witches. He's learned to summon a mental picture of himself as a brave little guy to help him cope when life gets difficult.

Such images can be based on your toddler's wishes and needs, rather than on the reality that he sees in front of him. These mental coping tools, or defenses, will grow increasingly complex as he matures, and will become part of his personality. Another kind of mental picture that will provide ballast when his sense of self is rocked is the symbolic image he is now able to form of you. He doesn't always have to be in your lap or within earshot anymore to keep an image of you fresh in his mind. Your toddler can actually recall the look on your face when you're feeling tender, or the strength of your arms as you sweep him up at the end of a long workday. His mental pictures of you are composites from all the interactions he's shared with you in various settings and at different times in the past. He can call upon those multisensory images to nurture him during lonely or sad times in his daily life.

In a very real sense, your toddler is no longer as dependent on you. Though he still needs you, he is beginning to retrieve symbols and images and use them to comfort himself. He'll soon be able to tap into the broader world of human culture, too, and draw pleasure and nurturance from the stories and rituals of the generations that preceded him. Before long his sense of self will be affected by the cultural values that you consciously and unconsciously transmit to him as the two of you talk, play, and go about your daily routine together.

For instance, if your cultural background celebrates rugged individualism and a can-do kind of spirit, you might be likely to use enthusiastic facial expressions and vocal tones when you read your child a story about Johnny Appleseed and his solo effort to plant trees, or when your child behaves assertively. On the other hand, if you come from a background that treasures consensus building and group action, you might light up when he is sharing a toy with another child. Your interactions convey your culture, and thus have an impact on the mental images your child stores and on how he views himself.

RAISING THE BAR

Your toddler's new ability to create and use ideas strengthens his ability to interpret the information he receives from his senses as well as the way he uses his muscles and sequences his behaviors. His delight in using words and pretend play to express his ideas and feelings will bring him running to you to share his good times. He'll be honing his fine-motor skills, too, as he manipulates action figures with you in mock battles. Because pretending to be Daddy or Mommy is lots of fun for him, your child will enjoy putting together complicated patterns of behavior as he plays make-believe. When he decides to tuck his teddy bear into bed, he'll be able to put together a whole string of different actions. Watch him turn down the covers, sing a lullaby to his bear, and give him a kiss goodnight, just as he's seen you do. In turn, your toddler's pretend play and conversations will gain polish from all this additional exercise of his muscles and senses, and over time will become more elaborate and nuanced. You'll see him incorporate telling gestures or use a tone of voice that's right on the money as he acts out different make-believe roles.

In this way, your child's continuing social interaction with you and the growth of his physical and mental abilities become intertwined. It may be easier to conceptualize this amazing interdependence by thinking of your toddler's new capacity for generating ideas as a braided rope that consists of his sensory skills, motor abilities, and interactive experiences with you. This rope is as strong as the sum of its interwoven strands. You thus have a wonderful opportunity to influence the strength of the braid, by offering your child many opportunities to build castles in the air as well as forts on the ground. As you talk about your creations together, and express your feelings, too, you will be strengthening one strand of the braid. However, you'll also be looking for opportunities to help your toddler voluntarily stretch reluctant muscles, and more actively take in the wonders of the world around him. Later in this chapter we will be discussing ways to strengthen various senses and skills. Let's take a closer look now at specific ways in which your interactions with your toddler can raise the bar on his ability to explore this exciting world of ideas.

PROPS FOR MAGIC MOMENTS

The best way to give your toddler more practice in building up his symbolic world is to spend more time with him. If you plan ahead and carve out 20- or 30-minute blocks of time during less-frenzied parts of your day, you'll feel more relaxed and your child will, too. Remember that it's perfectly all right to "hang out" and quietly relish your downtime together. Let your child enjoy your presence for a little while before adding complexities to the situation.

Try to have enough props on hand that will intrigue your toddler and stimulate him to express his ideas and feelings. Everyday objects that are safe to handle, such as combs, pots and pans and other cooking utensils, and toothbrushes will attract your toddler's attention because he's seen you use them often. Also, make plenty of room in your toy chest for play telephones, tea-party sets, plastic cookware, toy vacuum cleaners and brooms, and pretend rakes and shovels. *It's important to have such household objects and toys available so your child can play out real-life experiences. You can respond to your child's real desires by using pretend toys and implements.* For example, if he's thirsty, playfully offer him an empty toy cup. If he wants to go for a ride in the car, hand him a set of plastic keys.

Your toddler will probably copy your own everyday activities before he is able to put his own creative spin on what he sees. If there are a few dolls, puppets, or stuffed animals near at hand, he will use them to stage domestic dramas that arise out of his real experiences with everyday objects. As his play unfolds, and dolls start using telephones, or puppets start to cook spaghetti, look for ways to insert your own doll into the make-believe action. Get involved in the drama! Talk to the dolls, action figures, and stuffed animals directly. You could have your puppet pick up the receiver of one of the toy phones and announce that Mickey Mouse is on the phone and wishes to speak to your child's Donald Duck puppet, if he can pull himself away from the spaghetti preparations for a moment. Later on, *a specific set of action figures, puppets, or dolls can represent members of your family or other familiar figures in your child's life.*

It's important to give meaning to the objects your child is using in his play. Ask who is driving his racing car, and whether the rocket ship has enough fuel to travel to the moon. You might wonder out loud who's cooking dinner tonight, and whether any guests are coming over to the house or whether anyone has set the table yet, and so on. Expand the conversation as long as you can! Declare your living-room sofa to be a mountain, and use a spoon as a birthday candle.

Although your toddler may pattern many of his pretend dramas on the domestic activities he sees going on at home, he also gets some of his material from the fantasy worlds he sees and hears about in fairy tales and from the special children's programs he sees on television or in the movies. You can easily use characters like Mickey Mouse, Donald Duck, Mary Poppins, Aladdin, Peter Rabbit, or Barney to generate symbolic play. By reenacting familiar scenes or songs from these stories, programs, and films with your child, you can create new ideas and take special note of any characters or themes that your child may be afraid of or avoiding.

Don't forget to mine the many real-world experiences that are awaiting you and your child just outside the front door. Let him experience the thrill of riding a bus or subway train with you, of seeing airplanes take off from a runway, of splashing in a brook, of watching a chipmunk or a squirrel, or of going on a noisy merry-go-round ride. Before you know it, he'll be expressing his thoughts and feelings about these occasions in the make-believe games you play together. The two of you can flap your arms like airplanes coming in for a landing, drive a fantasy bus, or be puppies chasing a squirrel.

Sometimes you have to work a little harder than others to create magical moments during your pretend play together. If your three-year-old often seems disinterested in using props or initiating any play, first try to get a simple exchange of gestures going. You might hand him a favorite stuffed animal or doll, and wait quietly. Perhaps he'll silently nod his head, or turn away, and thus begin a gestural exchange with you. This small gestural opening is all the invitation you need. You could then try putting a doll on his lap and using a high-pitched voice to say, "I'm so sleepy now— will you rock me to sleep?" See what your child does next, without directing the action yourself. Remember, it's not important how your child responds or whether it is in a strictly logical, realistic way. The important thing is for him to take an interest in continuing your play together. The longer your make-believe sessions last, the more opportunities there will be for shared symbolic communication.

SMALL TALK

Try to set aside time each day for reality-based, logical conversations with your toddler. If his attention flags and his thoughts seem to drift, gently bring him back to the theme of your conversation while empathizing with his desire not to talk, or to talk about something else. It's helpful from time to time to ask him why he doesn't like what you say or why he doesn't want to answer your questions. Avoid turning this small talk into a inquisition, though. Give your toddler ample opportunities to spin out ideas and even argue with you. If he should ask you questions, however, don't deliver easy yes or no answers all the time. Encourage him to draw his own conclusions whenever you can. When he tries to wheedle another popsicle out of you, try asking him, "Just how hungry is that tummy of yours? Is it whimpering like a kitten or roaring like a lion?" When he replies, try following up by asking him if it's "as empty as a doughnut hole or as empty as a dried-up ocean." This kind of lawyerly hairsplitting will help him think on his feet, and will provide a nice balance to all the fantasy play and whimsical conversation that goes on between the two of you during make-believe sessions.

When you verbally spar with your toddler, you're giving him practice in taking your point of view into account and seeing things from a new angle. This skill, together with the ability to make quick decisions, is a good predictor of future intellectual ability. It's an effective way to help your child stretch intellectually, as long as you keep your tone generally playful. Not only will you increase his comfort in being assertive, but you'll also be priming his self-esteem. He'll feel as if his words and ideas and feelings must surely have merit if you're willing to wrangle with him about them!

On the other hand, rushing to introduce your two-and-a-half to three-year-old to formal academic skills may be counterproductive. Instead, enjoy exploring concepts of quantity with cookies or coins ("more" or "less"; "a little" or "a lot"). Use your hands to dramatize your games. If your child has already memorized numbers and letters, use them for thinking and interaction: How many cookies does he want? How many do you get? Can your child use the letters he recognizes to point to the animal he likes best (*Dog* or *Cat*?). In other words, enjoy pre-academic skills as part of a creative elaboration of ideas, not as a goal in its own right.

In general, number recognition and reading and writing the letters of the alphabet are heavily dependent on the timing and maturation of each child's individual nervous system. Earlier is not better. Relax, and enjoy the marvelous ideas that pop into your child's head and out of his mouth! As early academic skills emerge, use them to help your child think.

BROADENING AND ELABORATING IDEAS

Now that your little boy is developing a new comfort in using words and playing make-believe with you, he has a wonderful new tool to express a wide range of themes and feelings that includes not just love, dependency, curiosity and assertion, but also anger, aggression, impulsiveness, and sadness.

Once your child can utter the words "Go away!" rather than simply withdrawing into silence or petulantly crying, he can begin to confront his feelings. He learns that although his words may anger or provoke you, they don't have the power to make you or him disappear permanently. He finds that the world still rolls on even when he's raging. Your toddler is thus emboldened to use words to ventilate and express his wishes—even when the words and wishes are unfriendly—because he sees that you can tolerate his intense emotions.

When you see your child act out intense feelings during your pretend puppet play together, have your character acknowledge the feelings that have entered the drama. It's a good idea to use an exaggerated tone of voice to convey a certain feeling, when specific words do not. For instance, mime hugs and make kissing noises as your puppet "remarks" to your child's, "Oh, Mommy loves you soooo much!" Your gestures should be histrionic enough to let your child know that you've caught the emotional drift of his gestures and words. It's fine to really ham it up.

In fact, your pretend games can help your child elaborate the feelings that he tries to avoid. When you observe that the animals at your child's tea party are always polite to each other, or are quick to kiss and make up if small squabbles erupt, try taking on the voice of one of the animals yourself. Issue a challenge along the lines of "I'm not ready to make up yet!" Then, your toddler will have the opportunity to explore his own confrontational or angry feelings more fully.

Similarly, if your little boy seems too caught up in aggressive shooting themes while the two of you play space invader games, gently broaden the emotional theme of his play by trying to have him give reasons for the character's behavior. Thicken the plot; help the characters become more complex.

LABELING IDEAS, FEELINGS, AND CONCEPTS

Another way to help your child become more comfortable using ideas is to name, or categorize, the themes and feelings that emerge during pretend play. When he's being particularly bossy, recognize his need for control by saying something like "I can see you like being the boss today." Then let him continue to direct the drama. If he gets a little feisty and pushes you away, try remarking, "Boy, you sure want to do things by yourself today!" You could then move back just a little from him, so your body language communicates the message that you're willing to give him some more room. Just remember that it isn't your job to change his feelings or ideas; instead, you're simply going to let him know that you recognize and are comfortable with what he's feeling and thinking. As you do this, however, also join in and interact. Be the "child" while he takes on the role of "Dad" and bosses you around. As you help him stay with those intense feelings for just a few extra seconds or another sentence or two, you're gradually expanding his tolerance for and use of ideas.

It's also important to label and discuss the abstract themes that arise in your pretend play together. Three-and-a-half-year-olds can begin to grasp the idea of opposites; good guy/bad guy, wicked/good, and scary/silly, so when you see your child create characters that possess these qualities, help him label them. It's okay if he insists on being the good guy most of the time and you're stuck being the villain, but try to reverse roles occasionally; your child will enjoy pretending to be mean and angry! Your make-believe play also gives you many opportunities to introduce concepts concerning time and space. Although comprehending how to tell time is way beyond the capabilities of your 30-month-old, he may very well pick up a sense of "now" and "later" from your pretend-play scenarios. For instance, when the two of you have lined up long rows of action figures to assault the bad guys, you can catch his eye, give him a sweeping hand gesture, and toot out a pretend fanfare as you bellow, "Attack, now!" If he previously has found it difficult to wait to launch the attack, your shaking head, cautionary hand gesture, and conspiratorial whisper of "No—later!" has taught him that "later" is something he has to wait for.

If the character you are playing is an explorer going "far away to the North Pole," dramatically kiss your child good-bye, tearfully wave, and disappear into another room. "Far" thus becomes a label for a distance that's out of eyesight and earshot. The concept of "near" can be labeled and played out when your doll is afraid of the approaching big, bad wolf and wants to huddle "near" a Mommy or Daddy doll.

PLAYMATES AND IDEAS

You may still be the center of your child's universe, but if you haven't already, now is the time to start introducing him to a few other children his own age. Ideally you should aim for four or five one-on-one play dates a week in addition to preschool or group activities. These need not last for long periods of time. Sometimes one hour is just right, other times, longer.

If given the opportunity, children actually begin going beyond parallel play in the second year of life. Together with our colleague Billy Press, we've documented stages children go through in learning to enjoy each other. Between the ages of 12 and 16 months, sometimes earlier, they play near each other, but occasionally become curious about another child's toy, or brightly colored hair, which leads them to grab each other at times. This may result in some crying or squabbles, and sometimes a gentle poke or two.

Between 16 and 18 months, there is a gradual increase in wanting to do similar things. Children may follow each other down a low slide or show a subtle increase in emotional signaling as they move toy cars and trucks around. This often leads to copycat-type interactions consistent with the complex social problem-solving behaviors described in the preceding chapter. With this increase in imitation and emotional gesturing going on between children, by 18 months or so a wonderful sense of shared humor may start emerging. If one child makes a funny face or drops a toy, the other might laugh with glee, and soon both may be hamming it up, clearly having a great time together. At this age, children not only squabble but also help each other as they move big toys together, for example.

As they warm up to each new playmate or small group, children may work through earlier interactive steps. Two-year-olds may at first simply watch each other's antics, and then enjoy parallel, or side-by-side, play, even though they can already interact. Before too long they may show

Dos and Don'ts as You Raise the Bar

- *Don't* rely on puzzles, books, structured games, video-tapes, or TV. to spark your child's use of ideas.

- *Do* get down on the floor and become a character—such as a bear or wizard—in a pretend drama of your child's own choosing. Ham it up! Interact, talk, and emote through your character.

- *Do* hold long conversations about anything that interests your child, from a new toy to his favorite or most despised food. Use games, TV, and videos as a basis for long back-and-forth conversations rather than as ends in their own right.

more and more curiosity about each other and copy one another. Gradually, two-year-olds will begin interacting and getting involved in shared pretend play, particularly in small groups. Large groups tend to keep the interaction at a level of running around and trying out new toys with less sharing of ideas going on, because groups of that size tend to be a bit over-stimulating.

As toddlers' imagination and speech develops, social (or interactive) play will become more complex. Toddlers bounce ideas off one another and become actors in each other's dramas. Even if your toddler seems perfectly content to play "Let's pretend" games with you or your spouse, do try to expand his horizons by introducing him to little girls and boys his own age. After all, two-year-olds provide each other with feisty company. With so much fun at stake, your toddler will be motivated to cede control to others from time to time. He'll learn more about patience as he tolerates taking turns being the boss with his peers. Exploring the world of ideas with a playmate his own size will become a special delight and expand his social and intellectual abilities.

A very useful way to encourage peer as well as sibling play and interaction is to do group floor time. With you on the floor along with all your children or one of your children and one or a few peers, try orchestrating floor time in the following way: Each child gets to be the leader for 20 minutes, while the other children are actors or helpers in his drama. If a tea party is under way, the leader may decide to tell all the children where to sit and give them their teacups. If the leader decides to be Superman, you and your child's other siblings or friends might run and hide while the leader goes after all of you in hot pursuit.

Group floor time is a great activity for parents when all their children want their attention at the same time. In group floor time, all the children are involved all the time—even preverbal toddlers can be coaxed to hide with you! In addition, we've observed that with group floor-time experience, children learn to play with each other not only when an adult is present, but also when they are on their own.

ENGAGING THE ENTIRE MENTAL "TEAM" IN PEER PLAY AND GROUP FLOOR TIME

We have discussed creating activities where your child is simultaneously looking and doing, listening and talking, negotiating space, moving in ever more complex ways, and using his imagination and ideas, with strong guiding intentions, desires, and emotions. There is no better way to harness his mental "team" to work together under the direction of his own desires or emotions than when he is playing with peers or siblings. Certainly, sometimes peers or siblings should play on their own, away from their parents, since children are at times more fanciful and fun than Mom or Dad. Parents can pop in periodically to creatively foster an expansion of an activity the children are doing that involves a child's entire mental "team."

OVERCOMING CHALLENGES: A BLESSING IN DISGUISE

When toddlers have difficulties using one or more of their senses, or coordinating their muscles, it's harder for them to explore the world of make-believe. If they have problems in experiencing how something looks, sounds, tastes, smells, or feels to the touch, the multisensory pictures that become ideas in their minds may be less fully formed. It is harder for a child to hold on to these hazier mental images and then later manipulate them in imaginative ways during pretend play. For instance, if your two-and-a-half-year-old finds it relatively difficult to pick up visual cues, it will also be more difficult for him to retain a true mental image of an object's appearance. When the two of you decide to be pirates in search of buried treasure, he may have trouble pretending that yellow pop-beads in a box are golden pieces of eight. It's hard for him to hold a visual picture of real gold in his mind and thus pretend that beads are treasure. When he sees beads, he thinks beads. His visual challenge may make him cling to the concrete world.

A toddler who has a tough time comprehending or paying attention to certain sounds and voices might similarly form a less-than-complete multisensory image in his mind. His inability to fully comprehend the sound of your falsetto voice as you pretend to purr and meow like a kitty-cat would necessarily limit the scope of his concept of "kitten." His ideas about kittens might arise from petting their soft fur, being scratched by their claws, or noticing the way they pounce, but the sounds they make wouldn't be as significant a factor to him.

Furthermore, if your child finds it difficult to hear and repeat certain sounds like the purring of a cat, it will probably be harder to him to connect the actual sound of the word "cat" with the visual images in his mind. In short, a child has to be able to hear the sound of a word in his own mind or read it (when he is older and capable of reading) to integrate this element into the picture in his mind and form a full symbolic label. Although most children learn to use the shorthand of words through the aural channel, some who have trouble speaking or who have auditory-processing difficulties eventually learn to label a word by associating it with a picture. If these children are shown certain combinations of letters printed alongside a picture, eventually the letters coalesce into a kind of visual shorthand for all the multisensory images represented by the word, its illustration, and the actual object itself. This enables them to compensate for their difficulties in identifying the word from its sound. Such children may actually read certain words before they are able to say them. Fortunately, there are many ways to form full or complete images, and sometimes a challenge in one area actually leads to very creative capacities in others, such as developing a great eye for detail.

As you interact with your own toddler during these months, you may find that your child's physical profile sometimes can interfere with his enjoyment of your conversations together, or the times you spend playing make-believe. Even routine events may occasionally overwhelm him. Because he is a smart little person, he may want to either control or avoid those situations that are hard for him or that overload him. Let's take a look now at how the parents of Kara, Brian, Emma, Will, and Max are discovering new ways to work with their children's challenges and helping them discover the world of ideas.

TODDLERS WHO ARE SENSITIVE TO TOUCH AND SOUND

As Kara approached her third birthday, her parents Ellen and Steve increasingly had the sense that she was able to hold her own during playtimes with her older brother and sister. True, five-year-old Joey still enjoyed getting a rise out of her by making sure to let loose a few blood-curdling yells as the two of them moved action figures back and forth in elaborate patterns. He turned a deaf ear to Steve's insistence that he use an "inside," or quieter, voice as he played with Kara.

Although Kara was always interested in joining Joey's efforts to build block castles or create pretend tents out of bed sheets draped over card tables, she usually hesitated before plunging right into play. It was as if she were waiting for the other shoe to drop and for her brother to emit a bellow that would unnerve her. Because she was so sensitive and easily overwhelmed by certain sounds, Kara was cautious about exploring certain play themes that could lead to noisy interactions. In fact, she said "No!" in response to a lot of her brother's ideas, because she had to work so hard to stay organized and in control. This negativity naturally annoyed Joey, and spurred him on to spook her even more. All this limited the kinds of ideas and concepts that Kara could explore in her play with Joey.

Finally Ellen took Joey aside and struck a bargain with him: If he let Kara "be the noise boss" for a while, he could be the noise boss with Mom and Dad. Joey accepted his mother's challenge. Ellen then had a separate conversation with Kara. Since Kara's verbal skills were really blossoming now, her mother felt quite confident that she could follow the gist of her idea. She explained to her toddler that Joey would try to let Kara be in charge of how loud or piercing the sound effects would be during their make-believe games together. Kara was told that she could control just how loud or soft their two voices would be, just like Simon in Simon Says.

For instance, every time the noise level rose too high during the children's play together, Kara could place her forefinger to her lips in a shushing gesture that would be Joey's cue to quiet down. When the little girl felt ready for a little more noise, she could wave her arms back and forth like a band leader. She could dictate the terms of her noisy interactions with

Joey with the authority of a Simon, and Joey would try to follow her lead so he could really make noise with Mom and Dad.

Before too many pretend play sessions had come and gone, Kara was showing a new kind of confidence. Ellen noticed over the next week or so that Kara seemed more willing to turn the volume up a little when the make-believe action got heated. Since she felt more regulated and in control as she played with her brother, she was less cautious about exploring certain themes. In the past, she had seemed more drawn to the kind of quieter pretend play that Joey disdained. Her favorite make-believe games—holding tea parties and playing house—explored themes involving loving, nurturing, and sociability and only veered into scenarios with angry or aggressive feelings when Joey introduced them. Now it seemed as if Kara more frequently permitted one of her dolls to retaliate when her brother's tried to elbow past it. She was beginning, gingerly, to handle her troublesome hearing sensitivities by tolerating a wider range of noise, without falling back into negativity or avoidance.

Ellen and Steve were thrilled. Emboldened by their success, they decided to see whether Rachel, their eight-year-old, could also help her little sister explore a wider range of touches. The whole family was well aware of Kara's aversion to tickly touches, loose, floppy clothing, and nappy textures. Clearly Kara could benefit from some pretend play that gently nudged her into exploring a wider range of touches.

Ellen thought of an easy way to introduce a nubby new texture into the pretend play that Kara so enjoyed with her big sister Rachel. Rachel permitted Kara (albeit reluctantly) to join her as she played with her dolls and stuffed animals, but she always reserved the role of "teacher" for herself or for her favorite Raggedy Ann doll. Kara usually had to make do with pretending that one of her teddy bears was a "student." Ellen decided to buy a new rag doll and affix some Velcro strips to the top of its head and over its stuffed ears. She then cut out some brightly colored felt pieces in the shape of a hat, eyeglasses, and a mop of hair.

She gave the doll to Kara one day, excitedly announcing, "Now you have your own new doll for your own! See how you can put glasses on him, or give him some curly hair or a hat? Here's how you attach the pieces and take them off." Ellen realized that the scratchy feel of the Velcro would normally annoy Kara, but she was counting on her daughter's curiosity about the new toy to overcome her natural aversion to touching such a surface. Her instincts turned out to be right on target. Kara's pleasure in bright colors, her pride in having her own new doll, and her pleasure in playing make-believe with her big sister made her eagerly reach for the new toy.

At first she was somewhat tentative as she affixed and pulled off the felt pieces, but soon she was eagerly running to her sister's room to show off her new doll. Later that day Ellen saw both girls deeply engrossed in a make-believe game with the new doll taking center stage. Ellen was delighted to see how Kara nonchalantly tolerated the feel of the Velcro tape on her fingers as she stuck a hat on her doll and called out in a high, piping voice, "Time to go out and play!" Kara's interactions with her sister became more imaginative as she learned to incorporate more tactile sensations into her pretend play.

TODDLERS WHO ARE UNDERWHELMED BY THE WORLD AROUND THEM

Stuart couldn't help but notice that his son Brian, now 30 months old, seemed a little less mature than the other ten toddlers in his preschool class. Stuart volunteered to help out in the classroom each week, and he was beginning to get an uneasy sort of feeling when he saw how physically adept and chatty some of the other kids were. Just recently he had helped comfort a little girl who had tripped and fallen on the playground and was struck by her behavior. When she fell, she started wailing, "Ow, ow, ow, my knee!" and got up and headed right in his direction. Amid her whimpers she also made kissy noises to signify that she wanted a grown-up to "make it better." Brian had behaved very differently when he stubbed his toe and tumbled to the ground earlier that morning. He merely turned his head from side to side in search of his father, forlornly looked down at his foot, and started to cry.

Stuart felt disheartened by this clear evidence that his little boy's language skills and ability to plan out a number of actions weren't nearly as sophisticated as the other children's in Brian's group. Stuart and his wife, Tammy, had long recognized that their sweet-natured toddler was what the pediatrician referred to as a "low receiver and sender," or a child who seemed especially insulated from all but the most insistent cues from the outside world. They had conscientiously tried to crackle with enthusiasm as they interacted with their son, and indeed had managed to establish a warm connection with him. His quiet, shy smiles, cuddles, and lisping phrases reassured them that they were succeeding in drawing him out. However, seeing that such a gap remained between Brian's abilities and his peers' shook Stuart's confidence. After he shared his observations with his wife later that day, the two of them decided to talk with their developmental specialist.

The specialist quickly reassured both parents that Brian was making steady progress, and that their energized floor-time sessions with him had in fact sold him on the joys of interacting with people and things in the real world. Brian was now enjoying relationships and was a sturdy walker, although he still had a little trouble jumping and climbing. He could name most objects he saw around the house and at school, and seemed genuinely delighted when his parents took him to the park and he could slither down the slide.

But the specialist went on to say that the sort of challenges that Stuart had picked up on in the playground were typical of many toddlers with Brian's tendency to underreact to cues. He hastened to add that not only were there lots of pleasurable ways for Stuart and Tammy to further enliven their interactions with their child, but they could help him work on coordinating his muscles at the same time. The specialist reminded Brian's parents that if a toddler has problems performing one action after another (motor planning), he may also face difficulties when he wants to play pretend games.

For instance, even if such a child comes up with an idea to toddle over to a toy chest, dig out a new puppet from the bottom, and then tug the puppet over his hand, his low muscle tone and motor-planning challenges may make the task daunting. His legs and hands aren't easily able to implement his well-constructed plan. He might well wind up cutting the motor pattern short and simply go to the toy chest and pause wearily. It wouldn't be surprising if frustration were to set in, and his behavior dissolved into a series of aimless, disconnected motions. The toddler would have to think through all these planned behaviors, whereas other children his age are able to translate their wish automatically into action. Indeed, many toddlers with this type of motor planning problem may gradually give up on expressing their imaginations.

It was thus doubly important to help strengthen Brian's motor-planning abilities. His parents' aim was to help him learn to further interact physically with his peers and to help him build up his social skills and self-confidence. It was even more crucial that Brian feel as free as possible to act out a wide range of themes, ideas, and feelings during pretend play and to use his body and muscles, even though it was often difficult. To a large extent, his ability to explore emotional ideas rested on his muscles' ability to string various actions together. After all, how much spark or creativity could emerge during the little fellow's pretend play if it was just too hard to jump down from a pillow fort and rescue the toy bears who were being threatened by a giant? Being stuck on top of the fort, or frozen on the side of the playground, was hard for a toddler as full of sweetness and untapped zest as Brian.

With the therapist's help, Stuart and Tammy came up with a two-pronged approach that would help their little boy stretch both physically and mentally. First of all, the therapist reminded Brian's parents that his flexor (bending) muscles were easier for him to use than his extensors (muscles that keep him erect). He needed to experience a few physical challenges during their pretend play sessions together that would subtly steer him toward using those extensor muscles in a series of actions. Tammy immediately came up with a make-believe scenario that she was sure would capture Brian's interest.

Brian always brightened up during their trips to the grocery store. There's no telling why this particular excursion always seemed to break through his usual reserve; perhaps his enthusiasm could be traced to the bright lights, colorful boxes and fruit displays, Tammy's animated chatter, or even the free sugar cookie that the lady in the bakery gave him. Tammy had a hunch that with a toy shopping cart and a selection of empty cereal boxes and milk cartons set up in their playroom, it would be easy to help Brian weave together a make-believe story in which he had to "shop" for different items in a specific order.

To give Brian's extensor muscles a workout at the same time, the therapist proposed putting some of the cereal boxes up on a shelf that Brian could reach only by picking up and moving a low step stool. Once the props were in place and the store was set up, the therapist cautioned, it was important for Tammy to remember to let Brian take charge of the fantasy. She should be as enthusiastic as possible, and speak in clear and insistent tones to catch his attention. If Brian were to become cranky or throw a temper tantrum, Tammy was urged to remain unintimidated. She could retreat a little and tone down the intensity of their interaction if her toddler should become temporarily overwhelmed. With an underreactive child, it's always better to err on the side of lively interaction. As long as Tammy remained soothing and empathetic, she should simply accept such ups and downs as part of the process of trying to help her little boy use his body more.

The therapist also reminded Tammy to be sure to break down all the many related actions involved in shopping into smaller parts. Brian needed to be reassured that all the pushing, reaching, and stretching motions he observed as his mother pretended to shop were easily imitatable. The therapist suggested that Tammy push the cart together with Brian for a while as they played. She could then show him how to fetch the step stool whenever their pretend game called for reaching an item that was perched up high. The key was to practice each step involved in the pattern of actions until the child had it down pat before adding another to the sequence, and making sure to let the child take charge of the drama.

The therapist went on to suggest a number of games, including "airplane," that would improve Brian's muscle tone even as he actively participated in make-believe. Stuart was instructed to hoist Brian up and have the toddler wrap his legs around his father's waist. With his arms supporting his son's hips, Stuart could spin around in a circle until Brian's torso was nearly horizontal to the ground. The toddler could then direct the speed of the imaginary airplane ride ("Go faster, Daddy!" or "Slow down!") or decide whether they should fly out to see Uncle Dave in New York or Grandma in Chicago.

A second activity that would tap into Brian's active imagination while giving his extensor muscles a good workout involved running games. Story lines could be worked into parent-child chases in which good guys could be in hot pursuit of villains, or a giant could race Jack to the beanstalk. If Brian could be cajoled into frequently changing the direction in which he was running during these chase games, his extensors would eventually become strengthened and he would enjoy his physical activities more. The therapist suggested having both Tammy and Stuart simultaneously join in on the fun, perhaps pretending to be two hounds, so that Brian could be the canny little fox who manages to escape them both by repeatedly switching directions. He reminded them to let Brian "beat" them most of the time, by giving him certain advantages. (As long as a child sees adults playing at full tilt he'll usually feel that the competition is legitimate, and lots of fun, too.)

Tammy and Stuart were eager to go home and try these activities. They were encouraged and were looking forward to helping Brian assertively use his muscles as he explored a world of ideas.

TODDLERS WHO CRAVE SENSATION

The video taken at Emma's third birthday party captured all of this toddler's wonderful but exhausting energy on tape. When it was time to blow out her birthday candles, there was Emma standing up on her chair seat, conducting a chorus of "Happy Birthday to You" like a maestro. During the peanut hunt in the park Emma sped by in a veritable whirl of motion. The camera went on to record her angry protests and attempts to elude her father Mike's arms as he corralled all the children when it was time to leave the park. Later on in the tape, Emma's mother, Laura, gently spun the blindfolded toddler in a circle before setting her off in the direction of a pin-the-tail-on-the-donkey poster. Emma kept right on spinning and spinning until she collapsed on the floor in a dizzy heap.

None of this came as a surprise. Because it was difficult for this toddler to process mild sensations, she was constantly on the move in search of more experiences and more intense feelings. Laura and Mike were at a loss when it came to figuring out how to relate to their rambunctious three-year-old without squelching any of her wonderful spirit. They were thrilled by her growing conversational skills but dismayed by her bossiness. She frequently barked at them ("That's 'nuff, 'nuff—go away! Now!") like a drill sergeant. Although she enjoyed playing pretend games and building block towers, Emma didn't seem to be able to stay very long at any one theme or task. Her middle-aged parents were desperate for a little more downtime with their daughter. As Mike put it, "We're not looking for miracles here. Emma's the light of our lives but it's as if she expects every day to be a three-ring circus!"

Emma's nursery school teacher pointed out that more talk and less action seemed to help the toddler develop a less frenzied and more reflective attitude. For instance, every time Emma clamored to have the teacher fetch a different stuffed animal and become one of the characters in her make-believe games, it seemed as if she was accustomed to receiving a quick "yes" or "no" for an answer. (As a matter of fact, Laura and Mike sometimes said "yes" when they wanted to say "no" simply because they lacked the energy to face her anger.) The teacher mentioned that she had started to handle Emma's demands a little differently. Instead of going to fetch another play animal, she would ask Emma, "How come we need another animal in our game? What's he going to do?" Emma would seem to take a moment and reflect on the meaning of the words. As she considered the images created by these words, Emma slowed down her usual shift into action and operated in the world of ideas for a while. She would then tell her teacher why the new pretend figure was needed.

If Emma were to gain more practice in manipulating ideas in her head, she might be more likely to savor mental workouts like playing "Let's pretend." She would be able to satisfy some of her cravings for new experience and feelings by exploring different options in fantasy. She might thus reduce her need to act on and control the real world quite so much. Her taut and springy muscles would still compel her to "shake her willies out," as the song says, but a more active life of the mind would satisfy some of her need for increased sensation and at the same time help her learn to pause, ponder, and communicate.

Indeed, Emma could be active *while* she played imaginatively. If she were to run after an imaginary unicorn who had magical powers, for example, Emma could be moving and exploring ideas at the same time. As she combined action and ideas together in a drama, she would eventually learn to modulate and regulate those actions because she might decide, with a challenge from another pretend character, to slow down to give the unicorn some water, or speed up to rub the imaginary animal's golden horn for good luck. Her pretend play could thus simultaneously be both action- and idea-oriented.

Laura began to notice that whenever she and Emma ran around in the park, or whenever she helped her daughter climb on the monkey bars, the pretend games that they played out once they were back home seemed a little calmer and lasted longer, too. The vigorous motor activities seemed to help Emma become more organized and centered, and reduced her need to expend so much muscle energy during pretend play. It freed up her ability to also enjoy the mental manipulation of ideas.

Since Emma was a little girl who craved activity, during pretend play her parents found ways to challenge her imagination in action-oriented dramas. Superhero dolls could climb up to the tops of mountains to rescue people from roaring dragons, rather than have the dolls reenact little tea parties. It's not very satisfying for an action-oriented child like Emma who's so full of vim and vigor to simply play out quiet domestic scenes. Her parents could use this preference for action-filled play to whet her interest in the world of make-believe, and over time balance it with some quieter tea-party fun, too.

Laura and Mike realized that they now had some tools to help their little girl become more engrossed in whimsical themes and emotional ideas. If they could successfully get her to weigh the pros and cons of a certain course of action, or to express her opinions or emotions with words or through pretend play, she would finally be able to pause long enough to take note of the sights and sounds that surrounded her. She would be able to derive a new kind of pleasure out of being able to see and hear some of the ideas, themes, and feelings that were coursing through her mind actually played out in her make-believe dramas. Although she still relied on lively interactions with her parents to deliver many of the sensations she so craved, Emma should soon be able to "stop and smell the roses" and use her imagination in richer ways.

TODDLERS WHO TAKE IN SIGHTS, BUT TUNE OUT SOUNDS

Will was nearly three years old now, and although he was still a man of few words, he was steadily bolstering his reputation as a junior architect and military strategist. His parents, Lisa and Dan, marveled at his skill and patience in crafting block forts in which he waged imaginary battles between good-guy and bad-guy action figures. Will loved it when his parents moved the figures through their paces with him, and the action during his pretend play seemed to be fueled by a variety of themes and ideas. Will would cuddle wounded figures, and resolutely march his heroes to the top of his towers. He was busy exploring such themes as nurturance, assertiveness, and aggressiveness. When his mother's or father's facial expressions broadcast the dismay, fear, or delight that their characters in the drama were feeling, Will would respond appropriately and frequently steer the action in a new direction.

It was clear to Lisa and Dan that Will was learning to act out his ideas and feelings during pretend play, and that he was very responsive to their visual overtures. However, sometimes their little toddler would simply bang his figures into their own when he became frustrated, rather than try to talk for his toys or express what he was thinking about out loud. Although he would occasionally produce a few appropriate sound effects ("Bam! Bam!" and triumphant "Ta-dah!"'s) as the make-believe unfolded, for the most part Will remained pretty quiet and only rarely tried to verbally engage his parents or the characters they portrayed.

Although Lisa and Dan tried to accompany their characters' actions with animated words and avoided using rapid-fire commands as they interacted with Will, he still seemed overloaded by quick conversational back-and-forth's. Will's parents had long been aware that it was much harder for their son to pay attention to auditory signals than to visual cues. Ironically, however, during the past few months Will did use certain verbal expressions with startling accuracy. He could be heard exclaiming "Dammit!" and "Oh, hell!" whenever his block towers toppled. Toddlers with auditory difficulties often mimic the swear words they overhear, even when they seem to avoid using other words, because those particular sounds are usually uttered during emotionally charged moments. These words and phrases make a big impression on the child because he associates the lively sounds with energized voices and faces and an exciting situation. He also gets a sense that certain words are taboo and enjoys being a little provocative. Fortunately, Will also sprinkled other more socially acceptable dramatic expressions into his conversations. His parents found that he repeated phrases like "Oh my goodness!" and "Wowee!" when he interacted with his playmates.

Dan became aware that he had been so careful to avoid overwhelming Will with his own noisy ebullience that he had almost exclusively geared his play to the toddler's strong visual sense and well-developed fine motor skills. Dan realized that he could now start helping Will express some of the ideas and images that flit across his mind as the two of them played. By keeping his words and phrases simple, but emotionally charged and meaningful, Dan could gently help Will to respond in character to the action unfolding right in front of him. For instance, when one of Dan's action figures chased up a block tower on the heels of one of his son's figures and growled "Move over, bud!" the figure could refuse to budge until Will responded verbally in some way. "No, go 'way!" would be a fine retort. The drama's in-your-face action would most likely compel the child to use words. By helping to set up a make-believe situation in which Will's desires were being thwarted by another character in the drama, Dan was increasing the likelihood that his son would use words to express his feelings about the action that was underway. Rather than simply listening to his own thoughts, or physically acting them out, Will would be able to see the immediate power that his own words had to convey an idea. The more such situations Dan could set up, the more practice Will would get in picking up verbal cues. The more cues Will picked up, the richer his mental images, or ideas, would become, and his imagination would really take off.

It is not surprising for toddlers like Will, who have difficulty taking in what another person is saying, to alternate between being aloof and provocative. Lisa mentioned her concerns about his stubbornness to her own mother during a phone conversation. "When it's time to go outside, and I tell him to go to the closet and get his coat and then wait for me while I lock up the back door, he'll sometimes look right at me as if I hadn't said anything at all. Other times he'll just plop down on his bottom and refuse to budge. When I tell him to go down to the playroom and put the blocks in the bin and the stuffed animals on the shelf, he'll pull the same stunt."

Lisa's mother reassured her that she was a gentle and supportive mom, and that it surely wasn't the tone of her voice that was getting Will's back up. It seemed more likely that the toddler was losing focus when too many words representing more than a single idea were coming at him. Her mother urged her to simplify, simplify, simplify: "Just ask him to do one thing at a time. Shorten your instructions!"

If instructions are broken down into stages, and commands are energized or charged with more emotion, it is easier for a child like Will to hold the sounds of the words in his head long enough to comprehend them. For example, when it was time to clean up his toys, instead of giving him a stream of instructions Lisa could break down her instructions into simple questions that were uttered in a lighthearted tone: "Where's the block box, big boy?" or "Which shelf do the puppets go on, Silly Willy?" Once Will responded with just a word or a phrase, Lisa could go on with her next cleanup instruction. Eventually more complex instructions could be strung together.

This same process could be used when ideas are exchanged during pretend play games. Lisa had long ago realized that a suggestion like "Hey Will, why don't you have Barney teach all your bears and monkeys how to climb a tree so they can spy on the creepy new neighbors?" would only bring a blank look from her little boy. Such a proposal contains too many sounds, too many ideas, and too many linked behaviors for Will to absorb. By breaking down requests or questions into simple, doable pieces, however, Lisa found that she could help Will understand. "Hey Will, where's Barney?" could be an opening question, and when he replied by word or gesture, a follow-up could be "Okay, what is Barney going to do?"

In fact, as Will became more adept at simple phrases, his mom began a game that took advantage of his motivation. Whenever he really wanted something, like to "Go out!", Lisa would announce that she needed a few things, like her "gloves and hat," and eventually her "coat, purse, gloves, and hat" in order to go out with him. With practice and over time, Will would surely grow more adept in holding these kinds of linked ideas and instructions in his mind and all those words would no longer feel like such an overwhelming barrage of sound.

TODDLERS WHO TAKE IN SOUNDS, BUT HAVE A HARD TIME FIGURING OUT SIGHTS

At two-and-a-half Max was a real chatterbox. As he went about his busy day, he kept up a running commentary about what he had eaten for lunch, how he could pull his big-boy pants up and down by himself, when was it time to go to the store, and where his new shoes were. Lynn and Jonathan were charmed by his loquaciousness but occasionally felt that their son was a little too "wound up." More often than not, Max's pretend play would randomly lurch from one theme to another. A story line about a lion roaring in the zoo would suddenly switch to a fantasy involving a baby pig looking for its mommy, which might then switch to a dress-up game. Max's pretend play was looking a little fragmented—especially when his parents compared it to the logical, fluid quality of his conversation—and they weren't sure what to make of it.

When Lynn and Jonathan next met with their developmental specialist and described Max's behavior, the therapist reiterated just how hard it was for their little boy to process, or comprehend, complex sights. He reminded them to take advantage of Max's wonderful verbal skills as a way to enter into pretend play with him, but to recognize that he needed more practice in picturing his ideas and feelings. He explained that children with visual/spatial challenges like Max's may well turn from one play theme to another in rapid succession because they can't create a picture of the whole forest and therefore flit from tree to tree.

For instance, when Max's eyes would dart away from the sight of his favorite lion toy and his eyes would next alight on a pig bath toy, a new story line would emerge that bore no relationship to the earlier sight of the lion. For a child like Max, whose visual attention jumps from one image to another, the challenge is to help him begin relating these images one to the other. The therapist suggested that Lynn and Jonathan deliberately try and reintroduce forgotten objects into his play. They would thus be able to help Max associate a number of different images by keeping older images alive even after he's turned his attention to newer ones.

For example, should Max discard his lion toy, forget about roaring, and begin to oink like the pig he next spies, his parent could continue to roar like a lion and ask the pig what happened to the lion and explore whether or not he could join in on the play, too. If the animal play immediately morphs into a game in which the toddler tries on Dad's shoes and hats, his mother or father could playfully put the plastic pig inside of one of Dad's shoes and ask with a piggylike grunt whether the shoes were a good fit. The key thing was to help Max keep various visual images a little fresher in his mind for longer periods of time, and to challenge him to truly observe and connect the mental pictures.

Although Max needed more practice in picturing things, he was also very sensitive to intense visual images that were particularly colorful or bright. It was therefore important to avoid overloading him with fleeting visual images that were too complex or scary. Make-believe dramas that featured masks or contorted facial features might well frighten and intimidate him. He needed to approach such images slowly and with emotional support so that he could digest them.

Max needed to develop abilities for observing his environment, and for solving visual and spatial problems. One technique the therapist suggested involved emphasizing play that builds visual skills during their make-believe sessions together. For instance, if Max decided to act out the story of Little Red Riding Hood and to take the starring role, Jonathan could first problem-solve with him and ask where he, the Big, Bad Wolf, should be hiding out. Should he be over there, behind the door? Or hunkering down in bed? Or lurking behind a tree? As they discussed various options, Max would be forming visual images of these locations in his mind before he weighed in with his first choice for the site of the ambush.

Another way to help Max become comfortable with different kinds of sights would be to use a variety of visually interesting props during pretend play. The therapist suggested that Lynn could do such things as put masking tape on the floor to make railroad tracks or roads, pretend that shining flashlights are lightning flashes during a big storm, or make-believe that bouncing tennis balls are frisky frogs leaping out of a pond. All of these visual attractions would help Max get tuned in and oriented toward following the action with his eyes.

Yet another way for Max to get some playful practice in navigating across space would be to offer him some make-believe opportunities to explore and go find things. Obstacle courses and treasure hunts provide lots of chances to figure out how to climb from one level to another, or how to search for objects by following visual and verbal cues. As long as Max was encouraged to launch a make-believe drama of his own choosing, his parents should feel free to challenge him with subplots and asides that would give him extra practice in incorporating his visual sense into his pretend play.

Lynn and Jonathan were able to come up with several other make-believe activities that gave their son a good visual/motor workout. The next time Max collected all of his colorful stuffed animals together for a pretend birthday celebration, Lynn or Jonathan could announce that "the brown guys are mad at the green and red guys because they had to eat spinach instead of cake and ice cream at the birthday party. They refuse to sit next to each other at the table!" Max would be likely to get up and help organize the toys by their color even as he helped stitch together another episode in this make-believe story.

"Looking and doing" games, in which Nerf balls could be flying squirrels that have to be batted or kicked away, and balance-beam exercises in which the participants pretend to be explorers crossing a raging river could also help to strengthen their toddler's visual/motor skills. Dancing and simplified versions of sports that involved looking and doing, such as soccer, baseball, dodge ball, and the like, would also help, especially if the ball was big enough for Max to have the satisfaction of connecting with it and seeing it fly from his bat or his foot. Max's pleasure in moving his body and using his facile tongue would hopefully ease him into trusting his challenged visual sense and making it a more integral part of his fantasy play.

FAMILY CHALLENGES TO EXPLORING IDEAS

Now that your toddler can use words to express himself during pretend play, there's a new clarity in your relationship. To some degree, The two of you are literally speaking the same language. For some of us, however, knowing what's really on our toddler's mind can at times be upsetting. While one parent may take delight in their two-and-a-half-year-old's torrent of questions, another may feel suffocated. Some parents become worried when their toddlers express aggressive or angry themes during their make-believe games together. Others may become confused when their child labels body parts, including the genitals. In short, your child's new ease in expressing himself is sometimes at odds with your own ideas, leading you to overcontrol, withdraw, or feel anxious.

A Need for Order

Take a moment or two and consider what makes you feel secure in various situations. Do you feel most in control, and therefore most relaxed, when rules are followed and everything's in its right place? Or do you think of yourself as more of a free spirit who enjoys spontaneity? If you fall into the former category, don't be surprised if your own need for order and structure increases your toddler's defiance. During your pretend play-times together, you may find yourself steering the action to create more orderly, logical story lines. Try instead to use your skills in organization to follow your child's lead and see how his creative pieces may eventually have a theme to them.

On the other hand, if you tend to float too many free-spirited ideas during pretend play, you may find that you are inadvertently making it difficult for both you and your child to see the forest for the trees. Your own creativity may overload your child's emerging creativity. You can try to slow it down a bit.

Some parents are particularly concrete, or reality-bound, and have actually forgotten how to play make-believe. They may be happy to sit down and piece together a puzzle with their toddlers, however, or companionably look at picture books. Such parents may be more than willing to patiently read nursery rhyme after nursery rhyme, or to point out various numbers and letters to their child. Although these activities are usually pleasurable experiences for both parents and children, they are not substitutes for floor-time fantasy play!

When you feel uncomfortable with free-wheeling fantasy, it may be tempting to retreat to quiet, more orderly pastimes. After all, you know that your child enjoys the closeness you share as you read together or build block towers. But do try to engage your child in the realm of make-believe, too. He needs your active involvement in playing a full range of "Let's pretend" games. The two of you can learn to pretend together. Let him teach you!

If your child gets angry sometimes, don't overpersonalize his negativity—he's just trying to get you to play with him the only way he knows how. If you don't greet his tantrums with dismay or anger that matches his own, they will tend to subside more rapidly. Instead, try sending him a warm look, and then suggest some floor-time pretend games. Let him be the boss and let him assign you a role in the drama: "Tell me who to be today, sweetheart. Should I be the Lion King or Curious George?" In short, once you recognize that you feel more comfortable when you're not pretending with your child, try to get down on the floor with him and relax anyway. Then open the gates to some unstructured, silly interaction. You might learn to enjoy it if you are very patient with yourself.

UNCOMFORTABLE THEMES

Let's assume that unlike the parents discussed above, you consider yourself to be pretty flexible. You love to put on puppet shows and stage domestic dramas with your child. You may really let your hair down during pretend play and have no problem letting your toddler direct the show. Most parents, for example, are very comfortable exploring themes involving dependency as they play pretend games with their toddlers. We thrill to see our three-year-old tenderly kiss a doll or enact a story about a Mommy dog nurturing her puppies, because we recognize that we've succeeded in giving our child the precious ability to love and care for others. Still, if you're like most of the rest of us, there will be certain emotional or thematic hot buttons that you won't want your toddler to push during your make-believe times together. When the pretend play veers toward hurting and mayhem, for example, you may feel the urge to steer it back to calmer waters.

It's important to ask yourself, "What emotional areas are my own hot buttons?" Be honest with yourself, and pin down whether you have trouble with anger, sexual excitement, assertiveness, aggression, or even dependency. How do you relate to your spouse when you become aware of these feelings in yourself? Is it easier for you to walk away and avoid uncomfortable situations, rather than use words to explore your thoughts and feelings? As you become aware of your own personal hesitancies in certain emotional areas, you'll probably realize that you may be inadvertently communicating a silent message to your child that certain thoughts or feelings are best dealt with by trying to ignore them.

If this is the case, make a special point to learn about those very same themes during pretend play with your child. He needs practice in learning about various feelings, and it's clear that you do, too. Pretend play gives you both permission to try on different emotions for size, and in doing so you'll both gain confidence in experiencing and expressing a fuller range of human emotions. Even if you continue to find it difficult to explore certain themes with any gusto, the mere fact that you're willing to let your child lead you into those areas during your make-believe play together will permit your little boy to explore, and eventually understand, a wider world of ideas.

HOW PRETEND PLAY CAN
PREPARE FOR CHALLENGES

One often-overlooked tool in every parent's coping arsenal is using pretend play as a way to help your child anticipate an upcoming crunch point. You can employ make-believe dramas for problem solving on an emotional theme that you know will soon be challenging your child, whether it's the imminent birth of a sibling, an approaching separation from a parent, or even a scheduled trip to the doctor or dentist. Pretend play can serve as a kind of dress rehearsal for real-life events.

Perhaps the most common event that upsets your three-year-old involves leaving him with a baby-sitter, or dropping him off at Grandma and Grandpa's for a few hours. During the days before the big event, you might try to insert this into your make-believe games and see what your child does with it. Explore how various stuffed animals feel when Mommy bear goes shopping. Consider what Grandpa Bear could do to make the other animals feel better. Then go out and have yourself some fun!

CREATING IDEAS

Now's the time to help your child tell you what he want or thinks, and to become a partner in his emerging make-believe play. You can pretend to be a puppy, or talk for a puppy puppet, and ask your child for a hug or a kiss or a dog bone, for example. You can also open up conversations with him about his desires and wishes, and ask, "What do you want to drink, milk or juice?" His reply of "Juice" could be met by your eager head nod and response of "Let's go and get it! Show me where to go." As he answers, "There, Mommy," while pointing toward the refrigerator, he'll know that he can get his needs met by interacting with you.

FUN AND GAMES

🐛 *Let's Chitchat*

Using your child's natural interests, see how many back-and-forth circles of communication you can get going using words, phrases, or short sentences. You can even turn your child's single-word response into a long chat. For instance, when your child points to the door and says, "Open," you might reply, "Who should open it?" He's likely to say, "Mommy do it," and you could shake your head from side to side and say, "Mommy can't now. Who else?" He'll probably turn to his father and ask, "Daddy do it?" Daddy might reply, "Do what?" When your child once again points to the door and says, "Open, open!" Daddy can walk toward him saying, "Okay, can you help me push the door open?" With his eager head nod, your little boy will be closing this long sequence of back-and-forth words and gestures.

🐛 *Let's Pretend*

Become a dog or cat or superhero in a drama of your child's own choosing. Ham it up and see how long you can keep it going!

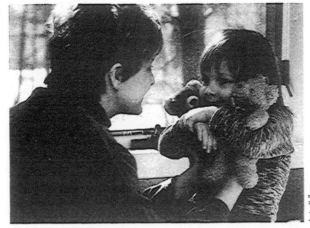

Janice Fullman

6

STAGE SIX:
BUILDING BRIDGES
BETWEEN IDEAS

WHAT THIS STAGE IS ALL ABOUT

By the time your child is three or four years old, she's moved way beyond some of the endearing behaviors of her babyhood and become increasingly comfortable sharing ideas with you that seem startlingly mature. You'll actually find yourself having debates with your little girl and suddenly realizing, "Gee, she made a good point!" Before too long, your child will start peppering you with "Why?"'s, "How come?"'s, and "Because"'s. She'll be supporting her wishes and desires with real evidence, and will require you to do the same. When you present her with some cooked spinach for dinner, for example, she may very well wrinkle up her nose in disgust and scornfully announce, "I don't like this stupid spinach because it looks yucky and it'll make me sick!" Between the ages of 30 and 48 months, she will gradually show you that she can connect one idea to another in a meaningful and logical manner. In the years ahead, achieving this exciting new milestone will support her ability to reason, to study, and eventually to work in a complex society.

When your child says, "I want to go outside", and you reply, "Why?, you are giving her a chance to logically tie her ideas to yours with a reason: "Because I want to play with my friend." Just a year ago, when she looked at you and implored, "Go out?" and you asked her, "Why?" she would simply reiterate, "Go out, go out, go out!" She wasn't able yet to connect her ideas to yours. At first blush, this ability to link her idea to yours, or string together two or three of her own ideas, may seem like a fairly simple accomplishment. However, when you stop and consider all the ramifications of this ability, it turns out to be a monumental stepping stone toward mature, rational thinking.

Your child is not only learning to be logical as she discusses her current desire to go outside or to get some juice. She is also learning to build bridges between her ideas in terms of a sense of time. The past, present, and future are starting to make more sense to her. When she asks to go outside, and you answer, "Not now, sweetheart," she's likely to counter with "When? When?" Your reply of "Give me fifteen minutes and we'll go as soon as you hear the buzzer on the washing machine" will probably be met with a wailing "No, no, NOW! No waiting!" This capacity to link her ideas to yours in terms of future or past behaviors doesn't develop overnight, but will become more and more apparent during the coming year.

Your child will also become increasingly adept at linking her ideas and yours in terms of space, or near and far. When she asks, "Where are you going?" and you say, "I'm going to the store," she might absently nod and be left with a comfortable feeling that you'll be back soon. Since she's been to the store with you many times before, she understands that it's nearby. She knows the difference between going to the store and going to Grandpa's house, which is very far away. In fact, if you tell her that you're going to Grandpa's she's likely to look more distressed and start protesting, "No, no, don't go!" or "Take me, take me!"

Your child is also learning to make connections between ideas that convey feelings. She may disarmingly ask, "Why are you sad?" when you look forlorn. She can also tell you why she is mad at her brother: "He took my doll and I want it back!"

During these months your child is also coming to understand events from many points of view at the same time. Even her daily activities are no longer viewed from one simple perspective, as they were in the past. At the age of two, when she was confronted with new objects she either liked them or she didn't. A cookie was yummy or it was yucky. Now, however, she has a far more complex relationship to the cookie and is able to ask herself, "How many cookies am I going to get from Daddy now, and when am I going to get more from him?" Your child can link two or three ideas into a unified thought: "I like cookies and they make me feel happy," or "The grocery store is nearby so it's easy for us to get more cookies." Even something as seemingly unidimensional as a cookie is now understood from many angles at once.

Like the blind men who each tried to describe an elephant after feeling different parts, a little child may be able to perceive only one part of the animal. However, when she grows older she is able to see the whole elephant because she can move around it and observe how all the different parts are connected. She need only glance at the elephant's trunk to remember where its ears, legs, and eyes are. As the child becomes able to connect ideas together, even the tiniest feature or event can evoke a more complex awareness of the world. Her ability to bridge ideas lays the foundation for what most adults think of as academic-type intelligence and its various components, such as reading comprehension, scientific reasoning, analytic skills, and the ability to self-reflect.

Your child's new experiences and mental abilities are linked to old ones. She is busy taking in experience through all that she tastes, hears, smells, and sees, and through what she feels and what she does. As she absorbs new pieces of information every second of every day, the information is combined with how she feels and what has just happened and what happened six months ago and with what will probably happen tomorrow. Not only can she connect all of her experiences together over time and space and through all her feelings and senses, but she also can recombine these ideas in an infinite number of ways. Your child's understanding of the world is mushrooming at an astonishing rate!

Another metaphor that captures the fantastic interrelatedness between all the thoughts that are now forming in your child's mind is an architectural one. Just as new cities require transportation, communication, energy, and many other interlinked systems so they can function as an organic whole, so your child's mind needs a variety of mental bridges to expedite, link, and create new thoughts. As you help her connect up various thoughts and feelings by interacting with her in longer and longer dialogues, she rapidly builds her own highways and byways. This mental infrastructure will provide her with the basis for understanding, and perhaps even changing, her world.

It's probably already obvious to you that your role during this stage of your child's development is a most critical one. You're about to become a debating partner, opinion seeker, and collaborator in exploring the world. This may seem like a tall order, and you're probably saying to yourself, "Hold up just a minute here; my head can only hold so many hats! It's difficult enough being a nurturer, reading my baby's facial expressions, and responding back in an animated way. As far as pretend play goes, I never thought I'd have to do that again! Now you're asking me to be a debater, negotiator, and structural engineer. That sure wasn't in the job description!" The good news is that most parents, educators, day-care providers and others who interact on a daily basis with children will realize that they're already doing a lot of what we're describing here without really thinking about it. And enjoying it, too!

Some parents find that this is in fact their favorite period during the preschool years, because they can have long and satisfying conversations with their children. Those who don't enjoy talking as much may find this stage more of a challenge. But in the final analysis there's really only one simple principle that parents need to keep in mind as they help their children master this new developmental level: Try to have longer and longer conversations with your child about everything she is interested in, and try to help her create conversations that make sense.

For instance, if your child is busy building a case for why she should be allowed to stay up a little later, try to patiently listen to all her reasons. If her arguments don't make sense, challenge her with a gleam in your eye to give you another reason. Try to be proactive, too, in seeking out her opinions about things, rather than simply testing her familiarity with various facts. If the two of you are admiring her new box of crayons, don't limit your comments to asking her to identify whether a shade is blue or green. Instead, ask her which color she likes best, and why. In this way she'll gain practice in building bridges between her ideas—*to think*. If you mistakenly place too much emphasis on having her parade her knowledge of facts, she'll simply be recalling isolated little words rather than learning to put two ideas together.

Your child's ability to exchange ideas with you concerning her own opinions and interests will become a new way for her to experience your warmth, closeness, and nurturing, along with the cuddling and kisses that have been part of your relationship since she was born. This new type of intimacy will bring joy to you, too. The persistent delight your child shows as she quizzes you about what she sees, hears, touches, and smells will be contagious. Her openness to new experiences will reawaken your own awareness of what is beautiful and strange in the world.

REALITY TESTING

During the past three years or so, the two of you have interacted in countless ways. Your intimate glances, gestures, conversations, negotiations, debates, and pretend games have gradually taught your child how to connect her ideas to your own. She's motivated to do this because she receives tremendous satisfaction in expressing herself, and in being understood by you. Even when the two of you spin out silly or fantastic story lines as you play make-believe, your logical two-way dialogues cause your child to consider your wishes, thoughts, and feelings as she responds to you.

This experience of exchanging emotional ideas during everyday chitchats and pretend play while remaining tuned in to the logical rhythm of conversation helps your child distinguish between what is real and what is not. This ability, which we call reality testing, will pave the way for all of her higher-level thinking skills. She'll rely on reality testing each time she has to do such things as correct her own math paper or search for the underlying meaning of a story. Her ability to reason stems from years of experience in bouncing her emotional ideas off something outside herself—you. Not surprisingly, the ability to connect "my" idea to "your" idea, as in "Why do you say 'no'?—I want to stay up!," is a bridge between what's inside and subjective, and what's outside and objective. Therefore, your child's ability to organize her experiences in the world in terms of a "me" and a "you," or "not-me," enables her to bridge her inner world of stored experiences and feelings with the outer, objective world that you represent.

EMOTIONAL THINKING

Up until this point in her development, your child's ideas were like separate little balloons of thought. She was able to visualize these multisensory images, or ideas, and could act them out using pretend play or words. Still, her ideas remained somewhat piecemeal and fragmented.

Years of exchanging logical, reciprocal gestures and comments with you, however, are now starting to ground her in reality. Her separate ideas are beginning to gel into sequenced thoughts. As you play pretend games together and engage her in reality-based conversation, she will begin to see that her balloons (ideas) and yours can be linked. One way you'll be helping her connect all the disparate parts of her pretend dramas will be to step right into a make-believe role yourself, and pose questions that help link up the various trial balloons your child has floated.

Sometimes your child will link her ideas to yours if your pretend-play character makes a statement that's a little over the top. If the two of you are packing for a make-believe trip to the beach and your doll announces, "Don't forget to bring your earmuffs and boots with you! All the fancy people wear them on the beach," your child will probably pick up on the absurdity of your doll's suggestion. Her doll might retort, "You're so silly! Nobody wears earmuffs on the beach. They wear bathing suits!" or perhaps she'll play along and giggle. In other words, friendly disagreements, as well as a shared sense of the absurd, can become a good basis for your discussions together. You needn't barrage your child with a string of questions to get her in the habit of cause-and-effect thinking.

With more and more practice in creating her own logical, sequenced links to your thoughts, your child's pretend dramas and real-life conversations will grow increasingly elaborate. As long as she tries to connect her thoughts to yours in a way that makes sense (even if her thoughts are wildly imaginative!), she's well on her way to becoming a logical thinker. She'll start negotiating her relationship with you in a more reality-based way, and will look to you for help in solving practical problems, asking, "Can I do this?" or "Will you get mad if I kick the ball inside the house?"

Remember, too, that as your little girl experiences the sights, sounds, touches, and physical aspects of things, she is simultaneously registering an emotional reaction to them. As we've discussed at some length in the previous chapter, your child's emotions organize her ideas into themes and categories. The emotional discussions she shares with you—whether it's talk about bedtime or fantasy play involving magic-carpet rides—will form the basis for her flexible thinking skills.

GRASPING ABSTRACTIONS

As your child becomes more and more capable of emotional thinking, she will begin to understand the link between the many experiences and feelings that define, identify, or give meaning to a particular abstract word. This will eventually enable her to comprehend abstract concepts like love, anger, sadness, and excitement. For instance, your three-and-a-half-year-old can understand an abstract term like "excitement" because she experiences hundreds of very different kinds of exciting circumstances, and you've spoken the word "exciting" and she and you together have labeled those experiences. The thrill she feels as you hand her a birthday present, the adrenaline rush that keeps her pumping as she overtakes you in a footrace, and the exhilaration that courses through her when her action figures knock down your castle are just a few of the many experiences that the two of you have shared that make up an idea as complex as "excitement."

SELF-REFLECTION

Your child will not only start to understand more abstract ideas during these months, but will also grow more adept at elaborating pretend and conversational themes of her own choosing. Each time you avoid falling back on easy yes and no answers to her many questions and requests, you'll be challenging your child to become more reflective. For instance, if she should tug on your hand and cry, "I want to outside now, Mommy!" a reply of "Gee! That's a great idea. What would you like to do there?" will get her thinking. Will she run or go on the slide or swing? As she ponders her response, your child will be considering a future course of action before she actually commits to it. In this way, she will also learn how to control her impulses rather than immediately act them out. She'll not only be learning how to plan actions, but will also be considering alternatives. Like the gritty sand that causes a pearl to eventually coalesce, these simple pauses of just a few seconds will eventually expand in the years ahead to form a habit of reflective thought.

TRIANGULAR RELATIONSHIPS

In addition to all her new thinking skills—controlling impulses, distinguishing between what's real and what isn't, understanding abstract feelings and ideas, and self-reflection—your child will soon become aware that her simultaneous relationships with more than one person are all connected. For example, as she learns how to negotiate a special relationship with each of her parents, she'll start becoming aware of new intrigues and rivalries and will use this understanding to her advantage. Sometimes we mistakenly think of this new cunning as simply being manipulative, but it's something far more important. It is evidence of a new ability to think in a complex way—to look at more than one relationship at a time.

If you should inadvertently ignore your sophisticated little preschooler, she may not be content simply to tug on your sleeve and say, "Come play with me *now!*" as she would have done in the past. Now she's liable to cotton up to your spouse to make you feel jealous, so you'll *want* to play with her. This sort of tactic is far more sophisticated than simply grabbing you, or coolly ignoring you. Your child is fast learning that sometimes indirect patterns of behavior yield more satisfying results than frontal assaults. She may even exploit her dual tie to both you and your spouse by playing both sides against the middle when she's negotiating for everything from additional playtime to more treats. She may turn to you with a look of wide-eyed innocence and insist that "Mommy [or Daddy] always lets me have two crackers." Certainly, most of us adults have occasionally played one friendship off another, or subtly manipulated office relationships. Even children as young as four are able to perceive similar kinds of intrigues and use them to their advantage.

Pretty soon, you'll notice that your child will periodically exhibit a marked preference for you or your spouse. She may seem to reject your friendly overtures. If you are temporarily odd man (or woman) out, it's hard not to feel hurt or jealous, even when you've been reassured by your mother, pediatrician, and friends that her infatuation will flip-flop from one parent to the other in the coming months. Your child may well be keeping you at a distance because she's afraid that your presence may jeopardize her intimate relationship with your spouse. Should this be occurring, it's a clear signal that you need to continue your efforts to be available. Your child is exploring new ways of relating but doesn't want to lose any of her closeness or security. Let her have the pleasure of rebuffing you and knowing you are still there for her. It's a wonderful gift.

Your child has taken on a big task; it takes a lot of practice to learn how to balance three or more people in an interactive system. In fact, this kind of thinking is just starting up during this developmental stage, and will really take off during her school years. Mastering the pushes and pulls of these more complex interactions will provide your child with a kind of checks-and-balances system. She'll learn that she can afford to get angry at one parent because she is still intimately linked to a second nurturing parent. Such a system buffers the intensity of her feelings and lets her consider more assertive and creative options.

These triangular relationships are your child's first attempts to establish her place in a broader pecking order. Her emotional world now extends way beyond the circle of your loving arms and includes other family members, friends, and children her own age. You'll see evidence that your child is beginning to think triangularly as you watch her play with two friends at the same time during informal playgroup get-togethers, or at preschool. She'll start taking obvious satisfaction in interacting with a group of children. Three- and four-year-olds may tease each other and quarrel about each other's toys, but they also gradually come to realize that they must delay gratification of some of their wishes and desires if they want to remain part of the group.

Triangular thinking will crop up during your toddler's make-believe play, as well. If you watch closely, you'll see her dolls and action figures explore complicated relationships that parallel those she sees around her in the real world. For example, you may notice that two of your daughter's dolls might decide to play a trick on a third. Perhaps she'll set up an even more elaborate triangular system, and move some of her action figures behind a castle she's constructed to try and trick your own action figures into believing that an attack is coming from the rear. Then, she might sneak her other figures to the side and launch her main attack!

Her new way of thinking may even be finding its way into how she understands motives in the stories you read to her, since she's becoming more aware of how other people feel. When a fairy-tale character is tricked by another character, she'll feel an empathetic feeling of "If I'm feeling angry, he [the character] must be angry, too." This represents a new level of intelligence that will stand her in good stead in the future, when she learns to interpret a novel from different perspectives or puzzle over a playwright's point of view.

HOW TO RECOGNIZE EMOTIONAL AND ABSTRACT THINKING

CONNECTING IDEAS

The dialogues that you'll soon be sharing with your child will be far richer and more logical than ever. You may even feel a pang when you realize how grown-up she is starting to sound. However, her new ability to spin wonderful stories and share fascinating thoughts will surely delight you. She will be connecting her ideas to yours in all sorts of imaginative ways, and even ordinary banter will seem more meaningful.

One day the two of you may be lying on your backs and looking up at a bright springtime sky. Your child may point her finger and cry out, "Oh, Daddy! Look at that cloud! It looks like a big giraffe! See the neck?" You might "oooh" and "ah" over her special cloud, and then point to another, remarking, "How about that puffy one right next to it? I think it looks like a mushroom." Your child may then come up with a story about her giraffe eating the mushroom. Your observations will build off each other's, and even mealtime discussions will develop along more logical lines: "Well, let's see what's in the cupboard. How about a peanut butter and jelly sandwich, sweetheart?" might be met by "No, No! I hate peanut butter and jelly. I want yogurt." When you remark, "Okay, but I don't remember which kind you like," she might fasten you with a knowing look and say, "Silly! You know I only like pink yogurt."

Such simple, related statements, uttered during her daily conversations and pretend-play sessions with you, let you know that your child is now *thinking*. Initially, these remarks consist of fairly straightforward statements, and contain few questions or complex ideas. Soon, though, your child will be ready for a more advanced kind of bridge building between her ideas and yours.

Who, What, When, Where, Why, and How

One way to help your preschooler build logical bridges is to pose questions that gently challenge her to consider your own ideas. But answering and raising *who, what, where, when, how, and why* questions are difficult and sophisticated skills for your little girl to master. Up until this point in her development, your child hasn't been able to easily sequence numerous ideas in her mind in quick succession, so when you posed questions, she often ignored you and went about her business. Now, however, she can create more complex connections between her ideas and yours. When you ask her, "What did you do at Grandpa's today?" she is able to visualize herself in another place and time and report back to you about her activities: "I played in the sprinkler and ate popcorn." You'll be hearing a lot of questions, too, and she'll demand that you respond to them. When she asks you a question like "Do I have to wear socks today?" you'll know that she's becoming increasingly able to manipulate ideas in her mind into logical summaries of her past behavior or future plans of action.

How exactly does your child do this? Over time, she has come to rely on your ability to read and respond to her ideas. Because she feels secure and comforted by the familiar rhythms of interacting with you, she will remain focused on your responses. She will eventually see how they link up to her ideas, and may actually visualize the images and feelings captured by your words. When you notice your child regularly answering *what* or *where* questions, and then posing some herself, you'll know that she's starting to be a real emotional thinker. She'll probably start answering *what* and *where* questions before *why* ones, because these questions refer to actual objects or places ("What toy would you like to play with?" "Where have you put Mommy's purse?"). Next, she'll probably start answering *how* questions, because they relate to functions and kinds of behavior that she has already experienced ("How do you fasten the snaps on your shirt?" "How shall we fix the doll's wobbly head?"). Soon, *when* questions will be answered as well as posed, since your child is now acquiring a sense of time.

Why questions are the hardest ones for your child to answer because they require her to examine the less than obvious roots of her own wishes, desires, or feelings. You'll find that your three- or four-year-old will initially answer *why* questions in a very simple, concrete manner ("Why did you throw your sandwich on the floor?" "Because I wanted to!"). Such responses don't necessarily mean that your child is being stubborn or belligerent; she's answering the best way she can. She's new to abstract thinking, and it may be months yet before she's able to survey her behavior and hold ideas in her head long enough to explain her underlying reasons: "Because I hate bologna and you should have remembered that!"

For this reason, a question such as "What do you want to do outside?" is an easier one to answer than "Why do you want to go outside?" If your three- or four-year-old has trouble with *what* questions, offer her a multiple-choice question: "Do you want to play on the swings or the slide or the teeter-totter?" If your child finds it hard to deal with multiple choices, make one of the alternatives so ridiculous that she'll probably break into giggles: "Do you want to play on the swings or go capture some ostriches?" When she answers you, you can rephrase her answer in a "why" format: "Oh, to swing—that's why you want to go outside!"

Your child's eventual ability to answer your "Why do you want to go outside?" question with "Because I want to play" is a far more sophisticated response than you might think at first. Her words reveal that she must clearly have a sense of an "I," or independent self, as well as an awareness that she has an inner desire, or "want," plus an idea for an action that will satisfy that desire in the near future, "to play." The fact that she can combine these ideas and concepts and build off your own ideas is an exciting indication that her thinking is growing increasingly complex.

Celebrate the Logic in *And*'s, *If*'s, or *But*'s, and *Because*'s, Too!

One of the telltale signs of more elaborate thinking in pretend play is action sequences of logically linked ideas. A doll's birthday celebration may feature cutting a pretend cake, followed by an imaginary exchange of presents. A space invader may zap a dinosaur with a pretend laser because the former comes from another planet where they are afraid of dinosaurs. Your child's plots will thicken because she now understands that certain categories of emotions logically match up with certain experiences.

One day soon, with impeccable logic, she may square her shoulders, fix you with a determined look, and announce, "I don't wanna go to bed yet because the sun is still up!" In fact, the word "because" is fast becoming one of the mainstays in your preschooler's vocabulary. By age four or four and a half, she'll understand not only that one idea can cause another, but that you'll listen to her with increased respect if she justifies her actions with a convincing excuse. (Of course, "I *had to* pull her hair because she took away my brand-new Beanie Baby!" may not convince you.)

When your child exclaims, "I pushed him because yesterday he pushed me," or when her doll marches over to yours and snatches the hat off her head because "your doll got to wear my doll's new hat this morning and that's not fair!" your child is showing you that she can reason by taking both time and feelings into consideration. A piece of anger arising in one time interval relates to a piece of anger in another time interval. She's now capable of giving you increasingly complicated answers as she reiterates all the reasons why she should be allowed to watch a favorite television show: "I'm not sleepy and I went to bed early last night, so tonight I get to stay up late!"

Not only can your child verbally connect two or more ideas in time, she can also connect ideas in terms of spatial problem solving. You may see her align blocks into adjacent rooms to form a palace for her doll, or construct separate block towers and then link them together with a tunnel to create an imaginary city. She will show you that she can manipulate space to create new play experiences.

It's important to note that your child's make-believe dramas can contain elements that are both realistic and fantastic. She can use everyday objects like bowls, spoons, and telephones as her pretend play unfolds, yet suddenly shift the action to the realm of superheroes. For instance, Batwoman could munch on very real corn flakes and then suddenly decide to fly to the moon because she wanted a piece of green cheese. As long as what is real and what is unreal are tied together with a logical connecting thought (hunger), your little girl is well on her way to becoming a logical, abstract thinker.

DESCRIBING FEELINGS

Your child's ability to describe a wide range of feelings is another hallmark of emotional thinking. Very recently, she might typically have expressed her ideas about anger through pretend play that featured bickering stuffed animals. A year ago, she might have merely acted out her angry feelings with aggressive behavior. Now, however, she's more than likely to express her stuffed animals' pretend fury with statements like "I'm really, really mad at you!" Similarly, during good times she might reflect on her own feelings and say something along the lines of "When Daddy came back home I felt so happy!" or have her dolls hug each other during pretend play and utter words like "I love you" or "Come back real soon!"

Some children may be able to express certain emotional themes, such as dependency or their need for nurturance, in only the most concrete manner—through actions, not words. They act out their needs directly, and hug or cling to you. You'll soon start noticing which emotional themes are easy for your child to verbalize, and which ones are more problematic. She may be able to describe feelings of curiosity and pleasure, but not aggressive feelings, or vice versa.

As your little girl explores various emotions and themes via pretend play and words, she will progress from linking two or more logically connected ideas to linking three or more complex ideas. Her emotional thoughts will express a broad range of themes, including:

* *Closeness and dependency.* A doll gets hurt and Mommy doll fixes it (36 months) and then the doll goes to a ball and dances with the prince (48 months).

Pleasure and excitement. The toddler says bathroom words like "doody" and laughs (36 months) and then turns to Mommy and says the same word, while waiting for her reaction (48 months).

Assertiveness and exploration. Good guys search for a missing Indiana Jones (36 months) and then have to fight spiders in the Temple of Doom (48 months).

Cautious or fearful behavior. A scary monster makes the Rugrats afraid (36 months) and then the Rugrats hide under the covers (48 months).

Anger. Good soldiers fight bad ones (36 months) and then trick them to defeat the enemy (48 months).

Limit setting. Only the good soldiers can hit the bad soldiers because of the rules (36 months). By 48 months, the child can set limits for herself by reasoning about consequences ("If I'm bad now, I'll be punished later"). Even though she doesn't always follow them, the child is now able to understand rules in terms of limits. She can also form abstract principles ("You shouldn't be mean to other people").

Recovering from anger, separation, and loss. The child uses pretend play to recover from anger and can pretend to eat the cookie she could not get in reality (36 months). By 48 months, the child can picture Daddy in his office when she's at home, and can verbally relate some feelings of sadness and loss ("He's away at work; I miss him a little, but I'm having a good time playing with my toys").

Continuing to engage in peer and sibling relationships, as well as with nonfamily members, while embracing a growing range of themes and feelings described above. A child needs increasing opportunities to play one-on-one and in small groups with peers (by 36 months). By 48 months there should be lots of continuing playtimes with peers so that a child is learning about having a real buddy or good friend. Similarly, interaction with siblings as well as nonfamily member adults should be developing and embracing a range of feelings. If your child needs extra practice in playing with peers, be a floor-time helper with the children. Join in and simply create opportunities for interaction.

WHEN AGGRESSION IS A
HEALTHY SIGN

Oddly enough, the appearance of aggressive themes in your child's pretend play and conversation during this stage can be another sign of developmental progress. As parents we want to foster feelings that fuel assertiveness and a healthy interest in power, yet control the acting out of aggression in which a child might hit, hurt, or break things. You'll see constructive uses of aggressiveness during your child's pretend play, when she takes on the role of the biggest and most powerful superhero who cuts the bad guys down to size, or becomes the most beautiful and talented ballerina in the company. You'll also notice when aggressiveness enters into her conversations with you, as she forcefully states her own point of view. Most parents try to promote this quality in their children; they don't want them to be timid or passive. They want their children to feel comfortable raising their hands in school, volunteering, participating in discussions, and holding their own during a debate.

All children need opportunities for exploring assertiveness, and rely on you to set behavioral limits that will keep their impulsive acting out in check. A lot of parents have special trouble dealing with their children's impassioned pleas for toy guns, swords, or space lasers, and feel appalled that their sweet-tempered children suddenly seem determined to ape the violence they see on television or at the movies. Parents should be encouraged to follow their own cultural and religious values, and allow only those toys in their home that they feel comfortable with. However, it is important to realize that if children aren't permitted to explore one avenue of assertiveness, they will need to explore another.

Many children will use their hands and fingers as pretend space lasers or guns despite their parents' best efforts to discourage violent play. It's important to recognize that you must offer your child some avenues of assertiveness. You want to help her use her words to elaborate *all* the themes of life, from power and assertiveness to sweetness and loving-kindness. If you cut out all areas of assertiveness from her experience, you'll be undermining a very important part of her emotional life. It's simply impossible for your child to avoid dealing with aggression. A child may manage temporarily to inhibit it but wind up becoming overly anxious or passive or controlled. The aggressive feelings may sneak out in more impulsive ways.

There are many ways within a variety of cultural and religious traditions to express assertiveness and to experiment with power using words and imaginative play. Perhaps a character could cast a magic spell on someone, or succeed in jumping higher than anyone else. Don't be surprised if Barney occasionally threatens to squash the other dolls in their beds! Even your child's accompanying dialogues may be filled with angry words.

Try not to overreact when your four-year-old temporarily becomes preoccupied with these aggressive themes. Each time she imagines herself to be bigger, stronger, and faster than the scariest creature that haunts her dreams, she regains a sense of control over her life. Combining her new interests with your warmth and empathy will, over time, help her join angry and loving feelings. This will enable her eventually to become a warm, loving, yet assertive, person.

As your child grows capable of linking her ideas into complex thoughts, she realizes that she is able to spark certain reactions in others. During make-believe sessions with you and others, she can assume the role of the bad guy and knock down houses and take aim at the good guys. She's waited a long time to feel powerful and in control, and now can safely test the boundaries of acting aggressively. The inviolate floor-time rules of never inflicting bodily harm or deliberately breaking toys provide her with a comforting set of limits; she knows you'll rein her in if her aggressive play gets too boisterous.

You may note an increase in your child's verbal feistiness around her fourth birthday. Because she's thinking more logically now, she's more willing to challenge your authority. After all, she can summon lots of good reasons why she shouldn't have to toe the line all the time. When you tell her to hurry up and get dressed, she may coolly inform you, "No, I won't get dressed. Clothes are stupid." Your child's bold words and aggressive pretend play give voice to her increased interest in power and grandeur, but she still has private feelings of being vulnerable. Fearful dreams may disrupt her sleep, and she may express daytime fears about aliens, ghosts, and monsters. These fears reflect an awareness of danger. Now that your child can mentally bridge her feelings of vulnerability to real as well as imagined threats, she may need extra time for loving, empathetic interaction with you to reassure her that bad things won't happen to her. She may even create an imaginary friend to provide her with an additional sense of security.

THE EMERGING IMPORTANCE OF FRIENDS, REAL AND IMAGINARY

Although children begin to play companionably during the toddler months, when they are between the ages of three and four they start to collaborate in pretend play, as well. They look forward to joining a friend in giving tea parties for their dolls, or in building sand castles that will be stormed by imaginary soldiers. They may push their toy tractors and bulldozers along the same path, and send each other's vehicles careening off the track. Disagreements among playmates are usually less intense than they were just six months ago, however; preschoolers increasingly understand that it's usually worth their while to share toys and even take turns because their fun is multiplied when other kids are around. At this age, children build on each other's ideas about how to play, creating elaborate plots together and sharing props.

If you notice that either your child or her playmate can't sustain the make-believe drama that's under way, it's perfectly fine occasionally to step right into the drama and see if you can start some interaction. If one of the children is getting ready to pull out, try to create some suspense or excitement to reel her back in. You may not get the child to stay a whole lot longer, but each additional minute of interaction provides her with that much more practice in logically bridging her thoughts to another child's.

Around ages three and four, especially as triangular thinking is increasing and children can maintain interaction among different relationships, some children can interact very easily in small groups. They effortlessly move from one friend to another or relate to two or three children together, such as when these children are playing house. One may be Mom, one may be Dad, and one may be the child. But other children need extra practice in relating to in a group. If that's the case, an adult can act as a facilitator and create situations that foster interaction, by saying such simple things as, "Can't you ask Suzie for the Batman cape?"

Sometimes a three- or four-year-old's percolating imagination will produce an imaginary friend. As a child learns to decide what is real and what is not, it can occasionally be very comforting to retreat to an island of fantasy. If you should hear your child chatter about a pretend friend, engage her in conversation about her sidekick. When you hear her talking to her imaginary friend, join in on the dialogue. By interacting even in this area, you're helping her create a bridge between her private world and her relationship with you.

The adventures of such imaginary friends enable your child to vicariously experience all the bad and good things that she thinks about, and are a variation on make-believe play with dolls and puppets. Over time she'll become increasingly aware that her friend is make-believe. If she seems a little too preoccupied with her pretend pal, ask yourself whether or not you've given her enough opportunities to play with real friends and with you and your spouse. By this age, in addition to preschool, which is more group-oriented, a child should have four or more chances to play one-on-one with other children each week, and daily playtimes with Mom and Dad. Usually, imaginary friends seem to vanish on their own once the child starts school and is enmeshed in the politics of the playground. However, some children hold on to their pretend buddies longer.

OTHER DEVELOPMENTAL LEAPS

As your child's abilities as an emotional and abstract thinker broaden, you'll see her making gains in various developmental areas involving language, sensory, motor, and cognitive skills. Keep in mind, however, that it is her emerging capacity to connect ideas into cohesive thoughts that gives birth to all these other specific skills. Without this glue, your child would not be able to operate as a fully integrated person, and her sensory and language skills, muscle coordination, and thoughts would all be functioning in a piecemeal fashion.

The chart that begins on the next page lists some of the motor, sensory, language, and cognitive capacities that are related to building bridges between ideas. Remember, these skills unfold at different rates in different children, and your three- or four-year-old may take her own sweet time in achieving some milestones while effortlessly mastering others. Growing up isn't a race! As long as she's progressing in the right direction, take time to savor the journey with her.

THE CRITICAL IMPORTANCE OF ABSTRACT AND EMOTIONAL THINKING

All of the emotional interactions that you have with your child during her busy day—whether it's idle conversation about eating or errands, fanciful pretend play, or opinion-oriented debates—create the thinking strategies

Capacities Present at 36 and 48 Months

MOTOR

- 36 months: Walks upstairs alternating feet, catches a big ball, kicks big ball, jumps forward, hops, copies circle, cuts paper, can unbutton buttons.

- 48 months: Skips and hops; rides tricycle; catches and bounces ball; holds pencil or crayon and copies six simple shapes, such as a line or a circle; shows hand preference; strings beads.

SENSORY

- 36 months and 48 months: Enjoys or tolerates various types of touch (cuddling, roughhousing, different types of clothing, brushing teeth or hair); is comfortable with loud sounds, bright lights, and movement in space.

LANGUAGE

- 36 months: Understands and constructs logical bridges between ideas with full sentences; uses *but* and *because*; answers *who, what,* and *where* questions; comprehends actions/verbs; uses plurals; uses two prepositions.
- 48 months: Comprehends complex *why* questions such as "Why do we need a house?"; can express ideas reflecting an understanding of relative degrees of feelings or wishes or intentions ("I am only a little mad"); can repeat a five- to ten-word sentence; can repeat four to seven random numbers.

COGNITIVE

- 36 months: Pretend play has logical structure to it (pretend ideas are connected); spatial designs are complex and interrelated

(a house made of blocks has connected rooms); child identifies "big" and "little" as part of developing a quantitative perspective; can identify objects by their function as part of developing abstract groupings.
- 48 months: Can point to pictures of objects in answer to questions such as "What do you eat with?" or "What makes food hot?"); can deal with concepts of quantity ("Which is biggest?" "Which box has more marbles?"); can identify similarities and differences in shapes and verbal concepts (triangle vs. rectangle, people vs. animals); can recall and comprehend experiences from recent past.

that she will eventually apply to the more impersonal world. These dialogues are the foundation for logical and abstract thinking, including reasoning about something as seemingly unemotional as number and quantity concepts. For instance, there is no better moment to learn the difference between three candy kisses and one more piece of candy than when a child's sweet tooth is acting up and she wants to justify more rather than less! Let's take a look at how this emerging ability to think emotionally evolves into self-reflection.

SELF-REFLECTION

In the recent past, your child may have been able to say, "I'm mad!" when she was steamed at her sister and just barely refrained from pinching her. Months later, she could say, "I'm mad and I *want* to pinch her," which was a great advance over actually doing it. Still, she remained caught up in the immediacy of her feelings. Now, however, she is actually capable of going a step further and linking her angry feelings to the reasons behind them. She can recognize that she's mad at her sister and wants to pinch her "because she took my new paint set without asking first!"

Self-reflection thus begins with using an idea to ponder a feeling or consider an alternate solution, rather than using the idea merely to justify an action. Your child is starting to step back a little from the rawness of her feelings, and enter into negotiations before rushing into behavior ("Daddy, it's not fair, it's my turn now!"). She can use words to reflect on her feelings in order to compromise or plan another solution with the help of another person. Later on, your child will even be able to picture herself in the future and imagine a solution that involves people or objects that are not right in front of her ("You're mean, I'm mad, and I'm going to tell Mommy on you").

After months and years of practice in linking her ideas to yours, your child will start to think more subtly—in grays, rather than black and white ("You're mean—but only a little mean"; "I'm mad, but only a little mad"). She'll be less caught up in an all-or-nothing view of things. Eventually, she'll be able to differentiate between what is true at a particular point in time and what exists at other times. She'll know that she feels a certain way right now ("You're mean! I'm mad at you!") and can also reflect on those feelings in relation to a more stable sense of herself and of you ("You were mean and I'm mad, but I'm a nice person so I don't have to get even with you. Most of the time you're nice to me so I guess I can forgive you"). Your child is thus developing a more cohesive and ongoing sense of self that helps her curb her own behavior.

MORAL CONSCIOUSNESS

Because she can now use her ability to reflect on ideas and understand consequences, your child is developing a true *moral consciousness*. The process unfolds in stages. First, as she reflects on her behavior she becomes able to anticipate the consequences of her actions ("If I hit or pinch my sister she'll cry and I'll be punished"; "If I hit or pinch my sister Mommy will catch me and won't love me as much"). The child's initial sense of right and wrong is thus fairly concrete; specific behaviors lead to specific consequences. Later on, she'll be able to think of consequences in terms of how the other person is going to feel. Initially, she'll understand this intellectually, but won't have true empathy. If you should ask her, "If you hit your sister, how will she feel?" your child may well answer "She'll be mad but I don't care because I'm mad!"

Over time, your child will begin looking at consequences in a less personalized way, and will consider what will happen to her sister (she'll be upset). Later on, when she's five and older, she'll sometimes want her sister to get very upset and other times she'll want her to be only a little upset. One day you may see that your preschooler is hopping mad and about to lower the boom because her sister was mean to her. If you were to ask her what she's planning, she might reply, "I'm going to hurt her because I want her to feel upset, to know what it feels like." If you were then to say to her, "Well, I'm proud of you for not going off and hitting her; tell me why you didn't," she might answer, "I'm not a hitter, Mommy—I just want her to feel a little bad." Starting at around four and a half, your child can begin to picture various consequences and intuitively begin doing things with some degree of proportionality. In other words, if a playmate starts pinching her, she'll pinch back and not necessarily escalate the warfare.

Your child's more nuanced sense of causality also leads her to want to do nice things for others so she'll receive a nice reaction in return. She thinks to herself, "I'll give my mommy a hug and a kiss because she'll give me a hug and a kiss back," or "My daddy hurt his toe so I'll rub it for him." She'll behave in certain ways because she knows she'll be rewarded with the signs of affection that make her feel happy and secure.

Obviously, the line between actions based on self-centered goals and pure altruism is a blurry one. But over time, being nice can take on a life of its own. At first, the child's sense of right and wrong is more focused on not doing bad things—or the worst of many bad things—that she could do (she could bop her playmate on the nose but she chooses only to give her a push). Her willingness to do nice things, like bringing Mommy the newspaper to read, or sharing a toy with her brother, has a lot to do with the patterns of warmth, nurturance, and caring present in her particular family. When there's a lot of warmth and enough emotional chicken soup to go around (without so much competition and rivalry that a child has to conduct guerrilla warfare to get her needs met), children are more likely to show both healthy assertiveness and a willingness to do nice things for others.

A child will initially do nice things because she's generally assured of nice consequences. She learns that she can count on you beaming with pride, or that Daddy will embrace her in a warm cuddle because she put milk in the cat's bowl when the animal meowed with hunger. A sense of morality will thus begin to build with both a wish to do positive things and an inhibition of some negative behavior.

How exactly do these moral rules get internalized? Your child will begin associating consequences with actions and will start to think things out in advance. Her feeling and occasional thought, "If I feed the cat some milk, Daddy will be proud of me" can now be internally guided. She can deliberately set up good feelings for herself: "I want Daddy to beam at me with prideful, loving eyes, so I'll go and feed the cat." Or, she might say to herself, "Taking my plate to the sink makes Mommy look at me with a big grin, and sometimes she even says I'm a great kid or gives me a hug and a kiss." As she performs a good deed, she initially does it in anticipation of Mommy or Daddy's reaction. These inner negotiations are often more at the level of intuitive feelings or images than words. Over time, however, as a part of her ability to string ideas together, she learns to anticipate your nodding warmth or big proud smiles. Eventually she will reach the point where she is able, in anticipation, to create the feeling that will come from you for herself. This ability to create a feeling, or image, or hear an inner voice, is as if she has a little mommy or daddy residing in a part of her mind, giving her a hug or kiss and a sense of security, or even issuing warnings when necessary.

Initially that inner warning or warm feeling comes in the form of the parent's image or voice, but eventually it is experienced as the child's own voice. She'll vibrate with a feeling of "I did the right thing," or "I'm a good person, and it's good to do nice things." This is similar to the inner glow adults feel when they do something nice for a friend, and has its birth in the warm smiles, hugs, or sense of closeness and approval that they experienced in their early relationships with their parents.

It's interesting to note that individuals can never fully provide *all* the inner warmth and security that they may want for themselves as they navigate through life. Some adults are able to provide more of it, others less. Some rely on their spouses or families of origin to keep supporting them with a steady stream of nurturing. Others, however, manage to get through even tough times at work when their colleagues may be critical, because they have an inner image or feeling or voice that tells them that they are doing the right thing. This internalized feeling and message sustains them for long periods of time.

This interior feeling, image, or voice has two components to it: the inner presence that guides you in a positive way, eventually with ideals and values; and another presence that can be critical or make you feel guilty or bad. Long before children can actually verbalize to themselves, "I'm a good girl," or "This is nice," they are experiencing these feelings. You can see that by the smile on their faces as they do something nice, or the proud posture of their walk, or the scared or nervous look in their eyes as they sneak another cookie out of the cookie jar.

Even at early ages, young children sense that doing nice things is good, while hurting other children is bad. When the child with her own well-developed inner rules steps over the line, she will feel bad. Her bad feeling may initially arise in anticipation of being caught or receiving a punishment, but later on it's experienced as an uneasy feeling. She'll want to avoid that guilty sensation, just as adults do when they behave in a way that they're not proud of, and feel badly about themselves.

When she says, "You're so mean" or "I hate you," and you look downcast or angry in response, she comes to understand that words have an effect. The ideas and feelings inside her become linked to an end result—your negative reaction. Your child is beginning to understand how her present acts can have an impact on the future, and that she can opt for good instead of bad, right instead of wrong. This new understanding gives her a growing ability to control her impulses. Now she can use ideas to picture negative feelings like anger, which allows her to anticipate the consequences of being angry and plan out ways to deal with her anger. She can sometimes even figure out why she is angry. Her newly awakened sense of right and wrong leads her to have opinions about good and bad ways of dealing with anger, and she may try to abide by her own rules. You may even notice her little face turning bright red and her arm trembling with the effort not to hit a playmate. This sort of self-control represents a giant leap in her ability to handle anger and should be applauded.

An inner moral guidance system thus gradually takes form, supported further by an emerging inner sense of values. What a child does, such as behaving nicely to her annoying little brother, can lead her to feel good about herself. By the time she is ten to twelve years old, she can sometimes actually verbalize the principles that are guiding her behavior and can make a distinction between what she is doing and what she should be doing. As long as you combine your positive expectations of her behavior with appropriate limits, your child should be able to strike a healthy balance between feeling good about herself when she chooses to do nice things, and feeling bad when she crosses the line into negative behavior.

Triangular Thinking

Your child's growing familiarity with *triangular thinking* also helps her set her own internal limits. She can often pass up pushing a playmate because she now takes into consideration how the other child would feel, how her mommy or daddy will feel about her action, or how she herself will feel. She may simultaneously have the bone-deep sensation that it would feel good to get even with her playmate since the latter broke her favorite toy. She recognizes that the playmate would get upset, but she doesn't care about that at the moment. She understands that her parents would probably disapprove. This faces her with a dilemma: What response will bring her the greatest satisfaction?

If she's more concerned about immediate gratification, she may disregard concerns about her parents and then push her friend. If she's more focused on securing Mommy or Daddy's approval, she may hold back. She can, in anticipation, feel their pride in her for coming and telling them how she feels with words ("I hate him, he broke my balloon"). Once she internalizes her parents' approval, even when they're not there, she may pass on an opportunity to push someone because she knows it's the right thing to do.

Why, in fact, would any four-year-old ignore her own thirst for revenge and side with what Mommy or Daddy thinks is best? If a child's parents haven't been providing enough nurturance and warmth, perhaps because they are overly busy, the child probably won't feel as if she's getting enough warmth and attention and is not going to be very motivated to adopt their perspective. Because she's angry and hurt by this state of affairs, she may also be more likely to lash out at her playmates, too. Alternatively, the child might not even think about anger if she fears her parents will punish her severely, or withhold the warmth she yearns for. In a family where there's an abundance of nurturance and warmth coupled with firm-but-gentle guidance and limits, however, the child will be aware of feeling loved and valued. Like any three- or four-year-old, she'll sometimes feel greedy or needy and make a play for more time, more fun, more games, or more toys. Since she's already gotten plenty, though, and simply wants a little more, her parents are in a position to convey a sense that enough is enough. The child can then learn to tolerate disappointment and live with not always getting her way. Such families teach their children how to do the right thing for the right reasons by providing *ample love with limits*. A child's sense of her parents' limitless warmth makes her feel good about them and good about herself, and creates a feeling of wanting to please them. The limits they provide her with help her control her greediness, too.

Maintaining Perspective and Mood

Now that your child is learning how to control her impulses, to choose good behavior instead of bad, and to see a cause-and-effect relationship between her ideas and your own during this developmental stage, she is also better able to *keep her perspective and maintain a more stable mood* while dealing with a range of intense feelings. Separating from you will be less of an ordeal because she can now evoke multisensory pictures of you and ideas about you for as long as she needs to make herself feel better. Because your child can now build bridges between ideas, she isn't as much a victim of the moment. Her thoughts can move in time and space and range from context to context, so that when she misses her father, she can say to herself, "I feel bad now, but when Daddy gets back home I'll soon feel better." She can anticipate feeling better and so may permit herself simply to remain subdued, rather than panicked. If she's had a hard day at preschool, she can think, "Mommy can make me feel better when she picks me up at lunchtime." Her ability to link images and feelings permits her to sense the big picture of her emotions rather than get lost in only one feeling. In this way, her mood is more stable.

Some children may habitually give in to the feeling of the moment. A child who reacts like this may have to deal with a situation where she feels she has been treated negatively and unfairly. She might begin to think, "Everyone in school hates me and they always will." She may then not only give up, but also behave meanly in response. She may keep recreating her negative circumstances and continue in her negative mood. You can help your toddler stabilize her mood and look beyond her immediate reaction by empathizing with her sorrowful feelings. Your warmth and empathy will put a feeling of acceptance alongside her bad feelings. When you say something like "Oh sweetheart, I know how hard it is to play by yourself when the other kids run away sometimes," your warmth will provide her with a bridge to more positive feelings. Later you can brainstorm together about solutions, such as seeking out some available children to play with. If you say, "Oh stop feeling sorry for yourself!" in a misguided attempt to toughen her up, such words will only confirm her feelings. She feels as if she is a bad or unworthy person, and such a message implies that she's a bad person for feeling like a bad person!

Once a child has a sense that tomorrow, or another setting, or another playmate can lead to happier times, she'll learn that one isolated experience doesn't have to pull her down. Furthermore, she'll begin to see that although she may feel bad on occasion, she can tolerate sadness, loss, and longing. Her situation may not always be pleasant, but neither is it catastrophic. Then, as your toddler comes to see a bigger picture, she'll also be more open to new experiences that are positive. Initially in the preschool years, children can get caught up in and exaggerate one emotion. Over time and with your soothing help they can learn to see the big picture and have a more stable mood.

THE DEVELOPMENT OF SELF-ESTEEM

Your little girl's *self-esteem* is developing during this stage because she is capable of building bridges between what she does, how she feels, and what she thinks, and the consequences of what you say, do, feel, and think. She can now tie together her inner state of mind with yours. Just a year ago, if she were happily playing a game with her baby brother, she would have been very aware of the pleased expression your face. She wouldn't have had an inkling, however, that it was her sociable behavior that made you smile. Now she can link these two ideas together, and picture or say to herself, "If I play with my little brother, Mommy will be proud and look at me with a happy expression on her face." This inner dialogue is conducted at the level of feelings or ideas (which may be a mix of images and words). It will let your child anticipate your future behavior and experience a taste of your approval before it actually occurs. Now her bridges are becoming even more elaborate; she can reason that "if I play with my brother, Mommy will be proud of me and take me to lunch with her tomorrow."

Similarly, a two-year-old would have to see a pony right in front of her before she'd be able to take any delight in the prospect of a pony ride. Your four-year-old can feel a genuine sense of excitement and sit in your car grinning from ear to ear before you're even in sight of the fairgrounds. She can smile and feel happy in anticipation because she can picture herself riding the pony. She's able to link her feeling of the moment to something that is going to happen in the near future. Her ability to construct this bridge over time to an upcoming pleasurable occasion creates a good feeling before the event actually occurs. She can actually sustain the good feeling over a longer period of time because it's not dependent on a pony actually being within eye- or earshot.

Your child's sense of self-esteem is now fueled by two sources: the empathetic warmth and approval supplied by you, her caregivers, and her teachers; and also the inner images she sees or inner voice she hears (arising out of your love and high regard for her) each time she does something praiseworthy. These images confirm her sense that she is good and valuable and thus form the basis of her positive self-esteem. If she receives disproportionately negative feedback from her playmates and parents, her inner voice is experienced as critical and anxiety-producing. This leads to a sense of defeat and low self-esteem. She is also beginning to get a sense of her own unique features and skills. Is she a dancer or a runner or a good arguer? She can relate your positive reaction to her sense of her own growing personality and abilities. It's helpful when parents can find real attributes of their child to truly enjoy.

ABILITY TO ENGAGE IN DIALOGUE

Another critically important skill that is mastered during these months is the ability to engage in *genuine dialogue,* which occurs when a child can build on another person's responses, or elaborate her own ideas after getting input from others. During this stage, your child learns to form bridges between various ideas, including her own and yours, and this puts her in touch with a fuller range of feelings, including those of other people. When she responds to and builds on the ideas of other people and not just her own, she is engaging in dialogue.

Some children communicate only their own ideas, and seldom build on other people's responses. A four-year-old child might come home from preschool and play out scene after scene of being a queen. She might even let her mother hold her imaginary ermine robe and scepter for her. However, this child might very well ignore the mother's casual questions about what the queen wanted to do next, or whom she wanted to play with. (In fact, we all know many adults who similarly like the sound of their own voices and show little interest in engaging others in truly organic, evolving conversations.) Fortunately, there are numerous strategies that you can use to help your own child build bridges to and from the thoughts of others, and we will be discussing them in detail in the following section.

Before moving on, however, let's consider the amazing increase in brain activity that is under way while your child is learning to think logically and make connections between a vast array of growing ideas. It has been found that during this period your child's brain experiences a growth spurt and metabolizes glucose (sugar) at twice the adult rate. Her brain is more active than an adult's (as measured by EEG recordings), and this activity occurs in two important language areas of the brain which are involved in the creation of words and the comprehension of other people's words.

While many of us tend to measure the importance of this stage (in terms of language development) by our children's spectacularly growing vocabularies—which often triple between ages three and five—the more critical development occurring now is the building of bridges between different ideas, words, and concepts. Your child's growing vocabulary is becoming a meaningful part of her thinking. Each of the approximately 2000 new words she learns is potentially linked to many other words and feelings in an almost infinite number of connections. It is these connections that enable her creative, logical, and abstract thought to grow.

HELPING YOUR CHILD WITH EMOTIONAL AND ABSTRACT THINKING

Your chief role during these months is to help your child connect her ideas and develop a logical understanding of the world. In conversation and pretend play, you'll be following her lead, all the while keeping an eye out for those areas in which she avoids making connections between ideas, feelings, and desires. Then, let her do the work of linking her ideas to yours! You don't want to spoon-feed connecting ideas to her, or she'll take the path of least resistance and passively accept your thoughts instead of creating her own.

In short, you'll be *eliciting* mental bridges from your child, rather than erecting them yourself. As we discussed in the introduction to this chapter, during these months you'll be busy trying to be a good play partner, a fellow debater, opinion seeker, and collaborator with your child. You will consciously be extending your conversations with her along logical lines. As simple as this sounds, going about it isn't always so obvious! The examples that follow in this section will illustrate just how you can interactively help your child elaborate her thoughts.

Let's suppose that your little girl takes her doll away from a tea party that's under way, and has the doll start playing with a toy space shuttle. You might create opportunities for logical reasoning by having your character ask her doll why she's gone exploring. Your child needn't reply the way you would, and her play may well shift from reality-oriented to illogical in the same play session. Her doll might pipe up an answer along the lines of "I have to go to Jupiter to get some special cookies for our tea party."

Even though the themes your child weaves between her ideas and yours may be quite fantastic, the structure of your joint dramas will become more and more logical because she is learning how to form a bridge between the creations of her own mind and yours. You can gently help your three- or four-year-old connect her ideas together logically when her flights of fancy lead her to become too self-absorbed, by acting confused and asking, for example, "How did we get from the tea party to Jupiter?"

If she gets bogged down in mechanical, noninteractive play, you can reach out to her with interactions that will help her link her actions and thoughts with yours. For instance, if your child seems content to have her dolls go up and down a slide, over and over again, rather than dramatically interact with each other, you could have one of the dolls ask, "Can we slide somewhere special?" Your toddler might then respond in a silly, but logical way ("We're escaping off the moon!"). If she continues to get trapped in monotonous or repetitive patterns as she plays, try to engage her in some fun with you. Then raise the *who-what-where-when-why-how* questions that create opportunities for logical reasoning.

SHIFTING BETWEEN FANTASY AND REALITY

Even though your child's wide-eyed belief in fairy tales and make-believe is delightful, it is important for you to help her distinguish between reality and fantasy. This will require time and patience on your part. After all, dreams feel real and it may take a lengthy conversation and lots of reassuring hugs to help your child accept the fact that there really aren't any monsters under her bed.

The fantasy interaction that develops during pretend play is different, however. Make-believe sessions are a time to respond to and elaborate on your child's ideas and feelings. You can facilitate these sorts of whimsical interactions by setting aside special floor times of a half hour or so at least once or twice a day.

You can help your child spin out her play sequences in a cause-and-effect manner, and yet still let her determine the direction the drama follows by introducing more characters or shifting the story's context. Your aim is to help your child elaborate the make-believe theme that she's already put into motion. If a doll builds a pretend fire to roast some marshmallows, your own doll could see if hot dogs could be part of the feast. Later on, if your child has her character trip and fall, your doll could become a doctor who takes her to the hospital. The introduction of a new character to the drama (the doctor), and having the scene of the action shift to an ambulance and a hospital, brings in many pretend elements that the child now has to link logically. This lends a cause-and-effect quality to the world of emotional ideas expressed in your child's pretend play. The increasingly logical nature of your child's make-believe interaction helps her appreciate reality and gradually create logical categories, including fantasy and reality, to classify her experiences.

As long as your child's ideas remain linked to yours and are supported by the logic of cause and effect, you needn't always hold up her fanciful thoughts to the harsh light of reality. By the time she's four years old or so, your little girl will likely be able to shift from superhero themes in which she possesses all sorts of marvelous powers, to a discussion of a child who was mean to her at school.

As the months go by, you will get an increasing sense that your child can comfortably shift between scenes of reality and fantasy, and won't mistakenly think that superheroes actually will fly into the cages she saw at the zoo. Her newfound ability to distinguish between fantasy and reality, even as she plays, is a sign that she can now organize her emotional ideas into larger categories. Your floor-time fun and your willingness to help your child elaborate her play themes and interact with new characters and situations will create a secure environment for her to play out emotional ideas and link them to yours, and in so doing become more logical. After all, in linking her ideas (which come from inside her) to your ideas (which come from outside her), she is bridging her inner, subjective world with the world outside her body and mind. As she creates these links in pretend play as well as in everyday conversations about lunch or friends, she is gradually building up her ability to figure out which ideas are real and which are not, as well as lots of other things about how the world works.

In addition, having numerous one-on-one play dates and interactions with other children in small groups furthers your child's ability to deal with ideas and feelings generated by others. A growing sense of reality helps fuel peer relationships, and in turn, friendship helps thinking and a sense of reality develop.

WHEN EMOTIONS BECOME INTENSE

As your child learns to link ideas, certain emotions may trouble her and sometimes cause her to become disorganized, anxious, or even withdrawn. Her thoughts may then be limited, or constricted, in those areas. When that happens, she may be less receptive to your own thoughts and ideas. You can help your child by becoming aware of which emotions at which level of intensity tend to push her into becoming disorganized or withdrawn. Then, you can be alert to the need to reduce the intensity of an emotion or provide her with more soothing or support and the use of ideas. For example, if your daughter should become overstimulated by a racing-car competition between your doll and hers, she might well start flinging her cars around. This sort of disorganized behavior is a red flag that will indicate to you that she's having some trouble handling feelings of competition or aggressiveness. After soothing some of her obvious anxiety, you can provide some structure, or limits, that will help her with the troublesome emotion.

How do you reestablish rapport with your little girl? First, be empathetic and let her know that you understand what she's feeling: "Boy, that car is sure revved up!" or "I know kids sometimes want to throw and pull things." Such comments focus on your child's tendency to get overly excited rather than on what's aggravating and disorganizing her. An oblique approach works a lot better than confronting the child with a question about why her dolly always has to win.

By empathizing with your child's tendencies, you communicate a supportive sense of connectedness to her. After a quick reminder that she's not allowed to hurt anyone or damage the cars by throwing them about, you can then go on to help her slow down long enough to reorganize her feelings. Adding certain logical sequences into the play may help her stay with the emotion she started to avoid. You might try doing something as simple as having a pretend red light indicate that both racing cars have to slow down.

Once you've helped your child slow down, you can reel her back into linking her thoughts and actions with yours by having your doll sympathetically ask questions like "Don't you hate going slow?" or "Do you want some new tires to speed like me?" She'll be more willing to let you help her build bridges among her thoughts if you hang in there even when she's not coping very well. Over many days, your play might explore the themes of winning and losing and fast and slow, and you can see what ideas emerge. Simply playing out difficult themes with soothing regulation and continuing elaboration of ideas is in itself very helpful and often enables a child to master a difficult feeling. Your camaraderie will thus encourage her to explore feelings and ideas that literally disrupt her train of thought. Your shared closeness will reduce her anxiety about those same feelings. Thus, reengaging with your child should be your first priority, and is far more important that getting her to return right away to the original story line the two of you were following, or having her explain where a new scene is heading.

One of the ways you can tell that your child is feeling anxious is when you notice a sudden disruption in a make-believe theme that the two of you are playing out, or a marked change in the gestures or mannerisms she uses. Imagine that the two of you have been playing house with a group of dolls, and all at once a new, frenzied quality enters your little girl's words and behavior. She may drop the Mommy doll she's holding, dart to the other side of the room to pick up a water pistol, frantically shoot at a dart board, then go back to her dolls and pretend to shoot one of the doll's arms off. Your child has worked a new theme—using a gun to express anger, or a need for protection—into an old plot.

This kind of disruption in a play sequence speaks volumes. It suggests that your child might be concerned about some danger, and feel a need to arm herself against it. She may have some worries about bodily harm, which is very common at age four. As you follow your child's lead through this pretend play, you'll let her know that all of her plot twists are interesting to you. Feel free to comment on the action you observe, with comments like "Look at that scary gun," but don't editorialize. If you were to try to assign too much meaning to her disorganized behavior by saying something like "Gosh, you seem so worried. What's the matter?" you'd be denying her an opportunity to construct her own bridges between various ideas. The more she works at forging these links (with your empathetic support and interactions), the richer and more varied her thoughts will be.

It's important to let your child play out her concerns symbolically using props such as dolls and action figures, because this permits her to dramatize her possibly anxious feelings. When she's able to re-link her feelings of vulnerability back to the family circle of dolls at the end of the play sequence described above, she will have succeeded in building a bridge from easy feelings to troubling feelings and back again.

You'll probably notice that your child will play out other concerns, such as dependency, or being separated from you, as your make-believe sessions involve Mommy, Daddy, and baby dolls. If your toddler suddenly has two or three of the dolls weeping or even fighting with each other when the Daddy doll goes far away, you don't need to rush in and give your child a hug because you assume she needs some reassurance about the constancy of your love. Your playing with her is very reassuring, and you want to let her play out her ideas without shifting the tone or direction of your interaction away from pretend.

Similarly, if your child screams out that she's angry, make it your business to quietly find out why she's feeling this way. Try not to send her to her room because you're feeling exasperated. Such an action might send a signal to the child that she'll feel less bad if she goes away from you. Have your response remain logically connected to her feelings and keep using ideas yourself even when your child's words or pretend play perturb you.

Two Voices

Sometimes it's useful to wear two hats as you play make-believe, that of a disinterested narrator of the action and that of an involved player in the drama. As long as you keep the sound of your two voices very distinct, you won't confuse your child. One advantage of taking on a narrator's role is that you can more directly translate actions and emotional expressions into words and concepts, such as "You're such a good mommy" or "You're giving your dolly a kiss." The narrator can summarize actions and emotional themes as the two of you play. Such comments can help the child stand back and observe her own behavior, and label it, yet not shift the direction of the story line. The narrator's voice is thus a useful catalyst to move the drama along when the child's attention seems to flag or her actions become repetitive.

Here's how two voices might play out during a floor-time session with your youngster. If you take on the voice of a hungry lion as you inch the stuffed animal toward the teddy bears manipulated by your child, you might roar, "I'm a tawny, scrawny lion and I'm coming to gobble you up!" Your child may respond by having her animals scamper away or by counterattacking. You'll keep trying to maintain the interactive dialogue, by growling such things as "I'm not going to let you escape from my clutches!" and she may well have her teddy bears rumble, "There are more of us and we're not afraid of you! We'll even get our friends the hippos to help us!" When that particular train of thought seems to reach a natural conclusion, you could consider dropping your lion persona and go back into your own voice as the narrator.

As a narrator, you might summarize the action with a comment like "That old lion looks like he's hungry and searching for his supper!" or "That was sure a good fight! I wonder what's going to happen next in the jungle." Your child will learn how to categorize your different voices, and respond to each voice differently. Listening more attentively will help her become a more active learner. This sort of cognitive head start is a wonderful foundation for the learning that will soon take place in preschool.

COMPLEX CHARACTERS IN PRETEND PLAY

In addition to joining in on your child's make-believe, and occasionally narrating the drama that is unfolding in front of you, you can add complexities to your characters. If you take on the role of a bad guy, try and have him demonstrate some tenderness over a hurt puppy. If you're Superman, occasionally have him look a little scared. Perhaps you could be a bold explorer who always forgets to tie his shoelaces and stumbles over his own feet. Your child may be a little confused at first, but after lots of interactions with a variety of complex characters, she'll learn to build bridges between the predictable and not-so-predictable aspects of their personalities. Eventually, she too may start creating characters that are more psychologically complex.

EXPLORING BOTH SIDES

Another way to help your child feel more comfortable with a complex range of feelings is to help her amplify each side of a theme that involves conflict. You may see her act out two contradictory themes nearly simultaneously. One of her baby dolls may hug a tearful Mommy doll, and then abruptly go off on a vacation by herself. Encourage your child to explore both of the themes present in her play—nurturance and separation. Have your own characters ask questions about how bad it feels to be left behind and how good it feels to go off exploring. You'll be heightening your child's awareness that it's possible to have very different sets of intense feelings in similar circumstances, and that her strong feelings are accepted and understood.

ENCOURAGING DEBATE

Each time you encourage your child to exercise her emotional logic and engage you in a conversational negotiation or debate, you enhance her ability to deal with anger and frustration while increasing her self-esteem. Your emotionally charged back-and-forth's teach your child that other people have desires and ideas just as she does. Because you show her that you respect what she says, even though you may not always cave in to her demands, she will eventually become more willing to compromise and use your thoughts as a springboard to new thoughts of her own.

During pretend play, you can help your child learn to grapple with your ideas by having your make-believe character stay in voice and chirp up, "Wait a minute, buddy! You didn't answer my question/follow my directions/get me what I wanted." As your child comes to consider your character's ideas and point of view, she will begin to understand that although it's sometimes frustrating to have to take in and process another person's conversation or pretend-play ideas, it's a price that's worth paying. You can also try a more direct approach, and have your character display an obstinate streak by asking your child's character, "Why do things always have to go your way?" During your conversations together, you can pretend that you're a little kid, too, and act just as stubbornly as your child. Little by little your child will loosen her insistence on controlling all the action, and learn the fine art of compromise. She'll find that bouncing ideas around and taking suggestions from other people sometimes makes playtime and conversation more fun and makes it last longer, too.

When you and your child disagree, encourage her to tell you why you're wrong. If you feel a little defensive, you can reassure yourself that it is natural to feel that way. Let her see that you enjoy hearty verbal differences of opinion, and welcome debate. Ask your child's opinions about everything! Even if she overrules your suggestions and doggedly insists on doing things her own way, she's still engaged in valuable interactive reasoning with you. The more lively and emotional (short of extreme emotions!) your debates, the more likely it is that your child will enjoy using her thinking abilities.

EMOTIONS, CATEGORIZING IDEAS, AND ABSTRACT THINKING

Emotions help us group ideas into categories: good and bad, similar and different. We use our emotions to help find patterns and meaning in the world, and to make sense of our environment. If your child's dolls are trying on clothes, your doll could ask your child's doll, "Which are your favorite outfits?" Such a question will encourage your child to group clothes into favorites and nonfavorites. When you ask a four-year-old "Why are these clothes your favorite ones?" her reply might be "Because they're pretty" or "fancy" or "cool." Be careful not to drill your child like a cross examiner, but have your questions be part of a fun discussion. If you overdo it, your child is going to back off and say, "Leave me alone! You ask too many questions." As long as there's an impish tone in your voice and a gleam in your eye, however, she probably won't feel badgered.

Your preschooler is learning how to use her emotions logically to compare and contrast a variety of ideas and see how they fit together into larger groups. You can help her learn about different concepts involving relationships (bigger/smaller, more/less, closer/farther) by posing questions that clarify things for her: "Who has the biggest dog?" or "Which toy fire truck has the loudest siren?" If the two of you are pretending to be frogs jumping out of a pond, ask whether you should jump "just a little bit high" or "way high." Later on, she will understand broad abstractions like love because they've similarly emerged out of multiple contexts in which emotions and qualities were compared and categorized. Love will come to mean hugging a lot, giving a lot, recovering from anger more easily, and usually putting the other person first.

SEEING BOTH THE FOREST AND THE TREES

Pretend-play activities and everyday conversations often challenge your child to draw details into a cohesive theme. When you're chasing each other around the house, stop a moment, look confused, and ask, "Why are we chasing each other, anyway?" Your play partner will have to explain the broad theme underlying your actions together. Then go ahead and get some details, asking, "What did I do that was bad?" or "What will you do when you catch up with me?" See if she'll list a number of reasons. Each of them will be details that support her main theme. As you encourage your child to talk on both the level of the specific and the level of the general, you will help her thinking become more flexible. Don't overwhelm her with too many clarifying questions, though. You don't want to undermine the spontaneity and joy of your dialogues together.

RECOGNIZING TALENTS, WORKING ON WEAKNESSES

It's important to recognize that not all three- and four-year-olds are equally gifted at understanding complex verbal sequences. Some children may not particularly enjoy dramatic play or storytelling, but are extraordinarily skillful at navigating their way around the rooms of their houses. Early on, these youngsters may show a marked preference for applying cause-and-effect thinking to spatial configurations. They build block towers that are architectural wonders, and delight in stacking pillows and boxes into elaborate space ships or corrals.

Although you may be trying to teach your child how to apply cause-and-effect spatial thinking to personal interactions, make sure she knows just how proud you are of her achievements *right now*. Show her you admire her talents by talking about her wonderful block house or city. Look for opportunities to build dramas about animals or people who live in the buildings your child constructs. With lots of opportunities to interact with you and other playmates while pretending ("I'm a brick layer!"), her intuitive understanding that if she places blocks in certain patterns she'll wind up with a castle will connect with the realization that the castle-building girl likes to hug and if she hugs Daddy or greets him in a certain way, he'll be very happy.

In the meantime, cater to your child's strengths and help her to more fully express her nonverbal thinking skills. These visual-spatial abilities form the basis for her sense of direction, reasoning about the physical properties of the world, and later comprehension of such subjects as physics and mathematics. Offer her opportunities to uncover hidden objects and navigate mazes. Treasure hunts, puzzles, card games like Memory, or variations on the old-fashioned shell game, in which the child tries to guess where a moving, hidden object lies, will all appeal to a visually oriented child. They will challenge her to figure out ever more complex spatial relationships, while enticing her to respond to and build on your verbal overtures as well. Encourage her to stage pretend play dramas in settings that she physically creates.

EFFECTIVE PRAISE

Obviously, a child who is adept at doing things, who has good motor control, who can tumble and catch a ball, or who can write her name finds it easier to accomplish things that she knows are worthy of praise. It is likely that her parents will express their pride in her abilities. She'll be aware of a warm, kindly feeling emanating from them many times during the day and will internalize a sense of their approval. On the other hand, a child whose body doesn't work as smoothly may knock things over and may have trouble learning to speak or write her name, or controlling her impulses. In such a circumstance, parents may offer lots of verbal encouragement, but their tone and gestures may convey disappointment.

In the past, childrearing books often advised parents whose children had various challenges to look for opportunities to shower verbal praise on them, but the impact of a parent's facial expression or tone of voice as he or she spoke to the child was often not sufficiently emphasized. Children believe their parents' nonverbal messages far more than their words. A weary, resigned tone in your voice would belie your cheery message of "Nice try" when your child drops her ball for the tenth time, and she'd probably see right through you. She'd then be more likely to internalize a disapproving inner voice that diminishes, instead of buoys up, her sense of self-esteem.

It's not surprising, then, that children with special challenges often have a harder time maintaining a stable mood and good feelings about themselves. Because their nervous systems make certain activities difficult, they get into experiences that are more negative. A child with such difficulties will sense your tension and come to expect negative consequences as you try to play with her in an area in which she is challenged. However, as we have seen with the five children profiled throughout this book, we can often restructure our interactions and turn many of those potentially negative experiences into positive ones.

By simply taking a realistic look at your child's true developmental profile, you can try to realign your expectations and take genuine pleasure in her very real accomplishments. Since a child's natural tendency is to be delighted by any new thing she can do, be sure to celebrate her progress each step of the way. She'll be closely watching you to see if you're resonating with her excitement or not. Clap with delight when your four-year-old successfully scribbles with a pencil, even if she's not able to write her name yet. She has no idea what the developmental norms are for any given stage, so be where your child is and share in her joy. We often worry that our child will compare herself to other children and feel badly. However, we need to realize that the ability to compare ourselves to another person is a highly developed skill, so it suggests great potential in social know-how if your child can already do this.

Children with even the most severe learning disabilities can enjoy great self-esteem if their parents communicate genuine pleasure and pride in their accomplishments. Your child's sense of self-esteem is closely tied to whether she feels valued because of all the varied aspects of her personality, rather than just a few select traits at which she excels. As she internalizes your high regard for her in all her idiosyncratic glory, her sense of self-worth will keep right on expanding.

LIMIT SETTING AND THINKING

As you encourage your three- or four-year-old to explore during pretend play a full range of her thoughts and feelings, including those of frustration and anger, you're not implying that she should act out these negative feelings in reality. By promoting your child's ability to express her angry or aggressive *thoughts* during pretend play, you strengthen your own right to set relevant limits—if they are needed—on her angry or aggressive *behavior*. Thus, playtime doesn't replace discipline; it supplements it. As we've said before, the rules for pretend play are simple: Your child can't hurt you or break anything. When she becomes distressed while playing make-believe and starts to behave in a disorganized way, it's time to step in and provide her with some comforting limits. If you're unable to distract her from a path of destruction, and toys or paint are flying through the air, go eyeball to eyeball with her and say in a warm tone, "That's not permitted." Don't overreact; your tone should convey a sense that even when you have to say no it's not because you're angry, but because your playmate needs some help in reining herself in. This will give your child confidence that her anger can be controlled and isn't so powerful that it can push you away. If she continues to get carried away, try to slow down the action and adopt a more soothing tone. Should she start breaking things or hurting you or another child, you'll have to move in quickly, and more firmly, with a no-nonsense tone of voice as you say, "No! Stop that now!" Sometimes you may even have to physically intercede between your child and a playmate or an object she's trying to break. In short, use varying degrees of firmness, as needed, making sure always to soothe your child. As you reestablish a background of structure and security during her playtimes, she'll be more likely to find better channels for her assertive side, as well as her loving side.

Although many children won't completely give up their aggressive behavior simply because they are able to express their feelings during pretend play, at this age most seem to respond to firm-but-gentle discipline more readily than at other ages. For the most part, they eagerly seek your approval and take pride in doing things to please other people. For instance, if you tell a four-year-old to be sure and wipe her muddy shoes on the doormat when you come in from playing outside, she may well turn to you and exclaim, "Look at my clean shoes! Aren't I a good girl?" On another day, though, when she's in a bad mood, she may calmly stare right at you and deliberately track mud onto the rug, as if she's daring you to discipline her. So savor her accommodating moments, but don't rely on them! You can foster her new spirit of cooperation by not coming down too hard on her when her actions become disorganized. Remember that your child's willingness to change her behavior depends to a large extent on her sense that you generally take pride in her and respect something special about her.

Your child's misbehavior will often reveal what troubling thoughts are on her mind, and why she's so angry or frustrated. Let's suppose that you've managed to calm down your little girl, and although she's stopped flinging her dolls around, it's clear that something is still agitating her. Perhaps she's darting from one side of the playroom to the other, and then sits herself down at a table and crayons a scribbled sketch on her drawing pad. When you take a moment and reflect on her actions, you may realize that her fragmented behavior first appeared when a fight broke out between the Raggedy Ann and Raggedy Andy dolls she was playing with. Her scribbling was accompanied by angry murmurs about stupid Mommy and Daddy, and it became more and more apparent that she was trying to work through some aggressive feelings that were upsetting her.

It's clear that your child has managed to regroup somewhat and face her troubling feelings. Your empathetic support and comments ("Boy, those two dolls were sure mad at each other!") helped her switch her activities and still focus on the same aggressive theme, albeit in a less threatening mode. Having art materials nearby provided her with another means to work through some of her intense feelings. Your gentle support ("Why do you suppose the two dolls were fighting?") should, in all likelihood, help her come up with some *because* answers that will link up her vague and upsetting feelings and ideas into more coherent thoughts.

When your child does require additional limits because she has misbehaved, it's important to increase your floor time together so that security and trust are increased. As you expect more from your child, always increase limits and floor time together. In addition, joining in on her play can help create opportunities for her to bring needy, scary, anxious, or angry private feelings out into the open, and can reduce her need to act them out in public. Still, there will be times when your child will behave aggressively and need you to reinstate some firm limits. In fact, by the time she's four years old or so, she can be a master of the indirect attack, or what is sometimes referred to as "passive-aggressive" behavior. For instance, when your preschooler is really mad at you because you have to pull her away from her cartoons at lunchtime, you may see her glass of milk "accidentally" spill once she's at the table. Or when her little brother has gotten the lion's share of Grandma's hugs, don't be surprised if his favorite pair of new bunny slippers go missing for a while.

When signs of passive-aggressive behavior begin to crop up, let your child know in a good-natured manner that you see right through her. Try and ferret out some of the reasons for her behavior, asking *who-what-where-when-why-how* questions in an unthreatening voice. Let her talk and verbally link up some of her feelings with the different ways she chooses to behave. As she tests her wit and cleverness against yours, she's gaining important practice in thinking. Now is not the time to lecture! Instead, quietly give your child firm limits that have real meaning for her. You might take away cartoon privileges for a while, or put away the new action figure for a time. Explain that you know it's hard to follow rules— it's hard for you, too!—and you hope that next time she'll be able to stay within your guidelines.

FOSTERING EMOTIONAL THINKING AS YOUR CHILD MATURES

As we have seen, your child's future ability to focus and plan, think abstractly, and test reality is being seeded during your conversations together. In the years ahead, these same dialogues will continue to build her intelligence. At college, passionate debates about love, life, and politics often generate more intellectual muscle than passive attendance at lectures. In a similar fashion, your child's ability to form bridges among her ideas and between the thoughts of others will eventually blossom into a capacity to step back from and reflect on her own ideas and emotions, which will be more valuable than most "enrichment" activities. Now she is capable of observing, "You banged into my toy car but I wanted my car to bang yours first"; in 20 years that same gift for self-reflection will be more fine-tuned and help her be a problem-solver at school, at work, and in relationships. With the ability to reflect on her feelings your child will be freed from acting them out.

The more practice your child receives in engaging you in whimsical play and conversation, the better she'll be able to comprehend written and oral stories. For instance, during the elementary school years a teacher will surely ask questions about a character's motivation in a story the class is reading. The child who has had innumerable opportunities to ask a lot of *where-when-why-how* questions, and who has received a lot of *because* answers that linked her ideas to another's, is far more likely to comprehend nuance and see patterns in the stories she reads.

Self-reflection and logical dialogue also help a child distinguish his or her thoughts from another person's. In a complex social setting like school or camp, a child who lacks such capacities would be more likely to think, "Nobody likes me," when she feels upset or anxious. She wouldn't be able to accurately assess outer reality and realize, "It might feel like no one likes me, but I know it's not really true." As your child's capacity for self-reflection grows, so does her ability to make reasoned judgments. Emotional thinking will not only foster reality testing and self-reflection, it will also help your child embrace planning for the future. Because she can connect her feelings and behaviors while being good with positive consequences, such as being praised or respected, your child is willing to delay gratification for a while. This gift of sensing that a positive end result awaits her efforts will enable her to plug away at arithmetic problems and patiently sound out words when she's a little older.

RAISING THE BAR

STRETCHING OUT DIALOGUES

When it comes to making conversation with your toddler, less is not more. More is more! Now's the time to get a running dialogue going about everything under the sun. When the two of you stand side by side brushing your teeth at the bathroom mirror, see if you can spark a toothpaste-filled conversation about the pros and cons of brushing fast or slow, up or down, front to back. When you're running errands in the car, try to pick up on her comments about the noisy fire engines whizzing by and then parlay her observations into a discussion about safety, or the exciting life of a fireman. During quieter rides make it a point to exclaim, "What a beautiful pond!" and see if the two of you can spin out a conversation about the ducks and frogs and water lilies. Bath times will provide you with another good opportunity for reality-based conversation, in which the two of you can talk about school and friends and life in general.

The more interactive your daily routines are, the more practice your child will get in building bridges between her ideas and yours. She'll have more opportunities to exercise her logic as the two of you discuss real-life situations. If your dialogues are conducted in a spirit of fun, and you don't sound preachy or take control of the subject matter, your little three- or four-year-old will tremendously enjoy chatting with you. Also, as long as you give your child plenty of time to craft meaningful responses and questions of her own, you needn't worry about exhausting or boring her. Another adult might be drained by your eagerness to keep the small talk going, but your little preschooler will usually thrive on it.

All of your reality-based back-and-forth's will give your child extra practice in building coherent thoughts, but it is the longer chats of 15 to 20 minutes at a time that really help develop your child's ability to sequence her thoughts. These free-flowing dialogues can range over a wide field of topics, including her friends, her preschool activities, stories she has heard you read to her, and even what's cooking for dinner.

There will be occasions, however, when your child will be more reluctant to chat with you than at other times. As we saw in Chapters 4 and 5, there are many gentle ways to keep a conversation going. Earlier in this chapter, we looked at various ways to elicit your child's opinions, or to help her elaborate new ideas. In general, when conversations start to lag, go back to building your questions around your child's actions, or your own. As long as you tap into her emotion of the moment, you're bound to engage her eventually.

For instance, at lunchtime one day your four-year-old may simply decide to be difficult and silently dismiss all your menu suggestions with a shake of her head. Perhaps she's giving you the silent treatment because you had to scuttle your plans to play mini-golf with her that afternoon. Even though she's angry, you know she's hungry and therefore has a vested interest in saying what it is that she truly wants to eat. You might try going to the refrigerator and deliberately taking out foods that you know she dislikes. "Oh look, how about some artichokes for lunch?" When she shakes her head in disgust, you can keep pulling out her least favorite dishes, and then even get downright silly. "Oh I've found just the thing! Rhinoceros stew!" If she isn't already giggling by this point, ask her for some help in finding something she'd *really* like. Rifling through the cabinets and refrigerator together will surely generate a conversation about food.

Why go to such lengths to rebuild your verbal connection with your child? Simply put, only you, or a loving caretaker who is focused on your child, has the time or the stamina to help her constantly refocus on linking up her inner thoughts to the outside world. These dialogues build up her ability to think logically and are the single most important thing you can do during these months to raise the bar on her intellectual, social, and moral capabilities.

MAGIC MOMENTS

In an ideal world, you'd always have the time and energy to be a fun-loving conversationalist and play partner for your child. For many families today, however, time is so strictly budgeted that playtime and even interludes of quiet conversation can get lost in the shuffle of a hectic day. Therefore, it's important to set aside a special time each day, lasting at least 25 to 35 minutes, in which you do nothing but play and chat with your child. Choose a time that is likely to be relaxed for the two of you, so you won't feel resentful or angry. Your spouse or other caregivers should also set aside at least one half-hour period each day to be available to follow your child's make-believe whimsies.

In addition, during the day be sure to look for any excuse to start up reality-based conversations and problem-solving discussions with your child. Some of your most memorable dialogues can occur when the two of you are doing something as ordinary as driving to the bus stop or walking out to the mail box. The more you lightheartedly insist on getting logical responses, and prompt her with words like "What else?" or offer her a contrary idea ("Isn't *X* the best cartoon show?" "No Mommy, no one likes it because . . . "), the richer your child's mental infrastructure will become.

BROADENING YOUR CHILD'S THINKING

As you help your child link her thoughts to yours in increasingly long chains, it's also important to put her in touch with a broad range of emotions and opinions. As we've explained in previous chapters, her ability to comprehend an abstract concept is directly tied to the multiple emotional experiences she has with that concept or word. She comes to know what abstractions like "love," "fairness," or "kindness" are because she eventually distills their meaning from all the various loving, fair, or kind experiences she has had. Thus, the more emotional experiences she has in the course of her day, the better she'll become at handling abstract concepts.

Helping your child identify and verbalize her feelings will increase her ability to think abstractly. The more she is able to talk about her feelings, the more she will be able to distinguish between her emotions and understand what triggers them. You can help your child find the words to describe her feelings by asking her questions about the events that set them off, and encouraging her to discuss the situation for as long as she cares to. You might even refer to an actual or invented incident that caused you to feel a similar way, or ask her to compare her feelings and think about their intensity.

Another way to help your child talk about her feelings is to seek out conversational areas that genuinely interest her. If she's enraptured with horses, strike up conversations about ponies and bridles and palominos. If baseball interests her, talk about your hometown team. Your chats won't disintegrate into rote recitations of different kinds of ponies or baseball stats if you try to broaden the scope of your discussions to engage her *feelings* about these things. Any number of stories about horses or baseball, from Black Beauty to Mark McGwire, can elicit powerful feelings. The more you tap into your child's genuine interests, the more motivated and logical her arguments will be. Introducing a little conflict and challenge into areas in which she shows a natural interest will ensure that your discussions will move beyond her own script and will include a broader discussion of feelings and ideas.

DEBATE AND COMPROMISE

A surefire way to help your child grapple with your own ideas and broaden your conversational and pretend-play base is to help her become aware that other people's ideas are worthy of consideration. You can provide her with practice in doing this each time you enter her make-believe dramas and become a feisty player with your own ideas and desires. While you follow her lead during your playtimes, try and mix it up by changing her script a little. When you adlib, she'll have to adlib back to keep the game going. This is how she'll learn that playing with you involves a spontaneous dialogue that's full of different ideas and opinions, rather than her own scripted monologue. If you make this fun, she'll occasionally be willing to compromise and let you have your way. Debates over household decisions, as we said before, also encourage flexible thinking.

You can underscore this lesson each time a playmate comes to the house and the two children play together by stepping into their interaction if your child insists that things can only go her way. Remind her that that's not always possible, and suggest taking turns. You can make the compromise more palatable by making it part of a fun elimination game, like "Eeny Meeny Miney Moe," or "Engine, Engine No. 9." Of course, you'll need to soothe whoever "loses," but even a disappointed four-year-old child can sense the fairness of the process and the need to take turns. Making your child more comfortable with the inevitable need to compromise teaches her how to function in the real world.

It's often very helpful for preschoolers to "practice" losing before they experience the real thing. Before your child's playmate arrives, discuss how it feels to take turns. Practice elimination games with your child and let her come up with the short end of the stick a few times. Talk about compromising, and help her anticipate letting her friend play with her new Play-Doh kit while she plays with the friend's card game.

Visualizing Social and Emotional Challenges

When your child knows that she will be facing a difficult emotional or social situation in the near future, like the necessity of sharing a new toy or having to face a mean child at preschool the next day, she's surely going to feel a little anxious and is bound to let you know it. The two of you can have problem-solving discussions every day in which you work on anticipating both the good and bad things that are in store for her. Let's assume, for example, that your four-and-a-half-year old comes home from preschool with a stricken look on her face and is full of complaints about a boy who pushed her during circle time. She may say something like "I hate him and I'm not going back to school if he's there." After putting an arm around your child and sympathetically letting her ventilate, try to shift your conversation over to a problem-solving mode.

Encourage your child to picture what circle time at school might be like the next day. Have her close her eyes and imagine the scene as if it were a television show. See if she can picture tomorrow's circle time, with the same mean classmate present, and have her describe to you what the scene might look like. You can prompt her by asking what the boy might be wearing, or where he might be sitting, or what the teacher might be doing. Try to ask about some of the details she's seeing in her mind's eye, so you can be sure that she's creating a vivid mental picture.

If your little girl finds it hard to visualize the scene, and says, "I can't do it! I can't make a picture on my screen,", you can help by asking, "Just tell me what you do see, sweetheart. Can you see what the boy's mouth might look like, or just a little bit of his face? Can you see his hands reaching out to push you?" After you help her pull these pieces together, she'll describe the people or the setting as best she can ("The boy is wearing blue shorts and a yellow T-shirt and he's wiggling around and he has squinched up his eyes and looks mean"; "My teacher is sitting on the other side of the circle and doesn't see anything"; "I'm wearing my dolphin sweatshirt and I'm sitting next to my friend, far away from the bad kid"). Don't worry if your child can't "see" too many details at first. Becoming a proficient visualizer doesn't happen overnight.

Once your child can "see" behaviors and people in her mind, try to have her picture the *feelings* that she might have during tomorrow's circle time ("I still hate him because he pushed me"). Then you could ask her to guess at the mean boy's feelings, which may be considerably harder for her to do. You might speculate with her about his emotions, and wonder aloud if he's feeling scared or bossy or lonely.

Next, try to have your child picture what she's likely to be *doing* during tomorrow's circle time, and have her describe her feelings and behavior to you. She may picture her actions a number of different ways ("Well, maybe I'll push him before he pushes me"; "I'll go tell the teacher what he did and make her punish him"; "I'll sit across the circle from him and stick out my tongue and make him feel bad"). You can empathically respond to all her statements, but try to build on one of the mental pictures she shares with you and help her come up with an alternative plan of action if she can't do it on her own. For instance, you might say, "Boy, I can just see you sitting across from him, giving him a mean look so he'll know he can't push you around anymore. I think that's a great plan! Maybe you'd better not stick your tongue out, though, because then the teacher might get mad at you instead."

A few days later you may find that your daughter decided to go ahead and wallop the mean boy instead of trying some of the alternate behavior she had pictured. Don't overreact or show her that you're displeased. Instead, try saying something like "Oops—remember what we said when we talked about this the other day? You decided that you could see yourself sitting clear across the circle from him and giving him a tough-guy look. Next time you're near him in circle time, take a second and even close your eyes if it's easier for you to picture what you should be doing that way." It's a lot easier for your child to commit to a future plan of action when she can "see" herself going through the motions. The visualization becomes a kind of dress rehearsal for how to behave during challenging real-life situations.

If your own child has problems pushing and shoving other children at school, and though able to visualize several alternate kinds of behavior finds it hard to stick to her plans, consider introducing some limits and incentives into the mix. For example, if she manages to follow her plan to use angry words or scowls instead of pushing, she might win a star from you (with ten stars she earns a trip to the toy store.) If she should revert to pushing, you can remind her to use her words, while giving her a warning: "Remember what we talked about; how you closed your eyes and could see yourself using angry words instead of pushing or shoving? Try really hard to see yourself using words instead of your arms next time. If you don't, we'll have to keep the TV turned off for two days." Should the pushing continue, be sure to hide the remote control. Limit setting only works if you carry it out!

As we mentioned earlier in this chapter, visualization not only reduces the sting of an upcoming event, it can also prolong its pleasure. When your child pictures tomorrow's trip to the zoo or a Christmas tree surrounded by colorful presents, she feels a sense of excitement that is a foretaste of the real pleasure she will soon be experiencing. Her wonderful new capacity to build bridges between her present and future emotions allows her to live beyond the moment and optimistically expect that the good times will roll on and on and on.

VISUALIZATION AND ACADEMIC SKILLS

Visualization skills can not only help your child anticipate social challenges, they can also give her a grasp of key mathematical and verbal con-

cepts long before she even enters kindergarten. Visualizing everyday objects that capture your child's interest can give her a genuine feel for quantity and numbers. Your goal is for your child to develop a good internal,
spatial sense of quantity, rather than have to rely on rote memory and par-
rot back that "Six plus four equals ten." You can help her master the basic
concepts of quantity by taking advantage of all the many compelling situations where your three- or four-year-old *really* wants something, and that
involve six items or less. Keep the numbers small but emotionally meaningful.

You'll have countless opportunities to explore the concept of quantity
with your child. Most children this age have a natural—even a passionate—interest in sweet foods like cookies or apples, and savory foods like
pizza. When you offer your hungry child some cookies, ask whether she
wants two or three. Count each cookie as you give it to her. What happens
if you take one away? Will she want more? Show her the cookies and ask
if two cookies are more than one cookie, or less. If you offer the healthier
apple alternative, ask her to show you with her fingers how much two apples would be if you put them side by side. Then have her show you how
much three apples would be, or four. Most importantly, have her then
close her eyes and see if she can picture five apples in a row, placed end to
end. Ask her to take two apples away and see if she can picture the remaining three. Remember that concepts are more fully mastered when a
child can close her eyes, picture the real objects that are in front of her, and
carry out your proposed operations by moving the objects in her mind's
eye.

Most children will take a look at a steaming pizza and if they're hungry
say that they want three pieces of pizza rather than two. (Their eyes, of
course, are frequently a lot bigger than their stomachs!) Try cutting a small
pizza into six pieces, and you'll probably be very surprised at your little
child's ability to grasp even more sophisticated concepts involving quantity. As you, your spouse, and your child are sitting around the kitchen
table getting ready to dig into the pizza, ask your four-and-a-half-year-
old, "How many slices of pizza should we take out of the box if each of us
is supposed to have one piece?" Then ask, "How many pieces are left in the
box if we each put two slices on each of our plates?" You could follow up
with "If Daddy takes one of those slices off your plate, how many will you
have left?" As you ask these questions, have your child close her eyes and
picture the slices of pizza on her plate. Nonfood items that lend themselves to this kind of mathematical interaction include shiny coins, mar-

bles, or intriguing blocks and seashells. The key point here is that the objects must be of compelling interest to your child.

Be sure initially to limit the numbers you use to six or less, so that any sequencing problems a child may have won't get in the way as much and interfere with her feel for quantity. In fact, it's far more useful to have your child add, subtract, multiply, and divide six objects than it is for her to be able to count to ten in a rote manner! Only when she's routinely able to do these sorts of operations by picturing them in her mind should she be encouraged to move on to larger numbers. Teaching your child to close her eyes and picture up to six objects in various combinations will give her the sort of spatial appreciation for quantity that gifted math students seem to be have.

These same visualization techniques can help your child develop an ability to grasp verbal concepts and reading comprehension skills long before she's able to read a single word. Now that she's become such a good thinker these past few months, she can become a more active participant in the process of understanding a story, rather than passively absorbing your words as you turn the pages of a book. Suppose the two of you are nestled side by side on the sofa, reading a storybook together. Try closing the book from time to time and asking her to close her eyes, too. Then, in an expectant voice, you can encourage her to paint a picture, or see a "movie" in her mind about the story you're reading together.

Let's say you've just finished reading a line about a boy going to a toy store. You could eagerly ask your child some questions about what she sees in her mind. What was the boy wearing when he decided to go to the store? Was he bundled up in an overcoat because it was cold outside? What color hat was he wearing? Did he remember to wear his scarf? You can build on her responses and help her flesh out the character she sees in her mind. How did he actually go to the store? What did he want to buy in the store and why? The more embellishments she is able to add to her mental pictures of the character and his surroundings, the more practice she'll receive in linking different ideas together to form multidimensional concepts.

As you depart from the written text every now and then, and help your child imagine a rich story behind the story, she'll be sharpening her ability to think in a cause-and-effect way. The two of you can discuss why the little boy chose a certain toy fire engine to take home with him. You could ask your daughter whether she would have put some different toys on the store shelves for the boy to make his selection from, saying, "Do you think the fire engine was the last one in the store?" "Were the other customers very sad when there wasn't one left to buy?" Ask her what would happen next if she were writing the story. Together, you can link atmospheric details, feelings, motivations, and consequences to the dry bones of the plot. All of your child's future reading and writing skills will be strengthened if they involve this kind of visualization.

Enabling Different Parts of the Brain and Mind to Work Together

Your little thinker is learning how to use all her senses, move her body in space, modulate her behavior, play make-believe games, take advantage of her improving gross and fine motor coordination, and engage you in interesting conversations, too. The more she is able to combine all these activities at once, the better a workout her nervous system will receive and the more efficiently it will operate. As you play together, keep one simple acronym in mind, FAT: Fun performing lots of Actions, while Talking logically at the same time. If you can manage to create opportunities in which your child accomplishes this, the two of you will be in fat city!

For starters, it's a good idea to let your preschooler enjoy a good physical workout at least three or four times a day, for periods of at least 10 or 15 minutes. A lot of motion seems to support the development of other parts of her nervous system, so it's especially beneficial—and fun—to join in on games that exercise her motor skills. It's not just the approving twinkle in your eye that makes your child feel good about the way her body works; an intrinsic sense of well-being will flood through her muscles when they are working well together. You've probably experienced this sensation yourself. When your bat connects to a ball with a resounding *thwack,* sending it soaring toward the outfield, your nervous system and muscles seem to hum. If you're a skillful dancer, getting up on your toes and gliding across the dance floor just feels good.

But if you've ever tried to use your left hand to shoot a basketball, and you're a righty by nature, your motions and actions won't feel as satisfying to you because they're not working in a smooth, flowing way. Similarly, if your child has some problems with motor control and you're trying to teach her how to throw a ball, she probably won't get much pleasure out of the action itself and may try to avoid it altogether. If she shies away from this kind of interaction with you, she won't get the practice she needs to become more proficient at throwing the ball, or get any pleasure out of the experience. Since she's not getting the sort of natural pleasure that a more coordinated child easily experiences within her body, and may not be receiving too many spontaneous shouts of approval from you, you've got to come up with another way to generate some genuine excitement about your activity together.

The method is downright simple: Make the activity so much fun that the external pleasure your child experiences will offset the lack of intrinsic pleasure in her body's movement. There are any number of ways to go about this. For example, if you're playing a game of catch, use an outsized Nerf ball that's at least as big as a soccer ball. If the two of you decide to play dodge ball, set up rules so that when you are "it" you can only play with one hand and have to crawl on all fours. Now your child will probably manage to hit you 70 percent of the time instead of a discouraging 30 percent, and she's bound to get a lot of enjoyment out of racking up points against you. Even if her motions are clumsy and the act of throwing isn't intrinsically pleasurable, eventually her increased practice will lead to smoother muscle control. At that point, she'll be able to tap into the easy, natural joy of physical activity.

You can also incorporate energetic movement into fun activities like obstacle courses and treasure hunts. Try setting up an obstacle course in which your child has to find something she wants by climbing through and going around, under, and over things. You can create a spooky tunnel by draping blankets over a table, or declare that the shortest route to the pirate's treasure is to be found by crawling under some chair legs.

Obstacle courses can not only be combined with imaginary play, they can also turn into complex treasure hunts that challenge a child to make full use of her auditory and visual-spatial processing skills. For instance, you might try announcing that a treasure hunt is under way for a prize that your child wants or values. At first, you might offer one or two simple clues ("The treasure is somewhere in the living room") that lead your child directly to the prize. Later you can make the hunt more complicated with three, four, and five-step clues ("Go to the living room and look for something green. Then look behind it and find a shoe box. Reach inside and find the treasure!"). Following your verbal directions will sharpen your child's auditory and sequencing skills; talking about how the treasure got buried in the first place ("Remember when the pirate ship sank nearby and they had to hide their gold?") will get her imagination cooking at the same time. You could even challenge her ability to think spatially by handing her a simple floor plan of the room with an "X" marking the spot where the shoe box is hidden.

Another example of an activity that engages all the various parts of your child's nervous system so that they function interdependently is setting up a good guy/bad guy chase. The entire house can be declared open territory with one spot designated as home base. If you can set up a low balance beam (for example, by laying a sturdy plank on two low boxes) and call it "home," you'll be able to spark a "FAT" game that involves thematic play with lots of verbalization, spatial thinking, and muscle coordination.

Here's how such a game could play out. If you are an evil mad scientist trying to rob Superwoman of her powers with a rock of kryptonite, challenge her to flee to safety toward the balance beam. Set up agreed-upon blockades and barriers before you start the chase, and challenge you child to think more architecturally. How can she get from the dining room to the living room without touching the carpet? Once she reaches "home," she'll have to maintain her balance on the beam, and control her muscles with confidence even as you gently barrage her with balloons or Nerf balls (a.k.a. "kryptonite"). As your child gamely bats the balloons/Nerf balls away while maintaining her balance, the two of you will keep up a running dialogue about how the mad scientist is enraged by Superwoman's amazing powers.

Dos and Don'ts as You Help Your Child Learn to Think (30 Months and Up)

~

- *Do* rely on jointly creating elaborate pretend dramas that have logical, interconnected plots. For example, tea parties and school scenes and trips to Grandma's can all be woven together.

- *Do* rely on enjoyable debates about everything from food and clothes choices to sharing toys.

- *Don't* simply tell your child what to do; explain *why* you want to do something. Discuss the pros and cons, and give your child plenty of time to argue her viewpoint. A good rule of thumb is that if your child's answers don't frequently surprise you, or if you have a single correct answer in mind, you are probably overscripting.

🐝 *Do* rely on reflective discussions. When your child wants something, don't simply say yes or no. Instead, ask "What/when/why/how . . . ?" In this way, you'll help your child give an opinion and reflect on her own wishes—the foundation for abstract thinking.

🐝 *Do* carry out these activities in peer, sibling, and small play groups. Children can debate each other or make funny pictures.

🐝 *Don't* solve problems for your child; let her solve them herself. Your role is to help her brainstorm or to offer any needed encouragement.

🐝 *Do* create experiences involving quantity, time, and space concepts that engage your child's strong feelings of the moment.

🐝 *Do* expose your child to a rich range of activities and encourage her natural interests and abilities. All these experiences will strengthen her ability to think abstractly.

🐝 *Do* enjoy stories, reading, puzzles, and other traditional activities as part of a vibrant back-and-forth discussion.

🐝 *Do* enjoy helping your child use words to describe all the different feelings of life, from anger to closeness. Discuss feelings during both pretend play and reality-based conversations.

This kind of complex activity is a useful way to raise the bar on your four-and-a-half-year-old's ability to look, listen, feel, touch, and act all at the same time! On other occasions, drumming or playing the piano or listening to music and moving to the beat can also provide your three- or four-year-old with a good rhythmic workout. By challenging your child on multiple fronts at once, or even on a few at a time, you'll be optimally helping her to build a healthy mind. She'll also be ready to play simplified versions of real games like dodge ball, basketball, or soccer. A game of catch in which the ball is randomly thrown to the right or left or high or low will get her going in such sports. As long as you level the playing field by doing such things as walking on your knees or only using one hand, and let your child "win" these contests at least 70 percent of the time, she's bound to enjoy herself thoroughly.

If your preschooler has trouble modulating her behavior, you could incorporate exercises in your pretend play that feature the need to run as quickly as you can from a group of scary giants, medium-fast so the princess can keep up with you, and slow-as-a-snail to escape the giants' attention. Similarly, your games can feature high-five's that are hard, regular, soft, and supersoft as you manage to kill off the monsters one by one, and you can shout, talk in a normal voice, and whisper as the two of you discuss the situation. If the excitement proves too much for your playmate, shift the action to slow motion for a while and help her modulate her behavior while still having fun.

Fine motor skills can also be an integral part of your games and pretend play together. At this age, most children love drawing games, finger painting, and scribble-scrabbling, and you can make up stories about the figures and shapes you see in each other's pictures. Some children who are particularly talented in the visual-spatial area and less confident about initiating conversations or following verbal instructions may enjoy drawing pictures and maps that help them make sense of their environment. For instance, if your child seems wistful because Mommy's gone on a trip, try getting out some paper and crayons and suggesting that the two of you draw a map that shows where Mommy is. As you stretch your child's visual skills and ability to coordinate the fine muscles of her hands, you'll also be helping her to feel emotionally close to her mother even when she's far away.

If your child has some trouble with her fine motor abilities and doesn't want to practice scribbling x's and o's or making shapes with her crayons, try to invent a game where she's motivated to move that crayon. You might suggest that you have to be able to copy any shapes she makes or you lose a point. Then tell her that if you are penalized a certain number of points she'll earn herself a trip to the toy store or the ice cream parlor. Be sure, of course, to be unsuccessful at copying some of her scribblings so you'll rack up points and she'll be able to win her treat.

The games we have been describing are also great activities to do with other children, peers as well as siblings. At this age it's often more fun for your child if one or more of her friends are involved. Small group games that stretch her abilities are very self-motivating because of her pleasure in being part of the group's shared fun.

BUILDING A COHESIVE SENSE OF SELF

As your child experiences all the different aspects of her personality (the angry side, the warm side, the loving side, the rejecting side, the silly side) while interacting with you, the parts themselves become interrelated because they coexist within a single relationship. Your joint relationship acts as a sort of glue that makes all the fragmented pieces of your child's personality combine into a seamless self capable of more cohesive patterns of thought.

Because her mind can now connect ideas in both time and space, your child forms a sort of composite, multisensory image of herself ("I'm skinny/stubborn/funny/pretty/nice," etc.). She can synthesize the piecemeal images she has of herself in the immediate past, present, and future, as well as in different settings (playing at nursery school, shopping with Mom or Dad). Thus, underlying her ability to sequence her thoughts logically is her growing sense of herself as an individual who has many different kinds of thoughts and feelings at different times and in different situations.

Through her empathetic relationship with you, your little girl is slowly getting in touch with a more integrated image of herself. A big part of this new self-image involves her fascination with all the various parts of her body. Preschoolers busily inspect their genitals and enjoy the pleasure they discover in those parts of their bodies, just as they relish all their senses. They laugh at any reference to elimination and like to shock you with their silly talk about "pee-pee heads" and "doo-doo faces." They know all the names of the major features on their bodies, and have a growing comprehension about how their body parts relate to each other.

Your child will probably express some concern about getting hurt. You may notice that a lot of themes about body parts falling off are now emerging during her pretend play. Your toddler worries about being able to protect her body, and reduces some of her anxiety by cavalierly lopping off other characters' limbs as she plays make-believe. Both boys and girls may experience a vague sense of anxiety when they observe differences between their own bodies and other people's. More frequently, however, girls and boys have many positive feelings about the specialness of their own bodies.

When your child expresses bodily concerns, it can sometimes be a symptom of how she's feeling about herself in general. Conversations about dolls' missing arms or legs can be a thinly veiled metaphor for your child's feelings of vulnerability in her relationship with you or others. On the other hand, when you hear your little girl hurling angry comments at you out of left field ("You're so mean"; "You're a crummy dad"), the words may actually be a clue that she's worried about challenges at preschool, such as a mean peer.

In general, though, your child's emerging interest in her body and the pleasure it brings to her will strengthen her sense of herself and her sense of others. She's starting to conceptualize what is inside her and what is outside, and to define the boundaries of her physical self. As she comes to be aware of her gender (in the childlike way of knowing that she's different from boys), her understanding of the real world is increased. Her growing sense of gender and sexual identity helps build her positive self-esteem.

Your role in this process is surprisingly simple. Try to be a warm, empathetic listener. If you're playing out a make-believe role, you can take extra care to keep the scariness of your character within boundaries that won't upset your child. When you're cast in the role of a protector or take on the voice of an observant narrator, use a comforting voice that will encourage your toddler to express all her fears and anxieties. Keep an even, calm tone, even when body parts are swirling all around. Although there is no need to offer up any solutions for your child's fears about harm coming to her body, or for her anxieties about differences between girls and boys, you can look for ways to help her link her ideas together and to consider what she would like to see happen next.

During this period, as your child's self image about her gender starts to coalesce, she may, through dress up and play, start exploring various possibilities. You may first observe some of this behavior as early as the second year of life. By providing her with appropriate nurturing and limits and a sense of security, coupled with encouraging her initiative, curiosity, and independence, you can usually support a healthy organized sense of gender in your child. If, however, your child seems angry, sad, or very confused and anxious about her body, it may reflect a deeper difficulty, and she may benefit from a professional consultation.

OVERCOMING CHALLENGES:
A BLESSING IN DISGUISE

Your preschooler's progress up through the developmental ladder has been an amazing journey. Perhaps your child, like Kara, Brian, Emma, Will, and Max, whom we've been checking in on in each chapter of this book, has had to put in a little extra practice before being able to pull herself up to the next rung. Since many children have various sensitivities or processing issues that range from negligible to significant, it's important to view these challenges as expectable aspects of normal developmental growth. Your willingness to take a clear-eyed look at where your child truly is on the developmental ladder, and then to woo her into emotionally rich interactions, has spurred her on to new achievements.

These days, she's gradually becoming not only a gifted conversationalist but also a debater, pretender, negotiator, and analytical thinker. There are times, however, when the process of learning how to think both logically and abstractly seems to bring her two steps forward, only to fall one step back. On any given day your four-and-a-half-year-old may be logical most of the time, building bridges between your ideas and hers while remaining attentive, warmly engaged, interactive, and creative, too. At some point during that same day, though, her thinking is likely to become disorganized and she may avert her eyes from yours, hide under a table, tune out your comments or stage a full-blown tantrum. She may shy away from linking her thoughts to yours because she becomes frustrated or feels uncomfortable handling certain emotions.

When your little girl developmentally regresses, she usually doesn't slide all the way back down to the bottom of the ladder. She may temporarily lose the ability to carry on a logical dialogue while engaging in imaginative play, or talk about her own ideas while ignoring yours. Occasionally, her regressions will be more marked and she'll refuse to play "Let's pretend" but remain involved with you and able to exchange emotional signals like smiles or gestures while making silly sounds or hiding under a table. If she's particularly stressed, she may well ignore your verbal overtures but manage to stay warmly engaged with you. When a fight with a playmate overwhelms her, she's likely to crawl into your lap to regroup for a while before she can become energized enough to tell you what happened.

When your child regresses, always try to increase your soothing engagement. Then, try to assess exactly where she is on the developmental ladder at that particular moment. Your goal will be to gauge how many rungs down on the ladder she's fallen, and to steady her at that level before helping her to retrace her steps. You'll be helping her get back in sync by taking a look at those early developmental capacities that she mastered long ago and assisting her to calm herself, pay attention, and remain engaged with you.

Take a moment and quickly run through the basic developmental stages in your mind, working from the bottom up to help her keep all the foundation pieces sturdily in place. Ask yourself: Do I have my child's attention? Is she looking at, listening to, or touching me? If you sense that your child has become disengaged, consider whether a gentle touch of the hand or lots of supportive gestures will help her engage with you. You may decide that sitting on the floor beside your child as she morosely plays with some of her toys might be a good way to recapture a sense of engagement.

Once the two of you are relating again, ask yourself if your three- or four-year-old is truly interacting with you in a more and more intimate way. Is her back still turned to you as she sits stony-faced next to you? Or does she indicate through her frowns and disgruntled expressions that there's some meaningful relating going on? If you sense that she doesn't seemed to be fully engaged, try joining her in an activity that she's already started, or being gentle and cuddly, to help break the ice. At that point you can try exchanging various gestures, from smiles and smirks to head nods. Usually when a child is upset or withdrawn and needs to be wooed, the simple act of handing her an item such as a crayon if she's drawing, or a new video tape if she shows an interest in getting the VCR to work, or even a snack to eat, will get communication going once again.

After you've mentally scanned your child's behavior and seen signs that she's effectively operating at these earlier developmental levels, you can take a look at whether she's able to actually problem-solve and chat with you. Once you feel there's some complex problem solving going on between the two of you, you can try approaching her at the level of ideas. Hopefully, at that point you can play pretend games or engage in logical conversations together.

More often than not, after quickly going over your mental checklist, you'll find that your preschooler only backslides a developmental rung or two at time. Suppose your four-year-old is yelling and screaming at you because you stood firm and only gave her two cookies, and has clearly become disorganized in her thinking. It's obvious that she's still engaged with you, however, as she grabs your apron and attempts to rip off the apron strings. She may even furrow her brow and mutter, "You are a stupid dopey Mommy." Certainly her gesturing, problem-solving actions, and words reveal that she's making at least partial use of all the earlier developmental levels, although her ideas are now fragmented and illogical because she's not handling her anger very well. You can help her go from these fragmented patterns of thinking to logical thinking by first helping her relax and quiet down. As she regains her calm, you can once again ask her questions that will help her link her own ideas to yours.

As a general rule of thumb, whenever your child regresses, your first thought should be to soothe, soothe, soothe. Use whatever calming technique works best—anything from a firm back rub, empathetic hand on her shoulder, and gentle stroking of her hair to offering warm eye contact. Soothing not only helps your child slow down enough to reorganize herself and take another step up the developmental ladder but also helps activate those earlier stages that are tied to her most basic emotions and body sensations.

It may take you just a few minutes or an entire floor-time session to help your child regroup, but it's time well spent. Each time you help your child reclimb the developmental ladder, you make her skills that much more stable. Don't feel unduly discouraged when she occasionally stumbles, or assume that you've somehow failed to give her adequate support. You'll be helping your child grow in her area of challenge each time the two of you return to and remaster an earlier interactive level. Since challenges can be met, and confidence can be regained, these regressions give you a chance to put your child's development on a surer footing. Now let's check in once again with our five special preschoolers and see how they and their parents are coping with their two-steps-forward-one-step-back climb into emotional thinking.

Preschoolers Who Are Sensitive to Touch and Sound

By the summer Kara turned four years old she seemed to have outgrown some of her earlier finickiness and hesitancy about certain touches and loud noises, but she still seemed bossy and controlling. In fact, her siblings, Joey and Rachel, now seven and nine years old, had long since stopped viewing her as the family's helpless baby and were getting increasingly annoyed by her attitude. Tensions had risen within the family to such an extent that Ellen, the children's mother, was getting worried. She decided to call the developmental specialist the family had previously been working with and set up an appointment.

Within a few minutes of being in the therapist's office, it became clear that Kara had made wonderful developmental progress during the two years that had elapsed since her last visit. She was able to leave her mother and father, Steve, behind in the waiting room as she engaged the therapist in easygoing chitchat. Their conversation together lasted a good 15 minutes, during which time Kara not only discussed a number of her own ideas but also responded to and built on some of the therapist's. Her ability to participate in long back-and-forth sequences about day camp and swimming in her pool was impressive, and she demonstrated a vocabulary ("My eyes got red 'cause the pool was too chlorinated") that was actually startling at times.

However, when Steve and Ellen reentered the office and started to take part in a make-believe game that Kara had initiated about a monster chasing Superman, it was evident that she still had hypersensitivities where loud noises and startling movements were concerned. At one point during the drama, Steve took on the role of the monster and made funny but loud noises. Kara visibly flinched and her patter remained subdued for the next few minutes.

After Kara's parents reviewed their usual patterns of behavior with the therapist, he suggested that it wasn't surprising that Kara found it so difficult to get along with her brother and sister and became so negative and stubborn when she played with them. She was a bright child, and intuitively recognized that she couldn't count on her siblings to calm her down the way her parents usually did when playtimes or conversations got too frenzied. She avoided interacting with Joey and Rachel in unstructured situations because she knew from experience that their rough-and-tumble play could easily upset her. Unfortunately, she avoided a lot of fun and joy and missed out on new games as she tried to protect herself. Her frequent whine "I don't want to do this anymore" made her seem like a spoilsport to her brother and sister, and they had simply lost patience with her apparent petulance.

In the past Rachel had seemed more than willing to help her little sister learn to tolerate various touches and sounds. The therapist suggested that when Kara pulled away from interacting with her sister, Rachel could be coached on how to soothe her, and keep the play going. Even rambunctious Joey could be made to understand that his little four-year-old sister probably felt bad about herself each time she had to shy away from playing with him.

However, the therapist also had a hunch that jealousy might be fueling the hostility between the three children. Steve and Ellen needed to devote a little more one-on-one time with their two older children. He suggested that Rachel and Joey no doubt harbored a natural resentment of all the attention that swirled around Kara and her special sensitivities, and that if they had at least one floor-time session each day with either Steve or Ellen they would probably be more willing to put up with their parents' limited attention at other times of the day when Kara was more demanding. Individual floor-time attention would provide them with an avenue for expressing their thoughts and feelings, and give each one a chance to be the top figure on the family totem pole for a while.

Steve and Ellen were encouraged to give their older children plenty of time and space to complain about Kara if they chose to, and not to criticize or judge Joey and Rachel's negative feelings. Turning the warm glow of their full attention on Joey and Rachel and sympathizing with the older children's frustration at having to be "nice" and "superquiet" around Kara would go a long way toward dissolving some of the antipathy that had built up over the past year or so.

The therapist also suggested that Steve and Ellen try to carve out even more time to stage some playtimes for the whole family, like the imaginary zoo game they had played together when the children were younger. By alternating who gets to be the boss during each session, each child—including Kara—would get a chance to set his or her own standards for having fun, and then hopefully learn to have a good time while following another person's lead, too. That meant that Rachel would have to let "the two shrimps" boss her around for a while, and Joey would have to be persuaded not to snicker when Kara's Lion King "roar" sounded more like a purr during their make-believe play. Even Kara could probably be coaxed into not covering her ears each and every time Joey started to beat his breast like Tarzan. Family-wide playtimes would be special occasions for fun that would promote the children's willingness to compromise and better tolerate each other's style.

Another way to promote Kara's flexibility and willingness to tolerate new sensations would be to have her interact more frequently with children outside the family circle. The therapist suggested increasing the number of days that Kara attended preschool from three to four, and having playmates come over after school two or three times a week as well. It was also critical to reemphasize to her teachers just how hard it sometimes was for her to tolerate the noise and rowdy touches of a large group of children. A simple accommodation like allowing Kara to play one-on-one with just a single child in a quiet corner of the room before the tumult of circle time each morning would make her transition to the noisy group less overwhelming.

The therapist urged Steve and Ellen not to feel embarrassed if their daughter exhibited some of her disorganized or aloof behavior in front of a playmate or two. He let them know that it was fine idea for them to occasionally step right into a role in the children's pretend play and soothe Kara when necessary, and then help her get back into the rhythm of logically responding to her friends' thoughts and creating some of her own. Kara would surely benefit from all these additional opportunities to learn how to read and tolerate other children's idiosyncrasies. Now that they better understood how to bolster Kara's ability to cope with her sensitivities to noise and touch, and had come to a new realization that *all* their children would benefit from more floor-time interaction, Steve and Ellen headed home armed with a new sense of optimism.

PRESCHOOLERS WHO ARE UNDERWHELMED BY THE WORLD AROUND THEM

What a difference a year makes! Just last year, Brian's father, Stuart, had been dismayed when he noticed how much less verbal his son seemed to be than the other children at nursery school. Now, as Brian was rounding on his fourth birthday, the preschooler spent whole chunks of time sprawled on his tummy, chatting up a storm as he lined up his action figures in elaborate configurations. Stuart and his wife, Tammy, were delighted at Brian's progress; he had been a "low sender" as a baby and had seemed frustratingly unresponsive to their energetic visual and verbal cues. However, early interventions designed to woo him into interaction by appealing to his well-developed visual sense and his delight in motion (involving lots of trips to the swing-set in the park) seemed to pay off. Brian had developed a real ability to play imaginatively for long periods of time and had no trouble describing the action to his parents.

Stuart and Tammy began to notice, however, that all of Brian's chatter was basically a monologue. Although he certainly appeared bright and verbal, he seemed to prefer his imaginary world to the real one. He needed to verbally "mix it up" with his parents and other children, to logically build his thoughts and pretend play in response to theirs. The more interactive conversations and pretend play Brian's parents could involve him in, the more chances they would have to go after his opinions and engage him in debates. The best way to do this was to talk about what he was doing and offer an opinion. "What if we put the action figure over here?" would spur Brian quickly to answer "No, over there!" Stuart also discovered that another way to elicit an opinion from Brian was to ask him how he felt about something. Questions like "Does that story make you feel happy, sad, or angry?" or "How do you feel when someone borrows your favorite toy?" often enticed Brian into sounding more like an expressive poet of his feelings.

Stuart and Tammy needed to engage their little boy in high-energy, rapid back-and-forth's while gently prodding him to answer their questions and build on their ideas. Making gains in this area was just a matter of practice. Instead of watching Brian manipulate his figures and offering summary comments like "Oh, what a marvelous fort you've built, Bri!" Stuart and Tammy tried entering right into the heart of the pretend play itself, even if it meant playfully raising their voices, waving their arms, or putting their faces near his. Their gestures, comments, and reactions caused his dramas to become more spontaneous and less scripted. Brian was more likely to bridge his ideas to theirs, since he wanted to prolong the fun they were having together.

Chase and follow-the-leader games, building forts and mountains made of pillows, and roughhousing also helped Brian focus his attention, engage in a dialogue, and think logically more than the elaborate but solitary games he had cocooned himself in. For that reason, Stuart and Tammy limited Brian's television and computer viewing to just a half hour a day. (In fact, all preschoolers should ideally be limited to no more than 30 minutes of television each day and another 30 minutes of computer games if they enjoy them.)

Brian needed his parents' help to connect all of his fragmented thoughts into long, related themes. If Stuart and Tammy let the high-energy quality of their interaction flag too soon, their son was likely to attend only to the beat of his own drum, and get lost in his own world. Brian's isolation tended to limit the depth and breadth of his thoughts. To counter this, his parents tried to energize their voices, and would ask him why he didn't answer their last question or respond to their pretend character's most recent comment. In this way, Stuart and Tammy would reel him back into connecting his piecemeal thoughts. As Brian grew more proficient in bridging his ideas to other people's, his social skills gained some polish, too. By participating in lengthier conversations, he had valuable practice in learning how to more rapidly assess the tone and vocal rhythms of other people's voices. This skill would help him to size up other children's intentions at school and on the playground, and would continue to serve him well when as an adult he had to work the crowd at a large party. Learning how to establish eye contact with a person, hold out a hand, and smile while saying "Hello!" is a pretty complex sequence of connected actions that are typically first practiced during this stage of development.

Because his motor tone was still somewhat low, Brian found it more difficult than some other children to complete certain motor actions before moving on to others both in real life and during pretend play. His pretend play appeared more fragmented. Brian's parents' job was to take on a role within the drama to help him return to the first action and complete it, or close the circle of communication before going on to the next theme. Games involving three or four steps might remain difficult for Brian to do, so it was important for Stuart and Tammy to provide him with some fun workouts that would improve his ability to coordinate his movements. They constructed mazes of cardboard boxes, pillows, and sofa cushions and staged lively hide-and-seek games that encouraged their little boy to link the movements of his body into longer, emotionally driven sequences.

Brian's parents also helped their son connect up his thoughts in real-life situations. For instance, if he wanted to stay up past his usual bedtime, he might simply announce, "I don't wanna go to bed now!" Stuart and Tammy encouraged a spirit of debate and lawyerly discussion with their son by playfully posing argumentative questions like "Give us three good reasons and maybe we can work something out." If Brian came up with "I'm not very sleepy" pretty readily, his parents could help him link up this thought with several others by asking "And you wouldn't have any interest in watching this television show with us, right?" or "What do you think about taking a nap tomorrow because you may be sleepy if you stay up late tonight?" Such emotion-based debates are an extremely effective way to grab the attention of underreactive children like Brian and pull them back into logically interacting with the busy, raucous outside world.

Stuart and Tammy also began increasing the number of times they played physical games with Brian to four or five times a day. They introduced running, jumping, and spinning games, and looking-and-doing games such as dodgeball and soccer, as well as treasure hunts. These activities are especially important for children like Brian who need extra practice in using their muscles.

PRESCHOOLERS WHO CRAVE STIMULATION

At four and a half Emma was still a little spitfire—energetic and verbal. More than most children, Emma spent a lot of her waking hours in search of colorful, noisy, intense physical and manipulative experiences because more subtle sensations left her hungry. She needed a lot of sensory input to "fill her up." She also appeared to be rigid or bossy when her sources of stimulation were being threatened.

It was obvious that the many distractions of school were making it hard for Emma to regulate herself without behaving aggressively. She felt unsure of herself and coped with that feeling by being active and keeping her distance from other children. This four-and-a-half-year-old needed some help in finding more socially acceptable ways to get a lot of sensory input.

The family's developmental specialist suggested that Emma would benefit from even more floor-time interaction with her parents, Laura and Mike, in the secure and controlled atmosphere of their home. It would be a good idea to have similar props to those used in preschool (animal figures, for example) on hand. Laura or Mike could then follow Emma's lead as she got an imaginary game involving the figures under way, being sensitive to her need to control the action. This meant that Emma's parents would avoid hovering over her, so as not to inadvertently make her feel protective of her toys. They could then offer—with soothing voices and slow, relaxed gestures—to help her group the animals into different corrals. As long as they approached their child slowly, and let Emma know that she was in charge, the odds were good that their little girl would be willing to link her thoughts to theirs during their imaginary play together.

Laura and Mike worked on modulating the pace of their play, having fast-moving lions become sleepy, slow ones. Laura and Mike did lots of soothing, too, after they introduced fun sensory play in which elephants stepped on people and animals in their path.

This sort of dress rehearsal for the more spontaneous pretend play that goes on in a preschool setting should help Emma learn to play with other children. If Laura and Mike were able to help her talk about her feelings as she played, and later discuss how hard it is to share toys sometimes, Emma would be less thrown by the actual give-and-takes that take place at school. Her parents could also make it a point to have extra rough-and-tumble play during their pretend-play sessions together, since that would help satisfy Emma's craving for sensation. Furthermore, they could encourage her to incorporate exciting themes into her pretend play; characters could go to Mars instead of the Safeway and farmers could grow diamonds and rubies instead of wheat. With practice, make-believe and melodrama could also satisfy some of her thirst for heightened sensation.

The specialist pointed out that a child like Emma, who single-mindedly goes out in search of exciting sensation, is more likely to overlook how her behavior might make another child feel. He felt that it was essential to follow up any "sharing" conversations between Emma and her parents with an increased number of after-school play dates—four or five times each week, if possible—to put the lessons into practice. The specialist went on to add that many additional opportunities to show concern for other people's needs would present themselves during the course of an ordinary day at home.

For example, Emma could be asked to pass the bread or salt to someone during dinner. If Grandma were to call and keep Laura on the phone for a while, Emma could be led to delay her gratification of a perceived need in the following manner: If she started tugging on Laura's arm to go out while her mother was speaking on the phone, Laura could remark, "Just give me five more minutes, sweetheart, I want to finish my conversation with Grandma." If Emma were to holler "I don't care—let's go now!" Laura could reply, "Maybe you should talk to Grandma and see if she wants to give me permission to go outside with you this minute or whether she needs to finish telling me something." Emma's next move might be to collapse on the floor and say, "I don't want to talk to her, I want to go out now!" If Laura were to respond "You'll just have to wait a few minutes, Emma," it would underscore the lesson that another person's needs might be more important than Emma's at that moment.

This sort of lesson in gentle but persistent limit setting would help Emma consider, and eventually tolerate, other children's ideas and needs when she was operating in the wider world of preschool. The more her parents were able to interact lovingly with their rambunctious child, and help her care about other people, the more willing she would be to curb her very real physical need to take the world by storm.

PRESCHOOLERS WHO TAKE IN SIGHTS, BUT TUNE OUT SOUNDS

Like Brian, Will was a little boy whose imaginary play was so absorbing that he sometimes found it easier to live in his own private world. Before preschool each morning, he would set up elaborate displays of the plastic dinosaur figures that his parents, Lisa and Dan, had bought for him, and roared and chirped as he moved the figures through imaginary swamps and jungles. Will was often oblivious to Lisa's repeated calls to come to the kitchen for breakfast. Sometimes Dan would have to flick the overhead light on and off in the little boy's bedroom, or give his shoulder a little shake, to interrupt his reverie.

Will's parents were amazed by his fascination with dinosaurs. His strong visual sense and precocious fine motor skills were evident in the pictures he painted of dinosaurs during art time at school. On paper his tyrannosauruses had recognizably big teeth and his brontosauruses' long necks were clearly featured. In spite of his obvious creativity and easygoing disposition, however, Will was viewed as something of a loner by his peers. At nursery school, he brightened up when it was time for art or when a classmate brought in an interesting item during show and tell, but his teachers reported that he seldom initiated conversations. Lisa and Dan had an growing sense that their youngster's auditory-processing challenges were interfering with his ability to make friends, and this dismayed them.

Children like Will sometimes retreat into their own thoughts and fantasies because processing verbal cues and other noises is relatively harder for them. As creative as they may be, they're not always able to build bridges between their own ideas and other people's verbalized ideas. Unfortunately, their ability to abstract and logically categorize thoughts can remain compromised unless their parents work to help them attend and link up verbal cues to their own ideas.

Lisa and Dan had to deliberately and playfully pester him to get a response: "Hey Will—what about my question?" If Will either fell silent or regressed to talking about his dinosaurs, Dan would pose the question in a singsong cadence that communicated a sense of silly fun that might snare Will's attention. He knew that it was especially important to keep up nonverbal back-and-forth cueing—head nods, smiles, and arm gestures—so that Will would remain emotionally tied into the dialogue, even when it was hard for him to listen to it and find the right words.

The important thing was to help Will respond to other people's thoughts and create ideas on his own, since it is through logical conversation and imaginative play that he would learn to create new ideas and build social relationships. For example, if Lisa and Will were playing with Raggedy Ann and Andy dolls, Will might do something like try to detach one of Andy's dangling arms. His mother could then fix her eyes on Will's and say, "Let me see if I understand what's going on. Raggedy Ann is about to pull Andy's arm off, right?" If Will nodded his head, Lisa could jump right into the character of Raggedy Andy and cry out in a strained little voice, "Oh, please don't hurt me!".

It wouldn't be surprising if Will ignored his mother's comment for a while, and then murmured, "I'm going to pull your arm off." Lisa might immediately reply in Andy's voice, "What did I do?" but her son might well choose to answer it only after the second or third time she repeated her question. By patiently joining in on his play and making sure that any discussion the two of them had involved the logical exchange of a few ideas, Lisa could help her son to respond to the outer world in spite of his auditory difficulties.

As adults we often make abrupt conversational transitions as new thoughts pop into our minds, but we alert our conversational partners to the fact that a new idea is coming with phrases like "Oh, that reminds me of the time . . ." or "You know, something like that happened to me recently, too." Good conversationalists and facile thinkers intuitively build logical bridges between new ideas and old ones. A child like Will, who finds it more difficult to take in and process sounds, doesn't have an inner voice that says, "Hey, wait, you've changed the subject," or "These ideas don't make sense when they follow the earlier ones."

There were ways Lisa and Dan could help Will cultivate this inner voice to warn him when abrupt transitions occurred during conversations. They could point out when his thoughts leapfrogged from one idea to another, and refocus his attention on ideas that were already in the air. If Will came home from school commenting on "the yucky food at snack time," and his mother were to ask him what the children were served, Will might well start talking about the pictures of lizards he saw in a book. At that point, Lisa could turn to him with a puzzled expression on her face and say, "Will, just a minute ago you were talking about snacks, and now you're talking about lizards. What are we doing, talking about snacktime or lizards?" Her aim would be to help her child see that he had switched subjects, and to help him follow his own thoughts in a logical way, and decide which thoughts he wanted to continue with.

Meanwhile Lisa and Dan enjoyed Will's very real gifts in the visual-spatial area. He was a whiz at puzzles and block designs. These visual skills proved helpful in other ways. Each night before Will went to bed, there was a series of bedtime activities that he had to perform but had difficulty remembering and following, no matter how many times Dan or Lisa spelled them out for him. They tried to make the instructions into a little song, to help him recall the steps he had to follow: "Just before Willy goes to bed/He has to brush every tooth in his head/Then he washes his cheeks, chin, eyes and nose/And looks for his jammies, and hangs up his clothes." The song was cute but ineffectual. Dan and Lisa found that they still had to prompt him each step of the way. Lisa's new thought was for Will to draw four different pictures of the activities involved in his nighttime ritual. He was an eager artist, and got a great kick out of drawing scenes depicting toothbrushing, facewashing, pajamas, and putting away clothes. After he finished the drawings, Will and his mother taped them up on the bathroom mirror. This visual prompt, accompanied by a playful chanting of the little rhyme each night, made it much easier for Will to remember the steps he heard outlined in the song. With practice like this, he would eventually learn to pay more attention to the sounds in his world because they could be linked to the visual information that brought him so much easy pleasure.

PRESCHOOLERS WHO TAKE IN SOUNDS, BUT HAVE A HARD TIME FIGURING OUT SIGHTS

By the time he was four and a half, Max was talking nonstop. He liked to regale his preschool friends with stories about his latest trip to Chuckie Cheese, or how his uncle showed him how to blow giant bubbles made out of soapy water. If it was time to learn a new song, Max would happily lead the classroom rhythm section and bang on the xylophone or drums while wiggling his bottom to the beat of the music. He seemed to be a happy fellow, full of energy and enthusiasm.

Yet both his parents, Lynn and Jonathan, and his preschool teacher had the sense that something was not quite age-appropriate in the way he spoke to other children. It was as if he required an audience to *perform* in front of, and he seemed to scarcely take any real pleasure out of low-key, one-on-one conversation. When Max asked another child a question, it was usually somewhat businesslike, and focused on getting a need or desire met. He often averted his eyes from the child's face, and consequently missed a lot of the facial gestures—bored expression, raised eyebrow, or quizzical frown—that would have let him know he was losing his playmate's interest. Many of his conversations, in fact, sounded more like monologues, or went off in different directions in a fragmented way.

Because they realized that Max had continuing problems in visually processing information, Lynn and Jonathan assumed that his slightly hyper school behavior was somehow related to this area of challenge. They were most concerned that his dramatic personality, although intriguing to other four-year-olds, would seem histrionic or even hollow to others when he got a little older. They wanted him to be able to share his thoughts and build on another person's ideas in an intimate way, and to learn to be more reflective.

Max's parents brought him into the developmental specialist's office in the hopes that the therapist could more precisely pinpoint why the toddler's ideas, although lively, seemed so fragmented. After observing Max for quite a while and engaging him in conversation, the specialist felt that this little boy was focusing on small pieces of the world because the "bigger picture" overwhelmed him. Max's talk was filled with rich imagery, yet it skipped abruptly from one thought or scene to another. He needed help to link all his kaleidoscopic images of the world into more coherent, and calmer, thoughts.

Max's gift for gab was obvious. Lynn and Jonathan realized that they needed to shift their attention to the visual part of his nature, and help him to picture his feelings and organize his thoughts. Each time they heard their son's conversation veer off into tangential details, Lynn and Jonathan could actively help him see the big picture and refocus on the main theme. For example, when the three of them were discussing *Goldilocks and the Three Bears*, Max's parents could ask him, "What's this story all about, anyway?" or "What do you think about Goldilocks going into a stranger's house and eating their food?" The more practice they could give Max in figuring out general themes and concepts, the more adept he would eventually become in building bridges between ideas.

Since Max had trouble with visual problem solving, activities like piecing together puzzles, searching for missing socks in the laundry basket together, and going on treasure hunts in search of hidden objects would provide him with a good mental workout. When Max played imaginary games, Lynn or Jonathan could plunge right into the action and follow his lead by having their bad-guy stuffed animal "hide" somewhere in the playroom while Max's own policeman teddy bear went in search of the rest of the gang. They could even assume the role of a narrator and issue comments like "You're getting hotter, hotter—nope, cold, colder now" or "Try looking upward" or "Just a weensy bit backward" to help him associate certain words with spatial concepts. Searches for everyday items could also serve as conversation starters and lead to two-way symbolic dialogues: "Oh Max, come help me find my purse. I think I might have left it on the counter in the kitchen or next to the garage door."

Lynn and Jonathan could further help Max comprehend spatial concepts during their pretend play together by asking questions about where their power rangers should hide from the alien invaders, or what's the best route back to the fort and safety. An active game like musical chairs would provide Max with a particularly beneficial workout, since it would combine the body movements and superior listening skills that came easy for him with the need to pay close visual attention, which was his biggest challenge. Max's parents could provide him with lots of verbal descriptions about what he was supposed to do as he played the game, and use hand signals and body language to illustrate the required movements.

Other visualization techniques could also be used to bolster Max's weaker visual skills. Just as athletes watch video tapes of other athletes fluidly performing difficult moves before they attempt to duplicate the moves themselves, Max could be taught to picture a series of pictures in his mind to help him organize his thoughts. For instance, when reading the bedtime stories that he so enjoyed, Lynn could set the text aside for a while and ask Max to picture what he thought the character looked like, or what sort of fairies and elves were hiding in the woods.

The more practice Max gets in picturing things in his mind's eye, the more he will be able to link the piecemeal images he picks up from the real world into coherent, organized concepts. Being able to "see the forest" and not simply "the trees" should diminish some of his anxious, attention-getting behavior, and free him up to take pleasure in the emotional warmth and intimacy of linking his thoughts with another human being's.

FAMILY CHALLENGES THAT INTERFERE WITH ABSTRACT, EMOTIONAL THINKING

Sometimes our own anxieties unconsciously interfere with our ability to help our children feel comfortable assembling their thoughts. For example, a father who has some issues about dependency and nurturance may plunk a baby doll in a toy car, rather than joining in on his child's pleasure in rocking and crooning lullabies to the doll.

Even though we all have emotional hot spots that we try and stay clear of, we reduce our children's ability to develop certain abstract ideas when we pull away from bouncing our ideas off theirs in these sensitive areas. It's by avoiding being overly concrete and literal, even when certain themes make us feel anxious, that we help our children to think deeply, broadly, and thoroughly.

Sometimes it is a certain set of circumstances, rather than a mom's or dad's emotional sensitivities, that interfere with a parent's ability to help a child organize her thoughts. A move, the birth of a new baby, financial setbacks, or the death of a grandparent are stressful events that might well cause a parent to become more rigid and concrete, or even to withdraw emotionally for a while. Even slight stress, like having to deal with a child's noisy siblings while trying to hold a one-on-one dialogue, may be enough to cause some parents to become overcontrolling, overprotective, or aloof.

Other adults who are usually in tune with the emotional needs of their child may become more fragmented in the use of ideas when they have to organize experience for a group.

The triangular relationships that develop during this stage can also make it hard to encourage emotional thinking. You may find that you have feelings of jealousy or resentment when your child openly prefers your spouse's company that cause you to pull away from both of them for a while. It's very human to feel the pain of a rebuff, but you have to remind yourself that your child isn't abandoning you; she simply needs to connect with your spouse for a while. Try to spend even more one-on-one time with your preschooler later that same day. In fact, each parent needs to spend time alone with his or her child so she'll learn to become more comfortable balancing the pushes and pulls of this three-way relationship.

Your four-year-old will probably focus on your negative features as she pulls away from you and temporarily woos your spouse. By undervaluing you for a time, your child is trying to become less dependent on you. Try to look for opportunities to form a playful alliance with your child, whether it's during a game or when the three of you are having a mild difference of opinion. Convey a sense of empathy and sympathy when you take her side. However, it is also important to communicate the basic understanding that *Mom and Dad are the primary alliance.* A single mom or dad should try to introduce another regular adult presence such as a grandparent or relative into a three- or four-year-old's life so that the child can also experiment with all the negotiations that take place within triangular relationships.

The tugs and jealousies that we feel in the midst of such relationships, coupled with our own emotional Achilles heels and the big and not-so-big stresses of everyday life, sometimes interfere with our ability to foster emotional thinking in our children. As with all problems, simply recognizing them is a big first step. The best way to overcome these stumbling blocks is to be flexible enough to work on your own inhibitions, anxieties, and conflicts, and of course to be warm and nurturing whenever you can. Then try and read your child's signals, and encourage dialogue involving her emotions, behaviors, thoughts and words. If she gets anxious and misbehaves, set effective limits using compassion and empathy, rather than making harsh demands on her. Remember: you have to give more before you can expect more.

LEARNING TO THINK

Help your child learn to think by holding long conversations with her in which you seek her opinions rather than simply trade pieces of information. For instance, when she expresses a desire to "Go out now!" you can ask her what she wants to do once she's outside. When she replies "Play on the slide!" she'll be linking her wishes with your thoughts and ideas. Try and pose open-ended questions to get her thinking, such as "Why do you like this color so much?" rather than "Which is your favorite color?" Enjoy debates about everything from bedtime to ice cream flavors! When your child clamors to stay up later, and you ask "Why should you be allowed to stay up so late?" she's likely to give you a lawyerly response of "Because you let (big sister) stay up and I'm almost as old!" Also, as you continue to be a pretend partner, try and come up with new plot twists. You might explore the dolls' feelings or let her be Mommy while you are a little child.

FUN AND GAMES

🍸 The Director Game

See how many plot shifts or new story lines your child can initiate as the two of you play make-believe games together. After the tea-party play becomes a little repetitive or lacks direction, you can subtly challenge your child to thicken the plot by announcing something like "I'm so full of tea my tummy's sloshing! What can we do next?"

🌱 "Why Should I?" Game

When your child wants you to do things for her, gently tease her with a response of "Why should I?" and see how many reasons she can give you. Then, offer a compromise, such as "Let's do it together," when she wants you to get her riding toy out of the garage, or pick out a new outfit to wear, etc.

Janice Fullman

7

FLOOR TIME:

NURTURING ALL SIX
LEVELS OF INTELLIGENCE
AND EMOTIONAL HEALTH
AT THE SAME TIME

As your child grows from infancy to school age, the importance of floor time goes far beyond just having fun. During floor time, your child will stretch his imagination and logical understanding of the world as he stages make-believe games and locks horns with you over rules. He'll use gestures and words to express his needs and to explore a broad range of emotions, from exhilaration to anger. He will also hone his physical skills as his muscles strengthen and grow.

You will be supporting your child's intellectual, emotional, and physical development through your interactive play. You can promote all this growth by simply following his lead and joining in! As you playfully relate to your child, incorporating as many of the six fundamental learning experiences as he has mastered up to the present time, you'll be helping him to calm down or become energized, to engage lovingly in shared fun, to initiate and respond to information by using gestures and language, and to build ideas and learn to think through imaginative exchanges and debates.

You'll also be making a special effort to tailor your interactions to his unique developmental profile. For instance, you'll be sure to be especially soothing if your child is sensitive or finicky, or animated if he's more laid-back. Because you'll be interacting with him in such a highly personal way, he'll feel increasingly secure and comfortable.

Admittedly, being an active, engaging partner when your child says, "Play with me!" isn't always easy. In a perfect world, floor time would happen spontaneously. For many families today, however, floor time has to be penciled into a mom's or dad's day planner. It is therefore important to set aside special times each day for play. Choose times that are convenient for you. It's important to reserve *at least* 20 to 30 minutes for each floor-time interaction with your child. A number of five-minute one-on-ones here and there do not equal floor time. You will both enjoy more and accomplish more when you give your relationship, playtime, and dialogue more time to develop. This special time with your child will allow you to reaffirm the intimate rhythm and sense of connectedness that the two of you have established and continue to nurture.

As our culture becomes more impersonal and technology-driven, our workdays lengthen and our free time seems to evaporate. With many families being supported by two breadwinners who often have demanding jobs, traditional patterns of nurturing have undergone a sea change. It's expecting a great deal of even the most devoted day-care provider to zero in on your child's unique play and learning style, the way you are motivated to do.

During floor time, you'll be getting down on your child's level, joining him in his world and on his terms. You'll be encouraging him to be the boss of all the drama that unfolds, and will follow his lead as an ever-willing sidekick—Sancho Panza to his Don Quixote.

THE BROAD PRINCIPLES OF FLOOR TIME

JOINING IN AT HIS LEVEL AND FOLLOW HIS LEAD

Until your child is well into his school years, you will frequently be interacting with him when he's down on the floor, where he feels most comfortable and where his toys and play things are located. When you are playing eye-to-eye with your child, you generate a sense of equality that encourages him to engage with you, take initiative, and act more assertively. However, you'll also be operating in his realm when you playfully make funny faces at him as you change his diaper, chat at the dinner table together, visit the supermarket, splash in the swimming pool, or go for a walk outside. Thus, "floor time" can occur anywhere and anytime the two of you are interacting in a way that lets him know that you are joining him on his own ground. His home turf consists of his interests, initiatives, and ideas.

Ideally, you should do what your child wants to do, even if it means playing dollhouse or superheroes for the umpteenth time. Any kind of playful sharing is valuable, however, as long as both of you find it enjoyable. If you wind up occasionally choosing the game, try to encourage your child to take over the lead and play as creatively as possible. Letting him make up new rules and ways of playing can be a way of building up his assertiveness, and getting him to take the lead.

You and your spouse may each prefer a different type of play. One of you may be good at acting out stories, while the other may enjoy art projects and more physical activities. It's fine to have different floor-time expertise, as long as each of you is an enthusiastic participant. Your child may sense what you enjoy, and initiate different types of interactions with each of you.

Please note that floor time is not a time for teaching rules. You can do that at other times. Nor is floor-time play an occasion to get controlling and bossy and start asking too many questions about the action that's unfolding. Floor time is the one arena in which it's safe to encourage your child to reign as a benevolent dictator! Even eight-month-olds want to be in charge of their own play as they decide that your nose makes a wonderful "toot-toot" noise each time it's tweaked. There's only one inviolate floor-time rule that you must step in and enforce if necessary: No hurting people, and no breaking toys. When limits do need to be set, they should be implemented gently-but-firmly, with lots of accompanying gesturing and verbal explanation. (We'll be describing this process at greater length toward the end of this chapter.)

Remember, your job is to *let your child set the emotional tone* of your play and then to *follow his lead*. Be very animated, using hand gestures and various facial expressions as you encourage him to choose any activity for the two of you to play. With a young baby, you should feel free to join in on whatever he is doing at that moment: clapping, making noises, or playing with a rattle. As you follow his lead, capture and mirror his gestures and emotional tone with your own expressions. Share his smiles and pouts. Most importantly, entice him to exchange his cute gestures with you.

If an older child is painting or building with blocks, gently try to join in. When your verbal child insists that you watch him paint a picture, follow his suggestion, but try gesturing to him and wondering aloud whether you could paint a little, too. If he winds up telling you five reasons why he is a better artist than you, and that you should just watch him at work, that creative interchange is floor time and the theme is "I'm better than you." Enjoy the playful debate!

Opening and Closing Circles of Communication

During floor time, when you make it a point to follow your child's lead and build on his interests and overtures, he will usually be inspired to build in turn on what you have done or said. As we've discussed throughout the pages of this book, this process is referred to as "opening and closing circles of communication." If your child moves his toy car and then you move your car parallel to it or say "Where are we going?" or "Can my dolly have a ride in your car?", you are opening a circle of communication. If he then gestures or verbalizes back to you, building on your behavior by saying, "We go to house!" or simply bangs his car into yours while giving you a knowing look, he is closing that circle of communication. Your play partnership with your child is based on his ability not only to take the initiative but also to respond to and use the information you share with him. This ability to tune into a partner and build on his or her response is what makes communication truly interactive. Even when a child's response is a simple "No" or "Shh!" he is closing the circle of communication that his partner opened.

BUILD ON YOUR CHILD'S NATURAL INTERESTS BY CREATING AN APPROPRIATE PLAY ENVIRONMENT

You will be wooing your child into playfully exchanging gestures and ideas with you during floor time while looking for an answering sparkle of interest in his eye. Once you've captured your child's interest, you'll be trying to inspire him to build on what you've done or said. One way to facilitate his ability to open and close circles of communication with you is to stock his play environment with a sampling of age-appropriate play materials, such as dolls, action figures, cars, and blocks. You and your child can use these manipulatable props together to pursue his natural interests. Try to become an extension of your child's props: When you pick up a stuffed frog, speak in a croak; as you push a toy car, make "vrooming" sounds. In this way you will not compete with your child's toys, but instead will be using them to promote creative interactions between the two of you.

Some children do better with a few select toys, while others enjoy interacting with you while using lots of toys. In addition to helping a child create brand-new dramas, dolls and action figures make it easier for many children to imaginatively explore some of the real situations and real feelings that they experience in everyday life, and to experiment with scary feelings, too. Avoid relying on board games and puzzles during floor time. Though such toys definitely have their uses, they tend to create more structured rather than creative and spontaneous interactions.

EXTENDING THE CIRCLES OF COMMUNICATION

As you participate in your toddler's or preschooler's floor time, try to expand the scope and length of his playful interactions with you. The best way to extend your child's drama is to interact constructively with him by helping him toward his goal. For example, you might notice that your 18-month-old is longingly looking and pointing at a toy circus train that is placed on a shelf that is too high for him to reach. When you retrieve the toy and turn to him and ask, "Want it?" and he reaches for it with a big smile, you are helping him to reach his goal and at the same time extend his interaction with you.

If your two-year-old is making loud noises with a hammer and bell, you could first acknowledge his activity with a comment like "What a terrific drummer you are!" Then you could put a duck puppet on your hand, pick up a toy hammer to bang the bell, and exclaim "Loud! Loud!" If your child shows an interest in your action or, better yet, tries to take the duck puppet and imitate you, you can expand the activity still further by getting out a dog puppet and starting a simple dialogue between the two puppets.

Sometimes you'll find that you'll be more successful in expanding your play or conversation with your child by interacting in a playfully obstructive manner. For example, if he's avoiding you during floor time, you might try positioning yourself between your child and the object or activity that is absorbing all of his attention. You can take on the role of a moving, talking fence that he needs to climb over or under to reach his favorite truck. If your child seems determined to move his toy trucks on his own, and tunes out your friendly overtures, you can try covering one of his trucks with your hand to create a "tunnel." When his truck doesn't emerge from the "tunnel" on its own, he may be motivated to search for it by picking up your hand.

BROADENING THE RANGE OF THEMES AND EMOTIONS EXPRESSED BY YOUR CHILD AS HE INTERACTS WITH YOU

As you talk and play and interact with your child, you will be looking for opportunities to add a new twist or plot line that builds on his interests. In this way, you will be engaging him in all the marvelously varied themes of life: closeness and dependency; assertiveness, initiative, and curiosity; aggression, anger, and limit setting; and pleasure and excitement. You will not only be relating to your little playmate in ways that will help him develop a full range of emotions, but you'll also be introducing him to themes involving right and wrong, and to various types of thinking skills, too. He'll develop a growing understanding of new words, as well as of spatial and mathematical concepts.

There will be many times when you'll notice that your child will avoid or neglect certain types of interactions, despite your best efforts to foster a supportive floor-time environment. At those times, it's appropriate to gently challenge your child in those emotional areas that he seems inclined to bypass. For instance, if your three-year-old tends to be wonderfully easygoing but a little passive when it comes to asserting himself and claiming his own toys during play group, you could do something as simple as move his favorite car away from his group of vehicles. Naturally, you'll want to appear impish, rather than malicious, so make sure you've got a big grin on your face and move the car away very slowly and deliberately, in a nonthreatening manner. Your three-year-old may very well assert himself and come after his prized jeep!

If your child's floor-time pretend sessions seem to center disproportionately around themes of anger and aggression, try to steel yourself not to interfere with the dramatic flow by asking questions like "Why is [the character] so mad?" or "Why doesn't [the character] behave nicely?" Instead, you might comment, "Gee, he really wants to bop those bad guys. He's going to destroy them in a hundred different ways. I bet he must have a good reason for that!" By acknowledging both the depth of anger that your child is portraying, and the fact that he must have good reason for it, you are empathetically helping him feel that you are on his side rather than a proponent of your own agenda. Your empathy is what eventually helps him learn about caring himself.

The imaginative and verbal expression of feelings usually helps a child learn to understand and regulate them. Strong feelings such as anger that aren't acknowledged tend to get acted out either directly with the child becoming aggressive, or indirectly, as he reacts in an opposite manner and becomes overly inhibited or fearful. Your acknowledgment of your child's feelings does not imply approval for acting them out in reality. In fact, recognizing a child's "pretend" agenda will help him use ideas rather than actions, and strengthen your ability to discuss and set relevant limits on aggressive behavior if it should emerge at school or at home during nonpretend times.

Floor-time play does not replace discipline—it supplements it. When a child is misbehaving, pretend play can sometimes help reveal what's on his mind, why he's so angry and provocative. Surprisingly, your acknowledgment of your child's negative, angry feelings may eventually help him to introduce positive themes in his dramas. Most children have a balance of feelings. If you convey an empathetic message that it's okay to explore aggressive themes during play, dependency, love, and concern will usually emerge, too. However, if your child senses that you don't understand his ideas, his frustration may cause him to polarize his feelings and opt for aggressive themes. It bears repeating that his experience of your empathy for *all* his feelings is the best way to teach empathy and compassion. You teach more by what you do than by what you lecture about.

BROADENING YOUR CHILD'S CAPACITY TO USE HIS MUSCLES AND SENSES AS HE PROCESSES INFORMATION FROM THE WORLD AROUND HIM

As you engage your child with sounds, words, sights, touches, and movements, you'll be making a conscious effort to appeal to many of his senses and to involve the muscles of his body at the same time. His wonderful "mental team"—all his wonderful emerging functional capacities—learns to simultaneously work together as he interacts with you in an emotionally meaningful and fulfilling manner. So when the two of you are having a floor-time session in which your child is the conductor of a toy trolley and you are his trusty brakeman, don't simply make the screeching noise of the brakes and ring the trolley bell or just call out stops along the line. Try to introduce some visual and spatial elements into your noisy play! See if the two of you can spy some robbers that are hiding behind a nearby chair, or perhaps wonder aloud if the thunderstorm that's raging around you will put you behind schedule. Can the conductor smell the storm coming? Is he getting drenched by the rain? How much does it cost to ride on his trolley?

In a similar manner, spatial play during floor time—such as building block towers and forts—can also promote your child's ability to broaden the range of his processing and motor capacities. Over time your fellow block arranger may start to build cities. You could become his assistant architect or construction worker, or step into countless other roles. After all, don't cities need someone to deliver food, to provide security, and to make sure that the monsters don't get inside? If your child is too fond of sitting, he may be motivated to leap to his feet and become Batman as he tries to scare the monsters away.

Extending your child's capacities, as well as your own, can combine great fun with great learning. But don't try to do too much too quickly! Just keep the basic underlying principles of floor time in mind and have fun with your child. In the years ahead when you look back on these wonderful interactive times together, you will realize that you really did help your child stretch his capacities far more than you realized at the time.

FLOOR TIME AT EACH DEVELOPMENTAL STAGE

The following outline is intended to be a guide to some of the many potentially useful and fun floor-time interactions you can share with your child. As he progresses through each stage, you can incorporate the capacities mastered at that stage *and all the prior ones* into your floor-time play together. For example, with your three-year-old you can foster logical thinking, imaginative problem-solving interaction, gleeful gestures, love and trust, and concentration all at the same time. This outline is in no way intended to be a comprehensive checklist that you must feel compelled to work through. Try to use this information and the examples throughout the book in much the same way you would consult a guide book to a foreign country. You might be intrigued by the numerous descriptions of all the many castles and museums, but realistically wouldn't expect or desire to see every sight.

STAGE 1: CALM, REGULATED INTEREST IN THE WORLD

- **Take note of your baby's or child's individual sensory and motor profile.**

Become aware of his unique style of hearing, seeing, touching, smelling, and moving.

- **Harness all his senses in enjoyable ways that simultaneously involve his hearing, vision, touch, smell, and movement.**

Entice him into the world.

STAGE 2: FALLING IN LOVE

- **Observe what kind of interactions—silly sounds, kisses, tickles, or favorite games—bring your baby or child pleasure and joy.**

Make the most of those "magic moments" of availability and relaxed alertness. Interact with her for 15- or 20-minute blocks of time at various points during the day.

- **Tune in to your baby's or child's rhythms, in terms of how she feels emotionally and uses her senses and movements.**

Peekaboo and hiding-the-toy-under-a-box are visual games that delight most babies, and rhythmic clapping games like pat-a-cake will especially intrigue babies with auditory strengths. Moving trucks will delight toddlers, and imaginative dramas will bring joy to most preschoolers.

- Follow your child's true interests, even if it's simply making silly noises, and you will foster pleasure and closeness.
- Become a part of an object she likes rather than competing with it.

Put a block she especially likes on your head, and make a funny face.

STAGE 3: TWO-WAY COMMUNICATING

- Be very animated as you exchange subtle facial expressions, sounds, and other gestures as well as words and pretend dramas with your child.
- Go for the gleam in your child's eye that lets you know he is alert and aware and enjoying this exchange.
- Help your child open and close circles of communication.
- Treat all your child's behaviors—even the seemingly random ones—as purposeful.

For instance, if he flaps his hands in excitement, you could use this behavior as a basis for an interactive "flap your hands" dance step. If his play seems a little aimless as he idly pushes a toy car back and forth, you might announce that your doll has a special delivery letter that needs to be carried straightaway to Barney. See if he takes the bait!

- Help your child go in the direction he wants to by first making his goal easier to achieve.

You could move a bright new ball closer to him after he points his finger and indicates that he'd like to play with it.

- Then, encourage your child's initiative by avoiding doing things for him or to him.

When it's time for him to go to bed, for example, see if your child can put his favorite teddy bear to bed at the same time, rather than relying on you to do it for him.

- Challenge your child to do things *to* you.

For example, when the two of you are roughhousing, entice him to playfully jump on you or climb up onto your shoulders, rather than simply picking him up and swinging him yourself.

Stage 4: Problem Solving

- Create extra steps in floor-time plots.

For example, you might try announcing "The car won't move. What shall we do?"

- Create interesting barriers or obstacles to your child's goals.
- Work up to a continuous flow of circles of communication.

Many toddlers can string together 30, 40, and even 50 back-and-forth's with your help.

- Be animated and show your feelings through your voice and facial expressions to help your child clarify her intentions.

If your child vaguely points to a toy and grunts, you might sometimes feign confusion, put a puzzled expression on your face, and fetch the "wrong" toy. Your child's gesturing and vocalizations will become more elaborate and perhaps heated as she works harder to make her wishes understood.

- Increase your child's ability to plan her movements and use her senses and imitative skills in different circumstances (such as hide-and-seek and treasure-hunt games).

Stage 5: The World of Ideas

- Support your child's use of ideas with meaning, intent, or affect, rather than by labeling objects or pictures.

- Challenge your preschooler to express his needs, desires, or interests.
- Encourage your child to use ideas both in imaginative play and in realistic verbal interactions.
- Help your toddler use ideas by fostering situations in which he wants to express his feelings or intentions.
- Remember WAA (Words, Action, Affect): Always combine your words or ideas with your affect (expressed feelings) and actions.
- Make a point of using words all the time; encourage chitchat with your child!

- Initially, encourage your preschooler's imagination by helping him stage familiar interactions during pretend play. Then, entice him into introducing new plot twists.

Challenge his dolls or teddy bears to feed each other, hug, kiss, cook or go off to the park and play. Jump into the drama he has begun by assuming the role of a character, and really ham it up!

- From time to time, switch from becoming a character in one of your child's dramas to taking on the role of a narrator or sideline commentator.

Your comments will thicken the plot.

- Periodically summarize the action and encourage your child to move the drama along.
- Encourage the use of all types of ideas.

Don't forget to incorporate ideas in the form of pictures, signs, and complex spatial designs, as well as words.

STAGE 6: BUILDING BRIDGES BETWEEN IDEAS; EMOTIONAL AND ABSTRACT THINKING

- Challenge your child to close all her circles of communication using ideas, both during pretend play and in reality-based dialogues.
- Challenge your child to link different ideas or subplots in a drama.

In this way, you will help her build bridges between various ideas.

- Pull her back on track by acting confused if her thinking becomes a little piecemeal or fragmented.

For instance, if her conversation about a neighbor suddenly shifts to a discussion about peanut butter and jelly sandwiches, challenge her to fill in the missing pieces of her thoughts: "Hold on a minute; I thought you were talking about our neighbor, but now you're talking about sandwiches. I'm lost! Which thing to you want to talk about?"

- Challenge your child with open-ended questions, those begin-ning with *who, what, where, when, why,* and *how.*

Your questions will help your child refocus in a logical way on her meandering thoughts.

- Provide multiple choice possible answers if your child ignores or avoids responding to your open-ended questions.

Throw out some silly possibilities for her to consider: "Did the ele-phant or the iguana visit your classroom today?"

- Create unexpected situations to challenge your child into greater creativity and new solutions.

- Expand your child's theme by placing it in different contexts.

- Challenge your child to broaden the emotional range in her drama.

- Encourage reflection on feelings in both pretend dramas and re-ality-based discussions.

Try posing open-ended questions such as "Why do you want to go outside?" or "What's the reason for the space invaders' attack?"

- Gradually increase the complexity of your preschooler's reflec-tive thinking by challenging her to suggest different motives, or to consider different points of view on various subjects.
- Follow up later on themes that are expressed during pretend play.

For instance, when your little girl returns home after preschool, you could inquire, "How is that new boy in school acting these days? Has he learned to share his blocks yet?"

- Challenge your child to give her opinion rather than recite facts.
- Enjoy debating and negotiating with your child rather than sim-ply stating rules (except when the rule is absolutely essential).

- Encourage and challenge your child's use of more and more ideas as part of logical, emotionally meaningful dialogues, instead of focusing on correct grammar.

As the two of you get a rich exchange of ideas going, your child will be learning to express herself logically. Her grammar will usually improve in a natural fashion as she becomes a better abstract thinker.

- Foster motor planning and sequencing capacities in your child.

You can even incorporate sketches and diagrams, as well as search games, obstacle courses, and building projects into your pretend play together.

- Encourage your child's understanding and mastering of time concepts.

Challenge her during real-life conversations and pretend play to incorporate concepts about the past, present, and future. For instance, you could pose questions such as "What are the cowboys going to do tomorrow?"

- Encourage the understanding and use of quantity concepts.

Negotiate with your child when she asks for an extra cookie or an extra slice of pizza. When the two of you play make-believe, speculate on how many cups of tea should be served to each doll at the tea party.

- Provide your child with an emotional, real-life understanding of basic concepts whenever you offer her any pre-academic or early academic work.

For example, you can negotiate using candies, cookies, or coins to learn the concepts of adding or subtracting. Keep the numbers small—under six—to avoid your child's having to rely on rote memory. Use visualization techniques (described in Chapter 6) to help your child get ready to read and comprehend.

- Keep challenging your child in both your pretend and reality-based conversations toward higher levels of abstraction by shifting back and forth between details and the big picture.

Periodically ask her how all the things she's been talking about fit together to help her "see the forest for the trees," or press her for details if she has a harder time seeing individual branches and trees in the green blur of the forest.

- Gradually expand your child's range of experiences—inside and outside, socially, and physically—because emotionally-based experiences are the seedbed for creative, logical, and abstract thought.

ADAPTING FLOOR TIME TO EACH CHILD'S INDIVIDUAL PROFILE

As you help your child master all six critical learning experiences—attending, engagement, two-way communication, preverbal problem solving, using ideas, and emotional and abstract thinking—during floor time, you'll also be catering to his individual developmental profile. By reading the previous chapter sections entitled "Overcoming Challenges: A Blessing in Disguise," you'll recognize whether soothing or vibrant, noisy or subdued, visual or aural, free-form or limit-setting approaches will work best for your child. You may recognize some aspects of your child's unique characteristics in the personalities of the five children—Kara, Brian, Emma, Will, and Max—profiled in those sections.

The Easily Overwhelmed, Sensitive Child

Some children, like Kara, are sensitive to light touches, certain sounds, bright lights, or abrupt movements. As you interact with them during floor time, they may be very cautious, and may need lots of time to adjust to anything new. They may also have a special need to be the boss of all the action and to control others. Children with sensitivities naturally want to test the waters of life only one toe at a time, and need to be wooed into pretend play gradually. It's vitally important to respect their need to be in charge, and to let them use your playtimes together as a way to experiment gradually with assertiveness.

THE UNDERWHELMED CHILD

These children, like Brian, are very reluctant to assert their wills by gesturing, using words, or playing "Let's pretend." Instead of always doing *for* the child, however, you need to woo or *entice* such a youngster into activity. Over time, the bits and pieces of opinions and assertiveness shown by the underwhelmed child will lead him to joyfully step into all sorts of make-believe roles. He'll relish being one of the people who are in control, like teachers, kings, and superheroes, and will grandly order Mom and Dad around the room in an active rather than passive manner. Often a child may need to manifest assertiveness or aggression through gestures and pretend play before he can express it with words.

THE CHILD WHO CRAVES SENSATION

Very active children, like Emma, provide a different challenge. Here your task is two-fold: You'll attempt to "go with the flow" and build on their natural interests, and also hold their attention and help them elaborate on their interests rather than flit from one topic to another. If such a child is not engaged in this flexible way, his craving for new sights, sounds, and touches may lead to frenzied, aimless behavior, rather than to active and organized play. But once his energies are focused on a theme he has chosen himself, he may be able to sit down and concentrate for 15 minutes or more. Try to mix in "modulation" games, going from fast to slow, noisy to quiet, to help him learn to regulate his behavior. Provide extra soothing, warmth, and pretending to encourage empathy and the use of ideas as well as actions. Remember to be gentle-but-firm, providing your child with guidance and limits.

THE CHILD WHO TAKES IN SIGHTS,
BUT TUNES OUT SOUNDS

These children, like Will, have a harder time figuring out certain sounds and often find it difficult to pay attention to their parents' words. Rather than simply naming objects, or pointing to pictures in a book, parents can use floor time to give lots of extra opportunities to practice understanding words. Pretend play in which a child is naturally motivated to "talk" for his dolls or action figures is a far more natural and fun way to support verbalization. Chatting with your child when you know he really wants something helps him pay attention to sounds, too.

THE CHILD WHO TAKES IN SOUNDS, BUT HAS HARD TIME FIGURING OUT SIGHTS

Treasure hunts, building things, visualization, and the use of visually exciting props during pretend play are all useful in enticing children like Max to pay attention to and figure out sights.

THE MANY BENEFITS OF FLOOR TIME

PROMOTING A FULL RANGE OF EMOTIONS

As your child's ability to use words and ideas grows, he will become more adept at articulating his emotions—saying "I'm sad" or "I'm mad." He'll make his emotions known not only through his spontaneous chatter, but also during the make-believe play of floor time. During your pretend games together, you can help him express as wide a range of emotions and themes as he can, including such negative feelings as anger, aggression, fear, and jealousy. Pretend play provides a safe outlet for your child to experience these emotions and also helps him find ways to moderate these feelings if they threaten to overwhelm him from time to time. To facilitate this, try to tolerate a range of emotions. Censoring the emotions that are expressed during play is not effective. Warmth, empathy, and support when your child acts out negative emotions during play, coupled with gentle-but-firm limits in non-pretend-play situations, serve as a real example that negative feelings such as anger can exist side-by-side with feelings of love. Through your availability and empathy and limit-setting guidance, your child becomes comfortable bringing all his feelings into one relationship. You are, in a sense, the unifier, or harmonizer, of all your child's various types of feelings because he is able to experience them in a single relationship.

INCREASING EMOTIONAL FLEXIBILITY

If your child becomes stuck on an emotional theme involving anger or aggression, you can tailor your own participation in his play in a way that will create opportunities to broaden his range of self-expression. If a child's entire play repertoire consists of only one or two roles, you can use floor time to create an opportunity for increasing the kinds of emotion he is comfortable with and able to express. This does not mean changing the basic theme that emerges in his play, but instead looking for opportunities to expand related roles. Your character can express a will of his own and gradually become more and more creative.

WORKING THROUGH NEGATIVE FEELINGS

Floor time is an invaluable tool when it comes to helping your child handle such feelings as fearfulness. If your child is clingy and full of tears when your baby-sitter arrives at your home each afternoon as you go off to your part-time job, your floor-time play sessions later in the day could well provide the key to helping him get over his fear of separation. Perhaps he'll announce that he is going to the store and that you should "be a big girl and not cry" because he'll be returning soon. Then, after stepping into the next room for a moment or two, he might pop back into the playroom and say something like "I back now. You big girl?" If your toddler should ask you such a question, be sure to stay in character and reply with something like "It's hard to be a big girl because I felt scared and I missed you too much." He'll very likely get a real kick out of having you play his accustomed role, the aggrieved child. Of course, one episode of make-believe probably won't completely dispel his separation fears, but it will surely help him to more fully understand what it feels like to be in control of the situation. In addition, he'll be comforted by the sense that you really do understand his fears.

Similarly, if you have been sent away on a number of business trips recently, and you sense that your child is anxious about being separated from you, his pretend play with you will probably reflect some of his continuing insecurity. During your floor time together, your child's initial reaction may be to show his general feelings toward you (warm, aloof, irritable, demanding, solicitous). However, he might slowly introduce some aspect of separation into his play. He could choose to play it out with animals leaving each other or with one animal being mad at another. If he is very troubled by his forced separation from you, he might also incorporate themes of devastation, featuring hurricanes or earthquakes, to show how he feels about your leaving him. Or he might quietly build a block tower and be noticeably low-key and undramatic in his play, as if to say, "I have no special feelings about you. I'm only interested in my tower."

When these floor-time behaviors appear, your job is really very simple. You'll want to respond to your child's overall emotional tone—being respectful if he is being cool or formal, warm if he is being loving—and encourage him to communicate all his feelings by creating a sympathetic atmosphere. You can use a similar approach as you help your child deal with nightmares and other fearful situations. A child who fears that a witch lives under his bed and will attack him during the night will often reenact some of his fears during floor-time sessions with you. As his witch attacks or "scares" you during pretend play, he learns that you are still there for him, and are tolerant of his "witchlike" feelings.

Your goal here is to be warm and caring, not to be an armchair psychologist or psychiatrist who can trace out all the unconscious elements of your child's floor-time play. It's not even particularly helpful to say things like "I can tell you're scared about that" as you empathize with your child. Simply try to create an empathic tone and have your character support more elaboration by introducing thoughts and questions such as "I'm scared," or "What's next?"

GROUP FLOOR TIME

We've been discussing the principles of floor time for individual children and their caregivers. These same principles apply to interacting with a small group of children. Siblings and/or peers can thus be involved in group floor time. There are two ways to get group floor time going.

One is simply to let each child be the leader for 20 minutes or so with the other children being actors or props in the leader's drama. Everyone follows the leader, whether it's playing school or good guys versus bad guys. The adult's job is to help the nonleaders follow along with the drama as it develops. Even toddlers can be included as fellow actors. They may run with you to hide in a closet, or sit in your lap while you are being served tea. A nine-month-old can be assigned a role as a friendly alien by an imaginative four-year-old astronaut. When it's the nine-month-old's turn to lead, you and the other children can simply try to open and close circles of communication with him. A four-year-old pretending to be "Mommy" might hand a nine-month-old sibling a rattle and see whether he will reach for it.

A second way to get group floor time going is to let the group find a common theme to engage in. This approach can work for three-to-five-year-olds or older children who play cooperatively. In this sort of group floor time, the adult subtly acts to help the children discover shared interests and initiate their dramas and expand them. Themes ranging from playing house, school, and exploring space to reenacting cartoons may get the drama going and the children will use their creativity to move it down interesting paths. The adult then has the pleasure of watching true improvisational themes unfold.

Both group floor-time approaches have the same goal: helping everyone get involved and interacting. In this way, all participants are attending, engaging, being purposeful, using lots of gestures, and, when it is age-appropriate, creating ideas and logically connecting them. Most importantly, everyone gets to have fun with Mom or Dad and with each other.

PROMOTING THE DEVELOPMENT OF LANGUAGE

Many toddlers and preschoolers enjoy practicing their speech, concentration, and motor skills during the excitement of floor time. Because these sessions can combine your child's natural pleasures and interests with his developmental skills, the learning that goes on is far more effective than that which is produced by structured teaching. Children who are lagging in any of these developmental areas require extra practice, and floor time makes the practice fun.

One of the biggest challenges for the child one and a half to five years old is to comprehend what is said *to* him. Frequently it is very hard for both parents and professionals to determine whether a two-and-a-half-year-old is being negative because he happens to be angry or because he is simply frustrated because he can't understand what someone wants from him. Integrating listening and doing games into floor time can often help. For example, your bear could play "Simon says" with your child's monkey. Go from "Touch your head" or "Touch your knees" to two- or three-step sequences: "Touch your head, touch your knees, touch your nose." If your child immediately stops playing the game and starts fiddling with his clothes, toppling toys, and generally being negative and provocative, come back to the game at a later time. Then, start with single commands and slowly work back up to two- or three-step sequences. In general, increase the complexity of your own words and sentences very gradually as part of your animated, interactive play.

LEARNING TO CONCENTRATE AND FOCUS

Floor time opens up wonderful opportunities to enhance your child's attention span. If your child is blessed with a long attention span, practice will occur naturally. On the other hand, if you find that your child is easily distracted, now is the time to work with him. When you first sit down with a highly distractable child, his play may appear to be very disorganized. He may pick up a doll for a couple of seconds, and then get up and buzz around the room, pulling books off shelves, spilling toys out of bins, and rolling his cars every which way across the floor. One floor-time exercise that can be particularly helpful in teaching your child how to respond to gestures and words is to vary the energy you put into your voice. If "Come here, sweetheart. Let's play with the car!" doesn't meet with any reaction from your child, you can more energetically declare "Hey, buddy, I need you!" or "Over here, pal!"

As your cadence and intensity increases over a few minutes, you may well get your child's attention. He may stay involved with you for 30 or 40 seconds. Once you have your child actively engaged with you, you'll want to keep adding a few more seconds to your interaction together.

The key to expanding the time you and your child spend in active attention and engagement is to zero in on activities that he finds interesting, and to open and close more circles of communication. The more fleeting his attention, the stronger your affect, or motivating spark, needs to be. Some children will stay more involved if you are being very physical, perhaps jumping and hopping, or when they throw or catch a ball. Others will be absorbed by the fine motor projects you do together—drawing, cutting, and painting. Still others are captivated by certain emotional themes, and stay focused as long as they are ordering you around or being taken care of. Go with your child's strengths, and first use those capacities your child finds easy to join in on. You can then gradually add activities that are a greater challenge to his ability to pay attention. By teaching your child—through the fun of floor-time activities—to become involved with you, rather than shifting from one activity to the next, you are helping him to expand his ability to stay focused.

ENHANCING FINE AND GROSS MOTOR ABILITIES

Floor time is a great way to painlessly practice fine motor tasks. Organized exercises, such as sitting at a table and writing down the letters of the alphabet, may be tortuously difficult for some children. On the other hand, crafting a pretend menu to hand out to the customers of your make-believe restaurant can cast similar fine motor exercise in an entirely different light. As long as you use your ingenuity and work these sorts of activities into the rhythm of your pretend play together, your child will surely have a lot of fun.

Gross motor activities will obviously be a big part of your floor-time games. Hopping, skipping, and dancing can all fit nicely into a lively drama. Chase scenes, mock rodeos, and ballet dances are good pretend-play ingredients, too. If these activities are too difficult for the child with significant gross motor problems, you could start off by suggesting simpler scenarios.

BUILDING PROBLEM-SOLVING SKILLS

In addition to the free-wheeling fun of floor-time play, it's important to set aside special one-on-one time for problem-solving discussions with your youngster. These dialogues will center around the routine daily activities that take place at home and in school. They can also focus on the "big" issues that your child may face: waking up at night, toilet training, hitting other children, throwing food on the floor, temper tantrums, or being mean to a sibling. Fifteen-to-30-minute chats—ideally not in the midst of a crisis—that take place over a period of days rather than a big one-shot discussion are most helpful.

If your own little preschooler is strong-willed, he may well spend the first 10 minutes ignoring you, changing the subject, or flatly announcing, "I don't want to talk about it." It's critically important to realize, however, that it can take 15 minutes of discussion for the child to recognize your interest. (Of course, not every child is this difficult to woo into interaction. Some can talk for an hour at a clip!)

Once you introduce a subject, try to listen to your child and empathize with his perspective: "I bet you could tell me lots of reasons why you think it's okay to pinch." Eventually he may give you his list of complaints: "He gets into my toys" and "You always take his side," and so on. Once you comprehend your child's point of view, you can then try to solve the problem at hand.

The more clearly you understand where your child is coming from, and the more you give him a chance to verbalize his complaints, fears, and wishes, the better chance you'll have of not only resolving the problem, but helping him grow emotionally. Don't assume you know what your child thinks and feels. And even if you do, *he needs to say it.* Make it a point to let him, and not you, talk for more than half of the time you spend together. Nodding or mumbling yes or no answers to your questions doesn't arm him with better problem-solving skills. The child who likes to talk the least needs to practice this skill the most.

You may notice that your child has difficulty seeing the "big picture". Even highly verbal and emotionally sensitive children may often become overwhelmed with their feelings of the moment. If your child has a problem in seeing the forest for the trees, you can draw his attention to the larger patterns that he's overlooking. Other children are fully capable of seeing the big picture but have a hard time describing details or recognizing shades of feelings. If this describes your child, try to pursue with great interest any conversational details he gives you: "Tell me what happened this morning; I have lots of time." Your interest in the particular aspects of his feelings will help your "big picture" child avoid overgeneralization.

Some General Principles of Problem Solving

- Anticipate tomorrow's joys and challenges.
- Value your child's perspective.
- Empathize with his feelings.
- Help him visualize feelings or events.
- Break down the task you are working on into its smallest parts.
- Set up requirements in such a way that your child is successful 70 to 80 percent of the time, to fuel his "can do" sense of mastery. Build up to harder tasks gradually.
- Always increase floor time as you increase time devoted to problem solving.

HELPING THE RESISTANT CHILD
BECOME MORE MELLOW

The child who is withdrawn, negative, or provocative, and the child who prefers to play with things rather than people, and the child who throws a tantrum as soon as you do something that doesn't suit him to a "*t*"—all particularly need the sense of pleasure and mutual understanding that develops during floor-time interactions.

Empathizing with a resistant child will not always be easy. Perhaps your three-year-old appears to be unaccountably withdrawn and sullen much of the time, although he's quite verbal and physically coordinated. He may not seem to enjoy the time he spends with you as much as you'd hoped. When he fails to show much interest in interacting with you in a spontaneous way, you'll probably feel a natural sense of frustration, and turn to a more structured activity, such as reading, instead. However, your little boy is still likely to remain a reluctant participant and, by the end of your story, may continue to look sad and disengaged.

If you're like many parents, you'll probably feel exasperated or worried at this point and you may decide to seek professional input from your pediatrician or from a developmental specialist. They're likely to suggest that if your child isn't responding to your intuitive approach, it's best to try another. You might try and tune in to the slower rhythms that he seems more comfortable with, and quietly sit beside him for five to ten minutes, letting him take the initiative. If he doesn't do much in response, you could make gentle overtures like putting an arm around him or extending an invitation to play with some blocks that are on the floor. This prelude, during which you simply extend warmth toward your child, is an important step on the road to true interaction.

Over time, his curiosity will start to show during your play together. He may initially criticize you or your spouse for putting a block or a doll in the wrong place, but eventually he will invite you to share in his many play ideas. Quite often, as play develops, a formerly resistant child will become enthusiastic about a baby doll or favorite stuffed animal, casting himself as a caregiver who has a sick baby to attend to. When you empathize with him he may explain, "My baby is always hungry. She wants more milk all the time. I have to feed her all day and then she is happy."

Such a child may be telling you indirectly that he needs lots of emotional filling up, and that caretaking is an important issue for him. The fact that he is able to express this theme during his play means that you are beginning to fulfill this need. His floor-time interaction with you will gradually help him become a more engaging and warm child.

Many childhood problems are partially helped through special floor times. Floor time increases security, trust, warmth, initiative, and a sense of being understood. It creates opportunities to make vague, "private" feelings—whether they are needy, scary, anxious, or angry ones—part of the world of ideas and relationships. It perhaps goes without saying that some children, as they become older, will want to engage in floor time without using toys or props. Their minds become the only tool they need to let their imaginations soar. When that happens, you'll follow your child's verbal productions just as you did his make-believe dramas. Daily chitchat about seemingly ordinary things—school, friends, TV shows, a new pair of shoes—can supply both you and your child with the key to his thoughts, fears, and wishes.

THE FLOOR-TIME APPROACH TO LIMIT SETTING

As we've said before, floor time does not replace discipline—it supplements it. When a child is misbehaving, floor time can sometimes help reveal what's on her mind, or why she's so angry and provocative. However, this special time for building a relationship has to be coupled with firm, consistent limits that are backed by your resolve. Your operating principle in setting limits should be: *Never increase limits without increasing floor time.* When you eliminate one avenue of expression—your child's impulsive or disobedient behavior—always give her another way to express her concerns. Successful limit setting, an ever-present challenge for parents, melds warmth and empathy with a rock-solid resolve. If you can couple an instructive, rather than a punitive, attitude with a respect for your child's underlying needs, you will be more likely to wind up with a child who understands limits.

MOBILIZING YOUR RESOLVE

Frequently, parents lament that their child "just won't listen." She "won't pick up her toys" or "she always throws her food on the floor" or "she pinches her brother." And yet most children don't scribble on the living-room wall more than once, because their parents have a firmer sense of resolve when it comes to having to repaint their walls than when they must pick up toys. Why, then, do many children feel free to continue strewing their toys around the house?

The answer is a simple one. Most children shrewdly pick their battles. They recognize the areas where their parents' resolve and intense feelings are clear, and generally only misbehave when they think they can get away with it. (Some children do write on the walls repeatedly, but they are definitely in the minority.) So the first step in limit setting is deciding which limits are really important to you and sticking to your guns in those areas. Resolve is communicated not only through your words, but also through your gestures.

TEACHING LIMITS

Limits are taught, not dictated. In fact, your child's transgressions, such as when she reaches for your favorite lamp, will provide you with many teaching opportunities. Once she is able to understand gestures, as well as a few words, you can get right in front of her and firmly shake your head from side to side as you say "No, no!" You can then aim her torso away from the tempting lamp, and reiterate "No lamp!" while she toddles away. She may cry in frustration, but your persistent use of head shaking and resolute-sounding "No's!"'s will show her that you're not going to give in.

Over time, your toddler will come to learn what your words and gestures mean, as she associates words, actions, and affects (feelings) with each other in the process we earlier labeled "WAA." On the other hand, if you routinely and silently pluck your child out of harm's way because it is easier (although in obvious emergencies you will of course do whatever is expedient), she will learn only that being picked up means "I can't do something."

If you're like most parents, you are very familiar with the helpless feeling of trying to set limits in a store when your child is grabbing an item and ignoring your command to "Stop it!" Many parents, after yelling and then physically reining in or giving in to their preschooler, go through the whole process once again the next time they go back to the store. If it's a repeating problem, you can be pretty sure that it isn't caused by the store's attractions. The child's misbehavior stems from the fact that she hasn't been taught to pay attention to her parent's wishes.

There are dozens of opportunities each day to teach respect for your words and guidance, so why choose the store to do your "toughest" teaching? Actively look for opportunities to teach when you and your child are on familiar turf, and not in a place where you will be embarrassed by either your own yelling or your child's. When you ask your child to pick up her toys, come to the dinner table, eat with a spoon and not her hands, get ready for bed, share her toys with a friend, or put on her coat, you'll have a chance to do some constructive teaching. Ask yourself the following questions:

- Do I have my child's attention?
- Does she understand what I want—for example, that I want her to pick up her blocks? Are my words or gestures clear and simple enough?
- If she is paying attention and understanding me, but is not choosing to obey, then why? Am I motivating her enough with positive regard, including respect? Am I prepared to motivate her with a reasonable sanction if needed?
- Am I willing to be more persistent and firm, and can I be gentle-but-firm if physical restraint is needed to protect my child from danger or from hurting someone else?
- Do I cultivate regular opportunities for empathy and dialogue through daily floor time and problem solving?

If the answers to these questions are all "yes", the limits you impose should be readily learned by your toddler.

Maintaining Empathy, Involvement, and Dialogue During Limit Setting

The natural human tendency is to pull away from empathy and closeness when you're involved in angry exchanges, power struggles, or limit setting. You may well ask yourself, "How can I possibly empathize with my child's desire to take her friend's new toy, or tease her sister?" The answer is that even while you must firmly set limits, you can empathize with how hard it is for your little girl to learn her new lessons. It is only through limit setting coupled with empathy that your child will eventually wish to please you. After all, your goal in setting limits is to teach greater empathy and respect for others, and your child will learn from what you *do* more than what you say.

While struggling to be empathetic, many parents find that they can't resist a desire to escape from their draining, angry children. It's natural to feel as if you want to get away from your child's nagging or whining. If you give in to this feeling, however, the escape pattern you set up will only succeed in making your child feel even more rejected, vulnerable, angry, and frightened. Your best approach is to take charge and reestablish a sense of security and control with your child by supplying her with extra floortime activities and problem-solving time. After a few weeks of reaffirming these special moments, your firm limit setting on your child's angry whining is both appropriate and helpful to her. Empathy, rather than escape, will help to reverse the cause of your distress.

CHOOSING YOUR BATTLES

Perhaps the hardest part of setting limits is deciding what to limit. Your own values and attitudes will lead you to pick your spots, but then you must be willing to set your boundaries wide and enforce them. In other words, *it is better to win a few important battles with sound teaching than to lose lots of little ones out of exhaustion.* Focus on just few key issues at a time. Work on table manners and leave cleanliness for later, or vice-versa. Don't make the tactical mistake of waging a war on three fronts at once or establishing very narrow categories for permissible behavior.

For example, don't punish your child for specific, narrowly defined kinds of transgressions such as hitting a playmate one day, spitting at another child on another day, or pinching a third child on yet another day. Instead, focus your discussions on the larger category of "respecting other people's bodies and therefore not hurting." The issue of "respect and not hurting" will cover any ingenious or lawyerly twists your child can create to defy you, such as "But I did too obey you! I didn't hit, pinch or spit on him. I just leaned on him really hard." Your goal is to help your child deal with general principles of behavior, and see the forest, rather than the trees of specific, niggling details.

REASONABLE SANCTIONS

As you decide on which kind of limit setting will underscore the seriousness of your resolve in your child's eyes, try to look for punishments that aren't developmentally detrimental. For instance, try to avoid restricting playing with friends, since that activity is too developmentally useful. Consider alternate sanctions like no television, no computer games, an earlier bedtime, or KP duty. Children need punishments that challenge them. As one four-year-old candidly said in response to a 15-minute time-out that his parent had just imposed, "That won't work. It's too easy for me!"

In fact, time-outs can suggest to your child that you are not able to withstand her anger. Going eyeball to eyeball with her or even asking her to think quietly in your presence about what she did may communicate greater resolve on your part. More importantly, some disobedient children have maturational lags, including their ability to comprehend what you say to them. They easily "tune out," and often get lost in their own fantasy world. The last thing they need is social isolation, which would permit them to daydream even more, and would further undermine their ability to test what is real and what is not.

When you consider that for many children, especially those who are inattentive or aloof, such isolation may be experienced as only mildly annoying and can in fact seem pleasurable, time-outs often turn out to be an ineffective way to set limits. Our developmental perspective lets us appreciate that it is the child's ability to balance intimacy, trust, and respect with anger that will lead to self limit-setting. Methods of punishment should never be cold, mechanical, or lack the very empathic values you are trying to teach. Constructive limit-setting takes place in the context of a warm, respectful relationship.

OVERPROTECTIVE PARENTING

Parents who are overprotective are often too fearful of or pained by their child's discomfort to set meaningful limits. If you find yourself backing away from effective limits ("I couldn't bear to take away three days of television—she would feel so unhappy and I would feel so mean!"), try to discuss these feelings with your spouse and explore the roots of such feelings in your own background. Instead of watering down sanctions, try to do something much harder: deal with your own inner pain and guilt over the situation by offering extra floor time and problem-solving time to your child. After all, you can't give your child too much of these! But make sure to *choose a limit that is genuinely meaningful to your child.* Since every child is different, you'll have to experiment and see whether a disappointed, stern look from you, days without television, restricted access to a favorite toy, or an earlier bedtime will prove to be more motivating.

TANTRUMS

When a tantrum erupts, parents feel a whole range of feelings: One parent might be mortified at the public embarrassment, whereas another might feel distraught because the child's anger "makes me feel like she hates me and I can't stand that." Still others may feel that their nerves are frayed by the sound of their child's high-pitched screeching. On the other hand, a bright little four-and-a-half-year-old may realize that yelling and having tantrums are like secret weapons. Parents don't know what to do and the child feels that she is getting even.

Tantrums can thus have different meanings and serve different purposes. There is a big difference between the child who cries at every little thing because she is overtired or ill and the child who wails in frustration because she can't tie her shoe, or the child who is uncontrollably angry at you because you won't let her eat a chocolate bar right before dinner. Knowing which kind of tantrum you are dealing with will help you handle it.

The overtired child needs you to help her calm down, by holding or rocking her, or reading or talking to her, or by drawing her attention to the colorful flowers outside her window. The goal is to teach her that even when she is really upset, she can settle down using certain calming tools. Her favorite sights, sounds, and movement patterns will help, as well as particular activities such as listening to a favorite story or watching a video while you hold her in your arms. Try not to get caught up in the feeling that "I'm being manipulated" when your child is overtired and fussy. She simply needs your assistance in helping her feel calm and regulated once again.

When your child becomes frustrated because she can't do something she is trying hard to do, like tie her shoes, realize that her tantrum is very similar to the anger you yourself experience when you hit your thumb with a hammer as you try to hang a picture hook. There are occasions in life when a person is entitled to ventilate! Remind yourself that when your angry four-year-old throws her shoe down in frustration, it is still an advanced communication involving gestures.

Firm limits are necessary if your child becomes destructive and tries to hurt someone or break something. For instance, if out of frustration your child flings her shoe directly in your face, it's certainly time to set a limit. Similarly, one day she may roughly discard a toy because she can't fit its pieces together. That's okay; but if she throws it down too hard, in a way that could break it, a limit should be imposed.

Since most of us are willing to sympathize with our fellow adult's moans and groans when they can't do something like figure out their new computer software, why not extend the same leeway to our own toddlers

or preschoolers? Try to empathize with your child's frustration and out-
rage over ornery shoelaces or complicated toys. Then, after she calms
down, see if she wants your assistance. If not, cheer her on from the sidelines as she tries again.

If your child wants your help, be a consultant, not a take-over artist. Ask
her how you might help and then follow her directions. If more assistance
is needed, you can offer some constructive suggestions, such as breaking
the task into small parts. For example, just crossing her shoelaces for her
may suffice for day one. If your child has difficulty planning out complex
movements, such as those required in tying a shoe or getting dressed, she
will really rely on your admiration for all her hard work and your willingness to offer her step-by-step advice. Your empathy and patience will
eventually spur her on to complete her task.

When your child throws a bona fide fit because you won't give her what
she wants or let her do what she wants, you'll want to do some strict limit
setting. Most parents find these sorts of displays of anger the hardest of all
to deal with, especially if their child is strong-willed and they themselves
are sensitive to loud noise or angry feelings. The most effective way to help
your child avoid these tense times is to first make sure that there is ample
warmth, closeness, nurturance, and respect in your relationship and then
to supply her with many opportunities to communicate her angry or frustrated feelings. Finally, it is important to establish a track record of limit
setting for earlier, serious infractions, such as hurting a sibling or violently
throwing toys

Now you are ready to guiltlessly deal with the tantrum itself. Try to convey an attitude of "I understand you're mad because you didn't get what
you wanted." Then, steel yourself to wait out the tantrum until the child is
able to communicate in words or gestures, and not just by crying, why she
feels that you have been unfair to her. It will only escalate her tension if
you yell back, or try to defend your position after you have made it clear,
or try to bribe her with compromises, or "jolly" her out of her angry facial
expression, or banish her to her room because you can't stand to listen to
the racket she's creating. Let her understand that if she chooses to let you
know how mad she is by using words or gestures, you are ready to listen.

You may notice that once you combine limit setting with extra floor
time, your preschooler may generally become warmer and more cooperative, but her tantrums may get more intense for a while. Any child worth
her salt will resist giving up her means of protest! If the tantrum brings
out a tendency for self-injury (biting or banging), for breaking things, or

for hurting you, you'll have to institute some immediate and firm limits. Containing her firmly in your arms will often do the trick. In such instances, be prepared for a real workout!

TEACHING NEW COPING STRATEGIES

Setting limits can also be an opportunity to help your child re-master all the earlier developmental coping skills that she has learned, to find new ways to get her needs met, and to feel a sense of self-respect rather than humiliation. By the time she is two, you and she will exchange words as you teach her how to use ideas in the heat of battle. Emotional ideas are a big advance over simply yelling, crying, or pouting—all of which are characteristic of the earlier, complex gestural stage. Similarly, when you and your three-and-a-half-year-old have a 20-minute discussion in which she contends that watching extra TV is a better idea than going to bed on time, your limit-setting negotiations are teaching her complex emotional reasoning. By entertaining her arguments you are not being a pushover; if she doesn't succeed in persuading you, you can still insist that she go to sleep.

It is relatively easy to discipline your preschooler when she covets and then swipes someone else's toy. But it is harder to try to figure out what needs your child may trying to meet by taking something that belongs to someone else. Perhaps her greediness stems in part from a hectic home life in which she is given lots of toys but little floor time. Her greed in this case may arise out of an attempt to feel important and respected. The question then becomes "How can I help her feel proud and secure in other ways? If I want her to equate importance with something other than the biggest and best toys, how can I help her realize that her interests, skills, silly jokes, and feelings of frustration and loss are important?"

As you put limits on your child's inappropriate ways of meeting her needs, you can also help her discover what those needs and motives are by offering a lot of floor time and problem-solving time. Whenever there are serious challenges to limits, you can bet that your child has basic unmet needs concerning such things as the parental relationship, sibling relationships, or problems caused by her own physical development.

RESPECT, RATHER THAN HUMILIATION

Power struggles with your child can be so infuriating that you become preoccupied with issues like not losing face. Not surprisingly, you may get so angry that you not only want your child to do what you want but to cry "uncle," too. However, intimidating and humiliating your child only teaches her that your "guidance" undermines her self-esteem. Helping your child save face and feel a sense of self-respect while following your guidelines lets her associate cooperation with feelings of positive self-esteem and success at overcoming a fussy or stubborn feeling.

Let's say your four-year-old is once again balking at going to sleep. After a long argument, you may finally win, and watch your little girl head toward her bedroom, chin tucked low. Once you sense that your child is capitulating, help her save face. You might tenderly tell her how good she'll feel in the morning after a good night's sleep, and then ask her with genuine interest about school and the next day's activities. If you get a response like "It's my turn to pass out the lunch bags tomorrow," you could respond with a supportive comment, such as "I know you'll do a good job." Now the former combatants are comrades-in-arms, and each of you feels respected.

Of course, don't be surprised if your preschooler is still somewhat angry at you and barks "Get out of my room! No goodnight kiss!" This is her way of trying to salvage some dignity out of the situation. Respect her need, and say something along the lines of "Gosh, I hope you'll let me kiss you goodnight tomorrow." After all, she *is* going to sleep, and is learning that limits are important, even though they may not be fun.

Janice Fullman

8

CONCLUSION:
GIVING MORE AND
EXPECTING MORE

Throughout the pages of this book, we've been exploring the six developmental stages and the related essential caregiving interactions that enable babies, young children, and their parents to master them and build intelligence and emotional health. It is our hope that familiarity with these milestones will enable both parents and professionals to recognize, create, and enjoy the interactive experiences that build a healthy mind. Understanding which type of interactions are most important also helps reveal which ones may be missing or less developed in a particular child, and how to fill in some of these developmental gaps. In this way, behavior that is intuitive for some parents can readily be learned by all.

Since we can all agree that childrearing is a complex process, it is important to highlight certain basic caregiving and parental attitudes that are particularly critical for a child's intellectual and emotional growth. These guiding principles embody many of the specific recommendations that appear in the preceding chapters. If there is a single golden rule of parent/child interaction, it can be summed up in just a few words: *Give more and expect more.* This axiom underscores the relationship between the amount of affection and empathetic interaction we offer our children and their ability to rise to challenges or to meet the demands we make of them.

Although it may sound simple, this advice is not easy for many of us to follow. There is a natural tendency to pull away and give our children *less* of ourselves when they disappoint or frustrate us. In the face of defiant disobedience, we sometimes become irate. Perhaps to stifle a more intemperate response, we may pull back, walk away, and occupy ourselves with chores. We may even mumble to ourselves, "After all I've done for him, he won't even . . . "

In such a situation, a child not only feels the pressure of your expectations, but at the same time also feels less nurtured. This double whammy will probably make him feel angry and frustrated. If he could clearly articulate his dilemma, he'd utter something like "What? Pick up my toys? When you won't even pick me up and cuddle me?" In general, a child will respond more enthusiastically to your heightened expectations—whether it's picking up toys, curbing aggressive tendencies with peers at school, or learning to share—if he feels he is receiving ample amounts of soothing emotional chicken soup, coupled with firm-but-gentle limits and guidance.

As you've gleaned from earlier sections of this book, the kind of nurturing we're prescribing has nothing to do with overprotecting or being indulgent. The most nourishing attention you can offer a child is lots and lots of floor-time interaction that encourages him to take initiative, interact, pursue flights of fancy, discover the joy of experiencing new sights and sounds, and lock horns with you during friendly debates. Such interactions help your child simultaneously harness all six developmental stages, or as many as he has mastered, while you provide him with firm-but-gentle guidance and limits. Each milestone involves both giving and expecting. If you're already "giving more" but neglect to challenge your child by raising your expectations of him, it's important to balance the equation by increasing your expectations. For instance, if you are responding warmly and often to your child's needs and wishes, you can encourage him to understand other people's needs and wishes by asking questions like "Well, how does your friend feel when you take away his new toy and play with it?"

Maintaining a basic attitude of giving more and expecting more also fosters your child's ability to meet expectable challenges without regressing into impulsive, demanding, or moody behavior. For example, if Mommy or Daddy has been working late for the past week and the whole household is snappishly on edge, a child may express his frustration by a lot of negativity. Consciously increasing the amount of warm attention and floor time during these crunch periods can create an atmosphere within the family that supports everyone's willingness to please each other.

It's probably obvious, but nonetheless should be mentioned, that in today's world it's nearly impossible to both do more and expect more when you're living on a financial shoestring and your free time is severely rationed. When both parents in a two-parent working family arrive home at 7:30 each night, that leaves only an hour or two before bedtime for the "giving and expecting" to take place. With the best of intentions, parents struggling to cope with such schedules may try and make up for lost time on weekends or during annual vacations. The fact remains, however, that children are more likely to thrive with a lot of giving and expecting from their parents or a devoted caregiver *during the course of each day.*

As we've discussed earlier, a useful childrearing rule of thumb is to try to have a parent or other loving adult available to the child during half of his nonschool waking hours. For two-parent working families, one possible childrearing plan is what we call the "four-thirds solution": Both parents work two-thirds time, rather than full time, or one parent works only part time while the other works full time. For other families, an affectionate nanny or grandmother can provide some of this key interaction and attention.

Of course, our "four-thirds solution" is not an option for a single parent who must work to put food on the table or for two parents who must work full time to supply their children with basic needs. Under those circumstances, parents should make a concerted effort to provide as much floor-time interaction as they can, and resist relying on TV to entertain their youngsters during the precious hours that they can spend together.

When we provide as much warm interaction as we can, our children tend to sense our caring and good intentions. By the same token, caregivers who have the financial resources and available time to engage and interact with their children, yet choose to pursue other options, may need to think about how much time it takes to truly provide the nurturance and guidance children thrive on.

In order to "give more and expect more," it is helpful to consider a parent's or caregiver's overall way of interacting with a child. We are all aware of the too often reported instances of abuse and neglect that many children in our society suffer. We need better economic and social supports and programs for families and parents to prevent these dire situations. We discuss this complex problem and the types of supports and programs likely to work in our books *The Growth of the Mind, Infancy and Early Childhood*, and *Infants in Multi-Risk Families*.

There are, however, patterns that occur in more typical interactions between parents and children that may benefit from a little scrutiny. These patterns are conveyed through a *parent's mood and emotional tone*.

A child can sense, through facial expressions, vocal tones, and posture, how we feel about things. If we grit our teeth in exasperation but manage to say in a very controlled voice, "You're such a good child!" because we want to maintain a positive attitude, most children will sense the true emotions that underlie our words. As first discussed in Chapter 3, a child learns to read our facial, postural, and vocal gestures long before he is able to use words. When there's a conflict between the words a child hears and what he senses from our gestures, he will almost always believe the gestures, just as we would correctly read the menacing posture and vocal tones of a stranger in a dark alley who beckons to us and says "I'm a nice guy—come here."

Does this mean that when we're angry we should go ahead and yell at a child and frighten him? Absolutely not! It does indicate, however, that the best time for praise may not be when we are angry or trying to control our frustration. Instead, deliberate praise is best communicated when we are relaxed and truly impressed with something a child has done. More importantly, as much as possible we need to try to stay involved in a continuous, supportive dialogue with and without words. Our children will forgive us for the temporary disappointments, annoyances, and anger they experience in our company if they feels that the overall tone of our interaction with them is one of warm support, caring, and love.

Many types of parental or caregiving emotional interactions can interfere with giving more and expecting more. Two important examples follow. A most troublesome one is a "here-but-not-here" pattern, where the parent or caregiver is not emotionally present. It occurs when a parent withdraws from interaction, or is available only intermittently. For example, immediately after a conflict or for no apparent reason at all a caregiver may emotionally withdraw and become quiet or preoccupied. Perhaps he or she is thinking about a problem that cropped up at work earlier in the day. The child is confused and only knows that he has a hollow feeling inside, in place of a warm, nurturing one. As adults, we're familiar with this feeling of loss because it happens at least some of the time in all of our intimate relationships. Spouses or friends may be distracted by work, sadness, depression, or anxiety, and simply not be there for us in a subtle emotional sense at a time when we need them. Even when the person may be physically present, and mouth the right words, we're aware of an empty feeling of noninvolvement.

Our children require more nurturing and support than we do, and are generally even more sensitive to the vagaries of our emotional tone. Older children or adults may be able to analyze their feelings when emotional support is withdrawn, but little children will often become confused by this shift in their caregiver's mood and may wind up blaming themselves for it. They may feel that they are somehow responsible for the situation, and that they are "bad." At times their guilty feelings are coupled with anger at their caregivers. It's therefore important for us to make a conscious effort to hang in there and continue to relate to our children as best we can. Everyone needs to learn to cope with a certain degree of uncertainty, but children need the reassurance of an overall emotional tone of supportive parental involvement. Of course, we need our rest periods as well. Try to set aside brief times to recharge, or to take an afternoon or evening for yourself while your spouse or a baby-sitter looks after your children.

Adults who have had a great deal of uncertain feelings about the constancy of their relationships as children may continue to feel badly about themselves, and frequently experience a barely suppressed sense of anger, especially if these patterns continue. They may try to cover these uncomfortable feelings with various coping strategies or defenses. They may simply avoid intimacy, or become easily humiliated, or insist in a self-righteous way that they are never wrong, or "bad." Nurturing, understanding relationships in the adult years can, however, be very helpful in dealing with such feelings.

Another emotional pattern (sometimes reinforced by words) that gets in the way of "giving more and expecting more" occurs when parents or caregivers don't withdraw, but instead frighten a child with their overwhelming anger and intensity. This scary pattern has an explosive quality to it; the parent may seem to seethe with annoyance. Even though the parent or caregiver may remain under good control most of the time, the child continually feels a sense of impending doom.

Since none of us wants to frighten our children, or appear emotionally vacant, we have to take stock of our own behavior and see if we can detect these troublesome patterns in ourselves. Often, our best helpers in becoming more aware of these patterns are our spouses or good friends, who may be more sensitive to the emotional tones and rhythms pulsing from us than we are ourselves. Although it isn't easy to change these often deeply ingrained patterns, simply being aware of them can make a big difference. This awareness fosters our ability to anticipate the pattern before it gets too strong, or to recover more readily. It can remove some of our natural defensiveness and free us up to feel more comfortable about asking our children how our behavior may have affected them. For instance, if you lapse into a particularly withdrawn or hostile mood, and later ask your child how that made him feel, he's likely to shake his head assertively and say, "I didn't like it at all." Such a question can be enormously helpful to the child, because the two of you can then reestablish a warmer, more empathetic connection.

Childrearing advice goes in and out of vogue. In some periods, parenting articles and books recommend more limits and structure and authority, while in others laissez-faire approaches are endorsed. We tend to cycle these debates every 30 years or so. Instead of such blanket advice, however, we need an approach that allows us to adopt the emotional tone and caregiving attitudes that are most helpful in meeting each child's unique needs. Parents should be wary of any "one size fits all" approach that oversimplifies something as complex as childrearing. Some children require firmer limits, while others need more soothing and collaboration. Most require a balance of a number of elements.

There are a number of parenting traps that we all can fall into, including:

- *Being either overprotective or overly challenging.* This is a particular problem with sensitive children who need extra soothing and support for being assertive. We can subtly overprotect a child by doing something as simple as putting a bread basket right next to him, rather than prompting him to take the initiative to ask or reach for it. We can overly challenge a child by trying to get him to do a new activity, such as swimming, too quickly rather than conveying a patient "get wet one toe at a time" attitude.

- *Being rigid and becoming locked into power struggles* rather than being extra flexible or collaborative with a defiant or stubborn child.
- *Being overly punitive or, conversely, helpless* with an active/assertive/impulsive child rather than providing extra opportunities for constructive activity, regulation, imagination, and caring.
- *Being disorganized* rather than creating longer and longer dialogues with the child who is inattentive.
- *Behaving in a laissez-faire, preoccupied way* with a self-absorbed child rather than offering extra wooing and engaging.

If, in spite of our best efforts, we fall back into these behaviors, we shouldn't be too hard on ourselves. Children will tend to eventually understand and respond to our overall pattern over many years, as long as the challenges they face are not beyond their ability to cope, and if we help them talk it out or play it out in an atmosphere of warmth and support.

Many books and articles also tend to focus a great deal on what we actually say to our children. While what we say is obviously important, our child's psychological dramas are being played out on a stage that is set by the emotional tone of our *behavior* with them. For instance, a quality like empathy, which most of us would like to see our children possess, isn't taught by telling children to be nice to other people or by instructing them to listen to what other people have to say. Such "guidance" may make a child act in a dutiful way, and he may go through the motions of being nice, but it won't create an empathetic understanding of another person's feelings. True empathy emerges out of two simultaneous experiences: being understood, and moving beyond strict self-interest.

A child who is empathized with in a gentle and compassionate way will understand at a deep emotional level what empathy is all about. As he grows older and can label these warm feelings with a word, his own positive experiences with coming to understand other people's feelings will cause him to want to engage with others in a similar manner. At the same time, if appropriate firm-but-gentle limits are placed on him and he's helped to take your needs, or those of a peer or sibling, into account by sharing toys or doing a few simple chores, he'll probably become increasingly able to see beyond his own immediate self-interest. He'll be better able to tolerate the limits that you place on his selfishness, and to develop more realistic expectations about your ability to meet his needs instantly. Your empathy, coupled with limits, will enable him to experience empathy and compassion.

In short, as you give more to expect more, your general emotional tone and posture are far more important than the specific things you may or may not say. Many of us lose sight of this general principle, and get sidetracked into issues of limited significance, such as whether or not we've properly praised our child in a certain instance or been a little undermining when we had to scold him. If your overall tone is warm and supportive, and you tune into your child's developmental capacities and unique characteristics while having appropriate expectations and limits in place, you are creating the opportunities for healthy emotional and intellectual growth that he needs, and should be leery about trying to be the perfect parent on every occasion. Just as a healthy tree can tolerate occasional droughts or downpours, your child can benefit from an array of manageable challenges as long as he is involved in supportive emotional and intellectual interaction with you.

As we have seen, the foundations of our intelligence and emotional health lie in a surprisingly straightforward set of interactions and experiences that all of us require throughout our lives. Ideally we try to provide these experiences for our children during infancy and the early childhood years, yet there is always time to provide these essentials. It is never too late to create opportunities for interaction, in which our children (or teenagers or young adults) can focus and engage, experience a range of feelings, create and share ideas and opinions, and learn to reflect and problem-solve in an atmosphere of warmth, acceptance, and empathetic guidance.

APPENDIX I:
THE FUNCTIONAL DEVELOPMENTAL GROWTH CHART AND QUESTIONNAIRE

~

THE FUNCTIONAL DEVELOPMENTAL GROWTH CHART

Just as we chart a child's physical growth during each checkup at the pediatrician's office, we should be monitoring his or her developmental progress. The Functional Developmental Growth Chart and accompanying questionnaire (page 374) can help you assess your child's developmental progress. It is a useful visual tool that shows graphically whether your child is showing expectable intellectual and emotional growth, or whether he or she needs additional support in certain areas. This developmental chart can also be used by clinicians, educators, day-care staff, and other child-care facilitators.

Historically we have been inclined to view children's development in terms of isolated abilities, such as motor development, sensory functioning, language and cognition, spatial problem solving, and social skills. As we look at these separate areas of development, we typically observe that a child can operate at a relatively advanced level in one area while having significant challenges in another. For instance, an early walker may turn out to be a late talker.

Although it is important to identify and assess specific aspects of development, for screening purposes it is more useful to look at a child's overall "functional" capacities: How does a child simultaneously use his or her whole mental "team" of specific abilities to meet needs, communicate, and think? Looking at how a child uses this "team" of abilities in a coordinated way to reach emotionally meaningful goals is a new and useful way to think about development. The early functional capacities, as we've discussed throughout this book, include the abilities to calmly focus and attend, to engage with others, to communicate needs intentionally, to engage in complex problem solving, to use ideas and words, and to combine ideas together with logical bridges as a basis for rational thinking.

If you find that your child is unable to master one or more of these six core experiences, or functional milestones, you can then examine specific components of development to see what might be contributing to his or her difficulties. For example, a mild motor delay may not significantly interfere with a child's relating, communicating, or thinking, but a very severe motor delay, or a mild motor delay coupled with severe family dysfunction, might derail one or more functional milestones.

On the Developmental Growth Chart, the six core developmental experiences (also referred to as stages or functional milestones) are listed chronologically from the bottom up on the left side of the chart. The child's age in months is indicated at the bottom of the chart. The heavy diagonal line shows the expected age ranges for mastering each functional milestone. As your child grows and develops, you can chart his or her actual mastery of each milestone in relation to the age at which the accomplishment is expected to emerge.

Record the age your child masters a particular developmental milestone, regardless of whether it is "on time," early, or delayed. If your child doesn't master a particular milestone within the expected time interval, record the last functional capacity that he or she has mastered by that point in time. In general, a child is considered to have mastered a milestone when he or she can engage in the behavior associated with the milestone most of the time. If your child can achieve the milestone only occasionally, or requires extraordinary support to perform it, he or she is not considered to have achieved mastery.

Normal development can fall above or below the chart's heavy diagonal line, but will be roughly parallel to that line. If your child is precocious (for example, three months ahead of expectations), his or her developmental line of progress will be parallel and a little above the heavy diagonal line. Similarly, if your child is a little behind (for example, three months behind on his or her functional developmental milestones), the expected line will be parallel but will fall just below the heavy diagonal line. If this is the case, it's a good idea to consult with your pediatrician and/or developmental specialist so you can receive some help in identifying what may contributing to the lag and what you might do to remedy it.

The accompanying questionnaire, which can help you figure out your child's developmental pattern, allows for a reasonably broad age range within which he or she may master each milestone. For example, babies usually engage in a relationship with their caregivers during the first four months of life. The growth chart expects this capacity to be present by five months. If these important functional capacities have not emerged reasonably close to the expected age range, it is important to try to figure out why. Your child may need a little more practice, or specific interventions may be indicated.

If your child's line of progress is not parallel to the heavy diagonal line, but instead arcs down and away from the line, be sure to seek an immediate assessment as soon as you notice the downward trend. Such a curve is a red flag that developmental delays are increasing as the child grows older, and often indicates that full evaluation and possibly an intervention program may be called for. In addition to professional consultation, you may find the following books helpful: Stanley I. Greenspan and Jacqueline Salmon, *The Challenging Child: Understanding, Raising, and Enjoying the Five "Difficult" Types of Children* (Addison-Wesley, 1995), and Stanley I. Greenspan and Serena Wieder, *The Child with Special Needs: Intellectual and Emotional Growth* (Addison-Wesley Longman, 1998).

THE FUNCTIONAL DEVELOPMENTAL GROWTH CHART

Developmental Stages

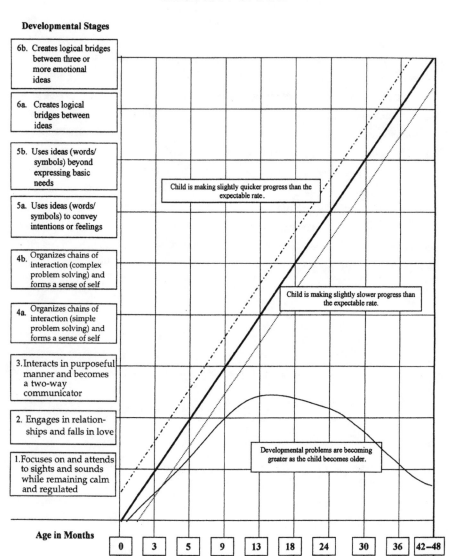

Developmental Stages	
6b. Creates logical bridges between three or more emotional ideas	
6a. Creates logical bridges between ideas	
5b. Uses ideas (words/symbols) beyond expressing basic needs	
5a. Uses ideas (words/symbols) to convey intentions or feelings	
4b. Organizes chains of interaction (complex problem solving) and forms a sense of self	
4a. Organizes chains of interaction (simple problem solving) and forms a sense of self	
3. Interacts in purposeful manner and becomes a two-way communicator	
2. Engages in relationships and falls in love	
1. Focuses on and attends to sights and sounds while remaining calm and regulated	

Child is making slightly quicker progress than the expectable rate.

Child is making slightly slower progress than the expectable rate.

Developmental problems are becoming greater as the child becomes older.

Age in Months

| 0 | 3 | 5 | 9 | 13 | 18 | 24 | 30 | 36 | 42–48 |

FUNCTIONAL DEVELOPMENTAL
GROWTH CHART QUESTIONNAIRE

To assess whether your child has achieved a new functional milestone, the answers to all the questions under that milestone must be yes. Even one no means that your child has not yet mastered the stage. Remember, the questionnaire and chart are simply tools to draw your attention to those developmental areas where your child is progressing as expected and to those where he or she may be facing some challenges.

STAGE 1: REGULATION AND ATTENTION (BY 3 MONTHS)

- Does your infant usually show an interest in things around him/her by looking at sights and turning toward sounds?

STAGE 2: ENGAGING IN RELATIONSHIPS (BY 5 MONTHS)

Ask the question from the prior category plus the new one from this category.

- Does your baby seem happy or pleased when he/she sees his/her favorite people: looking and smiling, making sounds, or using other gestures, like moving arms and legs that indicate pleasure or delight?

STAGE 3: INTERACTS IN A PURPOSEFUL MANNER AND BECOMES A TWO-WAY COMMUNICATOR (BY 9 MONTHS)

Ask the questions from all prior categories plus the new ones from this category.

- Is your baby able to show what he/she wants by reaching for or pointing at something, reaching out to be picked up, or making purposeful special noises?
- Does your baby respond to people who talk or play with him/her by making sounds and faces, initiating gestures such as reaching, etc.?

Stage 4: Organizes Chains of Interaction for Simple and Complex Problem Solving and Forms a Sense of Self (by 14 to 18 Months)

Ask the questions from all prior categories plus the new ones for this category.

- By 14 months is your toddler able to show what he/she wants or needs by using actions, such as leading you by the hand to open a door or pointing to find a toy?
- By 18 months is your toddler able to orchestrate more complex chains of interaction as he/she solves problems and shows you what he/she wants, including such things as getting food (for example, does he/she take your hand, lead you to the refrigerator, tug on the handle, and point to a particular food or bottle of juice or milk)?
- By 18 months is your toddler able to use imitation, such as copying your sounds, words, or motor gestures, as part of a playful, ongoing interaction?

Stage 5: Uses Ideas (Words/Symbols) to Convey Intentions or Feelings (by 24 to 30 Months)

Ask the questions from all prior categories plus the new ones for this category.

- By 24 months does your toddler ever respond to people who talk or play with him/her by using words or sequences of sounds that are clearly an attempt to convey a word?
- By 24 months is he/she able to imitate familiar pretend actions, such as feeding or hugging a doll?
- By 24 months is he/she able to meet some basic needs with one or a few words (may require parent saying the word first), such as "juice," "open," or "kiss"?
- By 24 months is he/she able to follow simple one-step directions from a caregiver to meet some basic needs, for example, "The toy is there" or "Come give Mommy a kiss"?
- By 30 months is he/she able to engage in interactive pretend play with an adult or another child (feeding dollies, tea parties, etc.)?
- By 30 months is he/she able to use ideas—words or symbols—to share his/her delight or interest (for example, "See truck!").
- By 30 months is he/she able to use symbols (words, pictures, organized games) while enjoying and interacting with one or more peers?

Stage 6: Creates Logical Bridges Between Ideas (by 36 to 48 Months)

Ask the questions from all prior categories plus the new ones for this category.

- By 36 months is your toddler able to use words or other symbols (for example, pictures) to show what he/she likes or dislikes, such as "Want that" or "No want that"?
- By 36 months is your toddler able to engage in pretend play with another person in which the story or drama makes sense? For example, does he/she have the bears go visit grandmother and then have a big lunch?
- By 36 months is your toddler able to begin to explain wishes or needs, for example: "Mommy, go out." "What are you going to do outside?" "Play." Your child may need multiple-choice help from you ("What will you do, play or sleep?").
- By 48 months can your preschooler explain reasons why he/she wants something or wants to do something: "Why do you want the juice?" "Because I'm thirsty."
- By 48 months is your preschooler able occasionally to use feelings to explain reasons for a wish or behavior ("Because I'm happy/excited/sad")?
- By 48 months is your preschooler able to engage in interactive pretend dramas with both peers and adults in which there are a number of elements that logically fit together? For example, the children go to school, do work, have lunch, and meet an elephant on the way home.
- By 48 months is your preschooler able to make a logical conversation with three or more give-and-take sequences about a variety of topics, ranging from negotiating foods and bedtimes to talking about friends or school?

APPENDIX II:
THE SIX ESSENTIAL DEVELOPMENTAL STAGES AND THE GROWTH OF THE BRAIN

Your Child's Developmental Goal	What You Can Do to Help	How the Brain Supports and Grows in Response to Each Developmental Stage*
Stage One Being Calm and Interested in All the Sensations of the World	Help your baby look, listen, begin to move, and calm down.	Neuronal connections are occurring immediately after birth in the areas of the brain that process sensory information and help the baby begin to initiate movement (i.e. primary sensory-motor cortex, thalamus, brain stem, and cerebellar vermis), and in areas that support the emotional interest in the world (i.e. amygdala, hyppocampus, and cingulate cortex)
Stage Two Falling in Love	Woo your baby into engaging with you with pleasure and delight	Further activity in areas supporting emotions, integration of visual sensory and motor areas, and right-sided neuronal connections occurs which supports the recognition of patterns (sights, movements) and promotes emotional relating, expressiveness and signalling (i.e. parital, temporal, primary visual cortical regions, frontal eye fields, basal ganglia, cerebellar hemisphere, beginning of cerebral cortex as well as continuation of limbic system).
Stage Three Becoming an Intentional Two-Way Communicator	Follow your baby's lead and challenge him/her to exchange gestures and emotional signals with you about his/her interests.	As the baby processes patterns and initiates more selective responses to environmental cues, growth in areas that support sequencing and reading and expressing gestures and emotion (two-way communication) are more active (i.e. increase in frontal cortex, including dorsal prefrontal areas).

Your Child's Developmental Goal	What You Can Do to Help	How the Brain Supports and Grows in Response to Each Developmental Stage
Stage Four Learning to Interact to Solve Problems and Discover a Sense of Self	Become an interactive partner with your toddler as he/she learns to use a continuous flow of gestures with you to pursue his/her interests and meet his/her needs.	Cerebral cortex is more active and continues so. Left-sided neuronal branching surges as toddler sequences sounds and occasional word(s) to problem-solve. Right-sided growth continues together with the ability to figure out larger patterns in the world and interact with a wider range of emotions.
Stage Five Creating Ideas	Enter your child's make-believe world as a character in his/her dramas. Engage him/her in long conversations about his/her interests, desires, and even his/her complaints.	Left-sided neuronal branching becomes denser as child comprehends, uses, and sequences more words and masters some of the basics of grammar. The visual-imaging parts of the brain grow as the child begins to engage more and more in pretend play. Both sides of the brain are becoming more specialized as language is rapidly being acquired.
Stage Six Building Bridges Between Ideas	Challenge your child to connect his/her ideas together by seeking his/her opinion, enjoying his/her debates, and enlarging his/her pretend dramas.	Brain undergoes growth spurt, metabolizing glucose (sugar) at twice the adult rate. Increased activity occurs in areas of the brain that deal with the creation and comprehension of words, and connections among words. Increased activity continues throughout childhood and then gradually shifts to the adult rate.

*See Chugani, Harry T., "Metabolic Imaging: A Window on Brain Development and Plasticity," *The Neuroscientist*, vol. V, no. 1, 1999 for further discusssion and references.

APPENDIX III:
TEN WAYS TO ENVIRONMENTALLY CHILDPROOF YOUR HOME

~

Young children, with their still-developing nervous systems, are particularly sensitive to the effects of toxins. The Children's Health Environmental Coalition (CHEC) provides 10 guidelines for safeguarding children from common household environmental toxins. CHEC's website (www.CHECnet.org) features the *Household Detective's* "Sherlock Homes" who leads you to further information on the 10 guidelines below as well as many in-depth resources.

1. **Check your house for lead paint.**
   Lead exposure in young children can slow physical and mental development. Before sanding, scraping, or removing paint, get your paint analyzed for lead if your house was built before 1980. Either call a certified environmental consultant (check your yellow pages) or call the US Department of Housing and Urban Development for a list of lead testing labs (1–800–532–3547).

2. **Prohibit smoking in your house.**
   Besides causing cancer, tobacco smoking increases children's risks of respiratory problems (including asthma) and ear infections. Direct those who wish to smoke to go outside. Because of air flow patterns in the house, merely keeping children away from an indoor smoking area is not effective.

3. **Eliminate pesticides in your home, garden, and yard.**
   Pesticides may be a factor in a range of health problems in children, from neurological impairment to cancer. Find natural, least toxic remedies to pest problems. Before using even least toxic pesticides inside your home, check with an expert. Write for *Least Toxic Control of Pests* to Beyond Pesticides, 701 E Street, SE Washington DC 20003. (www.beyondpesticides.org)

4. **Avoid exposing your child to paint fumes.**
   Paint is formulated from many chemicals that can affect a child's development. (It is only relatively recent that lead and mercury were eliminated from paints.) If painting is a necessity, open windows and ventilate well. If the painting is in the child's room, air it out for up to a month before allowing the child to spend time there.

5. **If you have a well, test the water yearly.**
   Many toxic chemicals present on the ground find their way into well water. Call a certified environmental consultant to check your water for such toxins as lead, pesticide residues, bacterial contaminants, and agricultural chemicals. This testing should be done yearly.

6. **Avoid using toxic household cleaners.**
   In particular, inhaling toxic household cleaners can affect children's nervous systems. Find non-toxic alternatives for such household products as air fresheners, rug cleaners, tub and tile cleaners, and oven cleaners.

7. **Vent fully all equipment and appliances heated by gas, oil, wood or coal.**
   Combustion by-products can be a factor in respiratory problems. To assure that these fumes do not build up indoors, turn on the exhaust fan when cooking over a gas stove. And inspect and maintain ventilation ducts

8. **Be alert to pesticide residues on foods.**
   Fruits and vegetables are always the best diet for children. But these foods may contain pesticides. To minimize exposure, wash and peel fruits and vegetables thoroughly and consider the option of organic foods, especially for those foods that are heavily consumed by your child. Pesticides on food affect children more than adults.

9. **Check your home for dampness, mold, and mildew.**

   Fungi related to dampness can cause allergies and respiratory problems. Dry out rooms with a dehumidifier and wash surfaces with equal parts vinegar and borax diluted in warm water.

10. **Avoid extreme heat conditions.**

    On high pollution days do not take your infant outside. Even on more mild days, avoid sun exposure. Infants should not use sunscreen lotions until at least six months of age.

ABOUT THE AUTHORS

Stanley I. Greenspan, M.D., is Clinical Professor of Psychiatry, Behavioral Sciences, and Pediatrics at the George Washington University Medical School and a practicing child psychiatrist. A supervising child psychoanalyst at the Washington Psychoanalytic Institute in Washington, D.C., and Chairman of the Interdisciplinary Council for Developmental and Learning Disorders, he was previously Chief of the Mental Health Study Center and Director of the Clinical Infant Developmental Program at the National Institute of Mental Health. Among his many national honors, he has received the American Psychiatric Association's highest award for child psychiatry research, and his work has been featured on PBS in a *Nova* documentary, "Life's First Feelings"; on ABC, NBC, and CBS News; on ABC's *Nightline*; on PBS's *News Hour*; and in stories in *Time, Newsweek,* the *New York Times,* and the *Washington Post.*

A founder and former president of Zero to Three: The National Center for Infants, Toddlers, and Families, Dr. Greenspan is the author of more than one hundred scholarly articles and chapters and is the author or editor of twenty-eight books for both scholarly and general audiences. These include *The Growth of the Mind* (with Beryl Lieff Benderly), *The Child with Special Needs* (with Serena Wieder, Ph.D., and Robin Simon), *Infancy and Early Childhood, Developmentally Based Psychotherapy, Intelligence and Adaptation: An Integration of Psychoanalytic and Piagetian Developmental Psychology, The Development of the Ego, First Feelings* (with Nancy Thorndike Greenspan), and *Playground Politics* and *The Challenging Child* (both with Jacqueline Salmon).

Nancy Breslau Lewis is a former medical writer at the National Institutes of Health, and a freelance newspaper columnist and features writer. She has edited books and articles on topics ranging from psychology to political activism, and is the mother of three children.

INDEX

and gestures, 135–136, 139
and imitation, 141–153
and interaction, parent/child, 153–154, 170–172
and language skills, 147
and limit-setting, 158–163, 196
and listening, 135
and morality, 150–152
and motor skills, 146
and muscle tone, 186–189
opportunities for, 173–174
and originality, 144–145
and peer interaction, 163–164
and pleasure, 143
principles of, 353
recognizing, 139–145
and sense of self, 137–138, 152–153, 174–182
and sensory skills, 146–147
and sight, 135, 191–195
and sound, 183–186, 191–195
as stage of development, 131–139
and stimulation, craving for, 189–191
and tantrums, 184–185
and touch, 183–186
and underreactive children, 186–189
See also Communication, complex gestural
Punitiveness, 369

Reaching out
and two-way communication, 87–88
Reading comprehension skills, 303–304
Reality testing, 257
Reflective pause, 201
Reflective thinking, 7
Regression, 365
and thinking, 311–313
Rejection
and two-way communication, 128–129
Relationships. *See* Peer relationships; Sibling relationships; Triangular relationships
Resolve
and limit-setting, 353–354
Respect
and limit-setting, 354–355, 360–361
Rhythm
and calm attention, 16, 17, 22, 31
Rigidity, 369
Rocking
and calm attention, 17–18

Sameroff, Arnold, 4
Sanctions
and limit-setting, 356–357
Scent, mother's, 35

Schanberg, Saul, 28
School
aggression in, 319–320
Security, 134
adult version of, 24–25
and calm attention, 23–27
and holding, 28–29
and overloading, 25
sense of, achieving a, 24–27
Self-absorption, 74
Self-awareness, 7
Self-esteem
and falling in love, 57
and limit-setting, 361
and thinking, 279–280, 288, 292
and two-way communication, 93, 95
Self-interest, 369–370
Self-reflection
and abstract thinking, 259
and emotional thinking, 272–273
and thinking, 295
Seligman, Martin, 89
Sensations
and calm attention, 16–20, 24
and ideas, 232
and security, 24–27
See also under specific senses
Sense of loss
and children's independence, 195
Sense of self
building, 66–68
and problem-solving, social, 137–138, 152–153, 174–182
and symbolic expression, 222–224
and thinking, 307–310
and two-way communication, 116–118
Senses
and floor time, 336
See also under specific senses
Sensory skills
and falling in love, 53
and problem-solving, social, 146–147
and symbolic expression, 210
and thinking, 270, 271
and two-way communication, 94
See also under specific senses
Separation and loss
and emotional thinking, 266
Sexuality
and parental inhibitions, 197
Shared bliss, 66–67
Sibling relationships
and emotional thinking, 266
and thinking, 313–315
See also Triangular relationships

Made in the USA
San Bernardino, CA
25 January 2013